LANGUAGE,

HERMENEUTIC, AND

WORD OF GOD

LANGUAGE, HERMENEUTIC, AND WORD OF GOD ঌ ঌ

The Problem of Language
in the New Testament and
Contemporary Theology

ROBERT W. FUNK

Grateful acknowledgment is made to the Christian Theological Seminary for permission to reprint Chapter 8, "The Old Testament Parable: The Good Samaritan," which appeared in a rather different form in *Encounter* magazine, Vol. 26, No. 2, 1956, pages 251–267.

FIRST EDITION

ISBN. 0-89130-225-5
LIBRARY OF CONGRESS CATALOG CARD NUMBER: 66–20776

K-Q

Contents

Abbreviations

---

*The following abbreviated bibliographical entries
are customarily employed in the notes:*

Barfield, *Poetic Diction*

Owen Barfield, *Poetic Diction: A Study
in Meaning* (2d ed.; London: Faber &
Faber, 1952).

————, *Saving the Appearances*

————, *Saving the Appearances: A Study
in Idolatry* (London: Faber & Faber,
1957).

Bultmann, *Existence and Faith*

Rudolf Bultmann, *Existence and Faith:
Shorter Writings of Rudolf Bultmann,*
selected, translated, and introduced by
Schubert M. Ogden (New York: Meridian Books, 1960).

————, *Glauben und Verstehen* I

————, *Glauben und Verstehen* I (Tübingen: J. C. B. Mohr [Paul Siebeck],
1933; 3d ed., 1958).

————, *History of the Synoptic Tradition*

————, *The History of the Synoptic Tradition,* translated by John Marsh (New
York: Harper & Row, 1963).

————, *Jesus Christ and Mythology*

————, *Jesus Christ and Mythology* (New
York: Charles Scribner's Sons, 1958).

————, *Theology of the New Testament* I, II

————, *Theology of the New Testament*
I and II, translated by Kendrick Grobel
(New York: Charles Scribner's Sons,
1951, 1955).

Dodd, *Parables*

C. H. Dodd, *The Parables of the Kingdom* (3d ed.; London: Nisbet & Co.,
1936; reprinted 1952).

Ebeling, *Nature of Faith*

Gerhard Ebeling, *The Nature of Faith,* translated by Ronald Gregor Smith (Philadelphia: Fortress Press, 1961) = *Das Wesen des christlichen Glaubens* (Tübingen: J. C. B. Mohr [Paul Siebeck], 1959).

————, *Word and Faith*

————, *Word and Faith,* translated by James W. Leitch (Philadelphia: Fortress Press, 1963) = *Wort und Glaube* (Tübingen: J. C. B. Mohr [Paul Siebeck], 1960; 2d ed., 1962).

————, *Theologie und Verkündigung*

————, *Theologie und Verkündigung. Ein Gespräch mit Rudolf Bultmann,* "Hermeneutische Untersuchungen zur Theologie," 1 (Tübingen: J. C. B. Mohr [Paul Siebeck], 1962; 2d ed., 1963).

Fuchs, *Hermeneutik*

Ernst Fuchs, *Hermeneutik* (Bad Cannstatt: R. Müllerschön Verlag, 1954; 2d ed., with Ergänzungsheft, 1958).

Fuchs I

Ernst Fuchs, *Zum hermeneutischen Problem in der Theologie: Die Existentiale Interpretation,* "Gesammelte Aufsätze," I (Tübingen: J. C. B. Mohr [Paul Siebeck], 1959).

Fuchs II

————, *Zur Frage nach dem historischen Jesus,* "Gesammelte Aufsätze," II (Tübingen: J. C. B. Mohr [Paul Sieback], 1960) = *Studies of the Historical Jesus,* translated by A. Scobie, "Studies in Biblical Theology," 42 (London: SCM Press, 1964). References to the English version are given in brackets, [ ].

Fuchs III

————, *Glaube und Erfahrung,* "Gesammelte Aufsätze," III (Tübingen: J. C. B. Mohr [Paul Siebeck], 1965).

Heidegger, *Being and Time*

Martin Heidegger, *Being and Time,* translated by J. Macquarrie and E. Robinson (London: SCM Press, 1962).

Jeremias, *Parables*	Joachim Jeremias, *The Parables of Jesus,* revised edition, translated by S. H. Hooke (New York: Charles Scribner's Sons, 1963) = *Die Gleichnisse Jesu* (6th ed.; Göttingen: Vandenhoeck & Ruprecht, 1962).
Kerygma und Mythos II	H. W. Bartsch, ed., *Kerygma und Mythos* II (Hamburg: Herbert Reich-Evangelischer Verlag, 1952).
Kerygma and Myth I	H. W. Bartsch, ed., *Kerygma and Myth* I, translated by R. H. Fuller (London: S.P.C.K., 1957; New York: Harper Torchbooks, 1961).
Kerygma and Myth II	H. W. Bartsch, ed., *Kerygma and Myth* II, translated by R. H. Fuller (London: S.P.C.K., 1962).
New Frontiers I	J. M. Robinson and J. B. Cobb, Jr., eds., *New Frontiers in Theology* I, *The Later Heidegger and Theology* (New York: Harper & Row, 1963).
New Frontiers II	J. M. Robinson and J. B. Cobb, Jr., eds., *New Frontiers in Theology* II, *The New Hermeneutic* (New York: Harper & Row, 1964).
Ogden, *Christ Without Myth*	Schubert M. Ogden, *Christ Without Myth: A Study Based on the Theology of Rudolf Bultmann* (New York: Harper & Row, 1961).
Wilder, *Language of the Gospel*	Amos N. Wilder, *The Language of the Gospel: Early Christian Rhetoric* (New York: Harper & Row, 1964).

Other Abbreviations

JBL	*Journal of Biblical Literature*
JBR	*The Journal of Bible and Religion*
JR	*Journal of Religion*
JThC	*Journal for Theology and the Church* (Harper Torchbook, issued at intervals)
NT	*Novum Testamentum*
NTS	*New Testament Studies*
RGG	*Die Religion in Geschichte und Gegenwart* (third edition)
ThLZ	*Theologische Literaturzeitung*
ThR	*Theologische Rundschau*
ThZ	*Theologische Zeitschrift der Theologischen Fakultät der Universität Basel*
TWNT	*Theologisches Wörterbuch zum Neuen Testament*
ZNW	*Zeitschrift für die neutestamentliche Wissenschaft (und die Kunde des Urchristentums)*
ZThK	*Zeitschrift für Theologie und Kirche*

Foreword

He who lays a violent hand on his tradition must beware of falling statuary. Knowledge of the imminent hazard goes hand in glove with the right grasp of the temporality, the historicality, of that tradition. And such knowledge makes one circumspective.

If, today, there is more caution on the one side, and more rashness on the other, we should not, by that circumstance, be forced to choose between them. Responsibility for the past, which carries with it joint responsibility for the future, can never be anything less nor anything more than circumspective: it has to take the risk of history in full view of the perils but without being deterred by them. Caution draws back from peril; foolhardiness does not comprehend danger. Circumspection seeks to disclose the risk the past lays upon the future, without any thought other than to take that risk upon itself as genuine responsibility for the past, and yet it knows, because it is circumspect, that it may well prove to be either overly cautious or merely foolhardy. It is that ultimate threat that requires the courage to be.

It is an easy matter to betray the future, and thus the past, by recklessness. It is an even simpler matter to betray the past, and thus the future, by excessive deference. In this time of gross disjunctures, it is perhaps the latter rather than the former that is most to be feared. Nevertheless, neither the one nor the other will be able to negotiate the transition from whatever it was that we were to whatever it is that our destiny has laid upon us.

The *theological* odyssey of our time is characterized by the quest for adequate circumspection. The quest has become incumbent upon us by virtue of our history. That is to say, of course, that the imposition of the quest hangs together with the way we read our history.

The problem our history poses for us is not yet manifest. It is taken for the most part, however, to be self-evident. This discrepancy is only the symptom of a deeper malady that resists diagnosis. Theology in the

modern period has assumed that it has two entities on hand, the
Christian gospel and the modern mind, and that it must seek the intellectual means of reconciling them. It is becoming increasingly apparent that this assumption is mistaken. Our problem is not how we
bring traditional doctrine of God together with our intellectual situation, how we translate the biblical message into modern terms, but
how we get the two things apart, how we gain critical leverage of the
one upon the other, whether we take traditional theological language
or situation as the primary term.

Theology and the way we experience reality have indeed come apart
at the seams. But that does not mean that theology thereby gains a
critical vantage point; it means that theology has abrogated its responsibility for touching and being touched by the real. Theology coming
out of the past hermetically sealed, as though it were handed down in
a time capsule, is only one more part of the historical litter with which
we have to reckon. And there is other historical debris, including
traditional litter in which that same theology has concealed itself, that
shapes and molds us even more decisively. No: our history has become
impregnably monolithic; it refuses to yield to our attempts to transcend
the past—that means, to live into our own authentic future—because
our horizon is fixed by that past itself. The impasse into which theological liberalism and theological orthodoxy have come is symptomatic of
our dilemma. We cannot move forward until we move back, until we
recapitulate our past critically and thus gain distance on it.

Circumspection is therefore the order of the day. It is required because we must learn to dismantle our history without getting crushed
by falling statuary.

Our history—the history we must seek to lay bare—is transmitted to
us largely in the form of language. It is therefore the linguistic tradition
that both bears and conceals our disposition to our history and to reality.
In his famous essay on language, Edward Sapir suggested that language
predetermines certain modes of observation and interpretation. He pre-
dicted that with the growth of scientific experience we would have to
learn to fight the implications of language. He was undoubtedly
correct, although the extent to which language pervades and shapes
our experience of reality can scarcely be measured solely in terms of
grammar.

What we see is presided over by what we can say. A literalminded
era takes the tyranny of one over the other for granted, but reverses the

relationship: what we can say is dictated to us by what we see. In that case, we have only to clean up our language, to free it from equivocal elements, to make it square univocally with what we see. If that project has now stumbled onto dimensions of language long lost to sight, it is only because man, the maker and user of language, does not dispose of language unilaterally. There is evidence that linguistics, another form of the preoccupation with language in our period, is also being driven into the abyss of meaning. Language does not merely stand at our beck and call; it is there before we are, it situates us, it restricts our horizon, it refuses us its total complicity.

The irony of our dilemma is that literalmindedness, which gives the priority entirely to seeing, is unable to honor that priority because it is held in bondage by the very language it believes it holds virtually at bay. Language so understood conceals a disposition to the question of the real that precludes fresh vision. Seeing is denied its rights because saying has been dispossessed.

Theology and phenomenology in some of their forms have consequently elected to attack the problem posed to us at the point of language. The struggle must go on in and with reference to language because it is here that our history dictates our present and foreshortens our future. The first task is to expose the roots of our linguistic tradition and the second, which is wholly concomitant, is to liberate language from the hegemony of prescriptive thought.

Biblical language is part of the linguistic litter that has come down to us in our tradition. It has become increasingly problematic to the modern mind. This fact is itself remarkable, not, to be sure, because of the tremendous gulf between the ancient and modern worldviews, but because of the difference in the relationship to language itself. This difference prompts the question whether our view of biblical language has not been decisively stamped by the linguistic tradition that delivered that language to us. One way of broaching the question is to take an aggressively passive look at the linguistic phenomena in the New Testament itself. It is barely possible that this process will teach us something about ourselves if not about the New Testament.

It does not require notice that language has erupted as a root problem in contemporary theology. That it has done so owes to the fact that nothing less than word of God—not doctrine of God—is at stake. It is apparent that if language is usurped finally by man, the possibility of word from God entering language is gone. It is thus not without good reason that contemporary theology has fought to restore to language its primordial rights.

By exposing the roots of our linguistic tradition we may perhaps gain some distance on our own linguistic heritage, distance that may make it possible to read that heritage in a wholly new light. And if in a new light, in a way that does not simply frustrate our own experience of reality. In that case, new language, or language with new bearings and power, may well up out of an unpredisposed confrontation with reality.

Once it has been grasped that because language is historical the way we experience reality is also historical, it is possible to mount the problem of the future of language. To say that language has a future is to say that it is not merely determined by what it has been. That means, of course, that the way we experience reality also has a future, and thus not determined merely by the way in which we have experienced reality. Man and world have been historicized, but not absolutely: there remains to man the ramp of his knowledge of his own historicity, which leads, not to the realm of the immutable, nor to the domain of his lordship over creation, but to his own authentic future, the future as it is given to him in that crossing over from what he was to what he will be. Crossing over is authentic only if man makes it his ownmost, i.e., only if it is tendered and seized as his ownmost history falling out as his ownmost future.

The future falls out in language: man lives out of and into language. To participate in that future means to live *out of* language as it gives itself to us and withholds itself from us, *into* language as it gives itself to us and withholds itself from us. That is also to say: to live out of the past as it gives itself to and withholds itself from the future.

The destiny of language seems to have made, or undoubtedly will make, theology in a traditional sense no longer viable. Theology must be prepared to submit to that destiny, to take the risk of that future, if it does not wish to become ghetto language, the cloistered tongue of the Christianized age.

The trajectory of the studies that comprise this volume is determined by the destiny of language as it has impressed itself upon the thought of Rudolf Bultmann and Martin Heidegger, Gerhard Ebeling and Ernst Fuchs, Owen Barfield and Maurice Merleau-Ponty, to mention only three pairs. While they and others, whose imprint may be detected here and there, may not consent to my specific reading of that destiny, it was nevertheless their circumspections which launched my own thought on its present course.

In the foreground of these reflections stand Amos N. Wilder, who has singlehandedly manned a sensitive post in New Testament studies in America for many years, and who was kind enough to scrutinize the manuscript in part; James M. Robinson, who has prepared a highway in the desert for those who would travel this way, and who troubled himself with the text in matters both great and small; Ray L. Hart, who advanced to me out of a rich fund that is presently to be paid out in full reasoned measure.

I wish also to acknowledge the generosity of Schubert M. Ogden, whose acute analysis of the presentation of his own position in Chapter 4 helped clear up a number of issues; of Charles Courtney, who reviewed Chapter 9; of M. Jack Suggs, who made pertinent suggestions with respect to Chapter 10.

There is something eminently unfair in the process by which the reader takes advantage of a man after he has set himself down in print. The poets know this, and so they set themselves down in a way that allows each reader to take advantage in his own way, only the reader discovers, if he is wise, that he has only taken advantage of himself rather than the poet. But the writer of prose is made to answer in perpetuity for a text that he may one day cease to espouse, simply because it is a matter of irretrievable public record. This is one of the differences between prose and poetry.

The theologian belongs to the latter rather than to the former of these categories. With every sentence he makes the noose more difficult to escape. Yet he does not mind really. Perhaps it is because he is more appreciative of human foibles on the part of both writers and readers. Perhaps it is because he is so quick to disown what he has written. If he is dimly aware of the pretension involved in speaking of God's word, revelation, truth and the like, his repudiation will come the quicker.

Since the chapters of this volume were written over a rather extended period of time, there is much in them that I would say differently now or not say at all. They are studies that can best be characterized as *under way*. To the extent that they pretend to lay down the conditions for the occurrence of word of God, I disown them in advance; to the extent that they represent a stage along the endless way, I gladly acknowledge them, but I do so from a certain distance.

In them I have taken advantage of others. It is only fair that I should suffer the same fate, and I willingly join, from this distance, with other eager executors of that fate.

ROBERT W. FUNK

Tübingen, Germany
July, 1966

LANGUAGE,

HERMENEUTIC, AND

WORD OF GOD

They were offered the choice between becoming kings or the couriers of kings. The way children would, they all wanted to be couriers. Therefore there are only couriers who hurry about the world, shouting to each other—since there are no kings—messages that have become meaningless. They would like to put an end to this miserable life of theirs but they dare not because of their oaths of service.

FRANZ KAFKA,
Parables and Paradoxes

Language, Hermeneutic,
and the Vocation of the Word

"You brood of vipers! how can you speak good, when you are evil? For out of the abundance of the heart the mouth speaks. The good man out of his good treasure brings forth good, and the evil man out of his evil treasure brings forth evil. I tell you, on the day of judgment men will render account for every careless word they utter; for by your words you will be judged, and by your words you will be condemned."—Matthew 12:34-37 (RSV).

The text gives warrant for taking speech seriously. It commends care in the use of words. It makes language the basis upon which men are called to account. Such deference for speech may be understood as aimed at the thoughtless and reprehensible use of unseemly and profane expressions. It may be taken as a call to avoid offensive language of all kinds, to make judicious use of words in every relationship between man and man. It may be interpreted, more formally, as the concern for premeditation and precision in discourse. While one or all of these may be implied in the text, it is a question whether observing the proprieties and consulting the dictionary will, in themselves, constitute a satisfactory accounting for the use of language.

The text indicates that speech is linked with the abundance of the heart or lack of it, with the vision of truth or blindness of spirit out of which speech proceeds. Care for language is thus not a matter merely of the propitious use of words. Furthermore, speech itself involves the ear upon which speech falls. Because speech is something which is heard as well as spoken it is possible to call its articulator to account for words carelessly uttered. Language enters into the history, personal and collective, of man and shapes it for better or for worse; it simultaneously creates understanding and incomprehension, it binds together

1

2

and it rends asunder. The constellation to which speech belongs, then, invariably has two poles, enunciation and audition, each of which sustains its own relation to language and bears, at the same time, responsibility for the other through speech.

Since the ear and the mouth, which are the two parties to speech, normally belong to different persons, language is understood as communication. One person seeks, through language, to convey something to another. The minimal condition for communication, therefore, is language that is already understood: understanding can take place only where language is previously understood. And so editors and advertisers, journalists and politicians, teachers and popular poets endeavor to confine experience and thought to domesticated language. Use comprehensible language, we are told, and communication must follow as the night the day.

It is doubtless the case that language sets the limits for understanding. Is it not possible, nevertheless, that experience and thought occasionally press the limits of *conventional* speech and spill over? That language already understood is sometimes inadequate to what is to be understood? In that case the language that sets the limits for understanding is not common parlance, but an idiosyncratic language or even a language as yet unborn. The authentic poet, for example, may be understood as one who has crossed the frontier of conventional parlance into uncharted linguistic terrain: he is seeking to hear, as it were, and to articulate for himself that which has not yet come to expression. In his case ear and mouth are united in the same person, but the responsibility of enunciation and audition to each other is no less for that.

When language is pressed to its limits, it is discovered that speech is more than words or even content of words, that it is more than sentences composed of subject and predicate. If the problem of communication lay only in words and sentences, the speaker or writer, if he wished to be understood, could provide a glossary and a grammar. Or another person, who understood what was being said, could translate. Perhaps there could be several translations from one into the same or different languages. But what would translation achieve if the subject matter spoken about were not understood? And how can understanding take place without understandable language? And if there is understandable language as a means of understanding, then is translation necessary at all? Does this not suggest that without previously understood language no understanding could take place?

Common parlance appears to presuppose a common view of reality: two people can talk with understanding about the same thing because they share the reality being talked about. Communication presupposes understanding, however imperfectly, of a common subject matter. Nonunderstanding and misunderstanding therefore arise where language does not refer to a common subject matter—where speaker and hearer, writer and reader, do not participate in a common reality, with reference to which meaningful discourse can be created. The problem posed by language may thus turn finally on whether common understanding precedes and makes meaningful speech possible. Put this way, it would seem that language is an epiphenomenon dependent on shared experience and joint understanding. This formulation obviously converts the previous suggestion that understanding depends upon language.

These considerations, then, suggest that the problem to be resolved is whether a common, understandable language depends upon a prior joint understanding, or whether joint understanding is dependent upon a previously understood language. To formulate the problem as a question of priority is to make evident that resolution is impossible. Such a formulation, moreover, obscures the root issue. In pressing the question, consequently, these two ways of putting the matter should be juxtaposed as a means of discovering what bearing they have on each other.

The initial difficulty is that the problem to be spoken *about*, namely speech, is bound up *with* the mode of language that must be employed in speaking about it. The problem of language can apparently be addressed only by means of more language. The problem of language has to be raised out of language as it is used and understood, into language as it is not used and understood. So long as that further language does not break out of the plane of language which constitutes the locus of the problem, the discussion will fall prey to itself—that is, to language as already understood. At the same time, any discussion of language must proceed from and in relation to language as it is known, used, experienced. The old house of language is to be dismantled and its materials used to build the new. Meanwhile, there is no place to dwell, no place to carry on the conversation, except in the old house.

Consider the artist who has before him a blank canvas. He has at his disposal the technical skills requisite to his craft and a tradition which stretches as far back as the Stone Age. The picture in his mind—the one he aspires to put on canvas—will not be the product merely of skills plus tradition. Skills and tradition are the basis of his work, but in the execution of the painting he is placing his skills and his knowledge of the tradition in the service of a tradition which is yet to be. The picture is there, in his mind, only by anticipation; the painting itself, if successful, will disclose to his own mind what he aspired to paint. It is this *out of* what is at one's disposal *into* what is not at one's disposal that constitutes the trajectory of creative art.

The "language of language" is analogous to the "language" of art. In confronting the problem of language one has to aspire to what is *not* at his disposal (an understanding, a language) on the basis of what *is* at his disposal (an understanding, a language). Out of language as it is understood, out of joint understanding, is to be won new language and new understanding. The new has to be projected onto possibilities which lie beyond the frontiers of common language and joint understanding. Only so can the new be genuinely new.

It has been noticed that common language and joint understanding go together in such a way that it is impossible to determine which is prior. This is because language conceals a commonly understood way of looking at things, and a commonly understood way of looking at things fosters sedimentation in language. Language and understanding give birth to each other; they also hold each other captive. A tradition is a common language and a joint understanding held in solution. A tradition falters when language and understanding are divorced.

It may be said, then, that the common reality which makes meaningful speech possible precedes speech in the sense that it is the reference, as yet unavailable to the common understanding, upon which creative speech is projected. It is the picture which is in the artist's mind only by anticipation. This common reality follows speech, however, in the sense that it becomes audible only as meaningful discourse is created. The picture in the artist's mind becomes visible, to himself and to others, only as it is put on canvas. The before-after relationship, since it must be taken both ways around, can best be expressed as simultaneity or reciprocity. Language and understanding arise together, are reciprocal. The common reality to which they refer both precedes and follows. It makes them possible, and yet the common reality does not become audible without language and understanding. Language and understanding both arise out of and invoke shared reality.

These reflections have now and then touched upon the subject of "reality." It was said, for example, that nonunderstanding and misunderstanding arise when speaker and hearer do not participate in a common reality. Is there any reality other than that which all men have in common? Is it not necessary to affirm a single, univocal reality, which is "out there," external to language and thought? However this may be, it is indisputable that reality can be and is disputed. Rational beings disagree about what is "really real."

If language and understanding are taken to be fully reciprocal, if they arise together, to what shall their rise (and decline) be attributed? To language invented on a whim? To capricious understanding? To the willful creation of rational thought? In any case, language and understanding are taken to be the product of human artifice. Some means must then be contrived in order to test whether language and understanding do in fact have reference to reality, whether they are "true." T. R. Miles has argued that philosophy, when properly understood, has the task of contriving just such tests. On this view philosophy is a second-order activity which comes into play only when someone has already made a first-order assertion.[1] The philosopher waits on somebody to say something, and then he endeavors to decide whether what has been said is true or false. Philosophy, of course, does not depend upon a single criterion, or even a set of criteria, but endeavors to discover criteria appropriate to various forms of discourse. This type of philosophy is known as functional linguistic analysis.

The point to be made over against functional linguistic analysis is that a second-order linguistic activity does not have adequate resources to enable it to arbitrate over first-order linguistic activity so long as it (*a*) confines itself to the "logic" already implicit in the language it is submitting to analysis, or (*b*) refers that language to the "logic" of some other order of discourse in order to determine the issue. Philosophy must itself investigate the grounds of first-order language if it wishes to dispute language and/or reality.

To put the matter abruptly, language and understanding have to be made to recoil upon the reality to which they allegedly refer. If common language and joint understanding presuppose a shared reality, the failure of language and understanding betoken the failure of that reality. Tradition fails because the reality which has supported it fails. In such a time, it is incumbent upon those who care for language and understanding to attend to the disjuncture between them and reality, and to attend to the reality that is striving to impress itself upon

---

[1] T. R. Miles, *Religion and the Scientific Outlook* (London: George Allen & Unwin, 1959), 63.

language and understanding. The reciprocity of language and understanding has to be grasped in relation to the question of the "real."

It was remarked that a tradition fails when language and understanding are divorced. A divorce of this order follows upon the disintegration of the reality to which understanding refers, while conventional language lags behind experience. "Understanding" in that case is a kind of not-knowing and not-having what language promises. Language goes dead when it forecloses rather than discloses understanding. On the other hand, understanding remains a not-knowing until language comes to its rescue. And both of them linger in limbo until the "real" breaks through the limitations set by the reciprocal dependence of language and understanding. Who knows what "worlds" lie buried behind our very eyes, under the rubble of countless language traditions!

*　*　*

Since the essays that follow are about language and written in language, the foregoing considerations have some bearing on how they are written and how they are to be read. These several studies are attempts to enter upon possibilities arising out of a disposition toward language as it is experienced and used today. This disposition is itself informed by various analyses of language, which are trained on both contemporary (Part I) and biblical (Parts II and III) language. Disposition and analysis form a circle, hopefully a spiraling and not a vicious one.

The problem language presents is keenly sensed in many quarters in contemporary theology. Because it has become problematical whether the Christian message can be addressed to contemporary man in meaningful terms, the language of theology has itself come into dispute. The bearing which word of God and theological language have on each other will be the underlying theme of Part I. The justification for attending to biblical language is that the disposition to language reflected in biblical language may afford some perspective on the problem of language as it is experienced today. It is possible that biblical language, if interrogated properly, will also shed some light on the relation of language to the question of the "real."

The essays presented here doubtless lack overt and "logical" coherence. While each may be read by itself, without reference to the others, the collection turns on a center as yet unfocalized. An element in the disposition, mentioned above, is a "soft focus" on the problem. A "soft focus" requires that the circumference and contours of the issue be permitted to emerge along with its center. The effort is made to allow the problem to present itself—to listen aggressively to what various modes of language are saying with reference to themselves. It will come as no surprise that the work lacks a definitive conclusion. My aim has been to uncover the problem and some clues pointing to its resolution by attempting to sketch a picture, or rather a series of pictures, I know only by anticipation.

Much of what is written doubtless stands in need of translation. Did it not require translation, it would not, perhaps, have had to be written. But into what can it be translated? It can be fairly demanded only that other pictures be drawn—perhaps an endless succession—each of which would suffer from the same deficiency, but the total impact of which might evoke understanding. In that event translation would become superfluous because translation would have taken place. The reader may bear in mind that other pictures have been and are being drawn by littérateurs, philosophers, and theologians, pictures which have founded and already considerably extended the series. To this series the present work aspires only to make a modest contribution.

These essays invite the reader not to founder on the words and sentences. The "logic" does not aspire to a rigid dialectic. What is to be listened for is what is struggling to come to expression. If it is borne in mind that something is being talked about which requires a deformation of our common speech, and thus our way of looking at reality, it may be possible to accord imprecise language a certain latitude. In any case, it is a curious not-knowing and not-having that is seeking its way into the clarity of expression.

It has already been intimated that this work has the vocation of the word ultimately in view. Vocation *of* the word may be understood either as the call of the word, its summons (subjective genitive), or as the task (vocation as calling) of articulating, proclaiming the word that summons (objective genitive). The reader may take it in either way, since hearing and speaking, attending and articulating, are taken to be coconstitutive: they are reciprocally enabling. He who aspires to the enunciation of the word must first learn to hear it; and he who hears the word will have found the means to articulate it.

It is not, however, to the hearing of the word nor its enunciation that these studies are immediately devoted. They reflect, rather, on language and hermeneutic as they enter into hearing and speaking. Such reflection makes it necessary to draw near hearing and speaking in order to "listen in" on the process; to participate, as it were, with a side glance at what is going on.

The word that is heard and spoken, spoken and heard, in the context of Christian theology, is called word of God. The subject matter of these essays is thus the Christian gospel. It is to the articulation of this word that the ministry of the church is called, and the pulpit is understood as the place where its enunciation takes place. Since the subject matter is word of God, it is appropriate to begin with some preliminary reflections on language, hermeneutic, and word of God as they bear directly on the vocation of the church's ministry. In this way the diverse perspectives from which the matter is subsequently viewed can be focused at the outset on the concrete issue of the proclamation of the word. This procedure may be welcomed by those to whom the terrain of contemporary hermeneutic is still largely unexplored, since these brief remarks bring together, in a practical way, themes which are later elaborated in a maze of detail. It is to be hoped that a practical introduction to a more abstruse discussion will not disappoint those who prefer a concise theoretical introduction to a more extended practical treatment.

I

This has been described as a time of the death of God.[2] The affirmation of the death of God is neither a scientific nor a philosophical assertion, but a *confession,* a confession that God is no longer "there," no longer available. It is useless to contest the point unless it is understood that the affirmation of the existence of God is not the contradiction of the death of God. The religious affirmation of God's reality, from the point of view of the death of God, is neither here nor there: it is simply irrelevant.

The testimony to the death of God bears witness to a correlative tragedy, namely, the failure of language. It is possible to claim that God has withdrawn only because man can no longer speak authentically of him. When God disappears, man falls silent. He falls silent in spite of the fact that he may even talk more. His talk, under the circumstances, becomes mere verbalization, vain prattle without ultimate reference. One may talk of God, to be sure, even affirm his existence or speak of his attributes, but such talk, if prattle, betrays its

---

[2] Cf. R. Bultmann, "The Idea of God and Modern Man," *JThC* 2 (New York: Harper Torchbook, 1965), 83–95, where further references may be found.

own emptiness and becomes inverted testimony to the death of God. This is the basis on which the observation is made that the religious affirmation of God's existence is at least irrelevant, at most testimony against itself.

If our specific concern is with the language of faith, with the message of reconciliation, with the proclamation of the gospel, it is not too much to say that the question of reality and language has everything to do with that concern. It is averred by those from whom one has a right to expect more than idle opinions that the preaching of the gospel has taken on the character of prattle. This means that the preached word no longer proceeds out of the reality to which it is supposed to give expression. "How can you speak good, when you are evil?" When preaching consists of words split off from the reality of grace, it has been reduced to talk. Under such circumstances, not only is God dead, but Christ, too, remains an inert figure in the tomb. It may therefore be said: the gospel is not really being preached because its claim is not being heard. If that sounds as though it has the matter backward, it is an intentional reversal: the articulation of the gospel depends upon the reality to which it refers becoming audible in language. The failure of language is commensurate with the disappearance of the reality to which it refers. To put it succinctly, when the language of faith fails, it is because faith itself has failed. Or, conversely, when the word of God invokes faith, man responds in the language that bears the reality of faith. When God is silent, man becomes a gossip; when God speaks and man hears, kerygmatic language is born and the gospel is preached.

There is no intention to argue the case for the failure of preaching in our time. Such an argument would itself be idle. The failure of preaching will not and cannot be demonstrated or even discovered until the gospel is apprehended afresh, in which case the need for argument will have ceased. In short, the only course ever open to those who are concerned with the proclamation of the gospel, whether or not they believe this is a time of the failure of the word of faith, is to learn to listen as never before, with ears sharply tuned for the tones that are suspected of having fallen on deaf ears; to seek to hear the silent tolling of grace as it echoes faintly from the traditional language of the church. Perhaps then, by some miracle, the sacred trust of the gospel, which comes not according to man nor from man, but through a revelation of Jesus Christ (Gal. 1:2), may be granted to this time and place.

The vital nerve of the hermeneutical problem—to introduce now the catchword—is therefore the failure of language. The failure of language, as it relates to preaching, is correlative with deafness, with insensibility to the word which God has spoken in Christ. If this fundamental connection between hearing and speaking, between reality and language, can be made clear, the relation of the hermeneutical problem to the minister's task will have been grasped. It will have been understood that the minister's work is essentially hermeneutical.

II

It is perhaps advisable to clear away some of the common misunderstandings which attach to the term hermeneutics, if indeed that term is any longer comprehensible at all.[3] Hermeneutics is traditionally conceived as the theory of which exegesis is the practice, i.e., has to do with the rules for the interpretation of scripture. Of the elements involved in the interpretation of a text—i.e., the text, the interpreter, the interpretation, and the rules governing interpretation—hermeneutics in its classical form concentrates on the last. With the rise of modern scientific biblical study, hermeneutics was gradually replaced by the critical historical method, now nearly universally known and practiced, and hermeneutics as a special subdivision of theology dropped out of sight.

Historical criticism as the modern counterpart to hermeneutics insisted, and rightly so, on applying to the biblical text the same rules that were used in the interpretation of other documents. It was under the tutelage of the historical method that the integrity of the text was discovered, and it is by this method that the victory over rigid, allegedly literalistic orthodoxies was achieved. Nevertheless, the historical method was seriously deficient at one point: it failed to take into account the limitations and biases of the interpreter. It was to remedy this deficiency that Rudolf Bultmann, taking his lead from Schleiermacher and Dilthey, added the existential dimension to the historical-critical method. Under Bultmann hermeneutic came to embrace all the elements involved in the interpretation of a text.

The presupposition which underlies the whole development from the rise of modern biblical criticism to Bultmann is that when one does

---

[3] For an extensive and illuminating discussion of the history and components of hermeneutics, see James M. Robinson in *New Frontiers* II (see Abbreviations), 1–77. Hermeneutics (plural) is used to refer to the traditional discipline, hermeneutic (singular) to the subject as it has been reintroduced into the current discussion, in accordance with Robinson's practice (*ibid.*, p. x).

exegesis he is interpreting the *text*. That is, it is the text that requires interpretation. Yet from historical criticism it had already been learned that the biblical text, like any other text, is composed of human language and is therefore culturally conditioned. It was but a short step to the conclusion that the New Testament is only a relative statement of the word of God. It was not until Barth's commentary on Romans that the force of this discovery began to be felt: if the text is a human word and therefore historically conditioned, it is not the text that is the word of God, but the text itself is already the *interpretation* of the word of God. Barth's methodology, as he describes it in the Preface to the second edition of the *Römerbrief*, is to live with the text until it disappears and one is confronted with the divine word itself. One sees emerging here the view that it is not the text that is to be interpreted— the text is already interpretation—but the word of God itself, which, of course, cannot be equated with any human formulation.

If it is God's word that is the object of exegetical endeavors, the process is at a dead end, for this word is not accessible to the exegete as an object for scrutiny. Yet this blind alley is precisely what led Gerhard Ebeling and Ernst Fuchs to the conclusion, remarkable as it may sound, that the word of God is not interpreted—it interprets! That is to say, it is indeed the word rather than the words with which exegetes have ultimately to do, but since they are in the embarrassing position of being unable to lay hold of that word, they can only permit it to lay hold of them. With this startling insight the direction of the flow between interpreter and text that has dominated modern biblical criticism from its inception is reversed, and hermeneutics in its traditional sense becomes hermeneutic, now understood as the effort to allow God to address man through the medium of the text.

It is precisely the assumption, endemic to the modern period, that man is the subject to which all things, including the word of God, must give account that led to the failure of language, and thus to disintegration of the language of faith. Implicit in the broader phenomenon is the assumption that the text is the object of interpretation; as "object" the text simply falls silent. The consequence has been the debilitation if not the collapse of preaching.

With man as the filter through which the word must pass, or, if you like, arbiter of the meaning of the word, it is inevitable that he will censor out what he does not wish to hear and audit only what he is predisposed to hear. Yet the word of God, like a great work of art, is not on trial. The work of art exists in its own right, to be viewed and contemplated, received or dismissed, but not reconstructed. The text, too, although shaped by human hands, stands there to be read and pondered, but not manipulated. With respect to the edifices in which men dwell, the late Winston Churchill once remarked, "We shape our buildings, and thereafter they shape us."[4] The view of hermeneutics which begins with the assumption that the text requires interpretation, that it is, so to speak, on trial, has the matter backward. It is not the text that requires interpretation, but—if the text is called forth by what it says—the interpreter! This reversal is what makes sense of the affirmation that the gospel is not being preached because it is not being heard.

Such an understanding of hermeneutic by no means vitiates the affirmation that the only authentic access to the true word which God has spoken in Christ is through the New Testament. Nor does it undercut the crucial function of the critical-historical method. On the contrary, this view allows both to come into their own.

It may be rejoined that the affirmation that the gospel is not being preached because it is not being heard scarcely needs elaboration. It is a matter which every conscientious minister understands well, and which the church has never forgotten. A look into the textbooks on homiletics, the church papers, and best sermons of the year is ample demonstration. But the issue cannot be contested in this way. The question being posed is not about what one says he does or ought to do, but about whether the language of the proclamation goes together with the reality of faith like new wine and fresh skins (Mk. 2:22). It is the question whether the words spoken from the pulpit and in the counseling chamber carry with them the reality of God's redemptive grace. It is the question whether the sermon gives presence to the Christ for both speaker and hearer. It is a matter of determining whether preaching any longer refers to anything real, or whether it merely continues to traffic in words and concepts which have long since been dashed to pieces on the rocks of a profane world.

The threat to the preaching ministry of the church is that it *thinks* it has not forgotten that hearing and speaking are correlative, that it *thinks* it has not forgotten what word of God says when heard. Those who mount the pulpit Sunday in and Sunday out before a sea of people are inclined to sail their ships into the harbor of Pharisaic intransigence. They do so, of course, in the interest of a firm anchorage. It is there, however, that one can forget and then forget that he has for-

[4] Quoted by Roy W. Larson, *Christian Advocate* IX, 3 (February 11, 1965), 15.

gotten. He cannot remember because he cannot remember forgetting. The horizon of the sea has become the mouth of the harbor.

Only as the memory is refreshed by the silent tolling of a largely vacuous language is it possible to recall that at one time, somewhere in the collective past, one ceased to hear. Therein lies the subtlety of the dilemma: those concerned for the renewal of the word cannot remind each other until someone is himself reminded, until someone is again addressed by the text of faith in such a way that hearing is restored.

III

It has been assumed that the vocation of the minister is to "preach Christ crucified, a stumbling-block to Jews and folly to Gentiles, but to those who are called, both Jews and Greeks, Christ the *power* of God and the *wisdom* of God" (I Cor. 1:23 f., RSV). That the minister as the servant of Christ is "the aroma of Christ among those who are being saved and among those who are perishing, to one a fragrance from death to death, to the other a fragrance from life to life" (II Cor. 2:15 f., RSV). The Pauline formulation may well meet some resistance in the American tradition with its strong activist leanings. If so, it is because the relation between word and deed has not been properly understood. The word to be spoken is not mere word, but the word that creates, brings into being. Like the word spoken in creation, it is the word that brings man from death to life or the word that condemns. By it men are lost, and by it men are saved. It is the word spoken in the name and therefore in the authority of God.

Such a word need not, of course, be phonetic. It may be a gesture, a deed, or even silence.[5] It is by no means limited to formal occasions on which ministers speak. Its essential characteristic is that it gives expression to God's word in Christ, that it speaks or interprets or translates the meaning of the saying, "The word became flesh" (Jn. 1:14). Such speaking, interpreting, or translating is always life-giving or death-bringing because it is the word of God coming to speech, the word which cannot fail.

This is hermeneutic as it is now understood. The hermeneut—the one who practices hermeneutic—is he who, having been addressed by

---

[5] The current use of the term language by one school of thought to cover more than vocables, i. e., more than the spoken or written word, is a metaphorical (nonliteral) use of the term. It is so used in order to call attention to a dimension of language long lost to view, viz., its event-character. On the word-character of deeds, cf. G. Ebeling, "Theology and the Evidentness of the Ethical," *JThC* 2 (1965), 119.

the word of God and having heard, is enabled to speak, interpret, or translate what he has heard into the human vernacular so that its power is transmitted through speech. If the minister is not a hermeneut, he has missed his vocation.

IV

Is this understanding of language and hermeneutic related in any way to the New Testament? Part II of this volume is devoted to a detailed examination of this question in connection with the parable of Jesus, and Part III in connection with the letter of Paul. It will suffice here to set out briefly the hearing of the text from which the preceding understanding of hermeneutic is derived. The concern will not be with hermeneutical theories, but with the substance of the gospel, for hermeneutic has now become the doctrine of the word of God.

The larger text for this preliminary sketch is the parables and parabolic deeds of grace to be found in the synoptic Gospels.[6] These would include such parables as the Prodigal Son, the Laborers in the Vineyard, the Great Supper, the Lost Sheep and Lost Coin, the Two Sons, and others; among the parabolic deeds of grace the story of Zacchaeus is typical.

Parables and parabolic deeds of grace are sprinkled liberally throughout the Gospel tradition. Considered as a group they reveal certain more or less constant features: (1) they are regularly addressed to, or acted out for the benefit of, Jesus' opponents; (2) they invariably cause offense to these opponents (usually designated as scribes and Pharisees); (3) they are also addressed to sinners, and normally produce joy and/or thanksgiving, either on the part of God and the angels, or on the part of the sinner who receives grace, or both.[7]

All three of these features are present in the parabolic deed of grace represented by the story of Zacchaeus (Lk. 19:1–10). That the context of this drama is the opposition to Jesus is indicated by the anonymous chorus of v. 7: "And when they saw it they all murmured." Making oneself a guest in the home of a chief tax collector who was rich could not help but evoke criticism. So the chorus says: "He has gone in to be the guest of a man who is a sinner." That is an exclamation of incredulity with a sharp edge of reproach. But Zacchaeus, we are told, jumped down from his perch and received him joyfully.

These three features provoke three questions: (1) Who really hears

---

[6] On parabolic actions, cf. Jeremias, *Parables* (see Abbreviations), 227 ff.

[7] On the question of audience, see *infra*, chap. 5, 143 ff.; chap. 6, 176–82.

the parable of grace, or really understands the act of grace? (2) What is the affront of grace which regularly induces deafness in righteous auditors? And (3) what is the courage which joy brings that enables the sinner to overcome the affront of grace and so to hear the word spoken for him? In answering these questions we may draw on the larger tradition.

With his diverse audience in view, Jesus aims the parables of grace in three different directions: (1) he sometimes directs attention to the poor and the sinners ("I came not to call the righteous, but sinners" Mk. 2:17 and parallels); (2) he sometimes invites the righteous and wealthy to consider themselves ("You brood of vipers" Mt. 12:34); or, (3), he may draw attention indirectly to God ("there will be more joy in heaven over one sinner who repents than over ninety-nine righteous persons who need no repentance" Lk. 15:7). But these distinctions are purely formal and tend to obscure the basic question: Who hears these parables? In the parable of the Prodigal Son, as it is called, there are the speaker, the father, and the three auditors: (1) the servants, (2) the elder son, and (3) the younger son. When the father sees the younger son approaching, he runs to meet him (an unbecoming act for an older Oriental), embraces him, orders a robe, ring, and shoes for him, and then crowns his welcome with a merry feast.[8] (All these eloquent deeds, incidentally, are in effect words!) Who in this circle of hearers understands these gracious and forgiving acts? Who now understands the meaning of the father's love? To ask the question borders on the trite. Nevertheless, the question pulls one up short when he understands what is being asked. For on this question the whole gospel turns.

Well then, the younger son heard. To be sure. He hears and understands the father's love. But who is the younger son? The younger son, of course, is the prodigal. And that means that he is the offender, the sinner. It is the sinner who hears and understands the parables of grace. The tax collectors and harlots hear and rejoice because this grace is for them.

But is that all? Does not the older son also hear? Does he not grasp that it is *his* father whose love is reaching out to the prodigal? Does he not recall that it is *his* brother who was lost and is found? The reply is unequivocal: indeed, he does hear and that is just the difficulty. Such grace as this, which is blind to merit, can only provoke anger. Who

---

[8] For the details, see Jeremias, *Parables*, 130 f.

among elder sons can tolerate a father who is utterly without discrimination?

It has to be said that, in the primary sense, it is the sinner who hears and understands. Zacchaeus jumps down and receives Jesus with joy; the laborers hired in the eleventh hour gratefully receive the wages which they did not earn; the tax collectors and prostitutes hear him gladly. It is the sinner who hears, for he alone understands grace. But the understanding of grace is not something brought to the parables or to Jesus either by squandering oneself morally or physically or by having the right theology. No, it is something one gains from meeting grace itself. The Apostle Paul learned the meaning of grace from his status as blameless before the law! It may be said, then, that from an encounter with grace one learns what grace is by learning that he is a sinner. One cannot be grasped without the other.

Consequently, it is all the same whether Jesus points to outcasts, to the righteous, or to God: those who stand in his audience will be able to identify themselves only as they understand his word of grace. And when they hear that word they will know. They will know not only who they are but who God is. They will understand themselves as sinners claimed by grace only when they know what God is; they will know what God is only when they understand themselves as sinners claimed by grace.

But the elder son also hears. The chorus at Jericho murmurs; the laborers hired in the first hour cry out for justice; the Pharisees are incensed because he goes in and eats with sinners. So the elder son, too, learns who he is when he learns what God is. Only he refuses to be identified as a sinner because he is righteous and so has no need for the grace of God. The word of grace and the deed of grace divide the audience into younger sons and elder sons—into sinners and Pharisees.

This is what Ernst Fuchs means when he says that one does not interpret the parables; *the parables interpret him*. The auditors are not invited to consider their response; they either rejoice because as sinners they are glad to be dependent on grace, or they are offended because they want justice on top of grace. They cannot go away and come back another day to give their decision. When man has been addressed by the word of grace, he has already been interpreted.

With this note one already strikes upon the affront of grace which turns so many listeners into elder sons. Such listeners are simply outraged that something so insubstantial as a word, even a word of forgiveness and acceptance, should be made the touchstone of their relation to God. They are horrified at the kind of undiscriminating and even irresponsible God that is coming to expression in such a word. But most important of all, they find it incredible that Jesus cannot see what they themselves see so clearly, namely, that the commandments and religion provide a handy means of discriminating between righteous and sinner. If he sees it, he has turned the criteria quite upside down.

In the parable of the Laborers in the Vineyard (Mt. 20:1–15)[9] those hired early in the day protest because (1) they are paid last, and (2) they are paid the same amount as those who worked only one hour. One is not to think here of labor problems. One is to think of the householder who says, "Is your vision evil because I am generous?" (v. 15: completely obscured in RSV!) In the parable of the Two Sons (Mt. 21:28–32), one of whom says he will but doesn't, while the other says he won't but does, Jesus draws this conslusion: "Truly, I say to you, the tax collectors and the harlots go into the kingdom of God and you do not." (Verse 31: comparison expressing exclusion, also obscured in RSV!) What could be clearer? The word that turns the righteousness (not hypocrisy!) of the Pharisee out, that cancels the loyalty of the elder son, that overlooks the perseverance of the early laborers in the vineyard, has something drastically wrong with it. And one does well to reject such a word and him who speaks it, in order to save the church and religion!

There is nothing wrong with such logic except that it fails to discern that it is man and not God who is on trial. It refuses to let God be God. *The Pharisees are those who insist on interpreting the word of grace rather than letting themselves be interpreted by it.* The elder son is he who insists that his loyalty counts for something: his loyalty must be the basis of interpretation, i.e., the condition of any view of grace acceptable to him. For that reason the grace in the parable strikes him as rejection. And so it is with the righteous—the term need not be self-righteous, merely righteous—who resist being exposed as sinners and are therefore constrained to hear the word of grace as blasphemy.

It is not so with the tax collectors and harlots. They hear the word gladly because it is the word for them. They hear it with the joy that attends the discovery of a priceless treasure. Out of that joy arises the courage to sell all they have in order to acquire it.

The word of grace is therefore the word of the cross. Jesus goes to

---

[9] Cf. Fuchs II (see Abbreviations), 219–26; 361–64 [32–38; 154–56].

the cross because he clings to the word of grace: that is at once the
offense to the elder son and the hope of the younger. It is an offense to
the elder son because he, unlike Jesus, cannot give up his claim; it is
the hope of the younger because he knows he has no claim. He who
hears the word of grace as a word addressed to him knows the
meaning of the cross. For just as Jesus invests everything, including
whatever title he had a right to claim, as well as his life, in the certainty
of that word of grace, so he who hears the word will know what it
requires of him. By hearing he has been claimed as a vessel of grace
and plunged into the way of the cross.

Who has ears to hear let him hear.

Theses Concerning the Deeds and Parables of Grace

1. Grace always wounds from behind, at the point where man thinks
he is least vulnerable.

2. Grace is harder than man thinks: he moralizes judgment in order
to take the edge off it.

3. Grace is more indulgent than man thinks: but it is never indulgent
at the point where he thinks it ought to be indulgent.

4. Grace is not something man can have at all.

5. Grace remains a mystery: it unveils itself as the ground of faith,
but evaporates like a mist before the acquisitive eyes of belief.

PART ONE

Language as Event
and Theology

The language of a people is its fate.
Amos N. Wilder,
The Language of the Gospel

Language as Event:
Bultmann and Heidegger

ERNST FUCHS AND GERHARD EBELING VIEW THEIR WORK as theology of the word of God. They understand word of God as language event.[1] Language event suggests a deliberate mutation of Rudolf Bultmann's characteristic phrase "salvation event" (*Heilsereignis*), as indeed it is. For this reason it is important to understand Bultmann's concept of salvation event and the relation of language to it, for it is his understanding of the word and the word alone as salvation event that is the immediate parent of the programs of Fuchs and Ebeling. Fuchs and Ebeling, furthermore, regard themselves as beginning with but going beyond Bultmann. Bultmann has thus mediated a concern for language to theology, although he did not foresee the developments that concern would precipitate.

The initial obstacle in the way of grasping Bultmann's disposition to language, as well as that of Fuchs and Ebeling, is that all three are dependent to a greater or lesser extent upon Heidegger's understanding of language. In view of the importance of the lineage, it is necessary to venture upon the hazardous task of providing a very elementary exposition of "language as the house of being."

The chronology of the development is somewhat confused. Bultmann is said to be dependent upon the earlier Heidegger, whereas Fuchs and Ebeling have taken their cues more from the later Hei-

---

[1] *Sprachereignis* (Fuchs) and *Wortgeschehen* (Ebeling) are both translated "language event." Fuchs has specifically repudiated ."speech event" ("Was ist ein Sprachereignis?" Fuchs II, 424–30 [207–12]), so the use of the term language is in the interest of avoiding confusion. Cf. J. M. Robinson, *New Frontiers* II, 54 n. 153. *Sprache* and *Wort*, *Ereignis* and *Geschehen*, respectively, are to be taken as synonyms, as will be noted below.

degger.[2] Be that as it may, it seems appropriate to place Heidegger between Bultmann, on the one hand, and Fuchs and Ebeling, on the other, since each borrows from a different side of Heidegger's work. In any case, Bultmann stands on his own feet and is quite capable of appearing first.

The explication of Heidegger will, hopefully, cast light both backward and forward, although it should be emphasized that Fuchs and Ebeling, like Bultmann, do not propose merely to lean on Heidegger.

I
LANGUAGE EVENT AS SALVATION EVENT
(*Sprachereignis als Heilsereignis*)

Rudolf Bultmann's insight that all mythological language objectifies God's acts by projecting them upon the plane of nature and history, thus making them visible, led him to reject the category of *Heilsgeschichte*.[3] He was concerned in this move to make it clear that faith does not permit itself any extrinsic basis in objective facts, certainly not in objective "saving facts." He was moved to point out, furthermore, that the language of faith, when it pictures God's acts mythologically, obscures the true character of faith precisely by its objectifying tendencies. Having gained his basic insight from mythological language, he could then transpose the problem to all theological thinking.

But the most important thing is that basic insight that the theological thoughts of the New Testament are the unfolding of faith itself growing out of that new understanding of God, the world, and man which is conferred in and by faith—or, as it can also be phrased: *out of one's self-understanding*. . . . If the scientific presentation of the theological thoughts of the New Testament has the task of pointing them out as the unfolding of believing self-understanding, it then presents *not the object of faith but faith itself* in its own self-interpretation.[4]

That is to say, Bultmann regards all theological language about God and the world as something which faith creates on the basis of its self-understanding.

[2] On the relationship of Heidegger to the theology oriented to the problem of language, see J. M. Robinson, *New Frontiers* I, 3–76; II, 43–49. Cf. Amos N. Wilder, *New Frontiers* II, 215 and n. 26.

[3] Cf. his review of Oscar Cullmann's book *Christ and Time*, in *Existence and Faith*, 226–40; *Kerygma and Myth* I, 10 f., 197; *Jesus Christ and Mythology*, 19 ff., 60 ff.; etc. (see Abbreviations).

[4] *Theology of the New Testament* II, 239 (italics his).

This conclusion is not surprising when one recalls that the history of religions school, as represented by W. Wrede, for example, regarded theology as the product of reflective thinking about the objects of faith and hence an epiphenomenon of the religious experience. While Bultmann is not willing to accept the history of religions view—because it does not understand theology as the "unfolding of believing self-comprehension"[5] —he does think that the legitimate meaning of theological statements is not grasped until one understands their existential reference.[6] For this reason it becomes a problem for him whether one can speak legitimately of God at all or not.[7]

Bultmann's view of biblical history, consequently, is linked to his understanding of biblical language. If biblical language is to be de-objectified or existentialized in order to make its intent clear, then biblical history can no longer be *Heilsgeschichte,* for *Heilsgeschichte* is inherently mythological. Salvation history, if we may so translate the term, is only the reverse side of secular history, in that both deal in objective facts, i.e., facts open to public verification, and hence are dominated by the same "logic." Modern man in particular is misled by this "apologetic antithesis."[8]

For *Heilsgeschichte* Bultmann substituted the term *Heilsgeschehen* or *Heilsereignis* in order to emphasize the event-character of God's acts.[9] This poses the question: How can an event of the past, i.e., God's act in Jesus Christ, continue to be eventful? Bultmann's answer is that

[5] *Ibid.,* 246.

[6] *Ibid.,* 247, 249 ff.

[7] "Welchen Sinn hat es, von Gott zu reden?" *Theologische Blätter* 4 (1925), 129–35 = *Glauben und Verstehen* I, 26–37. = "What Sense Is There To Speak of God?" F. H. Littell, trans., *Christian Scholar* 43 (1960), 213–22.

[8] The formulation "apologetic antithesis" is Fuchs's: *Hermeneutik,* 94.

[9] When Bultmann speaks of God's act in Christ as event, he means, of course, that it is event only as something *happens to* man: "God as acting does not refer to an event which can be perceived by me without myself being drawn into the event as into God's action, without myself taking part in it as being acted upon. . . . The encounter with God can be an event for man only here and now, since man lives within the limits of space and time" (*Jesus Christ and Mythology,* 68). The emphasis on the *pro-me-ity* is designed to exclude understanding the redemptive event as taking place on the plane of "natural" events (*Kerygma and Myth* I, 197) and, at the same time, to prevent it being understood as idea (*Kerygma and Myth* II, 192): natural event and idea are means by which sinful man holds God at arm's length in order to maintain his self-assertion. For this reason Bultmann can say, "the saving efficacy of the cross is not derived from the fact that it is the cross of Christ: it is the cross of Christ because it has this saving efficacy" (*Kerygma and Myth* I, 41). The point can best be understood perhaps if it is noticed that for Bultmann God's word (act) addresses man's *will* (*Glauben und Verstehen* I, 272).

the event of the past which is decisive for man's salvation is continually made present in the proclamation.

The "demythologized" sense of the assertion that Jesus Christ is the eschatological phenomenon that brings the world to its end is precisely this, that Christ is not merely a past phenomenon, but the ever-present Word of God, expressing not a general truth, but a concrete message, that Word that destroys and in destruction gives life. The paradox of the Christian faith is precisely this, that the eschatological process which sets an end to the world became an event in the history of the world, and becomes an event in every true sermon, and in every Christian utterance.[10]

If the call for demythologizing suggests a negative evaluation of language, at least of a certain understanding of language, Bultmann's understanding of the event-character of God's act in Christ requires a positive evaluation of language.[11] Indeed, Bultmann can speak of the event of Christ as word, as though its word-character were what made it eventful.[12] This suggestion is supported by Bultmann's observation that, while God encounters man at all times and in every place, he cannot be seen and heard just anywhere unless his word comes and makes each moment understandable in the light of the word.[13]

Ernst Fuchs and Gerhard Ebeling have taken up Bultmann's positive evaluation of language, which they indicate by altering *Heilsgeschehen* and *Heilsereignis* to *Wortgeschehen* and *Sprachereignis*, respectively. This shift in terminology goes together with their attempt to

---

[10] *Kerygma and Myth* II, 193.

[11] Bultmann reduces language to two types of statements: (*a*) those which convey information, and (*b*) those which demand a decision (S. M. Ogden, *Christ Without Myth* [see Abbreviations], 50). This dichotomy provides the grounds for both a negative and positive evaluation of language with respect to the kerygma. Cf. Paul M. van Buren, *The Secular Meaning of the Gospel* (New York: The Macmillan Co., 1963), 59 f.

[12] *Glauben und Verstehen* I, 289 f.; *Essays Philosophical and Theological* (London: SCM Press, 1955), 11 f.; *Kerygma and Myth* I, 206 f. The following passage is directly to the point: "For the love directed to *me*—and this alone can make me a new creature—cannot be demonstrated by historical observation. It can only be promised to me directly; and this is what is done by the proclamation. To go behind the Christ who is preached is to misunderstand the preaching; it is only in the word, as the one who is preached, that he encounters us, that the love of God encounters us in him. But once again, it must be emphasized that the word is what it is—namely, revelation—not because of its timeless content, but rather as an address that is brought to us here and now by common ordinary men. Therefore, *faith* also, like the word, is revelation because it is only real in this occurrence and otherwise is nothing. It is no disposition of the human soul, no being convinced, but rather the answer to an address" (*Existence and Faith*, 87). Italics his.

[13] *Kerygma und Mythos* II, 204 (*Kerygma and Myth* I, 207).

focus the salvation event in language itself. The discrepancy in terminology between Fuchs and Ebeling has no significance other than that
one takes the first Bultmannian term as his reference, while the other
takes the second; one hearkens back to Luther, the other reflects
Heidegger. *Wort* and *Sprache* are regarded as synonyms.[14] The striking parallelism to the Bultmannian terminology indicates that Fuchs
and Ebeling regard themselves as standing in the Bultmann tradition.
It is for this reason that the current movement in theology to understanding language as event should be approached through Bultmann.

We may take two characteristic formulations of Bultmann as our
points of departure. The first is from his essay on the word of God in
the New Testament.

The concept "Word of God" in the New Testament is likewise now understood [in the light of Old Testament usage] when it designates *the*
quantity for which it is predominantly used: *the Christian kerygma*. It is a
word which has power, which is effective. To be spoken is essential for this
word; it is preached and must be heard. It is instruction, command, and
must be done and kept.[15]

The second is found in the context of his defense of demythologizing.

The man who wishes to believe in God as his God must realize that he has
nothing in his hand on which to base his faith. He is suspended in mid-air,
and cannot demand a proof of the Word which addresses him. For the
ground and object of faith are identical.[16]

The second indicates that Bultmann permits speaking of God's deed of
salvation only within the relation of word and faith; the first, that the
word is what creates faith, effects faith, when it is spoken and heard.

Ebeling unconditionally affirms these two points in his own extended
discussion of Bultmann, but he is concerned to inquire whether
Bultmann has thought the relation of word and faith adequately
through to its ground.[17] Nevertheless, Ebeling is clear that Bultmann
has attempted to carry out a methodological justification of a theology

14 Cf. Fuchs, "Die Spannung im neutestamentlichen Christusglauben," *ZThK* 59
(1962), 41 [= Fuchs III, 292]; J. M. Robinson, *New Frontiers* II, 57.
15 *Glauben und Verstehen* I, 279 f. (italics his). Bultmann cites the New Testament
in a series of footnotes.
16 *Kerygma and Myth* I, 211.
17 *Theologie und Verkündigung* (see Abbreviations), 28 ff., especially 29 f.

of the word in his hermeneutical program.[18] Ebeling, consequently, understands himself as standing in the same relation to Bultmann as Bultmann at an earlier date did in relation to Barth, i.e., as more adequately executing the intention of this theological program.

It is not surprising, then, that Ebeling understands word event as a more precise formulation of Bultmann's own position. He defines word event in a variety of contexts, but always with the same two elements in view, referred to above. For example,

So we do not get at the nature of words by asking what they contain, but by asking what they effect, what they set going, what future they disclose.[19]

And again:

The Bible bears witness to a proclamation which has taken place and is the impulse to a proclamation which is to take place. And this event, which claims to be the Word of God, is not mere speech. But it sets something in motion, just as it itself was set in motion. It has to do with reality, which it changes.[20]

Going together with language as event is the exclusive connection of word and faith.

When God speaks, however, the content of the statement is identical with the will of God and therefore cannot be detached in any way from the person of the speaker. What God says, he also personally sees to, so that to believe the statements of God's Word—even if they should be statements of fact!—is not to believe "something," but by definition to believe God. That hangs together with the fact that the content of what God says always unconditionally concerns the person of the hearer, that is, that God's Word rightly understood is never statement but always address. A word is received as God's Word only when it is not in itself an isolated object of faith, but opens the way for faith to find its ground in God.[21]

The content of the word and the fulfilling of the word, its reaching its goal, are identical.[22]

18 *Word and Faith*, 310.
19 *Nature of Faith*, 187.
20 *Ibid.*, 183 f.
21 *Word and Faith*, 211.
22 *Nature of Faith*, 87.

Word event thus has to do not with the "logical" but with the "historical" function of words,[23] not with statement but with address, and not
only demands faith but evokes it.[24] "Historical" is contrasted with
"logical" because word as word event affects existence itself in its
existing; it does not simply supply answers, but waits for an answer,
gives power to answer. The very existence of man is at stake in word
event, for it empowers man to exist as one who answers.[25]

Fuchs, too, emphasizes the close relation between word and faith.[26]
His interest, moreover, is to press Bultmann's program to its conclusion so as to set the text, i.e., the word, once again in motion:

Rather one must let oneself be drawn by the gospel back to where space
and time make sense in terms of a movement, in terms of a path and
walking, as space for others and time for us. For this reason I have in this
course replaced Bultmann's program and method of demythologizing with
what seems to me a more radical existentialist interpretation, so as to bring
the text anew on the road and put it in motion. What resulted was at least
an analysis of Jesus' love. It should confirm itself as a movement of our own
existence. What in all of this is theory should be brought to an end for now,
in order that love itself can begin to speak. What does love say? "Arise, let
us leave theory!"[27]

Sprachereignis sets the text in motion in order to effect love. If the
word of God is not this, it is nothing.

II

A shift in the linguistic frame of reference may be of material
assistance in explicating language as event. It may be suggested that the
function of language in *Sprachereignis* falls under the heading of what
J. L. Austin has called performative discourse.[28] In this order of

---

[23] *Word and Faith*, 352.

[24] *Ibid.*, 29.

[25] *Ibid.*, 352.

[26] "Logos," *RGG* IV (1960), 437, 438, 440; Fuchs II, 429 [211].

[27] "Schluss der Vorlesung über das Johannesevangelium, Berlin S.S. 1958 (24. 7.
1958)," Ergänzungsheft to *Hermeneutik*, 13. Translated by J. M. Robinson, *New
Frontiers* II, 53.

[28] I refer to his essay "Performative Utterances," a BBC talk delivered in 1956 and
published in *Philosophical Papers* (Oxford: Clarendon Press, 1961), 220–39. The work
of Austin was called to my attention by Carl Michalson both orally and in an article
entitled, "The Ghost of Logical Positivism," *Christian Scholar* 43 (1960), 223–30. The
reference to Austin is on p. 224. Cf. the remarks of Frederick Ferré, *Language, Logic,
and God* (New York: Harper & Row, 1961), 55 f., 65.

discourse, a person is not merely *saying* something, he is doing something. The language itself is act. The vows exchanged in the wedding ceremony are good examples: one is not there reporting on a marriage—which means that the vows are not subject to verification—but indulging in marriage.[29] Other examples would be the sentence pronounced by a judge, the christening of a ship, the knighting of a hero, a provision in a will, an apology, a Presidential proclamation. This type of utterance cannot be adjudged either true or false.[30] It may, of course, fail of its aim, i.e., turn out to be mere words after all, which suggests that one should take care to observe the qualifications which apply to performative language.

Functional linguistic analysis is identifying, in much more mundane terms, something which those who study primitive cultures have known about for some time. I refer to the primitive bond between the linguistic and the mythico-religious consciousness, to use Cassirer's phrase, which fuses verbal structures and mythical entities; such verbal structures are "endowed with certain mythical powers . . . the Word, in fact, becomes a sort of primary force, in which all being and doing originate."[31] At this level language is a primal force. The *word* is often the instrument of creation, the *name* of the god is supreme in power, the individual is constituted by his *name*. The essential identity between the word and what it denotes lies at the base of this understanding of language. Naming does not mean inventing a convenient designation, but giving reality to the object, calling it into existence. By the same token, knowledge of the name gives power over the thing to which the name belongs. This is badly stated by virtue of the common understanding of name: what is meant is not that knowing the name gives power over something else; but power over the name, which *is* the thing. The unity of word and thing, the correlation of word and power, the performative function of language, are well known of course to students of the Old and New Testaments. The usage is well illustrated in Bultmann's essay "Der Begriff des Wortes Gottes im Neuen Testament."[32] Out of a wealth of material this one example from Psalm 33 will suffice:

[29] Austin, *op. cit.*, 222.
[30] *Ibid.*, 224.
[31] Ernst Cassirer, *Language and Myth* (New York: Dover Publications, n.d. [1946]), 45. Cf. the whole chapter "Word Magic," 44–62.
[32] *Glauben und Verstehen* I, 268–93.

6. By the word of the Lord the heavens were made,
   and all their host by the breath of his mouth.

. . .

9. For he spoke, and it came to be;
   he commanded, and it stood forth.

—RSV

If functional analysis is striving to overcome the restrictive view of language presupposed by verificational analysis, Cassirer and his predecessors, e.g., Herder and von Humboldt, were resisting the understanding of language which gained currency in the Enlightenment, viz., that language is derived from conscious reflection and is therefore something invented.[38] Neither verificational analysis nor the theory of language as an arbitrary system of signs and symbols is prepared to cope with the notion of language as power, with language as event. It is noteworthy that Austin calls for a two-fold investigation of all language—not just performative language as such—which would involve studying not only what a certain statement *means,* but also what *force* it has. He is persuaded that all language has *some* force.[34]

This brief digression has perhaps aided understanding by bringing *Sprachereignis* into an illuminating constellation. The effort to relate language event to the category of performative language is as much in the interest of saying how language event may not be understood as it is in that of saying how it may be understood. On the other hand, the primitive understanding of the word as power throws light upon this notion of language as event which is alien to the modern consciousness. It is Ebeling's conviction that it is the loss of this relation to language that accounts for the loss of power in the proclamation. The proclamation is no longer an event, but just talk, in which the claim of God is no longer heard. It takes place in a form of language which has become incomprehensible, which consists of the mere repetition of the traditional word of God. The word of God does not enter language in the present.[35] Ebeling shares this conviction with Dietrich Bonhoeffer, whose well-known saying he is fond of quoting:

It is not for us to foretell the day, but the day will come when men will be called to utter the Word of God in such a way that the world is changed and renewed. There will be a new language, perhaps quite unreligious, but

---

[38] Cassirer, *op. cit.,* 30.
[34] Austin, *op. cit.,* 238.
[35] *Nature of Faith,* 184.

liberating and saving, like the language of Jesus, so that men are horrified at it, and yet conquered by its power.[36]

Ebeling sees in this development the loss of the understanding of the word which characterized the Reformation. His first work, on Luther's hermeneutic,[37] has given direction to his theological program, based as it is on the doctrine of the word of God. He asks, why did words result in deeds of reformation? He passes to this radical answer:

The words in this case did not remain mere words and the deed occurred because the necessity for reform and the real event of reformation were grasped so profoundly that the Reformation could not, as a matter of fact, be understood as a matter of deeds but only as a matter of the Word.[38]

Luther could not claim the Reformation as his own work. How could he? He understood it to be the consequence of the word of God.

III

The place of Bultmann in this development can be viewed from another perspective, which may help expose the constellation of problems with which Bultmann has felt himself constrained to deal, and may, at the same time, indicate more clearly the route taken by Fuchs and Ebeling as post-Bultmannians (i.e., Bultmannians, but post). That perspective is the Jesus-Paul antithesis which has dominated New Testament scholarship and much theology for over a century.

It was Ferdinand Christian Baur who first set Paul off against the Jerusalem party, or the primitive Palestinian church, as a means of accounting for the evolution of early Christian history within the framework of a Hegelian dialectic. The antithesis between Paul and the Jewish church, advanced by Baur as early as 1831,[39] had, by the end of the century, become the antithesis between Jesus and Paul. The rationale for this modification need not concern us here, except to note

---

[36] Quoted *ibid.*, 184 f.; *Word and Faith*, 122, 286 f.; cf. Dietrich Bonhoeffer, *Letters and Papers from Prison* (rev. ed.; London: SCM Press, 1956), 140.

[37] *Evangelische Evangelienauslegung: Eine Untersuchung zu Luthers Hermeneutik,* "Forschungen zur Geschichte und Lehre des Protestantismus," X, 1 (Munich: Lempp, 1942; 2d ed., Darmstadt: Wissenschaftliche Buchgesellschaft, 1962).

[38] *Luther: Einführung in sein Denken* (Tübingen: J. C. B. Mohr [Paul Siebeck], 1964), 60.

[39] "Die Christuspartei in der korinthischen Gemeinde, der Gegensatz des petrinischen und paulinischen Christenthums in der ältesten Kirche, der Apostel Petrus in Rom," *Tübinger Zeitschrift für Theologie* 4 (1831), 61 ff.

that so-called liberal theology was activated by a lively interest in the historical Jesus. Owing to this interest, the poles established by Baur were shifted: one became Jesus, the other Paul, including the primitive church. The liberal antithesis has been retained down to the present day as the antithesis between the historical Jesus and the kerygma.

Bultmann had already set out in 1936 his view of the Jesus-Paul antithesis,[40] a view he has reiterated only recently with very slight modification.[41] In his earlier essay, Bultmann notes that the contrast between Jesus and Paul, as it was developed in the preceding or liberal period, arose out of the conviction that "authentic Christianity is the religion of Jesus."[42] The essential elements in this picture of Jesus' religion, however, had been separated out from the "husk" of Jesus' view of the world and history, that is, from mythological trappings. Jesus' message consisted of God the Father, providence, man as a child of God, and the infinite value of the human soul (Harnack).

The question of Jesus and Paul, according to Bultmann, was raised in a new form by the history of religions school, which pointed out that the "Christ-myth" had "its origins in contemporary mythology."[48] Wilhelm Bousset and Wilhelm Heitmüller, who belonged to this school, held, moreover, that the historical phenomenon known as Christianity is characterized precisely by this "Christ-myth," whether it is held to be Jewish or Hellenistic in origin.[44] These observations, all too briefly presented here, led to two conclusions: (1) the historical study of the Christian kerygma apparently signifies its destruction, if one assumes that this kerygma is mythological and that the mythologi-

[40] "Jesus and Paul," *Existence and Faith*, 183–201 (= *"Jesus und Paulus," Jesus Christus im Zeugnis der Heiligen Schrift und der Kirche*, Beiheft 2 zur *Evangelische Theologie* [Munich: Christian Kaiser Verlag, 1936], 68–90).

[41] "The Primitive Christian Kerygma and the Historical Jesus," in *The Historical Jesus and the Kerygmatic Christ*, C. E. Braaten and R. A. Harrisville, eds. (Nashville, Tenn.: Abingdon Press, 1964), 15–42 (= *Das Verhältnis der urchristlichen Christusbotschaft zum historischen Jesus*, Sitzungsberichte der Heidelberger Akademie der Wissenschaften, philosophisch-historische Klasse, Jahrgang 1960, 3. Abhandlung [2d ed.; Heidelberg: Carl Winter, 1961]).

[42] *Existence and Faith*, 184; cf. Adolf Harnack, *What Is Christianity?* T. B. Saunders, trans. (New York: Harper Torchbook, 1957) = *Das Wesen des Christentums* (Leipzig: J. C. Hinrichs, 1900).

[43] *Existence and Faith*, 184: From the Messianic mythology of Judaism come the figure of the Messiah-King, the Son of Man, and the doctrine of the two aeons; from the mystery religions derive the notion of the savior-god who dies and is resurrected and the sacraments through which the votary acquires a share in the destiny of the deity; from Gnosticism arises the myth of the redeemer who descends and ascends in order to prepare the way for the faithful to return to their heavenly home.

[44] *Ibid.*, 185; "The Primitive Christian Kerygma," 16.

cal has to be "peeled off" and discarded; (2) it also means that the religion of Jesus is not Christianity, that Jesus was not the "first Christian."[45]

The work of the history of religions school might have been interpreted to mean that the way was now really clear for a return to the simple gospel of Jesus, in which case it would also mean that historical Christianity was a distortion of the message of Jesus and had to be rejected. Bultmann was not prepared to give it this interpretation, as will be seen, but he was prepared to face the question posed by the antithesis in its radical form: "For such consideration can only serve to clarify what is really at stake, what Christianity authentically is."[46] No less was at stake for Bultmann than the nature of the Christian faith itself.

The way in which Bultmann grappled with the problem may be briefly summarized.[47] First, the history of religions school has made it clear that "it is not possible by returning to Jesus to obtain a Christianity that is free from mythology."[48] Even if the mythological kerygma is discarded, the message of Jesus still contains mythological elements, and by what right does one "peel off" those elements to get to his simple gospel? If one retains the mythological framework of the message of Jesus, then he is in no different position than he is in respect to Paul: in both one is confronted with mythological elements.

In the second place, Bultmann points out that the error in the preceding assessments of Jesus lay in not doing justice to his eschatological message. It is this message which contains the mythological elements, and it is also this message which brings Jesus into relation to Paul.

Furthermore, when the message of Jesus is demythologized—this does not mean stripping away the myth but interpreting it—it will be seen that Jesus and Paul are in fundamental agreement—when the message of Paul is also demythologized! "In other words, Jesus says nothing other in his call to repentance than Paul tries to make clear in his theology by means of theoretical argument."[49] Jesus' message is direct, without theoretical reflection, while Paul explicates the gospel by means of theoretical argument. In the last analysis (in demythologized

---

[45] *Existence and Faith*, 184 f.; "The Primitive Christian Kerygma," 19.

[46] *Existence and Faith*, 185; this point is the burden of the whole essay, "The Primitive Christian Kerygma."

[47] The summary is drawn from *Existence and Faith*, 186–96.

[48] *Ibid.*, 186; cf. "The Primitive Christian Kerygma," 28 f.

[49] *Existence and Faith*, 188.

form), whoever finds Paul's message a scandal and offense will find nothing different if he flees to Jesus. "Both men are in complete accord."[50]

Bultmann continues the argument in the form of a question: But must we not say that for Jesus God is always and utterly gracious, that he requires no special arrangements by means of which grace is appropriated, whereas for Paul there is need for faith in Jesus as the Christ, and that means that one must believe in the crucified and risen Lord if one is to have access to grace? This difference, Bultmann avers, is one in appearance only. "If Paul, like the earliest community, saw in Jesus the Messiah, he did nothing other than affirm Jesus' claim that man's destiny is decided with reference to his person."[51] Thus the christology of Paul is also the implicit christology of Jesus.[52]

It is important to notice how Bultmann puts the matter, which can best be done by juxtaposing two statements.[53]

But Paul says nothing else than that in Jesus God has unmistakably spoken his word of forgiving grace for everyone who will take refuge in him. That is, *for Paul, Jesus Christ is the forgiving word of God.*

While it is true that Jesus did not demand faith in his own person, he did demand faith in his word.

For Paul Jesus Christ is the forgiving word of God, the logos of God, and Jesus demands faith in his word. Bultmann is thus true to his basic insight that the salvation event has word-character, and that Jesus and Paul (and the kerygma) are in fundamental agreement on this point. The post-Bultmannians are likewise faithful to their teacher in fastening on this concept as basic.

Bultmann comes, finally, to the crucial juncture. In spite of the congruity between Jesus and Paul—to be affirmed over against the older liberal antithesis—there is a real difference between them: Jesus looks to the future; Paul looks to the past. Jesus directs his hearers to prepare for the coming reign of God, which is breaking in even now. Paul, on the other hand, points to what has already occurred; for him the turn of the ages had already taken place, the day of salvation is already

---

50 *Ibid.*, 193.

51 *Ibid.*, 196.

52 "The Primitive Christian Kerygma," 28 f. and n. 28 (with references to Fuchs, Bornkamm, Conzelmann, Ebeling).

53 Both found on the same page: *Existence and Faith*, 195 (italics his).

present. If, for Jesus, the decisive thing has still to occur, for Paul it has already occurred, and he can therefore proclaim the "now" arising out of the past. The dividing line between Jesus and Paul is the cross-resurrection (Bultmann never separates them, and indeed is supported by the New Testament is not doing so) : here is located the salvation event which marks the turn of the ages.

To conclude: Bultmann affirms the unity of Jesus and Paul in all points save one, but that one is crucial. It means that Jesus is the presupposition of the kerygma,[54] and hence the presupposition of New Testament theology.[55] For what Bultmann does—and here he runs diametrically counter to his predecessors—is opt for the historic form of the Christian faith, i.e., for the faith that arises out of the primitive church and Paul. We may let him put it in his own way.

If it is true that the kerygma proclaims Jesus as the Christ, as the eschatological event, if it claims that Christ is present in it, then it has put itself in the place of the historical Jesus; it represents him. Then there is no faith in Christ which would not also be faith in the church as the bearer of the kerygma; that is, using the terminology of dogmatics, faith in the Holy Ghost.[56]

In response to the criticism that he holds that "Jesus has risen into the kerygma," Bultmann rejoins,

I accept this proposition. It is entirely correct, assuming that it is properly understood. It presupposes that the kerygma itself is an eschatological event, and it expresses the fact that Jesus is really present in the kerygma, that it is *his* word which encounters the hearer in the kerygma.[57]

Having set out from the liberal antithesis between Jesus and Paul, Bultmann denies that Paul is the second founder of Christianity (W. Wrede),[58] but he affirms that what is only anticipation for Jesus has been realized for Paul, and that this difference marks off what is Christian from what is Jewish. Bultmann thus retains the antithesis, but in a radically new form, and elects, much to the consternation of

54 "The Primitive Christian Kerygma," 19.
55 *Ibid.; Theology of the New Testament* I, 3.
56 "The Primitive Christian Kerygma," 41.
57 *Ibid.,* 42 (with correction of the translation, but italics his).
58 Wrede is discussed in *Existence and Faith,* 183 f.

his critics, the opposite pole from his liberal forebears as the foundation of the Christian faith.[59]

This extended summary of Bultmann's relation to the Jesus-Paul antithesis is warranted for the reason that it exposes his ambivalence with respect to his concept of word of God, and also with respect to his understanding of language. The following remarks are confined to conclusions, the analysis and documentation for which are largely suppressed.

Gerhard Ebeling has noticed that Bultmann operates with a systematic-theological concept of kerygma, but is oriented to its concrete, historical articulation, particularly its New Testament form.[60] This double relationship fosters a certain ambivalence in Bultmann's use of the term which is not insignificant. Bultmann can affirm that faith "is man's response to God's word which encounters him in the proclamation of Jesus Christ. It is *faith in the kerygma,* which tells of God's dealing in the man Jesus of Nazareth."[61] Here he distinguishes word of God from proclamation, and presumably from kerygma, in that word of God is that which man can never lay hold of definitively, which always comes to man from beyond. At any rate, he often uses kerygma in the sense of particular historic formulations of Christian faith. On the other hand, he writes,

But the kerygma is just what theology can never seize in definitive form; it can always take hold of it only as something conceptually stated, and that means as something already theologically interpreted.

That the kerygma never appears without already having been given some theological interpretation rests upon the fact that it can never be spoken except in a human language and formed by human thought. This very fact confirms its kerygmatic character; for it makes clear that the statements of the kerygma are not universal truths but are personal address in a concrete situation.[62]

In this passage kerygma and word of God appear to be identical, whereas proclamation, theological statements, creedal formulations, and the like are already interpretations of kerygma. To be sure, for the

[59] "The Primitive Christian Kerygma," 15 and n. 1 (referring to H. Conzelmann).
[60] *Theologie und Verkündigung,* 38. Ebeling's lengthy discussion, *ibid.,* 26–51, is directed to the question of the relation of the two.
[61] *Theology of the New Testament* II, 239 (italics his).
[62] *Ibid.,* 240.

kerygma to be kerygma, it must be personal address.[63] To put the matter briefly, in contexts where kerygma and word of God are contrasted, the term kerygma takes on the meaning of human words; in contexts where kerygma and theological interpretation are contrasted, the term kerygma takes on the meaning: word of God—i.e., the word which comes from beyond. Even so, Bultmann regularly emphasizes that kerygma must become words in order to be kerygma.

The question which arises from these observations is whether Bultmann, when he calls for faith in the kerygma, is calling for faith in word of God, the word that comes from beyond, or in the historic kerygma. One would suppose, without further consideration, that it is the former. But in view of his resolution of the Jesus-Paul antithesis, this is by no means certain. In fact, when he says that the kerygma "has put itself in the place of the historical Jesus," and that faith in the kerygma is faith in the church and the Holy Spirit, it would seem that Bultmann is confining kerygma to its historic form. This view makes it possible to explain, without recourse to the problem of legitimation, why Bultmann refuses to go behind the historic kerygma.[64] Bultmann simply takes his stand on the kerygma of the primitive church.

This interpretation also accounts in part for Bultmann's conception of his program of *demythologizing:* that which requires existential interpretation, if the kerygma is to be made understandable to modern man, is the primitive Christian kerygma, and that is wholly mythological, as was observed earlier. What is not mythological does not require interpretation, not merely because it is understandable already, but because it is not part of the Christian kerygma. Can it then be inferred that word of God, for the primitive church and Paul, had to come to expression in mythological terms? If so, then the nonmythological elements in the message of Jesus are excluded by definition from the primitive kerygma, and Paul and John in fact do not take them up, as Bultmann notes.[65]

It is this apparent correlation of word of God, primitive Christian kerygma, and mythology that accounts for the contours of Bultmann's theological program. And it is this alliance that explains, so far as I can see, why Bultmann is willing to affirm the unity of the word of Jesus and Paul and yet posit a crucial difference between them.

What view of language, mythological or otherwise, is integral to

---

[63] Cf. Ebeling, *Theologie und Verkündigung,* 35 f., with references.
[64] Cf. Ebeling, *ibid.,* 41 f., 45, 55 ff.
[65] "The Primitive Christian Kerygma," 20, 38; *Existence and Faith,* 185; etc.

Bultmann's position? Schubert Ogden has rightly pointed out that
Bultmann reduces language to two types of statements: (1) those
which convey information, and (2) those which demand a decision.[66]
It should be noted, against the majority of Bultmann's critics, that he is
by no means disposed to a negative view of mythological language,
except insofar as it is understood as making assertions, i.e., conveying
information, about God and the world.[67] In fact, he proposes to rest
the Christian faith on the primitive Christian kerygma, which is
mythological. What Bultmann seeks is a means of expressing the
mythological kerygma in nonmythological *and* nonassertive language.[68]
It is thus clear that the language to which Bultmann is really adverse
is language understood as assertion. This is made evident by his
polemic against every attempt to make the kerygma serve objective
historicity![69] His negative view of language understood as assertion is
derived, of course, from Heidegger.

Bultmann has proposed no less than to end theology's dependence
upon the assertive character of language. To use Ian Ramsey's terms,
he has proposed ending the scale-model era in theology.[70] He sensed
that the positivistic use and understanding of language cripples language and thus theology. Rather than dealing with the root problem,
however, viz., the character of language itself, Bultmann took up
demythologizing as a means of overcoming the deficiency, and he
correlated this means with his interest in the historic form of the
kerygma.

If Bultmann, as a result of his background in the history of religions
school, was predisposed to a negative view of theological—i.e., mythological—language, in that such language is usually understood in a
positivistic sense, he learned the primacy of the *word* of God from Karl
Barth.[71] The conflict between these two allegiances gave him problems. However, the regional ontology of *Dasein*, provided by Hei-

---

[66] See *supra*, n. 11.

[67] Cf. *Kerygma and Myth* I, 102 f.: "Much of our ordinary language is based on
mythology in any case, and there are certain concepts which are fundamentally
mythological, and with which we shall never be able to dispense—e.g., the idea of
transcendence" (*Kerygma und Mythos* I [4th ed.; Hamburg: Evangelischer Verlag,
1960], 122). This statement should be set alongside one in which his objections to
mythological language are formulated, e. g., *Kerygma and Myth* I, 197.

[68] *Kerygma und Mythos* II, 187; cf. Ogden, *Christ Without Myth*, 56 ff., with further
references.

[69] E.g., "The Primitive Christian Kerygma," 24 f.

[70] Ian Ramsey, *Models and Mystery* (London and New York: Oxford University
Press, 1964), 4.

[71] See W. Pannenberg, "Dialektische Theologie," *RGG* II (1958), 168–74.

degger in *Sein und Zeit,* opened the way for him to solve the problem of interpretation: language about God, Christ, the world, i.e., mythological language understood in an objectifying sense, could be redeemed—i.e., interpreted, translated—by referring it to the existentials worked out by Heidegger. Since Bultmann took the existentials to be both nonmythological and universal in scope, they provided the means by which the import of New Testament language and other theological formulations could be translated into contemporary language, so as to expose the true intent of the gospel.

Fuchs and Ebeling along with other Bultmannians stand in this line. But as a consequence of Bultmann's limited assault on the problem of language, they are of the opinion that Bultmann left a residue of problems in need of solution. In particular, they believe that Bultmann's effort to overcome the deficiency of assertive language cannot ultimately succeed until the nature of language itself is reconsidered. Thus, while they continue to affirm Bultmann's program of demythologizing and take it as their point of departure, they think that theology must move beyond demythologizing, for its own sake and for the sake of the proclamation. Just how Fuchs and Ebeling propose to make this move will be considered in chapter 3.

If these considerations of Bultmann's position in the development have given preliminary direction, further consideration of language as event in theology must wait upon the extremely hazardous venture of sketching Heidegger's view of language.

IV
LANGUAGE AS THE HOUSE OF BEING[72]

"When *I* use a word," Humpty Dumpty said, in a rather scornful tone, "it means just what I choose it to mean—neither more nor less."

[72] In addition to Heidegger's works, important secondary bibliography includes: William J. Richardson, S.J., "Heidegger and the Origin of Language," *International Philosophical Quarterly* 2 (1962), 404–16. Hans Jonas, *Augustin und das paulinische Freiheitsproblem* (2d ed.; Göttingen: Vandenhoeck & Ruprecht, 1965); *Gnosis und spätantiker Geist* I, *Die mythologische Gnosis* (3d ed.; Göttingen: Vandenhoeck & Ruprecht, 1964) and II, 1, *Von der Mythologie zur mystischen Philosophie* (Göttingen: Vandenhoeck & Ruprecht, 1954); and *The Gnostic Religion* (2d ed.; Boston: Beacon Press, 1963), especially the appendix. Heinrich Ott, *Denken und Sein. Der Weg Martin Heideggers und der Weg der Theologie* (Zürich: EVZ-Verlag, 1959); *Dogmatik und Verkündigung* (Zürich: EVZ-Verlag, 1961); "Theologie als Gebet und als Wissenschaft," *ThZ* 14 (1958), 120–32; "Objektivierendes und existentiales Denken," *ThZ* 10 (1954), 257–89 = *Kerygma und Mythos* IV (Hamburg: Herbert Reich-Evangelischer Verlag, 1955), 105–31 = "Objectification and Existentialism," *Kerygma and Myth* II

"The question is," said Alice, "whether you *can* make words mean so many different things."
"The question is," said Humpty Dumpty, "which is to be master—that's all."[73]

Who is to be master of words is the question. If the development of logic and the linguistic sciences is taken to be an attempt to master words, to bring language under control, their very success, according to Martin Heidegger, would be their failure. The fact that modern man thinks he has language at his disposal indicates that his relation to it is destroyed.[74] And precisely at the time when he believes that he is master of words, he has fallen completely into the grip of his own technical terminology, and has thus cut out the light of the world. This tradition, which is now vested in language, cannot be broken or modified until man turns language loose, allows it to go free, reinstates it in its pristine power.

One may begin with the observation that Heidegger is a primitive with respect to language. This designation should not be taken to refer to what is ancient, although Heidegger does focus on the pre-Socratics and the Greek myths, and there is a clear affinity with the understanding of language in primitive cultures. Nevertheless, he would take it to

---

(see Abbreviations), 306–55. *New Frontiers in Theology*, J. M. Robinson and J. B. Cobb, Jr., eds., I, *The Later Heidegger and Theology* and II, *The New Hermeneutic* (see Abbreviations). Hans-Georg Gadamer, *Wahrheit und Methode* (Tübingen: J. C. B. Mohr, 1960); "Sprache II. Philosophisch," *RGG* VI (1962), 266–68; T. Bonhoeffer, "Sprache IV. Theologisch," *RGG* VI (1962), 272–82; Hans-Rudolf Müller-Schwefe, *Die Sprache und das Wort* (Hamburg: Furche-Verlag, 1961); Eberhard Jüngel, "Der Schritt zürück. Eine Auseinandersetzung mit der Heidegger-Deutung Heinrich Otts," *ZThK* 58 (1961), 104–22; Helmut Franz, "Das Denken Heideggers und die Theologie," *ZThK*, Beiheft 2 (1961), 81–118 and "Das Wesen des Textes," *ZThK* 59 (1962), 182–225; J. M. Robinson, "Heilsgeschichte und Lichtungsgeschichte," *Evangelische Theologie* 22 (1962), 113–41 = "The Historicality of Biblical Language," in B. W. Anderson, ed., *The Old Testament and Christian Faith* (New York: Harper & Row, 1963), 124–58; Heinz Kimmerle, "Hermeneutische Theorie oder ontologische Hermeneutik," *ZThK* 59 (1962), 114–30 and "Metahermeneutik, Applikation, hermeneutische Sprachbildung," *ZThK* 61 (1964), 221–35.

On Heidegger, further: T. Langan, *The Meaning of Heidegger: A Critical Study of an Existentialist Phenomenology* (New York: Columbia University Press, 1959); V. Vycinas, *Earth and Gods: An Introduction to the Philosophy of Martin Heidegger* (The Hague: Martinus Nijhoff, 1961); William J. Richardson, S.J., *Heidegger: Through Phenomenology to Thought* (The Hague: Martinus Nijhoff, 1963).

[73] Lewis Carroll, *Through the Looking-Glass*, chap. 6.
[74] Cf. Richardson, *Heidegger: Through Phenomenology to Thought*, 293. This mammoth and perceptive work came into my hands too late to be utilized in shaping this section on Heidegger.

refer .to the primary, or, to use his own terms, the primordial function of language.[75] He proposes to think through the problem of language beyond the understanding of language which is imbedded in the language tradition itself, to the understanding of language that would penetrate to the dimension out of which the subject matter comes to encounter man in language. In particular, he essays to track the metaphysical tradition in the West back to the soil out of which it sprang.[76] And that soil is language understood as the place where being comes to dwell.[77]

The primordial function of language is understood best by the true poets. Heidegger takes a text from Hölderlin:

> Full of merit, and yet poetically, dwells
> Man on this earth.[78]

What is man as poet? "Poetry is the act of establishing by the word and in the word."[79] The poet names being and so brings it to stand. Being calls to man, and in responding he, in turn, calls being out of chaos, so to speak, by giving it a place to dwell in language. But the act of naming is not to be misunderstood in accordance with the prevailing understanding of name:

This naming does not consist merely in something already known being supplied with a name; it is rather that when the poet speaks the essential word, the existent is by this naming nominated as what it is. So it becomes known *as* existent. Poetry is the establishing of being by means of the word.[80]

Are we to understand then that the poet creates being? By no means.

[75] William Barrett (in "Existentialism as a Symptom of Man's Contemporary Crisis," *Spiritual Problems in Contemporary Literature,* S. R. Hopper, ed. [New York: Harper Torchbook, 1957], 151) defines primitive as follows: "the primitive is the primary; and the valid search for the primitive is a search for the sources of our being which a too routinized civilization tends to obscure. In this sense, nearly all the art and literature that matter in the past half century have been primitive."

[76] Cf. Robinson, *New Frontiers* I, 23.

[77] Cf. Richardson, "Heidegger and the Origin of Language," 408 f., 413.

[78] Quoted by Heidegger in his essay "Hölderlin and the Essence of Poetry," in *Existence and Being,* Douglas Scott, trans. (Chicago: Henry Regnery Co., 1949), 270–91. The lines are cited on pp. 270, 282.

[79] *Ibid.,* 280.

[80] *Ibid.,* 281 (italics his). Cf. *Vorträge und Aufsätze* (Pfullingen: Neske, 1954), 223.

But the gods can acquire a name only by addressing and, as it were, claiming us. The word which names the gods is always a response to such a claim. This response always springs from the responsibility of a destiny. It is in the process by which the gods bring our existence to language, that we enter the sphere of the decision as to whether we are to yield ourselves to the gods or withhold ourselves from them.[81]

In other words, the poet is one who names by allowing being to speak. Authentic language is the voice of being naming itself through the mouth of the poet. For this reason Heidegger can say that the ability to speak and the ability to hear are equally primordial.[82]

In language, therefore, being itself is at stake. But man is also at stake, since he lives off of his relation to being, and a destroyed relation to language means a destroyed relation to being. Language affords the possibility of standing into the openness of the existent, i.e., in language being is disclosed and in language being is concealed.[83] Only where there is language is there world, and only where world predominates is there history. Language is the means by which man exists historically.

Language is not a tool at his disposal, rather it is that event which disposes of the supreme possibility of human existence.[84]

Since language really became actual as conversation, the gods have acquired names and a world has appeared. But again it should be noticed: the presence of the gods and the appearance of the world are not merely a consequence of the actualisation of language, they are contemporaneous with it. And this to the extent that it is precisely in the naming of the gods, and in the transmutation of the world into word, that the real conversation, which we ourselves are, consists.[85]

Language is thus the house of being.[86]

Heidegger's interest in the primordial function of language explains his interest in the poets, who name the gods, but what is the relation of

---

[81] "Hölderlin and the Essence of Poetry," 279 f.

[82] Ibid., 278; Being and Time (see Abbreviations), 206–208.

[83] Heidegger, Über den Humanismus (Frankfurt a. M.: Vittorio Klostermann, 1949), 16.

[84] Heidegger, "Hölderlin and the Essence of Poetry," 276 f.

[85] Ibid., 279. Cf. Heidegger, Introduction to Metaphysics, R. Manheim, trans. (New Haven: Yale University Press, 1959), 172.

[86] Über den Humanismus, 5; see also his Unterwegs zur Sprache (Pfullingen: Neske, 1959), 267.

poetizing to philosophical thinking? He answers this question in the essay, "What Is Metaphysics?"

> The thought of being guards the Word and fulfills its function in such guardianship, namely care for the use of language. Out of long guarded speechlessness and the careful clarification of the field thus cleared, comes the utterance of the thinker. The poet's naming is of a like origin. However what is alike is alike only in that it is something different from what it is like.[87] Although composing poetry and thinking are most alike in the care of the use of words, they are at the same time furthest separated in their nature. The thinker speaks being. The poet names the holy. To be sure the question must be left open here as to how, when thought about in terms of the nature of being, composing poetry and thanking and thinking are dependent on each other and at the same time different.[88]

It is this ambiguity which governs his own style, which vacillates between stilted, academic German and the poetic mode. This vacillation is characteristic of his earliest works, e.g., *Sein und Zeit.*[89] Heidegger's understanding of language as response to being and adhering to being also explains his peculiar way of doing etymologies.[90]

We must now step back from these observations and notice the approach which Heidegger makes to language in *Being and Time.*[91] This approach and where it leads him is the key to the path of his thought.

Being and Time is a phenomenological analytic of *Dasein.* It is a peculiar kind of phenomenology, to be sure, but it can be characterized as a kind of positivism in the sense that it takes as its raw data mundane subjectivity, the everyday mode of existence.[92] It is the peculiarity of Heidegger's approach that leads F. C. Copelston to wonder whether Heidegger is a logical analyst or a metaphysician.[93]

---

[87] Cf. his essay, *Identität und Differenz* (Pfullingen: Neske, 1957). = *Essays in Metaphysics: Identity and Difference,* Kurt F. Leidecker, trans. (New York: Philosophical Library, 1960).

[88] "What Is Metaphysics?" in *Existence and Being,* 360, as revised by J. M. Robinson, *New Frontiers* 1, 45. Cf. Richardson, "Heidegger and the Origin of Language," 413–16 and *Heidegger: Through Phenomenology to Thought,* 636 f.

[89] Müller-Schwefe, *Die Sprache und das Wort* (Hamburg: Furche-Verlag, 1961), 74, referring to the study of Paul Hühnerfeld, *In Sachen Heidegger* (1959), especially 72–86.

[90] Cf. J. M. Robinson, *New Frontiers* I, 51.

[91] Sections 32–38, pp. 188–224.

[92] Ray L. Hart, "Heidegger's Being and Time and Phenomenology," *Encounter* 26, 3 (1965) 311, 320 ff. Hart sets Heidegger's phenomenology against the development of the phenomenological movement as a whole.

[93] *Contemporary Philosophy* (Westminster, Md.: Newman Press, 1956), 178.

Nevertheless, Heidegger takes as the point of departure the under-standing of being manifested in everydayness. This understanding does not lie on the surface of things, but is to be gained only by painstaking and often violent analysis. After all, the everyday man does not simply will what his relation to being is. It is into this analytic that language is brought, and in the following way.

a. Words, language, can be encountered as things-on-hand (*vor-handen*). In this case language is objectivized and viewed as part of the furniture of the world, as part of the stock of tools which man has at his disposal. Verificational analysis, on Heidegger's terms, views lan-guage precisely in this way. Language is something we use consciously, deliberately, for certain ends, and in disposing ourselves to language in this way, we consider it to be among the tools on hand.

b. But words, language, can also be taken as things-at-hand (*zu-handen*), in which case language is also seized as a means of achieving something, but without reference to language in isolation. That is, language is seized within the context of a referential totality, entirely naïvely, and is not disengaged from that totality. As with other tools, language may be employed with its "in-order-to" structure still intact within the referential totality.

c. The analysis has not yet exposed the essence of language. These observations have to be brought into relation to *Dasein. Dasein,* as being-in-the-world, is already disposed in its thrownness to the world in some way. Its disposition to the world, which is what it essentially is, involves understanding. Understanding is the primordial (underived, pre-eidetic) grasp of the structure of existence, the grasp of the totality of involvements which reveals the categorical whole of a *possible* interconnection of the ready-to-hand.[94] This totality of involvements, this categorical whole, gains its significance from the possibility (note the word *possible* in the preceding formulation) upon which it is pro-jected. In other words, the structure of the whole comes into view only in relation to projection upon possibilities.

Now the significance of the projection upon possibilities gets articu-lated in what Heidegger calls primordial discourse. Primordial dis-course creates language; it is the foundation of language. Heidegger can say: "The totality-of-significations of intelligibility is *put into words*. To significations, words accrue. But word-Things do not get supplied with significations."[95]

[94] *Being and Time,* 184.
[95] *Ibid.,* 204. Italics his.

The articulation of significance in primordial discourse, in parlance, is given with the character of *Dasein* itself. Primordial discourse belongs, as a consequence, to being and not to man. But primordial discourse comes to speech, i.e., is brought into human language. These significations, in other words, get supplied with word-Things, with language.

d. Word-Things and language, of course, have their own history, as do other things-on-hand and at-hand in the world of *Dasein*. Of importance for the history of language in the Western tradition is, first of all, the metaphysical tradition of the Greeks which has entered language and decisively influenced the course of the Western language tradition. This tradition degenerated, at the close of the classical period, into logic. Logic as the exposition of the formal structure and rules of thought came only as the result of the separation of being and thinking. Logic delivers language over to the tyranny of thought or, to put it another way, makes thought the bar to which language must give account of itself. The correspondence theory of truth witnesses to the split between being and thinking, but endeavors only to sew a patch over this rent in the fabric of *Dasein*'s world. Logic dominates thinking and determines the understanding of language in the West down to the present time.[96] The subject-object split implicit in the logic of late antiquity was canonized by Descartes, who delivered being decisively and finally over to the tyranny of the subject-thinker. After Descartes, everything has to give account of itself to the investigating subject. The objective world is, of course, only the reverse of a predominating subject. For this reason, the objective view of the world is in fact the most subjective view.[97] Heidegger sees this development as the final stage in the decay of language, which is still working itself out in our period.[98]

The last point leads to the observation that when one takes hold of language naïvely, when language is grasped as something-at-hand in relation to the totality of significations which is understood by *Dasein*, he is brought under the tyranny of its history. More than that, language itself is the primary medium of history, and thus provides the horizons of the possibilities in which *Dasein* has its being.

It is now possible to see what Heidegger was about in his analysis in

[96] Heidegger, *Introduction to Metaphysics*, 121.
[97] Heidegger, *Der Satz vom Grund* (Pfullingen: Neske, 1957; 2d ed., 1958). Summary by J. M. Robinson, *New Frontiers* I, 27 f.
[98] *Introduction to Metaphysics*, 51.

Being and Time and why he abandoned the project. In that early work he was attempting to carry out the analysis of *Dasein* within the language tradition of the West. He did so in the interests of attempting to overcome the tyranny of that tradition. For this reason, Heidegger claims that the first step forward is a step back, i.e., one must first of all participate in the dismantling of the tradition in order to penetrate to its ground. It may be agreed that this "step back" is a necessary one. However, this phase of his thought has been given the categorical label: the early Heidegger.

Who then is the later Heidegger? Already in *Being and Time* Heidegger noted that listening, hearkening, and keeping silent are existentials which belong to primordial discourse. Only he who hears can speak, and only he who hears can hearken, and only he who has something to say can keep silent. These elements belong to primordial discourse as such.[99] On the other hand, *Dasein* in its everydayness is given to prattle, idle talk. This is because *Dasein* in its everydayness takes everything as already understood. One merely hands around opinions, one merely traffics in words. Prattle closes off understanding, idle talk indicates that language has been split off from its ground. As a result, prattle no longer knows the need to keep silent, to listen, to hearken. It can dispense with these because it takes the opinions of everyone as its own. Because it has forgotten the true origin of language, it talks all the more.

If the recovery of authentic speech is possible at all, it requires, first, that listening, hearkening, and keeping silent be rediscovered in relation to language, and second, that the tyranny of the Western language tradition be broken by means of new language, which is to be created not by artifice but by attending to being. New and powerful language must, so to speak, create itself. The role of man in this process is one of active passivity: he must learn to listen away into silence. Listening of this order is not simply receptivity, but resolute and violent attention.[100]

Both of these elements may be observed at work in the later Heidegger.

[99] Richardson, *Heidegger: Through Phenomenology to Thought,* 457 f.: The poetic dialogue, considered in its origins, unites hearing and speaking, in that the poet is hailed by the Holy and hails the Holy in return. Being hailed requires the power of "attending" (*Hörenkönnen*) and hailing in return is the origin of utterance (*Sagen*).

[100] This point may be put metaphorically: the Western tradition is like a fast moving train with no stops. If one wants to get off, he must descend at a point of intense discrepancy between his own movement and the underlying terrain.

The middle Heidegger saw that his attempt in *Being and Time* to overcome the tradition in the language of that tradition, while a necessary step, would eventually lead to capitulation before the power of the language tradition against which he was struggling. The tendency to poetize is already present in *Being and Time,* and any reader can attest to the strangeness of the language. Nevertheless, the later Heidegger is the student of the Heidegger who taught that the power of the language tradition can be effectually broken only through poetic silence and the rebirth of language.

The thought of being guards the Word and fulfills its function in such guardianship, namely care for the use of language. Out of long guarded speechlessness and the careful clarification of the field thus cleared, comes the utterance of the thinker.[101]

He has therefore retreated to the Black Forest and leads the life of the recluse, meditating in silence, pondering language, and exhibiting an increasing tendency to the poetic mode.

It is in the poetic mode that language is born.

Hence poetry never takes language as a raw material ready to hand, rather it is poetry which first makes language possible. Poetry is the primitive language of a historical people.[102]

The poet, as the Shepherd of being, listens to being and allows being to come to expression in words. The poet creates linguistic traditions. Heidegger aspires to be the philosopher-poet, and it is probable that only the combination is adequate to the task, although what Heidegger is about is being carried on elsewhere by littérateurs and artists. In any case, Heidegger has hearkened to Hölderlin in observing that "poetically man dwells on the earth."

The attempt has been made to develop Heidegger's understanding of

---

[101] "What Is Metaphysics?" *Existence and Being,* 360, as revised by J. M. Robinson, *New Frontiers* I, 45. Cf. the assessment of Müller-Schwefe, *op. cit.,* 76: "Heidegger executes a step-back in his thinking of language. He dismantles the metaphysical understanding of the understanding of Dasein. He thereby reaches the place at which the call meets man, at which he becomes a speaker out of the call itself. But he has no philosophical language to express it; language fails.

"This tarrying at the place where Dasein occurs is something great. For in fact the way back to the event of language, the step-back of the question is so against the trend of Western thinking that the second step *must not yet be taken*" (italics mine).

[102] "Hölderlin and the Essence of Poetry," 283 f.

language as the necessary backdrop for the work of Fuchs and Ebeling
in relation to the so-called "turn" in Heidegger's thought, for this turn
is decisive for those who regard language as a root theological problem.
In so doing it is not being proposed that the early Heidegger is no
longer relevant, or that the later Heidegger can be understood in
isolation. Rather it is suggested that Heidegger understands the course
of his own path to be determined by an inner necessity, to which each
phase of his work is in turn entirely relevant. In short, the later
Heidegger has followed the course set by the early Heidegger. The
discrepancy between the two Heideggers is of concern only to those
who wish to elevate one phase of his thought to normative status.
Fuchs and Ebeling are alert to this path and so have pushed to new
ground in rethinking the problem of the language of the Christian
tradition.

Language as Event:
Fuchs and Ebeling

ᴪ 3 ᴪ ────────────

LANGUAGE AS EVENT HAS BEEN TAKEN UP, IN THE WORK
of Ernst Fuchs and Gerhard Ebeling, into a whole theological program. The interrelation of language event, hermeneutic, and theology
of the word of God is evident in this formulation of Fuchs:

Being emerges from language, when language directs us into the dimension
of our existence determinative for our life. Is that the "meaning" of the
word of God? Then hermeneutic in theology would indeed be nothing else
than the "doctrine of the word of God" (Ebeling), faith's doctrine of
language. The reverse is also true: The theological doctrine of the word of
God would be the question as to being in the horizon of Biblical language.[1]

Since the doctrine of language pervades a wide array of theological
topics in the writings of both men, the modesty of the aim to explicate
their understanding of language as event is immediately endangered.
Some restraint must be exercised if the analysis is not to turn into the
representation of two theological programs. Certain aspects of the
concept, language event, have been chosen as the best means of
illuminating their fundamental position, while others, which might
well have been included, are only touched upon or omitted altogether.

It would be revealing, for example, to consider the law-gospel
dichotomy, in terms of which Fuchs and Ebeling have attempted to
distinguish their work from that of Heidegger,[2] or to inquire after the

---

[1] Fuchs I, 115, translated by J. M. Robinson, *New Frontiers* II, 55. Cf. Robinson's
remarks, *ibid.,* 67.
[2] Cf. Ebeling, "The Necessity of the Doctrine of the Two Kingdoms," *Word and
Faith,* 386–406. Robinson, *New Frontiers* I, 32 and n. 63, 75 f.; II, 49 f. and n. 134.

relation between the Old and New Testaments.[3] Similarly, the distinction between philosophy and theology,[4] between thinking and language,[5] and the relation of word and deed[6] would throw considerable light upon their understanding of language as event, but they are touched only in passing. The subject-object dilemma will come into view only obliquely, although it is clear that both men are concerned to overcome the Cartesian tyranny of the subject.[7] Passed over in silence are the relation of historical criticism to the theological task, a problem which has been given special attention by both men,[8] and the subject of eschatology, which has recently come to the fore.[9]

Themes peculiar to each man do not, as a rule, come up for direct consideration. These would include Fuchs' notion that "the essence of language is its movement toward love,"[10] Ebeling's development of the concept of conscience as hermeneutical principle,[11] and his particularly interesting contributions to the study of tradition[12] and the unity of the theological disciplines.[13]

It would have been desirable to give further attention to their

[8] A question to which Ebeling has recently devoted attention in his "Hermeneutic Problems of the Old Testament: Theses for the Seminar," prepared for a seminar held at Drew University, fall semester, 1963–64. Mimeographed.

[4] E.g., Ebeling, "Verantworten des Glaubens in Begegnung mit dem Denken M. Heideggers. Thesen zum Verhältnis von Philosophie und Theologie," ZThK, Beiheft 2 (1961), 119–24; "Theologie und Philosophie I, II, III," RGG VI (1962), 782–830. Cf. Robinson, New Frontiers I, 75 f.

[5] E.g., Fuchs, Hermeneutik, passim; Fuchs I, 171–74, 180; II, 428 [210 f.]; etc.

[6] E.g., Ebeling, "Luthers Tat," in Luther: Einführung in sein Denken (Tübingen: J. C. B. Mohr [Paul Siebeck], 1964), 58–78.

[7] Cf., e.g., Fuchs, Hermeneutik, 135 ff., Ergänzungsheft, 5.

[8] Ebeling, "The Significance of the Critical Historical Method for Church and Theology in Protestantism," Word and Faith, 17–61; Fuchs, Hermeneutik, 159–66; II, 55–65, 219–37 [32–47].

[9] To E. Käsemann, "Die Anfänge christlicher Theologie," ZThK 57 (1960), 162–85, Ebeling has responded with "Der Grund christlicher Theologie," ZThK 58 (1961), 227–44, and Fuchs with "Über die Aufgabe einer christlichen Theologie," ibid., 245–67. Käsemann's rebuttal is "Zum Thema der urchristlichen Apokalyptik," ZThK 59 (1962), 257–84.

[10] Fuchs, e.g., New Frontiers II, 241; cf. ibid., 60 f.

[11] "Theological Reflexions on Conscience," Word and Faith, 407–23. Cf. ibid., 332, 432 f. Cf. Fuchs, e.g., I, 137.

[12] G. Ebeling, Kirchengeschichte als Geschichte der Auslegung der Heiligen Schrift (Tübingen: J. C. B. Mohr, 1947); Die Geschichtlichkeit der Kirche und ihrer Verkündigung als theologisches Problem (Tübingen: J. C. B. Mohr, 1954); Wort Gottes und Tradition: Studien zu einer Hermeneutik der Konfessionen (Göttingen: Vandenhoeck & Ruprecht, 1964). Cf. also Word and Faith, 335–39.

[13] See especially "Discussion Theses for a Course of Introductory Lectures on the Study of Theology," Word and Faith, 424–33.

respective assessments of the contemporary situation, the time of the death of God, the time of the world come of age, for it is at this point that some difference in stance between the two is to be detected.[14] Such remarks as are made are confined to an appendix to this chapter on the "Language of God."

The presentation does not attempt to distinguish their positions, but rather emphasizes the basic area of agreement. It would be carrying coals to Newcastle to labor the point that Fuchs and Ebeling are attempting to carry through the radicalization of the doctrine of justification by faith launched by Bultmann. In any case, that this is their aim is evident in every line they have written.

Ebeling grounds much of his work in Luther, Fuchs in the New Testament, particularly the parables of Jesus.[15] But both men have been influenced by, or are to be understood in relation to, the so-called later Heidegger, as was suggested earlier.[16] As a consequence, they understand themselves to be going beyond Bultmann in certain crucial respects. Their positive evaluation of language, which indeed derives from one side of Bultmann's understanding of language, tends, nevertheless, to cancel out Bultmann's negative evaluation. On Fuchs' terms, Bultmann's theology of history is hostile to the word, despairs of it, because it confuses faith and thought. Because Bultmann does not see that proclamation and the linguisticality of existence belong together,

[14] Cf. Ebeling's essays on Bonhoeffer, *Word and Faith*, 98–161, 282–87; "Rudimentary Reflexions on Speaking Responsibly of God," *ibid.*, 333–53; and "The Message of God to the Age of Atheism," *Oberlin College Bulletin* IX, 1 (January, 1964), 3–14, with Fuchs' essay "The New Testament and the Hermeneutical Problem," *New Frontiers* II, 111–45 and his "Response to the American Discussion," *ibid.*, 232–43. Missing from Fuchs is the note of the questionableness of the gospel, its tragic powerlessness in a world come of age. Cf. Ebeling, "Die Evidenz des Ethischen und die Theologie," *ZThK* 57 (1960), 350 ff. (= "Theology and the Evidentness of the Ethical," *JThC* 2 [1965], 96–129) and Robinson's remarks, *New Frontiers* I, 71. It is perhaps not accidental that of the two only Ebeling has taken up the Bonhoeffer legacy.

[15] Of particular help in understanding Fuchs have been the essays of Amos N. Wilder: "New Testament Hermeneutics Today," in W. Klassen and G. F. Snyder, eds., *Current Issues in New Testament Interpretation* (New York: Harper & Row, 1962), 38–52; "Form-History and the Oldest Tradition," in *Neotestamentica et Patristica* (Leiden: E. J. Brill, 1962), 3–13; and his essay in *New Frontiers* II, "The Word as Address and as Meaning," 198–218. Wilder's recent book, *The Language of the Gospel* (see Abbreviations), although it came into my hands after this essay was virtually complete, is likewise helpful.

[16] Fuchs, I know, denies (*Hermeneutik*, Ergänzungsheft, 5) that his understanding of language is bound to the "later Heidegger," since he set out on his own way before the latter emerged. Yet Fuchs acknowledges that he sensed the real direction of *Sein und Zeit* already in 1927 (*ibid.*). In any case, Heidegger provides the relevant backdrop against which to read Fuchs and Ebeling.

he does not grasp that the language of the text has priority over the thought of the interpreter.[17] Since Bultmann is exercised over the opaqueness of biblical language, he wants to demythologize it. For Fuchs and Ebeling, however, what requires demythologizing is not so much the language of the text as modern man.[18] Modern man is to be interpreted by the text, not the text by modern man.

The immediate link between Fuchs and Ebeling and Heidegger is the linguisticality of existence. There is another, nonconceptual link, however, between Fuchs and Heidegger. It has been noted that Heidegger's style of writing, the strangeness of his language, and the inclination to the poetic mode go together with his understanding of language. Together they disclose his mood.[19] The same is true, *mutatis mutandis,* of Fuchs. He has concentrated on language as event and he is an illustration of his own point of view. He is the practitioner of free, untrammeled speech, if one may apply to him the phrases he applies to Jesus.[20] While the elaboration of language event as language gain, in what follows, is carried out primarily from the side of Fuchs, it is done rather more prosaically and systematically than Fuchs would do it. It is to be hoped that the flavor of Fuchs' language will not be entirely lost in the process.

Ebeling, on the other hand, is deliberate, careful, concise. He has occupied himself with vast historical problems. The consequence is that his writings tend to be more lucid to thought, more available to critical reflection. While Ebeling is less visible in the presentation, his succinct phrasing will often salvage a point in danger of being buried under an avalanche of verbiage.

It is fortunate that two men whose dispositions and styles are so different are at work on the same problem. They serve to illuminate each other.

It remains to say a word about the organization of the presentation. It is necessary, first of all, to explicate the linguisticality of existence as the root concept (I). It will then be possible to show that the proclamation as language event is to be understood as word of God (II), in which case, as traditionally understood, it is bound to a text (III),

---

17 Fuchs II, 430 [211 f.].

18 Fuchs, *Hermeneutik,* Ergänzungsheft, 13; cf. Fuchs I, 113 ff.; "The New Testament and the Hermeneutical Problem," *New Frontiers* II, 117. However, Bultmann (*Kerygma and Myth* I, 5 ff.) expresses a similar notion: the challenge presented to the New Testament is *modern man's understanding of himself.*

19 Cf. *Being and Time,* 172 ff.

20 Fuchs II, 270 [75].

derives from Jesus, who is the real text of faith (IV), and requires translation (V). In this way the theological program of Fuchs and Ebeling is properly focused in language event and hermeneutic.

I

THE LINGUISTICALITY OF EXISTENCE

In his *Hermeneutik* (section 6, pp. 126–34), Fuchs affirms Heidegger's position that reality is constituted linguistically. The world in which man lives is given to him in language. The question whether there is any reality apart from language is to be answered in the negative. "An eternal silence would be the dissolution of reality."[21] By language Fuchs does not mean only an audible report of sense-content, for language is not necessarily talk.[22] "Language is rather primarily a *showing* or *letting* be seen, an indication in the active sense: I intimate to you or instruct you what you yourself 'perceive' (take notice of or watch out for). . . . That can take place through a simple movement, even by turning away from another."[23] That is to say, language in the wider sense, which includes primordial discourse, is what gives being a presence, what brings it to stand. Man does not live in relation to being as such, but in relation to being as it is present to him, and that means in language.[24]

The world which is invested in language is largely inherited. The world which belongs to common understanding, which is inherited with the language tradition, involves self-understanding, for the reason that world embraces self. Behind all verbal formulations, even those in which the object (i.e., the self) is, so to speak, the subject, stands another subject, the real subject, the logical subject of the structure of the assertion. That subject is the posterior "I." "The I-relationship of the objects takes precedence over the reality of the objects."[25] This self-understanding, which embraces the posterior "I" and hangs together with world, is passed on in the language tradition.[26]

[21] *Hermeneutik*, 131. Cf. Richardson, *Heidegger: Through Phenomenology to Thought*, 293, for an identical statement of Heidegger's position.
[22] *Hermeneutik*, 131; cf. his reply to Bultmann, "Was ist ein Sprachereignis?" II, 424–30 [207–12].
[23] *Hermeneutik*, 131 (J. M. Robinson, trans., *New Frontiers* II, 54 f.). Italics his.
[24] Cf. Fuchs I, 124–29; cf. I, 115 (*New Frontiers* II, 55); II, 286 f. [89 f.], 425 f. [208]; "The New Testament and the Hermeneutical Problem," *New Frontiers* II, 242. Cf. Ebeling, *Word and Faith*, 248 f.
[25] Fuchs, *Hermeneutik*, 132 f., especially 133.
[26] *Ibid.*, 135 ff. See also Fuchs I, 112 f. and "Proclamation and Speech-Event," *Theology Today* 19 (1962), 349.

It cannot be contested that the pre-understanding transmitted in language is constantly thrown into question by fresh experiences, new observations and the like. Such "crises" may be minor, involving only the readjustment of certain aspects of the way in which man regards the world without a corresponding shift in self-understanding. That is to say, the whole continues to hang together in the traditional way. However, there are major crises, i.e., which involve a readjustment of the whole of reality, including, or beginning with, the I-relationship, self-understanding. Major crises indicate a break with the common understanding.[27] Now if the common understanding is administered by language, it follows that a decision in such a crisis is a decision with respect to language.[28]

The individual is not in a position to preside over the breakup of a linguistic tradition by himself, if for no other reason than that the linguistic tradition is not at his disposal. When his self-understanding is called radically into question, he is left suspended, so to speak, between the call and his inability to answer. This is one way of formulating the contemporary problem of the crisis of language suggested by Bonhoeffer, Ebeling, and others. Fuchs has formulated this problem in relation to language event:

This power of speech which creates unity [the unity of decision and language] is what I call the "speech-event." For in speech I do not remain self-contained as I do in thinking. In speech I expose those mental images which I have unified to the agreement or contradiction of others. That is by no means to say that we live dialectically. Our speech moves rather in a being which, as that decision concerning the unity of our mental images, is indeed always my being; but in that it is always my being, it reveals the situation in which the being of others strives after an adjustment with my being. That means that we have a common understanding, whether friendly or hostile, of how we present ourselves, because we speak with each other. The real content of speech, that which is event not only in speech but also precisely as speech among men, is therefore being-itself. But because being-itself discloses in speech something like our situation, as that which is ever and again understood between us, I term being-itself *situation*. Situation is the essence of the "speech-event."[29]

While this passage reflects many facets of the concept of language event, the point to be noted here is that the individual is and remains dependent upon language and hence upon the common understanding.

[27] Fuchs, *Hermeneutik*, 137; "Proclamation and Speech-Event," 349.
[28] *Hermeneutik*, 70.
[29] "Proclamation and Speech-Event," 349 f. (italics his).

So what results as self-understanding in this situation is never dependent on the individual alone. For this reason this self-understanding cannot be communicated directly, but can be "understood" only belatedly, in the language produced *anew* in a contested or *newly occurring* common understanding. This new language will have to distinguish itself from the old, and at the same time still make clear the call involved in understanding, in which we are to respond "with ourselves." Then we say to each person, or, better, we give him to understand, what is to be expected of him, for him to be able to live in common agreement with us—in case we do not withdraw ourselves from him completely.[30]

The dependence of the individual on language poses for Ebeling the problem of *concepts,* a point at which the structure of the hermeneutical task becomes evident. The structure is a twofold relationship, one to the linguistic expression and the other to the object which comes to expression therein. This means that to deal with concepts responsibly, one must be bound to two points: "attentiveness to the history of language and openness towards the reality that confronts us."[31] The relation between the two points is reciprocal interaction.

The fact of reality's confronting me and the manner in which it does so are conditioned by the language spoken to me. And again, the understanding of language spoken to me, together with my own ways of using language, are conditioned by the way in which reality confronts me and the manner in which I let myself be confronted by it.[32]

Given this structure, it is clear that for Ebeling, as for Fuchs, the individual is subject to the world bequeathed him by language until he broaches the history of language or disposes himself in a new way to reality. In either case he must pull the other in its train. For this reason Ebeling regards a particular language tradition as something to which one may fall prey if he disregards the history of that tradition. On the other hand, if one loses contact with reality, his concepts, and hence his language, turn into empty shells. If Ebeling is prediposed to concentrate on the history of theological language and attentiveness to present reality, Fuchs is inclined to major in the reality which biblical language mediates.

It is in this connection that we are to understand language event as

[30] Fuchs, *Hermeneutik,* 137 (J. M. Robinson, trans., *New Frontiers* II, 241 f. n. 2). Italics his.
[31] Ebeling, *Word and Faith,* 248.
[32] *Ibid.*

communication. Communication can mean the imparting of information, but it can also mean providing a means for sharing. Ebeling distinguishes the two in this way: in the first I have experience of a *thing,* even if the communication should have to do with a man; in the second I experience a benefit, that is, something happens to me. "In the first case I take part simply as an observer, in the second I really share in an encounter."[33] The debate over objectifying language in theology arises in part out of this distinction, owing to the fact that it is unclear whether communication in the first sense can give rise to or even tolerate communication in the second sense.

Language event as communication brings us back to the concept *situation,* introduced in the lengthy quotation above. Fuchs' remarks are reminiscent of a paragraph from Heidegger:

We are a conversation—and that means: we can hear from one another. We are a conversation, that always means at the same time: we are a *single* conversation. But the unity of a conversation consists in the fact that in the essential word there is always manifest that one and the same thing on which we agree, and on the basis of which we are united and so are essentially ourselves. Conversation and its unity support our existence.[34]

But the single conversation that we are has a history. This would imply that being, too, has a history in its self-manifestation. The history of being is etched in language because the word which is essential, if it is to be understood and so made a common possession, must become ordinary. Accordingly, the true word cannot give a direct guarantee of itself, that it is essential. The counterfeit word masquerades as the essential, and the essential looks in its simplicity like the unessential.[35] We have, therefore, to reckon with the rise and decline of language traditions.

Historical times are marked by the rise of new language traditions. The essential word, authentic language, announces a new time, it determines the situation of man anew by calling, so to speak, a new world into being. The world which it calls into being is the world waiting to be born; the time it announces is the time of that time. The time which Hölderlin announces, according to Heidegger, is the time

---

[33] Ebeling, *Nature of Faith,* 86; cf. 84–95, 186 (italics his); *Word and Faith,* 326, 327.
[34] "Hölderlin and the Essence of Poetry," 278 (italics his).
[35] *Ibid.,* 275 f.

of the departing gods and the not-yet time of the god that is coming; it is the time between.[36]

According to Fuchs all language announces the time. The language of the family, which announces the time for this and the time for that, reveals this characteristic trait. Fuchs can then say: language does not create something new, it announces what it is time for.[37] The announcement of the time is determined out of and determinative for the situation: it is determined out of the situation because being-itself is disclosing itself in the announcement of the time, and it is determinative for the situation because the new language qualifies the situation.

We are now in a position to attempt to explicate several key issues which have greatly exercised both Fuchs and Ebeling. Those selected for consideration, from among many, are the question of why the proclamation is bound to a text, which is the basic item in the agenda of Fuchs' *Hermeneutik;* the issue of the historical Jesus, which is now taken up into the question of "language gain" and the ground of faith; and finally, the problem of translation, which becomes acute for a theology oriented to language event.

II
THE WORD OF GOD

The entree to these questions is, as has been indicated, the linguisticality of existence, which both Fuchs and Ebeling bring into relation to the word of God. The position of man is this:

Man exists linguistically between call and answer. In this relation language advances him what he may really "let be." Reality certifies for him only that which has been linguistically advanced to him. His behavior towards reality is the mirror of the answer which he has given to the call of language which went out to him.[38]

Heidegger's lament that the language of the Western tradition is worn out and used up, that it is broken down and hence reflects man's corrupted relation to reality, only attests to the fact that man has learned to lead a false existence by means of language which he has

---

[36] *Ibid.,* 289.

[37] *New Frontiers* II, 125–30, 133, 140; "Muss man an Jesus glauben, wenn man an Gott glauben will?" *ZThK* 58 (1961), 55 [Fuchs III, 262 f.] (= "Must One Believe in Jesus if He Wants To Believe in God?" *JThC* 1 [1965], 156).

[38] Fuchs, *Hermeneutik,* 133.

taken over and destroyed.[39] Man's abuse of language also affects the
word of God, for the word of God is subject to the vicissitudes of the
same linguistic tradition.[40] On the other hand, when the word of God
comes into language, language itself is redeemed and with it man's
relation to reality.

When God speaks, the whole of reality as it concerns us enters language
anew. God's Word does not bring God into language in isolation. It is not a
light which shines upon God, but a light which shines from him, illumin-
ing the sphere of our existence.[41]

The advent of authentic language, which the word of God is, means
the creation of a new language tradition out of which man may then
live. As Ebeling formulates it:

And when the event of the word is an extraordinary one, it is creative of
language, that is, it creates new possibilities of addressing and understanding the reality which approaches us, and becomes the source of light which
can again and again lighten up the darkness of existence.[42]

It is therefore clear why Fuchs can say of the proclamation that it
"brings not merely a conception to speech, but decides where the Christ
as the one who assembles us is present, in the event we attend the
proclamation and therefore have faith."[43] The proclamation as language event gives a presence to the Christ in that it allows him to
qualify our reality. In holding that the proclamation as language event
assembles, constitutes the body of Christ, Fuchs is giving expression,
in relation to his understanding of language, to the Reformation doctrine of the word of God.[44] Since man exists linguistically between call
and answer, the call which comes to him out of the word of God is
responded to as the responsibility for language. The responsibility for
speaking resides in language itself. Language is gift, out of which man
is born; and the word of God is gift, out of which faith is born.[45]
Word of God and faith go together.

[39] *Ibid.*, 63 (cf. *New Frontiers* II, 50).
[40] Ebeling, *Word and Faith*, 335–39.
[41] Ebeling, *Nature of Faith*, 190; cf. Fuchs, *Hermeneutik*, 71.
[42] *Nature of Faith*, 188.
[43] Fuchs II, 426 [cf. 208].
[44] *Ibid.* (cf. *New Frontiers* II, 58).
[45] Fuchs II, 427 f. [210]; *Hermeneutik*, 63 (cf. *New Frontiers* II, 50, 58).

Fuchs agrees with Bultmann that man does not have faith at his disposal, but he attributes this in the first instance not to the fact that man is a sinner, but to the fact that faith is dependent upon the word, God's word. As sinner man attempts to domesticate language by making it subservient to thought.[46] In so doing, he leaves God "speechless."

III
THE TEXT: LANGUAGE EVENT AS LANGUAGE GAIN

The Christian faith, however, claims that God once spoke to man in Jesus Christ. In the strictest sense Jesus is therefore the "text" of the proclamation.[47] As word of God, he is the language event which illuminates man's situation, which announces the time of God's drawing near, which gives faith the "space," i.e., linguistic room, in which to dwell. Faith, for its part, responded to the event of Christ with confession, which, formally speaking, leaves its deposit in the New Testament as "text." What then is the function of the New Testament as "text"? Why is preaching and hence faith bound to a "text"?

This question Fuchs regards as crucial for the church which proposes to understand itself in relation to the New Testament. As a matter of fact, it was the growing hiatus between the text and preaching, between scientific biblical scholarship and theology, that drove modern theology upon the hermeneutical problem in the first place.[48] The question, then, is whether and how the text is to be understood in relation to contemporary proclamation. Or, to put it the other way around, what is to be interpreted in the exegesis of the New Testament?[49]

Since the text preserves the situation, by means of its language, in which one has to speak of God, i.e., announce the time of God's arrival, then preaching is dependent upon the text for the illumination of that situation.[50] Now in the conventional orientation to the text, it is the text itself which requires interpretation. That is to say, the text, without the aid of exegetical help, remains opaque. But Fuchs proposes to turn this relationship around: what is opaque to him is not the text, but *our* situation. The text is obscure because our situation is ob-

---

[46] Fuchs II, 428 f. [211].

[47] Fuchs, "Proclamation and Speech-Event," 353.

[48] Ebeling, *Word and Faith*, 96, 308; cf. the essay "The Meaning of 'Biblical Theology,' " *ibid.*, 79–97.

[49] Cf. Fuchs' essay of that title, II, 280–303 [84–103].

[50] Fuchs, "Proclamation and Speech-Event," 350, 353 f.; II, 287 [90]; etc.

scure.[51] When he then says that preaching is dependent upon the text for the illumination of that situation, what he has in mind is not merely the situation of the first disciples, but our situation.

. . . and it must surely be said that the decisive function for the illumination of our existence belongs to the text itself. The text itself is then (as "language gain") a *hermeneuticum,* so that exegesis must always be driven on-since it comes to its terminus only in the proclamation. Proclamation and linguisticality of existence belong together. *What is therefore exposited is actually the present, exposited with the help of the text.*[52]

Why then is there still a hermeneutical problem at all? "To the extent that *it is not dependent on our good pleasure to know the truth, insofar as the truth has us ourselves as its object."*[53] It is a question, if we may return to Humpty-Dumpty, of who is to be master, the text or the interpreter.

It is not only relevant to investigate the conditions under which the text becomes understandable, but thereupon to inquire likewise after what is to be disclosed *through* the phenomenon of the "text." The text is therefore not only the servant which preserves kerygmatic formulations, but much

[51] Cf. Ebeling's formulation, *Word and Faith,* 318:
"It is usually taken for granted that the reason why hermeneutics has to do with the word-event is, that verbal statements pose the problem of understanding. Now however much the need for hermeneutics does in fact arise primarily from difficulties of understanding in the word-event, it is nevertheless completely false to take this situation as the point of orientation for one's basic grasp of the relation between word and understanding and of what is ultimately constitutive for hermeneutics. The superficial view of understanding turns matters upside down and must therefore be completely reversed. *The primary phenomenon in the realm of understanding is not understanding* OF *language, but understanding* THROUGH *language.* The word is not really the object of understanding, and thus the thing that poses the problem of understanding. . . . Rather, the word is what opens up and mediates understanding, i.e. brings something to understanding. *The word itself has a hermeneutical function.* . . . It is to my mind not unimportant for the proper grasp of the hermeneutic problem whether we set out from the idea that a verbal statement in itself is something obscure into which the light of the understanding must be introduced from elsewhere, or whether, on the contrary, we set out from the fact that the situation in terms of which and into which the verbal statement is made is something obscure which is then illumined by the verbal statement" (emphasis Ebeling's).
[52] Fuchs II, 430 [cf. 211 f.]. Italics his. Cf. Ebeling, *Word and Faith,* 331: *"Thus the text by means of the sermon becomes a hermeneutic aid in the understanding of present experience.* Where that happens radically, there true word is uttered, and that in fact means God's Word."
[53] Fuchs, *New Frontiers* II, 143 (italics his).

more, a master which initiates us into the linguistic context of our existence, the context in which we exist "before God."[54]

To use the pejorative analogy of the New Testament, the Pharisee is the one who insists that he is the interpreter of the text, whereas the sinner allows himself to be interpreted by the text.

Concomitant with the rise of the Christian faith, consequently, is the rise of a new authentic language tradition. Fuchs refers to this new linguistic tradition as "language gain."[55] Man always lives, of course, in relation to the linguistic tradition in which he finds himself. And, while he may abuse this tradition by taking possession of it or objectifying it, he cannot kill it off. The possibility of the rediscovery of its depth is always present. This accounts for Ebeling's interest in the Christian tradition, which he proposes to recapitulate in order to rediscover its ground, much in the same way as Heidegger has dismantled the Western metaphysical tradition in order to reach its primordial roots.[56] Fuchs, like Bultmann, however, thinks primarily of the direct relation between the biblical language tradition and our own situation. In either case, faith lives out of this language gain and so must take pains, when its peculiar language tradition has been obscured or lost, to recover it authentically. Required for this is the proper doctrine of language, a hermeneutic of the word of God:

For the language of faith is the language of existence which understands itself. We live out of the language gain of the witness of faith transmitted to us as New Testament and not out of the treasury of good works laid up in heaven or elsewhere. The language gain of faith requires a doctrine of language *of its own.* Hermeneutic in the sphere of theology is the doctrine of the language of faith. The doctrine of language no longer interprets the

[54] Fuchs II, 429 [cf. 211]. Italics his.

[55] *Hermeneutik,* 271; Ergänzungsheft, p. 15 to p. 137; Fuchs II, 181, 430 [212]; *New Frontiers* II, 241 f. and n. 2.

[56] This aim is evident in virtually all of Ebeling's work. Note especially, *Kirchengeschichte als Geschichte der Auslegung der Heiligen Schrift* (Tübingen: J. C. B. Mohr, 1947), and the programmatic essay, "The Significance of the Critical Historical Method for Church and Theology in Protestantism," *Word and Faith,* 17–61, which first appeared as the lead essay in *ZThK* (47 [1950], 1–46) upon its reorganization. The former has now reappeared in *Wort Gottes und Tradition: Studien zu einer Hermeneutik der Konfessionen* (Göttingen: Vandenhoeck & Ruprecht, 1964), 9–27, along with other relevant essays. More general remarks, *Word and Faith,* 248–52. Further, *ibid.,* 26 ff. (on theology and tradition), 81 (on biblical theology), 335–44 (on the doctrine of God), 429 f. (on the study of church history), to cite only a few examples. On this basis Ebeling can understand himself as a systematic theologian and church historian at the same time.

language of faith in the horizon of reality, but in the horizon of time itself, and discloses the time to us as the authentic "place" of existence before God.[57]

IV
JESUS AS THE TEXT OF FAITH

It has already been noticed that, strictly speaking, it is Jesus who is the "text" of faith. Formally he is text because he is word of God. In relation to language event, one could say that the language gain of faith stems ultimately from Jesus.[58] The new linguistic tradition which goes together with the Christian faith arises in the situation which is qualified by Jesus as a radically new situation, i.e., as the time of man's existence before God. It follows that if *that* situation is taken up into language, it will have to take up Jesus as part of the situation, since he belongs, as word of God, intrinsically to the situation he qualifies: the word became flesh. Jesus is not just any chance part, to be sure, but the essential part which makes the situation what it is: the time of God's visitation.

The concept of the situation as the essence of language event thus makes it clear why Jesus belongs to the content of the proclamation. It also makes it clear why Jesus' person belongs to his own proclamation as well as to the proclamation of faith in him as formulated by the early church.[59] That is to say, Jesus' person and world belong together, i.e., cannot be separated out, as that language event which opens up the room in which faith may dwell: "Whoever speaks of God as Jesus does, alters and fixes the situation of man, and thereby of being, as the content of speech."[60] As a consequence, the language gain of faith roots in Jesus.

What has been said may be taken as sufficient justification for the renewal of interest in the historical Jesus. Yet the legitimacy of the interest is by no means self-evident on this basis alone, for what is missing is an account of why the historical Jesus is to be held over against the confession of faith in the kerygma, as though the two things were separate entities. Putting it this way gives warrant for correcting one basic misunderstanding: referring the christological

[57] Fuchs, *Hermeneutik*, 271. Italics his; cf. iii, 101 f.; *New Frontiers* II, 241. Cf. Ebeling, *Word and Faith*, 332: "Theological hermeneutics is the doctrine of the Word of God," and the whole essay, "Word of God and Hermeneutics," 305-32, *passim*.
[58] Fuchs, *New Frontiers* II, 241 f.; *Hermeneutik*, 139.
[59] Fuchs, "Proclamation and Speech-Event," 350.
[60] *Ibid.*

kerygma to the historical Jesus does not mean the comparison of two independent objects—that would be the comparison of two christologies or two ethics—but inquiring whether and how the christological kerygma is an appropriate response to Jesus as God's word.[61] Jesus as the language event which determines the situation in which faith dwells is thus understood as that which holds faith to itself, i.e., keeps it being what it is.[62] Going behind the primitive Christian kerygma, contrary to Bultmann's assertion, does not mean going behind the word to certifiable facts, but going behind a word which stands in need of interpretation to the language event which is presupposed therein.[63] It is for this reason that Fuchs and Ebeling can say that the historical Jesus is interpreted by means of the kerygma, and the kerygma by means of the historical Jesus.[64] This is because faith and Jesus go together, because faith clings to Jesus.

According to Ebeling, christology must not be loosened from either the historical Jesus or our own reality.[65] This prompts Fuchs to reflect that faith must be understood in relation to its experiences, for the real problem for faith arises precisely out of its experiences. Not only does faith encounter the power of evil, but it also stumbles on its own good works, to which it is vulnerable. Such good works, like the Easter experience, may become stronger than faith itself and so pose a threat to faith. That is to say, faith may lay hold of its own assurances of the future as a means of avoiding the brute reality of the present. Now bringing the kerygma into relation with the historical Jesus is holding faith in relation to its experiences, holding it in relation to the situation. Among other aspects of his ministry, the preaching of Jesus reflects the experiences which faith has. What is to be noticed in the first place about Jesus' preaching is not the content of his words, but the fact that he speaks at all. The situation which is reflected in the fact that one calls upon God in prayer causes one to marvel at the fact of the prayer.

61 Cf. Ebeling, *Word and Faith,* 201–206.

62 Ebeling, *Nature of Faith,* 70 f. Ebeling's characteristic phrase is Jesus as "the ground of faith": *Word and Faith,* 108 n. 5, 110, 238, 303 f.; *Theologie und Verkündigung,* 29 f., 32.

63 Ebeling, *Theologie und Verkündigung,* 56. Ebeling's remark in *Word and Faith* (295 and n. 1) that historicism is built on a depraved view of word—i.e., it abstracts from live word event and reduces it to mere statement—could be taken as referring to the resistance which has met the "new quest."

64 Fuchs II, Vorrede, 164 [28], 166 [30 f.], etc.; *New Frontiers* II, 135 f. Ebeling, *Nature of Faith,* 70 f.; *Word and Faith,* 202 ff., 298–304; *Theologie und Verkündigung,* 30 ff., 51–82.

65 *Word and Faith,* 204.

In the same way, the fact that Jesus speaks of God as he does is remarkable in itself, since it calls attention to the way in which the whole of reality is concentrated in his speaking of God.[66]

Beyond the fact that Jesus speaks is the content of what he says. Are we to understand his teachings as a compendium of opinions and pronouncements on various points, "a conglomeration of more or less unrelated views?"[67] By no means. To be sure, Jesus calls upon a person to listen and to listen with regard to himself. But *"Jesus also gives his hearer the exhortation to take along with him on his way! . . . Jesus bestows his word upon his hearers as a gift.* He formulates it so that *the hearer has something to hold to in the future also, as if a model of faith were given him to take along. . . .* Hence there belongs with faith a word that not only calls forth faith but also accompanies it. *Faith has a particular relation to language that is all its own. This experience is the most characteristic experience of faith."*[68]

In sum, keeping faith close to reality means keeping it close to the language event which Jesus constitutes, on the one hand, and close to our own linguistic reality, on the other. For the same reason the experiences the early church had in faith, experiences which are embodied in the language of the church, must be referred to the reality of the situation in the early church (by means of historical criticism!) as well as to the situation of Jesus. Jesus is common denominator of all the experiences that faith has, serving, so to speak, as the paradigm of faithful existence.

These remarks scarcely do justice to the complexity of the issue of the historical Jesus as it is being raised by Fuchs and Ebeling. The aim has been merely to point the way to the horizon of the problem. The issue would be greatly illuminated if one were, for example, to take up Fuchs' work on the parables. For in the parables Fuchs finds the most characteristic expression of the word of God.[69] Beyond that, there is the question of Jesus' words and deeds taken as a whole, and the relation of that whole to christology. These issues have here been opened up only in a preliminary way.[70]

---

[66] Fuchs, *New Frontiers* II, 118–23.

[67] *Ibid.*, 123.

[68] *Ibid.*, 123 f. Italics his.

[69] Fuchs II, 329 [125]. Cf. *infra*, chaps. 5–8.

[70] See, further: Fuchs, "Die Frage nach dem historischen Jesus," II, 143–67 [11–31]; "Glaube und Geschichte im Blick auf die Frage nach dem historischen Jesus," *ibid.*, 168–218; "Jesus und der Glaube," *ibid.*, 238–57 [48–64]; "Die Theologie des Neuen Testaments und der historische Jesus," *ibid.*, 377–404 [167–90]; and Ebeling,

V
TRANSLATION

If the inner connection between the word or language and faith is the basis upon which the text becomes a problem for preaching, and the basis upon which the question of the historical Jesus is renewed, although in peculiar form, it is also the basis upon which the problem of translation not only becomes acute, but gets transformed.

The problem of translation is the reverse side of the question of the text: the text becomes an obstacle or perhaps a false friend to the preacher who no longer knows what its function is; translation is the problem of preaching viewed from the standpoint of the text, i.e., it is the question of what the text says. It has already been noticed how the interpreter gets taken into the question of the text, and the remarks here presuppose that discussion.

Why has the problem of translation become acute? In a general way it may be answered: because of the distance that separates the modern from the ancient world. This distance is relative, however, and presumably can be bridged to a greater or lesser degree by means of historical knowledge. The general answer, therefore, requires further specification. It appears to be the case that the proclamation presupposes faith on the part of the hearers, or at least a common frame of reference within which faith is possible. But such a presupposition strikes many as demonstrably false for the present age. The contemporary world is a world come of age, to use Bonhoeffer's phrase, in which religion is not the presupposition of anything. This in turn is advanced as the reason why the language of faith is no longer eventful: it does not speak to modern man.[71]

In one respect this discovery might be taken as bringing our age into direct touch with early Christianity, for the reason that the infant church was not able to presuppose Christian faith on the part of those to whom it addressed its missionary preaching. On the other hand, in the first century there was a great deal of "religion" in the air, stemming in part from Judaism and in part from the Mysteries, of which the proclamation could make use, sometimes to its own detriment.

"Jesus and Faith," *Word and Faith*, 201–46; "The Question of the Historical Jesus and the Problem of Christology," *ibid.*, 288–304; *Theologie und Verkündigung*, 19–26, 83–92.

[71] Cf. Ebeling on Bonhoeffer, *Word and Faith*, 124 f.

The second aspect of the situation in the first century may be said to constitute the problem of biblical language, viz., that it attaches itself to a general religiosity which is no longer viable. The first aspect, on the other hand, is a kind of "rediscovery" arising out of the contemporary situation. And this discovery is now to be turned to positive advantage. If the proclamation seeks to bring about faith, it cannot take faith as the criterion of understandability. The nonbeliever, rather than the believer, becomes the test of the proclamation.[72] Fuchs can then assert that what faith preaches is to be made understandable to everyone; preaching has the difficult task of translating the language of faith as confession into the language of unfaith.[73] *"The proclamation loses its character when it presupposes confession."*[74] This criterion, moreover, is not superimposed upon the biblical text, for the biblical text on its part ultimately demands nonreligious interpretation.[75] Nonreligious interpretation is referred, like demythologizing, to the biblical text in this way.

If the problem of translation has become acute because the biblical language or the traditional language of the church no longer qualifies the situation of modern man, no longer addresses him, it is also possible to see why the problem of translation has shifted. Gadamer identifies this shift as the crucial advance beyond Bultmann.

In [Fuchs'] essay on "Translation and Preaching" it becomes clearer to what extent this hermeneutical doctrine seeks to transcend what Bultmann meant by existentialist interpretation. It is the hermeneutical principle of translation that points the direction. It is incontestable that "the translation should create the same room that the text sought to create as the Spirit spoke in it."[76] But the bold and yet inescapable consequence is that the word has primacy over the text, for the word is language event. This is obviously meant as the assertion that the relation between word and thought is not that of belatedly catching up with the thought by means of the word expressing it. Rather the word is like a flash of lightning that strikes.[77]

---

[72] Ebeling, *ibid.*, 125, 136.

[73] Fuchs I, 9 f.

[74] Fuchs II, 166 [cf. 30]. Italics his.

[75] Ebeling, *Word and Faith*, 136. Cf. Ebeling's remarks in "Jesus and Faith" on Jesus' understanding of faith (*ibid.*, 232–38); likewise Fuchs' "nonreligious" interpretation of the parables.

[76] The quotation is from Fuchs II, 409.

[77] Hans-Georg Gadamer, "Hermeneutik und Historismus," *Philosophische Rundschau* IX (1962), 263 (J. M. Robinson, trans., *New Frontiers* II, 63).

Fuchs claims, as the basis of his hermeneutical doctrine, that language is not the abbreviation of thinking, but thinking an abbreviation of language.[78] The understanding of the word is different for those who think out of existence and those who think out of concepts. For the one, word is communication, for the other, a medium of knowledge.[79] If language has primacy over thought, translation cannot consist of the reduction of two diverse language traditions to common conceptualities. Rather, what came to expression in the text must be allowed to come to expression anew, and that means that the word can be spoken anew only if it is heard anew.[80] The affinities of this doctrine of the word with Heidegger's understanding of the poetic function are unmistakable.

Fuchs observes that the phenomenon of translation as he understands it is to be observed already in the New Testament. The New Testament itself provides evidence that it was successful in translating Jesus for people of the Hellenistic world so that they understood him in their own language; it was able to do this without in the end having to give up Jesus' own proclamation. Their own language was by no means merely the sequence of words in the Greek Testament. It was rather the linguistic preparation for the answer which they were to give to the proclamation with their own faith in Jesus. The New Testament succeeds in putting the question understandably to them whether they are willing to be one with Jesus.[81]

Jesus is translated, then, when he becomes the question to us whether we are willing to be one with him.[82] The historicness of New Testament language drives us to translate the truth revealed to us there into our own language; but it also gives us the task of forming our language anew in relation to our hearing. The latter, more important, task goes beyond demythologizing.[83] What is the relation of translation, understood in this way, to the text?

The *text* is neither transmuted nor modernized. It is also not replaced by something different. The text is rather to be exactly what it is: a linguistic complex, requiring understanding, which stands written. There follows as a consequence for the sermon that it also is to let the text be what it is. The

78 Fuchs II, 428 [210].
79 Fuchs I, 91 f.
80 Ebeling, *Nature of Faith*, 191; Fuchs, *New Frontiers* II, 144 f.
81 Fuchs I, 34.
82 *Ibid.*, 35.
83 *Ibid.*, 151.

sermon as the work of the preacher will therefore be his own word. Preaching is not exposition but proclamation. Although preaching may also say the same thing as the text, it then in no case says the identical thing.[84]

The text wants to speak; this is its vocation. But in order for it to speak, it must be placed "there" where it speaks to us. Its proper "there" is where it becomes language event for us.[85] The hermeneutic which goes with language event understands the three senses of *hermeneuein*—to speak, to interpret, to translate—to be essentially one:[86] to translate requires interpretation, since the language which qualifies one situation has to be interpreted for the new situation into which it is directed, but translation and interpretation do not reach their goal apart from a new speaking, for the reality which came into language can come into language anew only as event of language.

We may allow Ebeling to summarize the matter:

Man speaks because he is addressed. Language is the manifold echo to the question of God. So the event of the Word of God is necessarily bound up with the entire life of language. For if the Word of God brings the whole of our reality into language anew, then the reality which is already in language is necessarily addressed anew.

This touches the root of the vexatious linguistic problem in the Word of God. The happening of the Word of God has created a linguistic tradition of its own, to be seen not only in many forms in the Bible, but also in great variety and indeed disharmony in the history of the church. And now the Word of God, with this tradition, wishes to aim at reality in present-day language, it wants to express it anew and so express itself anew. The difficulty is only apparently solved by the manipulation of language, by modernizing words and making use of fashionable jargon. God's Word is expressed anew only when it is heard anew, with tense attention to how the traditional Word manages to make itself understood in the real circumstanc s to which our lives are exposed. This listening combines two things in one: an upright perseverance in experience, and a patient waiting upon understanding. If the Word of God were heard anew in this way, it could also be spoken anew with the authority proper to it. And that would transform our linguistic problem; for though this seems to be a linguistic problem for the Word of God, it is in truth our own linguistic dilemma.[87]

84 *Ibid.*, 94 f., and cf. 91; Ebeling, *Word and Faith*, 331.
85 Cf. Fuchs, *Hermeneutik*, 109, 111; *New Frontiers* II, 138.
86 Ebeling, *Word and Faith*, 321; "Hermeneutik," *RGG* III (1959), 243.
87 Ebeling, *Nature of Faith*, 190 f. For a lucid exposition of theology as translation see J. M. Robinson's essay, "For Theology and the Church," *JThC* 1 (1965), 1–19.

LANGUAGE OF GOD

It is not possible within the confines of this essay to develop the implications of the concept language event for the question of whether and how meaningful discourse about God is possible. Indeed, the proper foundation has not been laid. It is appropriate, however, by way of appendix, to broach the subject by drawing the lines—of necessity in extremely laconic form—along which the problem is to be thought out, if the concept language event is taken as the point of departure. Suggestions are confined to those provided by Ebeling.

1. Contrary to expectation, it is the general belief in God that poses the problem of whether Christian theology can speak meaningfully of God any longer. The question of God has been assimilated to what everyone knows, with the result that, where God is spoken of at all, such speech comes with ease and is taken as self-evident. But it is equally evident that the God that is generally believed in is no God at all.[88]

For this reason, the phenomenon of atheism, which is widespread but complex and difficult to assess, is welcome to and shared by those who wish to take the question of God seriously. The distinction between vulgar and authentic atheism is difficult to make, to be sure, but in its authentic form it is not to be taken, as is increasingly the tendency by "religionless" theologians, merely as preparation for talk about God in the traditional sense; rather, it is to be viewed with ultimate seriousness when it takes the form of a-theism—viz., non-theistic in the metaphysical sense which dominates the tradition.[89] As such it can contribute positively to theology. In this respect theology has yet to learn—and must learn—what it means to speak of God godlessly.[90]

Theology, consequently, is being thrown back upon its ground: can it speak of God without presupposing God?[91]

2. In the phrase, language of God (or message of God, if the

---

[88] *Nature of Faith*, 72 f.; *Word and Faith*, 193. Cf. Ebeling's remarks on Bonhoeffer's reservations with respect to the term God (*ibid.*, 107, 126 and n. 1).

[89] *Nature of Faith*, 77 ff.; "The Message of God to the Age of Atheism," *Oberlin College Bulletin* IX, 1 (January, 1964), 7–12.

[90] *ZThK*, Beiheft 2 (1961), 124.

[91] Again, Ebeling's analysis of Bonhoeffer's view of the contemporary situation illuminates his own assessment, which in most respects is identical: *Word and Faith*, 128–41, 148–55.

proclamation rather than theology is in view), "of God" can be taken either as an objective or as a subjective genitive. If theology is understood as language *about* God, it is to be asked whether and to what extent its language is *from* God. In view of the contemporary situation, the problem may be formulated the other way around: if theology is understood as dependent upon language *from* God, i.e., upon language event as revelation, then to what extent is talk *about* God still permissible?[92]

It is not only the present situation, however, that leads Ebeling to pose the problem in the second way, but also an understanding of that upon which knowledge of God is founded: ". . . the linguistic event which is constitutive of the knowledge of God is, rightly understood, not a word about God, but Word of God. For it is only as one who himself speaks that God can reveal himself as God."[93] Now, of course, word of God understood as the speech of a supernatural being presents insurmountable difficulties, whether understood literally or symbolically. If, however, the point of orientation is "the Word became flesh" (Jn. 1:14), it follows that God's word is always encountered concretely in human words, and that means in Jesus as the incarnate word and in the proclamation. And both are conditioned by historical linguistic traditions. In that case, word of God should be understood as God turning to man in his (God's) humanity.[94] But how then can one distinguish between word of God and word of man? Word of man, according to Ebeling, is God's word when God comes to speech in it, when it communicates faith.[95] The revelation of God takes place as word, with the result that occurrence of God's word and faith go together.

3. In view of what has been said, theology has the responsibility of reflecting upon the language event which roots in Jesus as the incarnate word of God, since this language event is normative for our understanding of word of God.[96] It then remains to be seen whether these reflections are relevant to the problem of language about God.

In his analysis of the relation between faith and Jesus in the Synoptic tradition, Ebeling makes the following points. First, Jesus' understand-

[92] Cf. Ebeling, "The Message of God to the Age of Atheism," 4.
[93] *Word and Faith*, 352; cf. *Nature of Faith*, 87 f., 94. Cf. Fuchs, *Hermeneutik*, 71.
[94] *Nature of Faith*, 92, 94.
[95] *Ibid.*, 90–95, especially 94.
[96] Note Ebeling's response to Althaus' criticism of the so-called Christomonism implied in this position: *Word and Faith*, 110.

ing of faith, as revealed by his words, is nowhere explicitly said to be faith toward God. *Pisteuein* and *pistis* are used absolutely. This does not mean that faith does not imply, even require, God, for the point is that faith is letting him work who has the power when all other human resources fail. Nevertheless, Jesus does not elicit faith in God or confessions of faith apart from faith in concrete encounter with his power.[97] Secondly, neither Jesus nor the Evangelists speak of Jesus' own faith. Jesus identifies himself so closely with faith that he found no need to speak of his own faith at all. He devotes himself rather to awakening faith. In the Synoptic tradition, in contrast to John, Jesus is never the object of faith. Yet he is always linked with faith because he is the one who awakens faith.[98] In the third place, Jesus' word is not about faith but is faith, and in a double sense: (*a*) it is a word spoken before God, a word of which God himself is the guarantor; (*b*) it is a word with which Jesus identifies himself, so that it gives expression to his own surrender in faith to God. Jesus and his word are therefore one.[99]

4. On the other hand, Jesus' word as language event does not wait upon confirmation from the hearer. It is so constituted that it does not need to ask for response, it simply necessitates response. The hearer is given the certainty of faith which goes with the word, to which he may cling or not. In either case he has made a decision.[100] Jesus' word, moreover, concentrates the whole of existence in a concrete situation to which faith is related. Thus Jesus never calls for faith in general, but faith in relation to a concrete situation, which is so intensified that it serves as a paradigm for the whole of reality.[101] In so doing Jesus sets a question mark against faith: he calls faith into question as something which has an object to be believed in, something appropriated in thought, or something inherited. His word makes the difference between faith and unfaith acute, and in such a way that unfaith is usually joined with traditional faith.[102]

These characteristics of language event are all embraced in the parable. It is for this reason that Fuchs can say that the parable is the most characteristic expression of the word of God.[103] The parable

[97] *Ibid.*, 232 ff.
[98] *Ibid.*, 234 f.
[99] *Ibid.*, 237 f.
[100] *Ibid.*, 288.
[101] *Ibid.*, 239–45.
[102] *Ibid.*, 239.
[103] See *infra*, 128 ff.

concentrates a totality of significations, a world, in a concrete situation. This totality, this world, is radically qualified by God, and it is to this world that Jesus has surrendered himself. Nevertheless, neither God nor Jesus "appears" as an object in that totality. It is a world, furthermore, into which the hearer is invited; he is invited to comport himself with that world as Jesus does, i.e., to follow Jesus. The hearer must decide, as he listens to the parable, whether he will be drawn into that world, i.e., whether he will have faith, or whether he will resist and withdraw.

5. These considerations may be briefly followed up. Taking the cue from Jesus' word, it may be said that Jesus does not give his diciples a word to speak about God, nor does he give them a word to speak about himself. On the contrary, he gives them the word to speak which he spoke. This word does not take faith as its presupposition; rather, it takes godlessness as its presupposition. In fact, it sets a question mark against traditional faith. Thus it may be said that the proclamation can, perhaps must, be articulated in a language that is "godless." For this reason theology must set a question mark against the traditional doctrine of God and the traditional christology, thereby perhaps rediscovering the import of theological predication, e.g., in the New Testament.

6. The preceding reflections by no means indicate that for Ebeling theological language about God is no longer permissible or possible. Theology should indeed ask "how far God's Word makes words about God necessary and also possible, and thus how in answer to God's Word there can be, and as a highly necessary thing also must be, in actual fact talk about God, doctrine of God. But the doctrine of God that founds on God's Word will in the first instance have to make it its purpose to understand this its ground."[104] Reflecting on its own ground means that theology must think concretely what it means by God, not beyond and apart from real life, but in strict relation to it, "so that God and ourselves are together in the one sentence."[105] This is what Ebeling means by such phrases as "Theology and Reality," "Rudimentary Reflexions on Speaking Responsibly of God," and "Worldly Talk of God."[106]

Going together with this concern is the concern about how the gospel as gospel comes to speech. Ebeling regards this problem as the

104 Ebeling, *Word and Faith*, 352.
105 Ebeling, *Nature of Faith*, 75.
106 *Word and Faith*, 191–200, 333–53, and 354–62, respectively.

one basic problem of theology. In distinction from proclamation itself, it is the business of theology to give a critical-reflective account of language event.[107] The need for responsible talk about God is self-evident: in no other way can the obstacles and distortions which threaten language event be overcome, even if, by achieving its goal, theology ever and again makes itself superfluous.[108]

[107] "Hauptprobleme der protestantischen Theologie in der Gegenwart," *ZThK* **58** (1961), 125 f.
[108] Ebeling, *Word and Faith*, 425.

The Language of Theology:
Van Buren, Ogden, Ott

ᔭ 4 ᔧ ————————————————

THE DISTINCTION BETWEEN THEOLOGY AND THE KERYGMA as word of God addressed to man is basic to Bultmann's thinking, as John Cobb rightly notes.[1] More precisely, Bultmann distinguishes among the self-understanding arising out of response to God's word,[2] the kerygma which proclaims God's act in Jesus Christ, and reflective theology, which seeks among other things to present the second as the self-interpretation of the first.[3]

It is to be observed that the kerygma or proclamation can be understood (1) as God's call, which encounters man in human words, or (2) as faith's self-understanding coming to expression in theological thoughts.[4] To put it schematically, the kerygma comes on both sides of faith: it is that which evokes faith, which gives rise to the self-understanding that is faith, but it also occurs as confession, as theologically formulated sentences which express faith's self-understanding. It is thus both call and answer. That the kerygma composed of theological sentences can be call, rests on the paradox characteristic of Christian preaching, viz., that God's call always comes in human words. That the same kerygma is answer follows from the character of faith as self-*understanding*: the understanding of self, world, God which is inherent

[1] John B. Cobb, Jr., *Living Options in Protestant Theology* (Philadelphia: Westminster Press, 1962), 236 f., following Fuchs, Diem, Ott.

[2] Always existential self-understanding and not an objective anthropology: *Theology of the New Testament* II, 239.

[3] Cf. *ibid.*, 237–41.

[4] Cf. *supra*, chap. 2, 21–26; Bultmann, "Preaching: Genuine and Secularized," in *Religion and Culture: Essays in Honor of Paul Tillich*, W. Leibrecht, ed. (New York: Harper & Brothers, 1959), 236–42, especially 237 f.

in faith must necessarily come to expression. The linguistic explication of believing self-understanding is a movement within faith itself.[5]

For its part, systematic theology presupposes the proclamation as occurring word of God,[6] and is to be understood, therefore, as "a kind of phenomenology of faith."[7] Insofar as theology seeks to interpret the theological thoughts of the kerygma as the explication of believing self-understanding, i.e., to interpret theology and self-understanding in their inner unity,[8] it participates in "the character of address that belongs to the sermon."[9] In this sense systematic theology is indirect address, in that it keeps faith to that self-understanding without which it would not be faith. But insofar as theology presents the theological thoughts of the kerygma as "right doctrine," i.e., as the object and content of faith, theology is itself misunderstood because the word of God it presupposes is misunderstood.[10]

Although self-understanding, kerygma, and theology can never be simply and sharply distinguished from one another, at least not in practice, theology, nevertheless, must keep these differences constantly in view.[11]

Bultmann's understanding of faith, kerygma, and theology in their relations and differences has been determinative for subsequent theological discussion, even in quarters where his influence is not explicitly recognized. Alternatively, it could be said that Bultmann has merely exposed the problems with which contemporary theology has to deal if

[5] Bultmann, *Glauben und Verstehen* I, 178, 186; *Theology of the New Testament* I, 318 f.

[6] Fuchs, *Hermeneutik*, 99.

[7] John Macquarrie, *An Existentialist Theology: A Comparison of Heidegger and Bultmann* (London: SCM Press, 1955), 6, cited by Schubert Ogden in *Christ Without Myth*, 23. Bultmann so describes it: *Existence and Faith*, 94.

[8] Bultmann, *Theology of the New Testament* II, 251; *Existence and Faith*, 93 f.

[9] *Existence and Faith*, 93.

[10] Bultmann, "Preaching: Genuine and Secularized," 239 f.

[11] Bultmann, *Glauben und Verstehen* I, 186; *Theology of the New Testament* II, 240. In these passages the distinction is made between kerygma and theology, but it must be made also between self-understanding and kerygma since the theological thoughts of the kerygma are never simply equated with self-understanding. The knowledge inherent in faith is knowledge of self, i.e., new understanding of one's self (*Theology of the New Testament* I, 318), and not the specific content of the kerygma. It is for this reason that the kerygma must be demythologized: only in this way can the self-understanding which lies within the kerygma be made clear. This tripartite division is implicit also in the discussion which stems from Bultmann, as shall be seen.

it aspires to be cogent. In either case Bultmann's work cannot be conveniently set aside.[12]

Fuchs and Ebeling, as their work has been presented, have concentrated on language and hermeneutic as the key to residual problems, with the consequence that the sequence, faith's self-understanding and its linguistic explication, tends to get reversed.[13] Among other theologians who have responded to Bultmann's challenge in rather different ways are three younger men whose work is to be considered here. For the latter the problem of theological language has gravitated to the center. The reason is that it is no longer clear what theology is, and specifically whether and in what sense it is legitimate to speak of God theologically. They have turned emphatically to the third element in Bultmann's tripartite division, viz., theological language in the narrower sense, because the theological enterprise itself is seen to be under threat, as indeed, in its classical sense, it is under Bultmann's hand. It may not be purely accidental that two of them, Paul van Buren and Heinrich Ott, have been students of Karl Barth, whose massive *Dogmatik* was presumably designed to settle just this question. The third, Schubert Ogden, is the product of a philosophical tradition peculiarly American, which has been highly resistant to the encroachment of dialectical theology. Ogden's work reveals the upheaval that results from a direct and serious confrontation of the two.

The following discussion is focused on the problem of theological language and, insofar as possible, is confined to that theme. It will be seen that theological language, particularly God-language, is understood to be under direct or indirect attack. The point is less evident in the case of Ott, who restricts himself to a redefinition of theology's task without raising the wider question explicitly. All three men are addressing the question in the terms in which Bultmann has set it or at least identified it.

I

Bultmann asks: "What sense is there to speak of God?"[14] Ebeling is also exercised with this problem, as we have seen.[15] It is the task of theology, traditionally understood, to speak *about* God. But it is this

---

[12] Cf. Ogden's strong statement, *Christ Without Myth*, 22 and 125.

[13] *Supra*, chap. 3.

[14] "Welchen Sinn hat es, von Gott zu reden?" *Theologische Blätter* 4 (1925), 129–35 = *Glauben und Verstehen* I, 26–37 = *Christian Scholar* 43 (1960), 213–22 (Franklin Littell, trans.).

[15] Chap. 3, 67–71.

function, indeed the right, of theology to speak about God that has been called into question. What is theology to do if it loses the right to speak about God? Can it be "theology" any longer? And would the silence of theology also not mean the end of Christian faith?

Theology is based on, or takes as its raw material, the language of faith. Faith's language arises as confession and proclamation, out of the knowledge inherent in faith, and thus as the human words and sentences in which faith seeks to explicate itself linguistically. Broadly defined, the language of faith is what the man of faith confesses, what he "hears" as he attends to the word of God. Christian theology looks to the language tradition of faith, especially to the biblical language, but also to the length and breadth of the tradition, including contemporary expressions of faith. Without this raw material theology would presumably fall silent.

It follows that the language of faith, and hence theology, is founded upon the "experience" of faith and upon faith's experiences: by the former is meant the "experience" of that power which sets a limit to human calculation and control, i.e., a transcendent power;[16] the latter may be taken to refer to the contingent character of every act of faith, viz., its dependence upon a particular locus in a spatial-temporal continuum, in history. If the term "experience of" is unacceptable, the phrase "response to" may be substituted. On the basis of this "experience," as a response to an encounter with the transcendent, faith produces its confession and/or proclamation.

Bultmann asserts that the language of faith in the New Testament is a mythological objectification of the "experience" of faith. It is mythological because it speaks of the otherworldly or transcendent in terms of this world or what is immanent, and it is objectifying because it projects the transcendent, i.e., God and his acts, onto the plane of nature and history. In order to preserve the intention of this mythological language—the transcendence of the transcendent and the self-understanding awakened by it—it is necessary to translate the language of the kerygma into self-understanding, which embraces self, world, God. The language of faith is comprised of statements about God which are at the same time statements about the self, and statements about man which are at the same time statements about God. But both types have to be understood basically as faith-statements, i.e., as "God-for-man" statements or as "man-before-God" statements. To isolate one element or the other is to vitiate the intentionality of the language.

---

[16] *Kerygma und Mythos* II, 183 (Ogden, *Christ Without Myth*, 25 f.).

This brief sketch provides the framework for identifying the specific points at which van Buren, Ott, and Ogden elect to attack the problem of theological language.

It is sometimes averred that the contemporary man of faith does not in fact "experience" anything that can legitimately be called "God." That is to say, whatever the contemporary man of faith calls "God" is certainly not the transcendent to which the New Testament kerygma points, and the current edition of the man of faith, when he is put under pressure, must simply confess that he has no "knowledge" of God. Modern man is taken to be without resources for the "experience" of the divine. The problem which theological language posits, therefore, is the problem of faith's "nonexperience" of the transcendent. If theology talks in God-language, this man cannot possibly understand what is being said because he can provide no existential reference for the language.

This is the setting for the problem as van Buren conceives it. Van Buren, however, does not seize the problem of the "nonexperience" of faith; he takes secular man's inability to understand God-language as indicative of a shift in language stock and nothing more. He therefore restricts himself to the establishing of a theological language stripped of transempirical elements.

It is clear, nevertheless, that faith once experienced something it called "God." What was that something? Can it be translated into modern terms—terms which are devoid of God-language? Or is the problem more far-reaching and critical, viz., that theology must dispute the nature of reality with secular man in order to make meaningful translation possible?

Bultmann takes it for granted that the fundamental difficulty is *translation*. He assumes that if the kerygma is put into proper other words, understanding of faith will follow. He does not claim that *faith* necessarily follows, but he does presuppose the possibility of faith, i.e., the possibility of the "experience" of the transcendent. His answer "to the assertion that for modern man the idea of God above or beyond the world is either no longer viable or is perverted in a religiosity which would like to escape the world" is unambiguous: "By no means! Only the idea of God which can find, which can seek and find, the *unconditional in the conditional*, the beyond in the here, the transcendent in the present at hand, as a possibility of encounter, is possible for modern man."[17]

---

[17] Bultmann, "The Idea of God and Modern Man," *JThC* 2 (1965), 93 f.

Schubert Ogden sets out from this point. While affirming Bultmann's analysis of the problem and his constructive proposal in principle, Ogden finds it necessary to take exception, in the first place, to Bultmann's insistence that faith is a possibility in fact only because of Jesus Christ. The necessity of exception arises from the fact that this proposition contradicts Bultmann's other axiom, viz., that faith is to be demythologized, interpreted exhaustively as authentic self-understanding. If Bultmann's program of demythologizing is then carried through consistently and exhaustively, Ogden discovers, in the second place, that Bultmann is without adequate resources to speak of God at all, since he appears to use Jesus Christ as a God-surrogate. The final and demanding task, as Ogden sees it, is to develop the philosophical resources which will enable theology to speak of God in an "objective" but nonmythological and nonontological (classically conceived) sense, to speak of God with an "objectivity" that is appropriate to existential philosophy. Thus, for Ogden theological resources have failed primarily because philosophical resources have failed, and the route to success is to overcome the inability to articulate adequately what is already known.

Heinrich Ott comes at the issue from the Barthian side. This prevents him, on the one hand, from giving weight to Bultmann's analysis of the situation of modern man so decisive for Ogden: God has manifested himself in Jesus Christ, and that manifestation in no way depends on the circumstances under which it is to be received. But Ott allows, on the other hand, that theology may fail if it misunderstands itself. So long as theology thinks in objectifying concepts and uses objectifying language (here Ott is also directing his remarks against Bultmann), it holds God at arm's length. Such a procedure thwarts the "experience" of faith and denies to theology its experiential character. The language of theology, like the language of poetry, should lead to the "place" where one stands before and in the presence of God. The model for this understanding of theology is Heidegger's primal thinker. Ott apparently believes that his Heideggerian view of theology accords with Barth's intention.

Ott is of interest in this context because he is being driven onto the same problem as van Buren and Ogden, but from a distance. Where his work will lead him remains to be seen. Nevertheless, he has approached the problem with a sensitivity that is surprising, considering his apathy to all talk of the modern world. Perhaps his sensitivity has been acquired vicariously though not explicitly from Heidegger and Bultmann.

The understanding of language as word event suggests that the prior question cannot be posed precisely in the way any of these three poses it. If language is understood as word event, the problem of theological language is not merely a matter of translation in the sense of transposing one language into another, for that requires other cor-responding words, and cor-responding words cannot be raked up from just anywhere. Nor, on this view, can it be a matter, fundamentally, of disputing the character of reality ideologically, since theology in that case would be trying to make it possible to believe, i.e., to entertain God-language, without coming to faith. It is the lack, rather, of the word, the true word, in the house of which faith may again dwell. In and out of the true word theology could perhaps again enter the lists and dispute reality. It is indeed a matter of the misunderstanding of language, but it is questionable whether the correct understanding of language will itself produce salutary language. A sound understanding of poetry is not necessarily conducive to the production of poetry.

In brief, these three men presuppose, as it seems to me, what is at issue. Yet they have stood into the question in a way that places us all in their debt. The measure of the sting—if there be any—in the following analyses is intended to be commensurate with the measure of the critical relevance of their work.

II

Paul M. van Buren[18] finds himself caught between the theological "right" (Barth) and the theological "left" (Bultmann, Ogden), between the conservative concern for christology and the liberal concern for contemporary ways of thinking. Going together with this divergence is the tension between historical expressions of the Christian faith and the inability of modern secular man to "place" traditional theological language. Van Buren is of the opinion that philosophical linguistic analysis may be able to step into the breach with aid if not comfort.[19]

While van Buren has brought together a relatively unique constellation of elements, it is clear that he is exercised by the same problems

---

[18] Primary sources for this analysis include his *The Secular Meaning of the Gospel Based on an Analysis of Its Language* (New York: The Macmillan Co., 1963); "On Doing Theology," a mimeographed lecture presented at the Second Consultation on Hermeneutics, Drew University, April 9–11, 1964. On *The Secular Meaning of the Gospel* cf. Langdon B. Gilkey, *JR* 44 (1964), 238–43 (= *New Theology No. 2*, Martin E. Marty and Dean G. Peerman, eds. [New York: The Macmillan Co., 1965], 39–49).

[19] *The Secular Meaning of the Gospel*, 17 f., 57.

that trouble Bultmann. It will be illuminating to observe how he proposes meeting them.

The hermeneutical task, according to Ebeling, is bound by two points: the history of language, and the reality that confronts us.[20] The hermeneutical problem is the problem of interpreting the traditional language of faith in the face of reality as it is experienced. Theology, as a consequence, must take account of the present "experience" of faith as well as the past "experience" of faith; it must seek to establish the living language which cor-responds to traditional language, if, indeed, there are correlative terms. This is the Bultmannian formulation of the problem, as we have seen, but without the assumption that translation, except in the root sense, can bridge the gap.

Van Buren's program is to be interrogated initially with respect to the question of the reality that confronts modern secular man.

Van Buren does not take the term "secularism" firmly in hand,[21] but he is willing to define it as disposition, as attitude marked by certain characteristics. Secularism is possessed of certain empirical attitudes, of a deep interest in questions of human life this side of the "beyond," and of a lack of interest in metaphysical speculation.[22] The secular man, van Buren avers, is not "out there," outside the church, to be addressed from "in here," inside the church, but is in the man of faith himself.[23] This modern, secular man, who is also the man of faith, mirrors the culture in which he lives: he thinks empirically and pragmatically.[24]

It is this style of thinking that constitutes the problem with respect to theological language.

The empiricist in us finds the heart of the difficulty not in what is said about God, but in the very talking about God at all. We do not know "what" God is, and we cannot understand how the word "God" is being used.[25]

The term "God" allows of no verification and is simply and plainly meaningless to secular man. This assertion, to be sure, reveals van Buren's own empirical attitude, but he is also convinced that such a stance is much more common among contemporary "believers" than

20 *Word and Faith*, 248; cf. *supra*, chap. 3, 53.
21 *The Secular Meaning of the Gospel*, xiii, 194.
22 *Ibid.*, xiii f., 20.
23 *Ibid.*, 2, 11, 20.
24 *Ibid.*, 17.
25 *Ibid.*, 84.

either Bultmann or Ebeling recognize, and that the cogency of his program depends on the extent to which "a method consistent with such attitudes is found to be helpful for the reader."[26]

It would appear to be certain that van Buren is appealing directly to the reality which confronts modern secular man, viz., to a reality devoid of any trace of the transcendent. As Langdon Gilkey sums his position up: "all theological references to God, and so presumably all religious dependence upon him, must be deleted."[27] Religion, for van Buren, is not a misuse of the God-relation, as it is according to some forms of "religionless" Christianity, but stands for "*any* relation to God, for any relation beyond one's relations to things and persons."[28] As such, religion itself is not viable for secular man.

This interpretation is supported by van Buren's response to the question about the transcendent God of classical Christianity. On van Buren's view, it is asked, is theology any "more" than ethics?

Our answer takes the form of another question: In a secular age, what would that "more" be? It is our inability to find any empirical linguistic anchorage for that "more" that has led to our interpretation.[29]

It is the lack of "empirical linguistic anchorage for that 'more,' " the fact that the world is encountered in a completely secular, i.e., godless, way, that makes it impossible to speak meaningfully of God.

It does not help, van Buren charges, to speak, as Ogden does, of an "experienced nonobjective reality," by which God, or the transcendent, is meant.[30] It is equally meaningless to speak "analogically" about God.[31] For Bultmann and Ogden apparently think that something can be made of the word "God," that secular man can be taught to speak of God correctly. Van Buren obviously doubts that secular man can make anything at all of God-language. "Simple literal theism" is wrong, "qualified literal theism" is meaningless.[32] For this reason, the Bultmannians have left the problem of speaking about transcendence unsolved. They substitute some oblique language for the word "God," but this only begs the empiricist's question.[33]

[26] *Ibid.*, 83 f.
[27] *JR* 44 (1964), 238.
[28] *Ibid.*, 238 f. Italics his.
[29] *The Secular Meaning of the Gospel*, 197 f.
[30] *Ibid.*, 64 f.
[31] *Ibid.*, 65 ff.
[32] *Ibid.*, 99.
[33] *Ibid.*, 79. On this point cf. further, 11 f., 195.

Van Buren appears to assert that modern secular man lives in a secular, i.e., godless, landscape, and that this is the basis of the further assertion that God-language in any form is meaningless. The contemporary "man of faith" has no "experience" of the transcendent comparable to that reflected in traditional theological language, with the result that the secular Christian should either (a) give up his faith, or (b) reconceive it without divinity. It is possible, of course, that a secular version of the Christian faith is the only legitimate "translation" of the historic faith; that lack of God-consciousness in the modern world is the true heir of the God-consciousness of the primitive church. This is the possibility to which van Buren is attracted, and which he attempts to work out. The prospect is breath-taking.

Nevertheless, the words "appear(s)" and "presumably" in these descriptive statements and in Langdon Gilkey's formulation, cited above, are to be noted. It is by no means certain that van Buren thinks that he and secular man (the two are not to be distinguished) are quite as "godless" as some of van Buren's statements would lead us to believe. This should not be interpreted to mean that van Buren is of the opinion that secular man is not "really" godless after all. If this were the case, then van Buren would be holding a frivolous parade, the only possible object of which would be to entertain the "God-seekers." That he is not engaging in sleight of hand is indicated by the fact that he addresses himself to himself and to those in the church. He disavows apologetic interests.[34] It may be taken to mean, however, that the real problem is not godlessness, but language adequate to express the "experience of faith" in nontheistic terms. That is to say, is "experience of faith" the given term, which "godlessness" can frustrate but not thwart, but for the translation of which secularism sets the terms? Does the godlessness of the secular man of faith mean simply that he does not have adequate nontheistic language at his disposal "to raise the knowledge inherent in faith to the level of conscious knowing"? If this is the case, the further question arises whether the language van Buren offers is really nontheistic, or whether he, too, smuggles the transcendent in by some devious means. It is in order to explore these questions.

In summarizing the consensus of such analysts as Hare and Braithwaite, van Buren notes that there is "the implicit or explicit conviction that the language of faith does have a meaning, and that this meaning

---

[34] *Ibid.,* 11; cf. xiv, 20, *et passim.*

can be explored and clarified by linguistic analysis."[35] This conviction goes together with van Buren's view

that the difficulty lies rather in the character of the language of faith, that the problem is not so much one of bad religion as it is one of bad, or at least unworkable, language.[36]

The secular age, consequently, does not present us with the problem of faith itself, but with the problem of the logic of an apparently meaningless language.[37]

When the problem, as van Buren conceives it, is posed the other way around, it takes on a slightly different color. In this form, the question is not whether faith is possible, but whether it is able to give account of itself. Such an account need involve only the empirical placing of faith's language.

The language of faith may be viewed from two perspectives, that of secular man, and that of the biblical witness. Van Buren's interest is to get them together. What happens when he juxtaposes two dissimilar "language-games"?

In the language of faith, for Bultmann and Ogden, statements about God are statements about human existence, and statements about man are statements about God. Bultmann believes, however, that theology can only make use of man as the head term. If we say that we know God only as God-for-us, and man only as man-before-God, it does not follow that we can speak of "the-for-man-God"; we can speak only of "the-before-God-man." Bultmann imposes this restriction in order to protect the transcendence of God, who can never be spoken of as object.[38] Aside from the question whether God can stand as the head term, it is clear that for Bultmann such statements are reciprocal: statements about man-before-God are statements also about God, and statements about God-for-us are also statements about man.

The Nietzschean cry "God is dead!" on this view must be taken to assert something also about man, viz., that he is godless. According to van Buren, however, this cry is meaningless. For the statement to mean something, man would have to have experienced the death, or absence,

[35] *Ibid.*, 99 f.
[36] *Ibid.*, 81.
[37] *Ibid.*, 84
[38] Cf. Bultmann's essay, "What Sense Is There To Speak of God?" (*supra*, n. 14), and *infra*, chap. 9, 239–42.

or lack, of God. But for secular man the *word* "God" is itself dead. It cannot, therefore, mean anything.[39] Van Buren's position is decidedly odd for someone who aspires to fathom the *meaning* of traditional theological language. One might have thought that if the term "God" were dead in one case, it would also be dead in the other, since secular man is the touchstone in both cases. Is van Buren going beyond Nietzsche, or is he going behind him?

This observation leads to van Buren's complaint with reference to the *vice versa* of the Bultmann-Ogden position: why, van Buren asks, do Bultmann and Ogden add "vice versa" to their assertion that statements about God are also statements about man?[40] When secular man speaks of dying, is he really speaking about "God and his activities"? Or do Bultmann and Ogden have the language of theology in mind when they make this remark? It shouldn't really matter to van Buren, who wants to translate God-language into nontheistic terms, and who, therefore, should not be concerned about the vice versa. What should concern him, however, is whether the other avenue is not also closed off. How is it possible to look for meaning in statements about man-before-God when the term "God" is dead? That is to say, is it really crucial to van Buren's position to differentiate between God as the head term and man as the head term, as Bultmann does? Or, does not the fact that he cancels "God" out of the language put an end to one form of the statement as well as the other?

Van Buren is not prepared to go quite so far in emptying the "experience of faith" of meaning. He presupposes, as was noted, that the language of faith has some meaning. How can this meaning be expressed in language barren of transempirical elements?

The first person pronoun is utilized as the basis of a "blik" (R. M. Hare, I. T. Ramsey), which "involves a perspective entailing a commitment."[41] What is of special interest is the "logic" of this "I-language." Van Buren puts it succinctly:

The language of faith, by referring to a transcendent element, indicates that something has happened to the believer, rather than that he has done something.[42]

[39] Van Buren, *The Secular Meaning of the Gospel*, 103.
[40] *Ibid.*, 66.
[41] The definition of a "blik" is found *ibid.*, 91. For "I-language" see 88 f., 89 n. 15, 103, 105, 106, 129 f., 154 f., 171, 195.
[42] *Ibid.*, 140.

It is for this reason that the "blik" of faith is said not to be chosen by
the believer, but that he is "grasped" and "held" by it.[43] The disciples
did not choose Jesus; he chose them.[44] And the reference to the "Holy
Spirit" indicates that their new freedom and perspective were understood as gifts.[45] This passivity is also characteristic of the language of
the resurrection appearances,[46] and the attitude which goes together
with the doctrine of reconciliation is that the man of faith should treat
other men as if they were pardon*ed* and accept*ed* in some "final"
sense.[47] And finally, this passivity is what gives the gospel its "objective" reference.[48]

Van Buren certainly knows that the passive construction is often
used in the New Testament as a circumlocution for the divine name.
This passive therefore conceals God-language. Van Buren's secular
version of the language of faith looks very much as if he were conceal-
ing a reference to the transcendent in a passive construction. He may
be using the passive as nothing more than a surrogate for God. The
passive voice is ambiguous, to be sure, when the agent is not expressed.
It therefore becomes incumbent on van Buren to explicate the logic of
his use of the passive. In the absence of such explication, one can only
conclude that the passive is van Buren's means of dodging the fundamental issue: to what does faith attribute itself?[49]

If faith, in its traditional form, attributes itself to a transcendent
agent, if it asserts that something happens to the believer, van Buren
must be prepared to do more than to supply passive language. What
does he propose to name as agent?

In view of his whole line of reasoning, one expects him to name
Jesus. But this is not the case. With Bultmann, he claims that there
were no Christians before Easter, that knowledge of Jesus does not
produce faith, that Jesus did not cause his disciples to share his freedom.[50] Easter is the mysterious experience that comes between Jesus

---

[43] *Ibid.*, 140.

[44] *Ibid.*, 134.

[45] *Ibid.*, 136.

[46] *Ibid.*, 129.

[47] *Ibid.*, 150.

[48] *Ibid.*, 169 f.

[49] It goes without saying that the man of faith also understands his faith as his own
act, as his own response (*ibid.*, 141). The issue is how to account for the fact that the
language of faith attributes faith both to a human and to a transcendent agent.

[50] *Ibid.*, 124 ff. On 197 he unequivocally rejects a "Jesusology" and opts for Easter.
Cf. his repeated assertion that Jesus without Easter is not sufficient basis for the Christian
faith, e.g., 145, 197.

and the first Christian.[51] In this, too, he shares Bultmann's position. Unlike Bultmann, however, van Buren can give this experience only a passive reference.[52] He is willing to concede that with Easter Jesus gained a new power, or began to exercise one he already possessed, and that this must be the experience of transcendence to which the disciples bore witness.[53] It does seem exceedingly odd to use the name "Jesus" in this context, as though a dead man were in a position to exercise any kind of power at all! However that may be, one might have expected van Buren to conclude that the disciples' *memory* of Jesus began to effect a change in them, or that Jesus' *word* at last hit home, and they understood what he had been talking about all the time he was with them. But this van Buren will not allow. No, the disciples could not refer their faith to the historical Jesus, and they could not refer it finally to their own memories or decision: they *had* to refer it to the risen Jesus, who was now seen to be Lord over the whole world.[54]

If Jesus of Nazareth is not the author of faith and the Holy Spirit has been eliminated, what then? Logically and historically, van Buren argues, the believer's expression of faith depends upon that of the apostles![55] That involves a very high doctrine of the church indeed, even for an Episcopalian. Nevertheless, it is still another item which van Buren has in common with Bultmann. The only point at which they appear to part company is where Bultmann is willing to affirm that faith must refer itself to God, who breaks into man's history from outside, but not in any observable (empirical!) way. Van Buren prefers to use the passive circumlocution.

Van Buren confesses, half-way through his study, that he has not said how far the empirical attitudes of secular man will carry him, nor to what extent he shares them.[56] Nevertheless, he claims that he does not require transempirical language, that he does not need circumlocutions for God as a means of articulating the meaning of faith.[57] He believes it is entirely possible to be agnostic about "otherworldly" powers and beings and still be a man of faith.[58] One may gather from these remarks that secular empirical attitudes can carry the theologian

[51] *Ibid.*, 126 ff.
[52] *Ibid.*, 129.
[53] *Ibid.*, 132.
[54] *Ibid.*, 133 f.
[55] *Ibid.*, 137.
[56] *Ibid.*, 106.
[57] E.g., *ibid.*, 171. Cf. 170, where he proposes to carry the program of the theological "left" to its conclusion and not speak of God analogically or any other way.
[58] *Ibid.*, 195.

the whole distance, and that they are fully shared. In spite of this impression, van Buren insists that he is concerned to *understand* the apparently transempirical aspects of the language of faith.[59]

This analysis alleges that van Buren leaves the tension between secular man and faith unresolved, or at least concealed in a passive circumlocution. The allegation is based on two points: (1) van Buren is unable to take the claim of faith's language seriously because he is burdened with a deficient view of language; (2) he cannot accord secular man his final rights because he has not grasped the interdependence of language and reality.

To take the second point first, van Buren fails to see that when language fails reality fails, and the other way around. If God-language is meaningless to secular man, it is because he has no reference for the term "God." His landscape is indeed secular. The transcendent reference in the traditional language of faith cannot be accommodated in secular language until that language is itself redeemed—unless, of course, secular man does know the "experience of faith," but has forgotten that it used to be referred to "God"! The godlessness of secular man is made over into a piece of potential piety by the clever process of pouring the gospel into his ready-made language. The question theology has to face is whether faith is a possibility for secular man, given his language and thus his world.

On the other hand, van Buren comes to language with the understanding of language predominant in philosophical linguistic analysis: language is an arbitrary system of signs, devised to convey information. Because he takes this definition as his starting point, he is constrained to opt for a noncognitive "blik" as the basis of faith. This alternative is dictated by the type of linguistic analysis that wants to restrict cognition to the kind of knowledge that can submit to "hard" empirical reference, and thus to the verification principle. But there are other modes of cognition, to which the imagination, metaphor and symbol, and the language of poetry are parties. It could be said that van Buren is attempting to devise a theology for a literal-minded era. It is doubtful, to put the matter briefly, whether the "experience of faith" is amenable to literal language, with or without God.

Were the theological program devised by van Buren to succeed, it would be the end of theology. There is, perhaps, no special cause to grieve in that prospect. It would be a pity, however, if theology, which presumably deals in knowledge of some order, were to be dispossessed on the grounds that its raw material, the language of faith, turned out

[59] *Ibid.,* 196.

to be noncognitive. Theology would arbitrate, as it were, between competing "bliks," but what would it do for criteria?

Paul van Buren, like most of us, is really three men. He is a secular man who finds that the traditional language of faith can no longer be "cashed." He is a linguistic analyst who recognizes that the problem of language has become chronic. And he is a theologian who is committed to the significance of the Christian faith for men in all times. Van Buren the secular man is the most intriguing, but he surrenders in the end to the other two, and it is by no means certain that van Buren the language analyst is able to bring van Buren the Barthian to heel.

III

Schubert M. Ogden,[60] like Paul van Buren, finds himself under stress as a consequence of the tension between classical expressions of the Christian faith and the world view implicit in modern philosophy and the sciences. As in the case of van Buren, this stress takes the form of tension between the theological "right" and the theological "left." Ogden, no less than van Buren, wants "to maintain constant conversation" with classical theology and yet take account of the present situation.[61]

---

[60] Primary sources for this analysis include: "Bultmann's Project of Demythologization and the Problem of Theology and Philosophy," *JR* 37 (1957), 156–73; "The Situation in Contemporary Protestant Theology, IV: Systematic Theology," *Perkins School of Theology Journal*, XII, 2 (Winter, 1959), 13–20; "The Debate on 'Demythologizing,'" *JBR* 27 (1959), 17–27; *Existence and Faith: Shorter Writings of Rudolf Bultmann*, Schubert M. Ogden, sel., trans., and intro. (New York: Meridian Books, 1960); "The Lordship of Jesus Christ: The Meaning of Our Affirmation," *Encounter* 21 (1960), 408–22; *Christ Without Myth: A Study Based on the Theology of Rudolf Bultmann* (New York: Harper & Brothers, 1961); "The Significance of Rudolf Bultmann," *Perkins School of Theology Journal*, XV, 2 (Winter, 1962), 5–17; (with Van A. Harvey) "Wie neu ist die 'Neue Frage nach dem historischen Jesus'?" *ZThK* 59 (1962), 46–87 = "How New Is the 'New Quest of the Historical Jesus'?" in *The Historical Jesus and the Kerygmatic Christ*, C. E. Braaten and R. A. Harrisville, eds. (Nashville, Tenn.: Abingdon Press, 1964), 197–242; "Bultmann and the 'New Quest,'" *JBR* 30 (1962), 209–18; "The Understanding of Theology in Ott and Bultmann," *New Frontiers* I (see Abbreviations), 157–73; "What Sense Does It Make to Say, 'God Acts in History'?" *JR* 43 (1963), 1–19; "Beyond Supernaturalism," *Religion in Life* 33 (1963–64), 7–18; "Zur Frage der 'richtigen' Philosophie," *ZThK* 61 (1964), 103–24; "Theology and Philosophy: A New Phase of the Discussion," *JR* 44 (1964), 1–16; "The Temporality of God," in *Zeit und Geschichte: Dankesgabe an Rudolf Bultmann zum 80. Geburtstag*, Erich Dinkler, ed. (Tübingen: J. C. B. Mohr [Paul Siebeck], 1964), 381–98; "Theology and Objectivity," *JR* 45 (1965), 175–195.

[61] *Christ Without Myth*, 16: "Our situation today is defined both by the renewed determination to pursue theological work in obedience to the kerygma and in critical openness to the entire Christian past and also by the concern to do justice to liberal theology and, in particular, to face in all seriousness the fundamental problem with which the liberal theologians sought to deal."

In contrast to van Buren, however, Ogden does not regard himself as caught between Barth and Bultmann, but unequivocally opts for Bultmann, whose work he regards as of "extraordinary significance"[62] for contemporary theology. In Bultmann Ogden finds that the proper tension is maintained between traditional theological formulations and the demand for restatement meaningful to modern man. Bultmann's significance resides in the fact that he has grasped the problem rightly, has focused it properly, and has provided the primary resources for its resolution.[63]

As the basis for pursuing Ogden's relation to Bultmann, however, it will be illuminating to consider Ogden's assessment of the contemporary human situation, and thus put to Ogden the same question that was put to van Buren, viz., the question of the reality encountered by modern man.

Ogden himself approaches this question, following Karl Barth, from the side of the theological situation. Theology must be constantly developed anew and *ab ovo,* it can no longer maintain the simple identification of the kerygma with various types of orthodoxy, and it has come to see that the constructive work of liberal theology was less than adequate.[64] The liberal theologians were correct, however, in accepting the challenge of the modern world, since they rightly saw that the continued existence of the church and its message depends upon radical criticism of traditional theological formulations.[65]

Neo-orthodoxy,[66] on the other hand, overlooked the virtues of liberalism in this regard, and simply assumed that traditional theology could be addressed to the contemporary situation without further ado. "It has rarely asked itself whether the character of our modern situation may not make such an assumption gratuitous."[67]

The situation of contemporary theology, as distinct from both liberalism and neo-orthodoxy, is characterized by an ambivalence that is a consequence of its double heritage: it is quite willing to concede that its only legitimate task is to articulate the "understanding of reality

[62] *Ibid.,* 18; cf. "The Significance of Rudolf Bultmann," 5–17, especially 5–7, 12 f.
[63] *Christ Without Myth,* 125.
[64] *Ibid.,* 14.
[65] *Ibid.,* 42; cf. "The Significance of Rudolf Bultmann," 8.
[66] The term is used here in a more or less literal sense to characterize so-called biblical and kerygmatic theologies constructed in this century in extreme reaction to liberalism.
[67] Ogden, *Christ Without Myth,* 16.

that is implicit in authentic Christian faith." But it is "unwilling to take for granted that this task is still a real possibility."[68]

Contemporary theology is faced with this dilemma as a result of its having learned that theological work is to be carried out in obedience to the kerygma and in openness to the Christian tradition, and as a result of its sensitivity to the stance of modern man. The juxtaposition of the two creates a crisis of major proportions for theology, one that it can avoid only at the risk of vacating its commission.

The modern man to whom the gospel must be addressed is the man who can accept many assertions of the New Testament only at the price of a *sacrificium intellectus*.[69] Ogden, following Bultmann, unconditionally affirms:

If the price for becoming a faithful follower of Jesus Christ is some form of self-destruction, whether of the body or of the mind—*sacrificium corporis, sacrificium intellectus*—then there is no alternative but that the price remain unpaid.[70]

This same man does not understand himself as "open" to invasion by alien or supernatural powers. "He views himself, rather, as a unified being and attributes his experience, thought, and volition to his own agency, not to divine or demonic causes."[71] Unless such a man is accorded the status of a free and responsible being, who takes responsibility on himself for his own existence, " 'salvation' and all it implies must be meaningless" to him.[72] It follows that a history of salvation which attributes saving efficacy to certain historical events, whether miraculous or not, is not only incredible but irrelevant.[73] Bultmann therefore asserts that there is no honesty of another or higher type than that which "requires me to hold nothing as true that contradicts the truths which are the factual presupposition of the understanding of the world that guides everything I do."[74] Ogden is fully persuaded that Bultmann's characterization exposes the "stubborn reality of the mod-

[68] *Ibid.*
[69] *Ibid.*, 35.
[70] *Ibid.*, 130.
[71] *Ibid.*, 35.
[72] *Ibid.*, 136.
[73] Cf. *ibid.*, 36, again citing Bultmann.
[74] *Glauben und Verstehen* II (Tübingen; J. C. B. Mohr [Paul Siebeck] 1952), 235 (*Essays Philosophical and Theological* [London: SCM Press, 1955], 261), cited by Ogden, *Christ Without Myth*, 134.

ern world," not only for those outside the church, but also for those inside the church, and that means precisely also for the man of faith.[75]

The reason Ogden finds Bultmann's theological work of extraordinary significance and yet finds himself compelled to go beyond Bultmann has been lucidly set out in *Christ Without Myth*.[76] The matter may be briefly reviewed.

Faith, for Bultmann, is obedient response to the word which issues from the New Testament. The New Testament word, however, is clothed in mythological language, which mirrors an understanding of the world and man that modern man cannot accept. Mythological language is unintelligible, incredible, and irrelevant to modern man as a consequence of three characteristics of myth: (1) myth "objectifies" a reality that is not an "object," viz., the unworldly, the divine, the transcendent. (2) It attributes certain occurrences to supernatural or superhuman causes; events are "open" to the incursion of transcendent powers. (3) Myth always takes the form of a report or narrative the characteristic content of which is nonnatural or supernatural occurrences.[77] The second and third characteristics are really of a piece, and constitute a basic reason why modern man finds myth unintelligible and incredible. For scientific thinking, and thus for modern man, the world is "closed" to the incursion of otherworldly powers; modern man lives out of the basic assumption that one does not need to appeal to a supernatural causal antecedent as the explanation of anything.[78] The first characteristic may be understood, however, as the reason mythological language is regularly *misunderstood*: myth reduces the transcendent to just one more factor in the known and observable world; this reduction has the effect of belittling the divine and robbing it of its transcendence. This is not, however, the intention of mythological language.[79] On the other hand, modern man may take quite another view of the "objectifying" tendency of myth: he may reason that myth "objectifies" the transcendent, which is to say it objectifies *nothing*, in consequence of the fact, affirmed by Bultmann and Ogden, that he can no longer conceive of transcendence as invading the world, i.e., he can no longer conceive of it mythologically. Because for him transcendence and mythology are inseparably linked, transcendence

---

[75] Ogden formulates this characterization in a number of unambiguous and trenchant statements, *ibid.*, 127–37.

[76] The first three chapters are devoted to just this point.

[77] *Ibid.*, 23–27.

[78] *Ibid.*, 36.

[79] *Ibid.*, 26.

does not fall within his purview; he takes his world to be devoid of transcendence altogether. It is thus not only the fact that myth "objectifies" that creates problems, but also that it refers to "transcendence" in the first place. Nevertheless, Bultmann and Ogden elect the former rather than the latter of these alternatives as the principal obstacle for the man who lives in an Einsteinian universe, on the ground that it is possible to conceive transcendence nonmythologically.

Bultmann has shown the way out of the impasse between the mythological language of the New Testament and modern man's understanding of himself and his world by showing that myth intends to express a certain understanding of human existence. When mythological language is demythologized, it is seen that myth is not making affirmations about the divine in this-worldly terms, but is actually asserting something about the way in which man understands himself and his world. Demythologization, then, is nothing other than the translation of myth into "self-understanding," which is the appropriate and valid means of exposing the true intention of myth. For this reason Ogden regards Bultmann as having defined the problem confronting theology and as having shown the way to its solution.

Bultmann's own particular solution, however, is untenable, according to Ogden, because it incorporates two mutually contradictory propositions: (1) "Christian faith is to be interpreted exhaustively and without remainder as man's original possibility of authentic historical (*geschichtlich*) existence. . . ." and (2) "Christian faith is actually realizable, or is a 'possibility in fact,' only because of the particular historical (*historisch*) event Jesus of Nazareth. . . ."[80] These two propositions are contradictory, Ogden reasons, because man cannot be held to be always responsible for choosing between alternatives, one of which is not open to him apart from Jesus Christ.[81] On Bultmann's view, man before and apart from Christ does not really have the choice between faith and unfaith and so cannot be made responsible for it. Ogden is therefore obligated to attack Bultmann's "christocentrism"[82] in the interest of giving the first proposition, stated above, its full weight. In this Ogden believes that he is meeting "the demand for demythologization that arises with necessity from the situation of modern man,"[83] as well as that arising from the New Testament itself.

[80] *Ibid.*, 112.
[81] *Ibid.*, 117 f.
[82] Specifically mentioned, e.g., *ibid.*, 143, 145 f.
[83] *Ibid.*, 127. Italics in original.

What is at issue when the gospel is addressed to man, according to Bultmann, is whether the intention of the mythological language of the New Testament is valid, viz., whether man can become free only in dependence on a transcendent power. Faith affirms this truth, even though it is not bound to the New Testament way of representing it.[84] To this Ogden gives his assent. But when Bultmann goes on to add that the transcendent power at work in faith is made accessible only through Jesus Christ, Ogden demurs. He takes his difference with Bultmann to lie in the role ascribed to Jesus Christ. As a responsible and free being, man must have the possibility of faith ever before him—if faith is a possibility at all; to bind faith to Jesus Christ is to imply "a quasi-Gnostic conception in which man is understood as the helpless and irresponsible victim of fate."[85] Bultmann has therefore left a mythological residue in his theological program.

Ogden's opposition to Bultmann's "christocentrism," for whatever good and sufficient reasons, drives him to deny that faith can be bound, not only to the Christ event, but to any particular event or to some particular events; it must be universally accessible. Ogden proposes no less than to incorporate transcendence into the structure of reality. The prospect is intriguing, if not entirely new.

But the question then becomes, with respect to Bultmann's view, whether Ogden has not modified the intention of the mythological language of the New Testament as Bultmann understands it. That Ogden has done so would have to be established in the face of his own express statements to the contrary, and thus in relation to the wider reach of his work. It is possible, moreover, for Ogden to point to Bultmann's recent essay, "The Idea of God and Modern Man,"[86] as lending support to his own view. Nevertheless, there are some indications that when Ogden demythologizes the New Testament he comes out with a slightly different version than Bultmann. We must confine ourselves to a few points.

As the basis of his assertion that faith is factually possible only in Jesus Christ, Bultmann adduces the New Testament.[87] Ogden counters, however, that the New Testament never doubts that each individual is responsible for his final destiny, that the only basis of salvation in the New Testament is the everlasting love of God primordially active

---

[84] Ibid., 39 f., with appropriate references to Bultmann.
[85] Ibid., 119.
[86] JThC 2 (New York: Harper Torchbook, 1965), 83–95.
[87] Cf. Ogden's summary, Christ Without Myth, 73–75.

in creation, preservation, redemption, and that "the only final condition for sharing in authentic life that the New Testamtent lays down is a condition that can be formulated in complete abstraction from the event Jesus of Nazareth and all that it specifically imports."[88] These formulations may be accepted as reflecting certain aspects of New Testament thought. The difficulty they present is not so much in what they assert, as in what they are taken to exclude. It is by no means clear that the responsibility of man and the primordial love of God, of themselves, exclude the connection between faith and Jesus Christ, also posited by the New Testament. In any case, the New Testament evidence is clear. Bultmann's *Theology of the New Testament,* as indeed all his exegetical writings, show that this connection is the fundamental datum for primitive faith, and Gerhard Ebeling has remarked that we must learn anew to marvel at the close connection between Jesus and faith in the tradition.[89] The nature of the connection cannot be taken for granted, to be sure, and it is clear, furthermore, that the connection is not rightly construed as that between belief and object of belief, as in some orthodoxies. It is possible that the close relation of Jesus and faith, Ebeling suggests, witnesses to the correspondence of *sola fide* to *solus Christus.*[90] On the other hand, it is the more remarkable, in view of the primitive Christian tradition, that Jesus himself apparently uses the term faith in a nonreligious way, i.e., without reference to God.[91] Thus, contrary to Ogden, it could be said, on the basis of the New Testament evidence, that faith is either connected with Jesus Christ or used in a "secular" way. The juxtaposition of these two within the New Testament may indicate that primitive Christian faith understood itself to be dependent upon Jesus without taking him as object; Jesus may be the source rather than the object of faith.[92] In any case, Ogden is hardly correct when he asserts that a "christocentric" reading of the New Testament significantly alters its own express emphasis,[93] and he is by no means justified in assuming that when the Christ event is demythologized, the connection between faith and Jesus is dissolved. It is possible that demythologizing binds faith to Jesus all the more closely, as Ebeling thinks.

---

[88] *Ibid.,* 141–44; the quotation is from 143.
[89] *Word and Faith,* 204.
[90] *Ibid.*
[91] *Ibid.,* 232 ff.
[92] *Ibid.,* 238.
[93] *Christ Without Myth,* 143.

Ogden presses his criticism of Bultmann not so much because of the New Testament evidence as because of Bultmann's other principle, which Ogden makes the cornerstone of his own work: that Christian faith is to be interpreted as man's original possibility of authentic historical existence. Bultmann and Ogden alike emphasize the freedom and responsibility of man. Both insist that faith acknowledges itself as God's gift. But in view of Bultmann's ontic differentiation of the historical events upon which faith is dependent, it has to be asked whether Bultmann and Ogden understand the freedom, responsibility, and hence guilt, of man in the same way.

Since the lines of Bultmann's constructive theology are derived from Paul (and John), it is worth noticing how Bultmann understands Paul to formulate the matter. Paul does indeed insist that man is responsible for his own existence,[94] and it is probably Paul's view that man becomes sinful by his own sinning.[95] On the other hand, Paul is also of the opinion that man has lost control over his own destiny in that flesh and sin are powers *"to which man has fallen victim* and against which he is powerless."[96] Bultmann insists that flesh and sin as powers do not constitute a realistic mythology, but express the fact that man has lost the capacity to be the subject of his own actions: he wills the good, i.e., life, but invariably winds up, apart from faith, in sin and death. The fact that he wills one thing and achieves another points to an inner division in the self, the two parts of which are at war with one another; this conflict witnesses to man's "memory" of his true destiny, but also shows that his ability to achieve it has been perverted.

While Bultmann would agree that man's freedom to opt for life is an original ontological possibility, he would insist that this possibility has been closed off under the conditions of human existence, since man has in fact taken up his other option, viz., to turn against the creator. But how is this closure to be understood apart from recourse to dualisms of one kind or another, or to alien powers of a mythological sort? In a little-noticed passage in his *Theology of the New Testament* Bultmann explicates what he takes to be the intention of Paul.[97] From the differentiation, e.g., in Romans 5:13 f., between sin for which man is responsible and that for which he is not responsible, the inference can be drawn that every man experiences himself to have been born into a

---

[94] *Theology of the New Testament* I, 227.
[95] *Ibid.*, 251.
[96] *Ibid.*, 245. Italics his; cf. *Christ Without Myth*, 72 ff., where Ogden summarizes the views of the New Testament and Bultmann.
[97] I, 253.

world where sin already reigns; by virtue of his solidarity with other men, the individual participates in sin for which he is not initially responsible, but to which he gives his complicity. He thus becomes jointly responsible for sin which is and is not dependent upon his own free choice.

Owing to the role which cohumanity plays in this understanding of sin and guilt, the concept "world" takes on correlative significance in the thought of Paul. Bultmann shows that the term *kosmos* in Paul often expresses a definite theological judgment; as such it is an eschatological concept.[98] From the perspective of faith, Paul views the world of men, mankind in its totality, as hastening toward its end, i.e., as under judgment. The present situation of mankind is revealed by the catastrophe toward which it is running. But *kosmos* also has "cosmic" dimensions: it is the sphere of the principalities and powers which have come to tyrannize man. While these antidivine powers owe their dominion to man himself, in that he grants them their authority by virtue of his sin, it is nevertheless the case that once man permits their sway, he loses the freedom to extricate himself from their grip. Just as the individual participates in the guilt of mankind, so he accedes to the tyranny of the demonic powers, and in the one case as in the other he shares the guilt for a state of affairs over which he no longer presides. But the *kosmos* in its wider reach is also on its way to destruction and is even now under judgment.

Human solidarity in sin is proleptically broken and the dominion of the powers overcome, according to Paul, through the victory of Christ. God acting in Jesus Christ does for man what he cannot do for himself, viz., bring the old aeon to an end.

Little as all this constitutes a realistic mythology, it must nevertheless be translated into nonmythological language. The point to be made in translation is precisely this: for man to gain the freedom to opt for authentic existence, it is necessary for the world in the sense of all men to be redeemed, and for the world in the sense of cosmos to be transformed. Man cannot opt for that which is dependent upon the redemption of other men and the cosmos, since he is not in a position to effect this redemption.

When one takes his bearings from Paul, it is easy to see not only why Bultmann grants that man's freedom makes him responsible for his sin, that his "memory" of his true destiny makes it possible for him to

---

[98] *Ibid.*, 256 f.; cf. *Glauben und Verstehen* III (Tübingen: J. C. B. Mohr [Paul Siebeck], 1960), 25, 209 f. For the corresponding Johannine concept, see *Theology of the New Testament* II, 15 ff., 26 ff.; *Glauben und Verstehen* I, 135–37.

clarify his own situation conceptually, but why Bultmann also insists that the possibility of faith in fact is simply not available to him apart from something done *to* him and *for* him, here and now. Bultmann thus counterweights man's freedom and responsibility with man's bondage. It is not a matter of mutually contradictory statements, but of man's original possibility being refracted in the prism of his ontic situation. By virtue of the perversion of his true destiny, man is exposed as a mortal rather than a god because he cannot "unmake" the world he has "made."

There is no counterweight to man's freedom, so far as I can see, in Ogden's proposal. He insists that Bultmann's distinction between "possibility in principle" and "possibility in fact" must be vacuous if Christian faith is to be understood as authentic historical existence, which man is always responsible for realizing. He alleges that modern man rejects "everything that violates the unity of man's selfhood by representing him as at the mercy of powers whose agency is independent of his own responsible decisions."[99] It is to be noted that the *same* point with respect to man's freedom is made in both of these formulations. He further alleges that a distinction between general and special revelation, and hence other ontic distinctions referring to God's relation to the world, must fall back on a mythology of some kind,[100] from which the inference may be drawn that all ontic distinctions reside finally within the domain of man's will. If Ogden now replies that his counterweight to the absolute freedom of man is the primordial love of God, everywhere effectively present, we can only conclude that God also appears to be placed at the disposal of man. It is possible that the understanding of *solus Christus* is only a rallying point, in the debate with Bultmann, for other, more fundamental problems.

It is of course the case that Bultmann holds that God is everywhere present in his creation. But God does not reveal himself just any-where—only where his word comes and makes him known.[101] Ogden appears to ascribe such a function to Jesus.

Likewise, when Jesus speaks of the forgiveness of God, his intention is not to describe it to the theoretical intellect, but, as one who is "sent" or authorized by God, actually to bestow it as an *existentiell* possibility.[102]

99 *Christ Without Myth*, 119.
100 *Ibid.*, 156.
101 See *supra*, chap. 2, 22 f.
102 *Christ Without Myth*, 162; cf. 161 f.

He previously qualifies this by saying that the word spoken in Jesus is no different than the word spoken everywhere "in the actual events of nature and history."[103] It is the more remarkable, then, that Ogden makes the word spoken in Jesus Christ the norm of all other words.[104] But he does this for a different reason: only by binding itself to the gospel can theology be theology in any meaningful sense.[105]

This leads me to remark, finally, that Bultmann takes his bearings from the phenomenon of faith itself, as that phenomenon presents itself in the tradition, primarily the New Testament. As a consequence, Bultmann does not reason from general ontological possibilities to the ontic situation of particular men when doing theology, but the other way around. He therefore constructs a phenomenology of faith.[106] That he does distinguish ontology and onticity is indicated by his presentation of the Pauline theology,[107] and I take his distinction between "possibility in principle" and "possibility in fact" to rest on the same basis. Ogden, as it seems to me, has his eye fixed intently on the ontological question, with frequent side glances at modern man. The two methodologies overlap but do not coincide. I take this to be the reason Ogden does not feel compelled to account for certain elements in the tradition, e.g., the connection between Jesus and faith, which exercise Bultmann so much. This remark is relevant only insofar as it illuminates why a rigorous and precise demonstration tends to trim the edges off the phenomena; but it also illustrates, hopefully, why precise demonstrations are necessary.

Turning now to Ogden's position vis-à-vis the modern man whose understanding of himself and his world has been the touchstone of so much theological debate, it is in order to inquire whether Ogden's formulations are any more viable for this man than Bultmann's.

It is clear that Bultmann takes the modern world view as his criterion for demythologizing in order to expose the real offense of the Christian faith. Demythologization reveals that the gospel is not bound to the biblical world view, and thus can be stated in nonmythological terms. But it also reveals that the gospel is not bound to any world view, including the modern.[108] This means that the real offense of the

103 *Ibid.*, 156.
104 *Ibid.*, e.g., 138.
105 *Ibid.*, 139.
106 *Supra*, 73.
107 Note, e.g., *Theology of the New Testament* I, 227.
108 For these and the following points, the reader is referred to Bultmann's *Jesus Christ and Mythology*, especially chaps. III and V, as well as to an interesting essay

Christian faith does not lie within the domain of world views at all, but within the domain of self-understanding. Within the latter domain, Bultmann is no less clear that for modern man's self-understanding— the one that apparently goes with his world view but in fact belongs to sinful man as such—the self-understanding of faith is a scandal and offense. Man resists understanding himself as dependent upon God's grace and attempts to secure his life and future by his own efforts. The gospel, on the other hand, calls man to throw himself upon the mercy of God, to live his life out of grace, and thus to be free from dependence upon himself: herein lies its offense. Now the modern world view, precisely because it does not and cannot take notice of transcendence as an explicit factor in natural processes, affords sinful man an acute temptation to link his self-understanding with his world view and to understand both as devoid of transcendence. The "crisis of faith," of which Bultmann was writing already in 1931,[109] although it is not really a crisis of world views, is nothing other than a crisis with respect to the transworldly reality called God, and therefore a crisis with respect to Christianity, for the historic form of the Christian faith, typified by Paul, depends upon a "salvation" of which God is the author. Bultmann is prepared to face this crisis, even if it means abandoning the Christian faith, but he does not think so radical a solution necessary, for the reason that the modern world view does not exclude the transworldly reality called God from the domain of man's self-understanding.[110]

Ogden acknowledges this crisis no less than Bultmann, and as his book *Christ Without Myth* unfolds (indeed already in the title itself), one gains the unmistakable impression that Ogden intends to purge whatever mythological element may remain from Bultmann's program in accordance with the demands of the modern situation. This impression is not in error, and the previous criticisms should not be allowed to dull it. That Ogden is attempting to cross the frontier to which Bultmann in part has directed him, there can be no doubt. The remaining question can be put simply: How will the man who regards himself as unequivocally modern regard the effort?

---

entitled, "Das Befremdliche des christlichen Glaubens" in *Glauben und Verstehen* III, 197–212, especially 207 ff. The same points are often made by Bultmann in other contexts.

[109] *Glauben und Verstehen* II, 1 ff. (*Essays Philosophical and Theological,* 1 ff.)

[110] Cf. *Existence and Faith,* 185.

Since Bultmann himself assumes that the Christian faith is entirely a matter of *existentiell* self-understanding,[111] Ogden can claim that he is carrying through Bultmann's intention in the formulation of his "first principle."

The first principle of such a solution is that the demand for demythologization that arises with necessity *from the situation of modern man* must be accepted without condition.[112]

I take this to mean that demythologizing must be carried through to the extent demanded by the situation of modern man.[113] This would seem to be unequivocal: theology cannot affirm anything that is not credible within the framework of modern man's understanding of himself and his world.

It will be helpful at this point to review the steps of the argument, including Ogden's own positive formulation of his solution. (1) Modern man cannot accept the mythological picture of the *world* for the reason that the world is a closed unity for him, i.e., it is not open to the incursion of transcendent powers. (2) Modern man cannot accept the mythological picture of *himself* either, since his own self-understanding asserts that he is a unified being, who is not open to the incursion of divine powers, with the result that this man attributes his experience, thought, and volition to his own agency. To these points, which he holds in common with Bultmann, Ogden now adds: (3) "man is a genuinely free and responsible being, and therefore his salvation is something that, *coram deo,* he himself has to decide by his understanding of his existence."[114] Ogden's point can be put in another way. Man's new self-understanding (faith), which he lays hold of and understands as his own responsibility, is not dependent upon the Christ event (against Bultmann), it is dependent only on *"some* event in which God's grace becomes a concrete occurrence and is received by

---

[111] Ogden, *Christ Without Myth*, 112, correctly interpreting Bultmann.

[112] *Ibid.*, 127 (italics mine); cf. 130 ff. Cf. 125 on Ogden's relation to Bultmann's intention.

[113] This is not to say that demythologizing cannot be supported from the side of faith as well. With Bultmann and Ogden, I believe that it can be. The point here, however, is the extent to which the situation of modern man determines theology's necessity. In "The Significance of Rudolf Bultmann," 10, Ogden hedges a bit on behalf of Bultmann: Bultmann does not demythologize because the modern world view demands it, but because the gospel itself requires it; Bultmann is not an apologist.

[114] *Christ Without Myth*, 136.

a decision of faith."[115] Unless this statement is true, "it is arguable that 'salvation' and all that it implies must be meaningless to the modern man."[116]

It has to be said that Ogden apparently takes a huge step in meeting the typical objection to the self-understanding of faith on the part of the man who resides in the modern world. He has conceived a brilliant and highly persuasive proposal which can only be regarded as an authentic effort to interpret faith in contemporary terms while remaining true to the gospel in its classical form. He has rightly grasped Bultmann's theological program and its significance for contemporary theology, while noticing that Bultmann's constructive work is less than fully satisfactory. The questions to be raised with respect to Ogden's solution do not derive from the judgment that he may not be fully orthodox. If anything, he errs on the side of orthodoxy. And that suggests that Ogden has not come entirely clean after all with respect to his own first principle.

In the first formulation of his solution, cited bove, Ogden introduces the phrase *coram deo*. What is the point of this qualification? The modern man characterized by points (1) and (2) can arrive at his own decision in the absence of as well as before God. What does *coram deo* add to the sentence? In the second formulation, *"some* event" would seem to be sufficient in itself. Why add, "in which God's grace becomes a concrete occurrence and is received by a decision of faith"?

That these qualifications do have some bite is indicated by yet another formulation.

The truth is that this possibility [Christian existence] is not man's own inalienable possession, but rather is constantly *being made possible for him* by virtue of his inescapable relation to the ultimate source of his existence. To be human means to stand *coram deo* and, by reason of such standing, to be continually confronted with the gift and demand of authentic human existence.[117]

This way of putting it suggests that man, in laying hold of authentic existence, must also understand himself as standing *coram deo*. And to stand *coram deo* means that he must finally be brought to see, if he achieves authentic existence, that authentic life is something which is

115 *Ibid.*, 123 (italics his). I take this to be Ogden's own position, though he prefaces the statement with, "So far as his [Bultmann's] argument goes, . . ."

116 *Ibid.*, 136.

117 *Ibid.*, 140 (italics his).

made possible for him, rather than something of which he is himself the author.

The modern man who considers this proposal within the framework of the set of presuppositions indicated will very likely register a protest. He will protest that he thought he was to receive the grand prize for his ultramodernity, but that he now finds that Ogden has loaded his proposal with similar if not the same reservations as Bultmann. He thought he was being assured that he need accept nothing that would violate his freedom, his responsibility for his destiny, as he understood it; now he discovers that authentic existence consists fundamentally in ascribing that life to God. He is summoned to live in radical dependence on God's grace. Whatever else it does, this proposal certainly contradicts his self-understanding as *he* understands it.

Ogden has the right, of course, to clarify what he is and is not saying. He is *not* saying that he proposes to reduce the content of the Christian faith to something that will simply be acceptable to modern man. He *is* saying that the Christian message has to be demythologized because any mythological representation of transcendence is unacceptable to modern man's picture of himself and his world. He is *not* saying that man can achieve his own salvation. He *is* saying that man is responsible for making the decision in favor of the self-understanding that is authentic existence.

He *is* saying, furthermore, that *coram deo* does not qualify man's freedom of decision (as Jesus Christ does in Bultmann's version); the possibility of authentic existence is ever before man as something he can choose or reject at will. He *is* saying that *coram deo* does qualify the content of the self-understanding which is bound up with authentic existence—or, better, which is authentic existence. The primordial love of God is made to coincide with man's own responsible decision in such a way that he can still understand it as his decision.

If modern man protests that the content of the self-understanding for which he is responsibly to decide, if he wishes authentic life, contradicts the content of his old self-understanding, so much the worse for him. Thus, even on Ogden's formulation, the contradiction which is offensive to modern man, whether it is bound to Jesus Christ or not, stands. So much the better for Ogden. In the meantime what has happened to the criterion from which we set out, viz., modern man's understanding of himself?

If the content of the self-understanding for which man is called to decide contradicts the means by which he reaches it, must it not be said that one or the other is extraneous? That is, what cogency does the content of this new self-understanding have if its first order of business is not to qualify the means by which it is reached? Let Bultmann put the answer:

> Faith is God-wrought to the extent that prevenient grace first made the human decision possible, with the result that he who has made the decision can only understand it as God's gift; but that does not take its decision-character away from it.[118]

Should Ogden agree, as he very likely will, this brings us back to the point made earlier in support of Bultmann: man's understanding of himself as a free and responsible agent *over against God* must be qualified precisely in the decision by means of which he reaches faith. Modern man, or man in any other age, can thus scarcely start out with his old self-understanding intact. Precision is achieved only by putting it paradoxically: he can't make the decision until he achieves new self-understanding, but he can't achieve new self-understanding until he makes the decision.

It is possible that Ogden would agree with this line of reasoning and still insist that, so far as his first principle formulation is concerned, an outmoded mythological conception of God is being rejected by modern man, or that his point has been missed. When the language of faith is demythologized, it is seen that the gospel calls for nothing other than for man to realize his original ontological possibility.

> To affirm that all "statements about God and his activity" may be interpreted without remainder as "statements about human existence" need mean nothing more than that one is prepared to accept without condition that the redemptive grace of God is always given to us and to all men in every situation of our lives, and therefore the authentic existence in faith and love it continually makes possible is something for which each of us is primordially responsible.[119]

This means that *coram deo* belongs to the structure of authentic existence as such, and *deus* to the structure of existence as such. To exist is

---

[118] *Theology of the New Testament* I, 330.

[119] *Christ Without Myth*, 141. This view is supported by Van Harvey's statement, which I take to be a twin of Ogden's formulation, that Bultmann's position undercuts his "own principle that every *existentiell* relationship presupposes more general ontological possibilities" (*JBL* 78 [1959], 165).

to stand before God, and to exist authentically is to live in dependence on the grace of God.

At this juncture our modern friend should have grasped the point. He will have seen that *his understanding* of his self-understanding was never really under consideration at all. His freedom to determine his own destiny, having been affirmed, was first modified in its structure (without the loss of its decisive character), and then circumscribed by choices which he, in his old freedom, is not prepared to accept. Like the hostage given the choice by the buccaneer of paying the ransom or walking the plank, he would prefer to take tea at four.

So far from being a flaw in Ogden's program, this resistance on the part of modern man may signal a strength. Or it is possible that the modern man under discussion is really two quite different people. The interrogation has merely attempted to establish what modernity it is that Ogden is unwilling to sacrifice to his Christianity.[120] So far it is not clear. But this much is clear: he is unwilling to sacrifice theism, at least in some form, to anyone.

That Ogden proposes to take up the theistic tradition, albeit in very different form, is evident in *Christ Without Myth,* even if he had not elaborated the point in subsequent writings. That very different form is occasioned by the problems Ogden encountered in working at conceptualities adequate to the articulation of the Christian (and any other) understanding of God. It is to his credit that he recognized that the classical theistic position was no longer tenable and that Bultmann, who was up against the same issue, had already taken a crucial step in the direction of meeting the problem. As Ogden sized up the situation brought to light especially by Bultmann's work, the choice theology had to make was either to complete the de-divinization of theology by dropping God out altogether, or—if I may put it boldly—to re-divinize the world by according God an essential place in its structure. Ogden felt compelled to elect the latter.[121]

Classical theism and its modern exponents can explicate faith's reference to a transcendent God only by denying or seriously obscuring the temporality and historicity of man; the more radical contemporary theologies, which are indebted either to an existentialist philosophy of Heidegger's type or to analytic philosophy, want to do justice to the

[120] *Christ Without Myth,* 132.
[121] Cf. Ogden's characterization of Hartshorne's work as a "secularized Christian theology" (doctrine of God), resting on a general ontology: *JR* 44 (1964), 9. Ogden's attempt to rescue the theistic tradition is supported by Bultmann's recent article, "The Idea of God and Modern Man," 83–95.

temporality and historicity of man at the expense of explicating "the
certainty of faith in its eternal ground." Ogden does not like the choice.
"On occasion, indeed, as with van Buren, this tragic choice is actually
put to us, and the real poverty of our situation is revealed." Ogden
seeks some means of escaping the dilemma, means which he has
identified and begun to elaborate as the doctrine of analogy and the
temporality of God.[122]

The momentous theological and philosophical issues opened up by
Ogden's proposals lie beyond the competence and scope of this essay.
What does lie within it, however, is the identification of the problem
and the way of approaching it. We must confine ourselves to the
salient points.

In the first place, it is clear that the antecedent problem for Ogden, as
for many others, is that the traditional language of faith, traditional
talk about God, is no longer meaningful or viable for much-celebrated
modern man. It will not do to ignore this fellow, as Paul Holmer
fondly hopes,[123] if only because he is in each one of us. The failure of
the linguistic tradition suggests, moreover, that language and reality
have come apart at the seams. While Ogden discerns the hiatus, it is
unclear whether he thinks he has accounted for it.

To put it another way, has Ogden taken account of his own assessment of the situation? Is this man, for whom a mythological picture of
the world and himself is unintelligible, incredible, and irrelevant,
simply open to more sophisticated talk about God? It is true that
Ogden so defines the mythological (following Bultmann) that talk
about God is not excluded in principle, provided one can conceive
nonmythological language in which to speak of God. But does this do
justice to the temper of modern man, *who wants to exclude whatever it
was to which mythological language was taken to refer?* That is to say,
will logical sleight of hand reinstate the reality to which mythological
language once witnessed? In short, Ogden walks a fine line between
sacrificing the referent of mythological language to the modern temper
and so reconceiving that referent that it is found to constitute no real

---

[122] "The Temporality of God," 394 ff. The whole essay is devoted to the second
point; for the doctrine of analogy, see "What Sense Does It Make To Say, 'God Acts in
History'?" 1–19. For his part, van Buren concludes that Ogden does justice neither to
the gospel nor to the way secular man thinks (*The Secular Meaning of the Gospel*,
79).
[123] "Contra the New Theologies," *Christian Century* 82 (March 17, 1965), 329–32.

problem at all. Herein appears the sleight of hand: Ogden reinstates with logical brilliance everything he appears to have given away.[124]

What Ogden does not seem to notice in the work of Ebeling and van Buren, for instance, is that both are struggling in hand-to-hand combat with *reality* as modern man experiences it as well as with traditional theological language. Ogden does not "notice" that reality or the fact of the struggle because he cannot "weight" them; all items in a purely logical program are "weightless."[125]

This criticism may be taken as mistaken (Ogden does "notice" them) or irrelevant, but the point is underscored, I think, by the way in which Ogden understands language. For Bultmann there are two forms of human communication: *existentiell* statements which confront the auditor with decision relative to his self-understanding, and *objective* statements which provide information about the world and the phenomena within it.[126] Ogden has shown that Bultmann, who utilizes existentialist statements that belong to neither of the two types identified by him, since they are the means of distinguishing between the other two, nevertheless understands existentialist language as sharing in the "objectifying" character of objective statements. This is so, he holds, because existentialist language holds existence at arm's length in order to inspect and analyze it. In this respect, Bultmann takes theology to be "objectifying" also. Ogden holds that faith (as *existentiell* self-understanding), proclamation (as *existentiell* language which confronts the auditor with an *existentiell* decision), and theology (existentialist language) lie along a continuum, between the poles of *existentiell* self-understanding and objectifying knowledge.

Ogden is concerned to show, indeed must show if his theological program is to stand up, that there is yet another type of theological statement which has God as its object, is cognitive, and is open to rational assessment or justification. Such theological statements belong to the same logical class as metaphysical assertions. "That is, they are assertions which at once have objective reference to 'how things are'

---

124 Ogden is constrained to manage the issue in this way because he is committed both to the modern spirit and to the Christian kerygma. "Theology today may indeed have become impossible, but if it is still to be theology in any meaningful sense, this can only be because its self-acknowledged task is one and the same with the perennial theological task of the Christian community" (*Christ Without Myth*, 139).

125 Cf. Ogden's use of logical consistency as his fundamental criterion: *ibid.*, e.g., 19, 95, 125, 136.

126 *Ibid.*, 50. Cf. *supra*, chap. 2, 35 ff.

and yet are true not contingently, like hypotheses of the special sciences, but of necessity, like the truths of logic and mathematics."[127] The dogma that has to be struck down in order to support this view is that no assertion can have objective reference and also be necessarily true.[128] Ogden believes that Whitehead and Hartshorne have succeeded in breaking this dogma, with the result that he can conclude: "If theological statements not only express faith, but also assert something about the divine reality in which faith understands itself to be based, then the question of how they are to be rationally justified is an altogether appropriate question."[129]

This understanding of the nature of theological language goes together with an assertion made in *Christ Without Myth:*

> It belongs to the nature of a true statement that, just insofar as it is true, it is transparent to the reality that makes it true. Indeed, *this reality itself is actually present "in, with, and under" the statement that seeks to express it.*[130]

Now, of course, if theological statements are taken both to be true and to have objective reference, the reality they seek to express is "in, with, and under" them.

This view might conveniently be called the "trickle-down" theory of language. If metaphysics and philosophical theology can make "true" statements about God, modern man will simply be faced with the reality that is "in, with, and under" those statements. And this is the "logic" of Ogden's program: he proposes to salvage the "experience of faith" by constructing a theological metaphysics which will make it possible, if not necessary, to believe in God.

That theology as doctrine of God looks first of all to word of God asserts itself ever more strongly in the modern period, as a consequence of the fact that the viability of word of God has been so seriously called into question. What requires asking is not the question of priority, but whether theology, taking the priority of word of God as its axiom, is intent upon discovering what and where the word is upon which doctrine depends. It would seem that Ogden is supplying the doctrine for which the word is missing, in an effort to breathe life into that

[127] Ogden, "Theology and Objectivity," 190.
[128] *Ibid.,* 191.
[129] *Ibid.,* 190.
[130] Page 161. Italics his.

word (characteristic of theologies of "translation" in the narrower sense). Ogden is far more sensitive to and perceptive of the real state of affairs, of course, than this criticism implies. Nevertheless, it is a legitimate question whether the structure of his theological program corresponds to that sensitivity.

Quite apart from the merits of the case Ogden builds with respect to the need for a cogent philosophical basis for theology—and it is doubtless true that faith could not long survive without giving a reasonably satisfactory intellectual account of itself—it remains that discursive theological language, i.e., the "necessary" truths of theology, falls on that end of the spectrum at greatest remove from faith as *existentiell* self-understanding. Furthermore, the pole to which discursive language must be tethered is "reality as experienced," in this case the "experience of faith."

If the possibility of the word of God being understood coincides with the possibility of man's understanding himself,[131] and understanding himself in the way for which the word calls, then the first question to ask is whether it is a possibility for modern man to understand himself *existentiell* in this way. The problem with which Bultmann, Ebeling, Fuchs, van Buren, Ogden, and Ott are grappling is precisely this: the possibility of understanding himself *existentiell* in the way for which the word calls is remote for modern man. In that case, Ogden is working on the far end of a continuum for which the *existentiell* or nearer end is missing. It is questionable whether a logical program of his or any other order can create or restore the near end of the continuum by logical fiat. The response of Ogden's modern man to Ogden's own theological program can scarcely be anything other than an *existentiell* Ho-hum![132]

It is for this reason that Ebeling is working with a different assumption in mind, however much he may sympathize with Ogden's project. He begins with the priority of word event on the basis that language primordially gives what is to be seen. Language in this sense has everything to do with reality as experienced, since it falls on the near end of the continuum, closest to *existentiell* self-understanding. In this sense, in fact, language is the medium of *existentiell* self-understand-

---

131 *Christ Without Myth*, 113, citing Bultmann with approval.
132 Cf. Bernard E. Meland, "Analogy and Myth in Postliberal Theology," *Perkins School of Theology Journal*, XV, 2 (Winter, 1962), 24: "I sense in Schubert Ogden, especially, a degree of confidence in the formulations of human reason comparable to that of Professor Hartshorne, which I am unable to share."

ing.[133] If the reality of God has failed it can only be because word of God, not doctrine of God, has failed.

Yet what Ogden does prove in his logical tour de force[134] is not without interest. He demonstrates in the first place that Jesus Christ is unnecessary to faith as a possibility in fact (against Bultmann). In the second place, for those to whom the vocable "God" has lost its meaning, he shows that God is unnecessary to faith as a possibility in fact (only *some* event is required).[135] And finally, he proves that the only understanding of faith that is possible for modern man is faith understood exclusively as authentic existence, as "clarified and conceptualized by an appropriate philosophical analysis."[136] In my judgment Ogden has forcefully and cogently set the problem. When he then proceeds on the assumption that authentic existence is a possibility in fact for modern man, he steps out of modernity and comes untethered from the *existentiell* situation. Furthermore, when he appeals to God as integral to the structure of existence, does he do anything other than what he accuses Macquarrie of doing, viz., begging the question at issue?[137]

IV

Heinrich Ott took up the study of theology under Karl Barth, who may have complicated his theological existence by assigning him the theology of Rudolf Bultmann as a dissertation topic. While engaging in an analysis and critique of Bultmann's theological program from a Barthian perspective,[188] Ott continued to immerse himself in the

---

[133] So Heidegger.

[134] Ogden anticipates that someone will undoubtedly characterize his demonstration as a tour de force, or perhaps that this is the only possible way to evaluate it (*Christ Without Myth*, 163 f.).

[135] *Ibid.*, 123.

[136] *Ibid.*, 146 (italics in original).

[137] The reference to Macquarrie is *ibid.*, 135. Ogden begs the question, of course, in an entirely different way from Macquarrie. Nevertheless, the question at issue is whether the "experience" of faith is itself a possibility in fact for modern man. Both Ogden and Bultmann are able to give an affirmative reply to this question on a priori grounds: "This non-objective reality, variously referred to as 'the unworldly,' 'the divine,' and 'the transcendent,' is *given* in man's self-experience as the ground and end of his own existence and of his immediately disposable world." *Ibid.*, 25 (italics mine). Cf. also 51, 55 f., and especially 160. A "godless" generation will hardly be moved by a logical confrontation with its "ontological possibility." The lack of prospect for such a logical confrontation with either the believer or the unbeliever is not the most important reason, however, for not embarking upon it. The most important reason is that a logical confrontation with an "ontological possibility" may in fact obscure and thus delay the emergence of the ontic question.

[188] Published as *Geschichte und Heilsgeschichte in der Theologie Rudolf Bultmanns,* "Beiträge zur historischen Theologie," 19 (Tübingen: J. C. B. Mohr [Paul Siebeck], 1955).

philosophical work of Martin Heidegger, in specific relation to which he eventually formulated his own program.[139] These three mentors continue to serve as the frame of reference for Ott's work, although he has explicitly launched upon a correlation between the later Heidegger and a theological program with a Barthian orientation.[140] In a way less determinative for his thought, Ott, too, finds himself in a press between the theological "right" and the theological "left," between theology in its classical form and modern man.

The course Ott has taken was clearly indicated already in the "productive criticism" he developed in relation to Bultmann. One must seek, Ott concludes in that study,

(1) a concept of reality of a historic type that overcomes the Bultmannian cleavage with a synthesis embracing both "significance" and "corporeality," "history" and "nature"; (2) a comprehensive interpretation of understanding as the actualizing of historic being that goes beyond the limits of Bultmann's hermeneutic; (3) a synthetic concept of time that takes into account both the eminent significance of the historic Now and the reality of past and future as such; (4) the primal essence of language.[141]

The influence of both Barth and Heidegger can be detected in these elements. Ott believes that Heidegger's work "may contain a flood of perspectives important for theology that have probably never been correctly exploited."[142] Ott then rounds off his summary in the following way: "Such productive criticism of Bultmann, however, will be oriented, viewed methodologically, more to the revelation itself, to the word of Holy Scripture which attests the revelation, than has yet transpired in Bultmann's case; the ontological structures will have to be read off from the theological subject matter itself."[143]

The way in which Ott rounds his criticism off betrays his Barthian heritage, which is subsequently elaborated in Heideggerian language. How he manages this synthesis of Barth and Heidegger is made evident in his contributions to the kerygma and myth debate and to the debate over the historical Jesus.[144] Since this point is central to Ott's position, it is in order to give a brief account.

[139] *Denken und Sein. Der Weg Martin Heideggers und der Weg der Theologie* (Zürich: EVZ-Verlag, 1959).

[140] See the perceptive analysis of James M. Robinson in *New Frontiers* I, 30 ff.

[141] *Geschichte und Heilsgeschichte*, 202; *Denken und Sein*, 7 (Robinson trans., in *New Frontiers* I, 31).

[142] *Ibid.*

[143] *Ibid.* (omitted by Robinson).

[144] Heinrich Ott, "Objectification and Existentialism," in *Kerygma and Myth* II, 306–35; "The Historical Jesus and the Ontology of History," in *The Historical Jesus and*

110 LANGUAGE, HERMENEUTIC, AND WORD OF GOD

The problem with Bultmann's view of historical reality, according to
Ott, is not that Bultmann understands history as "essentially an
encounter which actualizes human possibilities,"[145] but that he is
forced to posit a fundamental dichotomy in historical reality. Bultmann
is driven to do so because he also wants to affirm a mode of historical
reality that can be objectively verified. Since Bultmann affirms both
views of history, viz., history as existential encounter and history as
objectively verifiable,[146] he is left with two discrete modes of historical
being.[147] These two modes of historical being, historical (*historisch*)
and historic (*geschichtlich*), respectively, are correlative with two
modes of time: historical being which can be grasped as *bruta facta*
implies that an event can be pinpointed in time and that historical
events can be arranged at fixed points in a temporal sequence; historical science assumes a linear view of time since it takes for granted that
history is a "self-enclosed, dynamic continuum of events which can be
fixed as points of time."[148] Bultmann's concept of historic being, on
the other hand, presupposes a "punctiliar" view of time, i.e., one in
which "the exclusive horizon of genuine historical occurrence" is the
present moment, the "now" of decision.[149] Bultmann again affirms
both views, but holds that he who knows only the linear view of time
will have missed history and thus the possibility of authentic self-
understanding.[150]

the Kerygmatic Christ, C. E. Braaten and R. A. Harrisville, eds. (Nashville, Tenn.:
Abingdon Press, 1964), 142–71. These two articles appeared originally as: "Objektivierendes und existentiales Denken," *ThZ* 10 (1954), 257–89; *Die Frage nach dem
historischen Jesus und die Ontologie der Geschichte*, "Theologische Studien," Heft 62
(Zürich und Zollikon: EVZ-Verlag, 1960). In addition to the items already cited, the
following are also relevant to this study: "Der Gedanke der Souveränität Gottes in der
Theologie Karl Barths," *ThZ* 12 (1956), 409–24; "Theologie als Gebet und als Wissen-
schaft," *ThZ* 14 (1958), 120–32; "What Is Systematic Theology?" and "Response to the
American Discussion," in *New Frontiers* I, 77–111 and 198–212 (the former also
appeared in *ZThK*, Beiheft 2 [1961], 19–46); "The Problem of Non-objectifying
Thinking and Speaking in Theology," a paper read at the Second Drew Consultation,
April 9–11, 1964, published as: "Das Problem des nicht-objectivierenden Denkens und
Redens in der Theologie," *ZThK* 61 (1964), 327–52 (to appear in *JThC* 3, 1966);
"Existentiale Interpretation und anonyme Christlichkeit," in *Zeit und Geschichte* (see n.
60), 367–79.
[145] "The Historical Jesus and the Ontology of History," 145.
[146] *Ibid.*, 159.
[147] *Ibid.*, 146.
[148] *Ibid.*, 154.
[149] Ott, "Objectification and Existentialism," 317.
[150] Ott, "The Historical Jesus and the Ontology of History," 146.

In Ott's judgment, Bultmann is unable to come to terms with "the unitary nature of history"[151] because he clings to the scientistic, objectifying view of historical reality, over against which he must then define his own view. In the same manner, Bultmann operates with "punctiliar" time in an effort to distinguish his own view from the linear time of so-called scientific historiography, which he also accepts. Bultmann is left with an "eschatological paradoxical dualism."[152]

Ott endeavors to demonstrate, in opposition to Bultmann, "that the objective mode of knowledge is entirely inappropriate to historical reality because there are no such things as objectively verifiable facts."[153] This demonstration clears the way for the conclusion that "all true knowledge of history is finally knowledge by encounter and confrontation."[154] Facts are not appropriate to history because historical reality presents itself, by its very nature, as appearance, as a picture.[155]

Reality always impresses itself upon us through pictures, perhaps in different ways to different people at different times. As it impresses itself upon us it creates within us an exposition, an interpretation, an explanation, a point of view in the widest sense; this does not even need to be conscious. . . . However, a picture does not first arise when *we* create a picture for ourselves. Instead, reality itself is the first to impress itself upon us in the form of pictures. Therefore the picture is not at all something which originates only after the given facts have been examined. The pictures are primary; the facts are a secondary abstraction.[156]

Because historical reality presses itself upon man in pictures or images, the dimension of significance is integral to, indeed, constitutive of, historical reality as such.[157]

On this view, Ott reasons, Bultmann's dichotomy is transcended and the way opened for an approach to historical reality as a unitary field. This view makes it possible, as a consequence, to overcome the subject-object schema, as well as to take the temporality of existence in a radical sense.[158] Bultmann rightly wants to avoid the subject-object

151 *Ibid.*, 148.
152 Ott, *Denken und Sein*, 8.
153 "The Historical Jesus and the Ontology of History," 148.
154 *Ibid.*
155 *Ibid.*, 150.
156 *Ibid.*, 161 (italics his).
157 *Ibid.*, 158.
158 *Ibid.*

dichotomy in dealing with history,[159] but he does not fully appreciate that his affirmation of the "objectivistic" understanding of history requires the perpetuation of the inviolable subject-observer, who takes up a position external to history in order to view it. Or, if he does appreciate it, he regards the perpetuation as useful, perhaps even necessary. Ott believes that one can maintain Bultmann's view of history as encounter or confrontation only if one denies the validity of the positivistic view of history.

The positivistic interpretation of history, which views it as a complex of facts and which presupposes at bottom a subjectivistic attitude, is an abstraction. Facts in the sense of *bruta facta* do not exist at all. They are mere abstractions arising from a disregard of the significance which first and foremost constitutes historical being.[160]

Similarly, if one takes Bultmann's view that "to a historical event belongs its future"[161] seriously, then it has to be said that what once happened in a given time and place is still not the whole event; events cannot be neatly located at dimensionless points on a temporal line.[162] By the same token, it is no longer possible to reduce history as encounter to the existential "now" since neither can the "now" embrace an event in its entirety.

Ott's productive criticism of Bultmann may be arbitrarily terminated at this point in order to raise his own specific stance more directly into view. His criticism of Bultmann, however, has already marked out the course he intends to follow. Our interest is to expose this course to the questions previously put to van Buren and Ogden.

Ogden, as we noted, sets out from Bultmann's assessment of modern man's understanding of the world and himself, while van Buren begins with modern secular man, whose credentials are presented by a kind of popular pragmatism and, at a more sophisticated level, by analytical philosophy. Having begun here, they find it impossible to retain any aspect of a mythological view; the redemptive significance of the Christ event is to be understood, if at all, entirely in its *promeity* (*pro me;* Bultmann: as God for us). Ott, on the other hand, does not and cannot start with the present situation as "criterion" in any real sense. He cannot because he accords absolute priority to God's *pro se*

---

[159] See Ott's remarks on Gogarten, "Objectification and Existentialism," 310 ff.
[160] Ott, "The Historical Jesus and the Ontology of History," 157.
[161] *Ibid.,* 147.
[162] *Ibid.,* 147 f.

(God in himself), following Barth. The logic of this priority must now be explored for the bearing it has upon "experience" of faith, language, and theology.

Barth, so Ott asserts, advocates an existentialism, but a broadened existentialism. On what basis does this broadening take place? On the basis that God can only be *pro me* if he is also and in a prior way *pro se*. "God's *pro me* is a structural element of his *pro se*, the latter being ontologically prior."[163] Ott pursues Bultmann's line of reasoning to the *extra nos*, which Bultmann also affirms, but of which he cannot speak directly; Ott then includes the *extra nos* within the sphere of theology's subject matter on the grounds that theology must be able to speak of that event, apart from its *promeity*, which gave rise to theology in the first place, viz., the event of Jesus Christ. But the event of Jesus Christ, contrary to Bultmann, can retain its *proseity* without being objectified, and that means without its being understood mythologically. Minimally, one can say that "the divine action *pro me* is absolutely primary because all I can do is to respond to it by my decision."[164]

That the Christ event can be accorded its *proseity* without being objectified is demonstrated by Ott's previous considerations relative to the nature of historical reality. A historical event impresses itself upon us as an appearance, as a picture or image, and that picture or image is constitutive of the reality of that event. The event of Jesus Christ impressed itself upon the first disciples in just that way, the image of which is preserved in the New Testament.

We become involved in an encounter with Jesus Christ when we stand under the impression of his picture. To know Jesus Christ through the picture which the Bible presents is to believe in him.[165]

The point made with respect to Jesus, of course, has ontological bearings. With respect to historical reality in general, "we can have experience only of a picture, and there is no access to reality which precedes that of experience."[166]

From this basis it is but a short step to the conclusion that the contemporary human situation cannot finally qualify God's *proseity* and hence his *promeity*. Since the *proseity* of God is ontologically

---

163 "Objectification and Existentialism," 328 f.
164 *Ibid.*, 331.
165 Ott, "The Historical Jesus and the Ontology of History," 160.
166 *Ibid.*, 161.

prior, it is not merged with his *promeity*, i.e., it is never reduced merely to how anyone, or any epoch, experiences God's gracious act. Furthermore, since the there and then (*illic et tunc*) is never merged into the here and now (*hic et nunc*), the there and then remains relevant, one could even say effective, for the here and now. God has acted and his act continues to qualify history.

It is of the essence of historical time that although new moments occur, one moment is constitutive and determinative for the moments that follow.[167]

It is for this reason that all history is to be interpreted in the light of the history of Jesus Christ and not vice versa.[168]

Ott, like Barth, upon whom his dependence at this juncture is clear, cannot accredit the *Zeitgeist* of modern man for the reason that God's redemptive act in Jesus Christ is accorded absolute priority in and of itself. God's *proseity* is determinative of all subsequent history, including the modern period. Whether and to what extent modern man is open to the "experience" of faith can only be taken as questions relevant to the mode of address of both preaching and theology; the reality of God and the possibility of faith are simply assumed.

Ott claims to have derived the ontological foundations of his understanding of historical reality from the "later" Heidegger.[169] Whether his claim is justified can be settled only in the further course of the discussion. In the meantime, James M. Robinson has provided a provocative analysis of Ott's work to date which leaves the matter open.[170] It is possible, nevertheless, to pose certain questions to Ott, not only with regard to his relation to Heidegger, but also with respect to the internal structure of his own program, and thus with respect to the compatibility of the Barthian and Heideggerian legacies. The question of language may serve as the focal point.

Ott raises the question with Bultmann whether his concept of the kerygma as that in which word and act of God are identified is not

---

[167] Ott, "Objectification and Existentialism," 333.

[168] *Ibid.*, 325. How differently one can interpret all history in the light of the history of Jesus Christ is exemplified by Bultmann and Gogarten, who want to account for the de-divinization of the world, at least in the West, on the basis of God's act in Christ. Cf. Bultmann, "The Idea of God and Modern Man," *JThC* 2 (1965), 86. This implies, of course, that God as he is in himself, his *proseity*, has to be understood out of his *promeity*, rather than the other way around.

[169] He makes this claim, e.g., "The Historical Jesus and the Ontology of History," 152 ff.

[170] *New Frontiers* I, 30–63, with the conclusion, 73; Ott modestly agrees: *ibid.*, 198.

what allows Bultmann to concentrate the horizon of genuine historical occurrence exclusively in the existential "now." Ott wonders whether the objections of Bultmann's Lutheran opponents, although wrongly formulated, do not conceal a legitimate question.[171] For his part, Ott sees no reason why act and kerygma witnessing to it cannot be distinguished without falling (as the Lutherans do) into the subject-object pattern.[172] Since Bultmann has a "punctiliar" view of time, he cannot conceive the act of God and the word witnessing to it as in any way separate in time.[173] Ott's interest in distinguishing between the two goes together with the Barthian priority of the *proseity* of God: God's revelation of himself is in no way contingent upon human witness. If the event of Jesus Christ is understood as the self-revelation of God in history, then the following statement applies:

. . . it is not possible to speak of past events which are finished and done with. Nothing historical is finished and settled; rather everything historical extends its being—that is, its significance—into time, into the future and into the present of every knower.[174]

Such a statement is surely unguarded inasmuch as no mention of language is made in this context. Unguarded, that is, when one considers the understanding of language Ott has taken over from Heidegger. Yet it accords in its unguardedness, perhaps, with the Barthian viewpoint.

Ott is of the opinion, on the other hand, that

The essence of time is revealed in and by means of language. The word belongs to the structure of time. For the word expresses the continuity of meaning which constitutes time. It expresses the mutual dependence of its successive moments. The biblical word is the prototype for this. The unique and final event which occurred there and which decides our existence confronts us in the word of the Gospels.[175]

This view appears to accord with the previous assertion, mentioned earlier, that "we can have experience only of a picture, and there is no access to reality which precedes that of experience."[176] "Word" and

[171] "Objectification and Existentialism," 319.
[172] *Ibid.*, 317.
[173] *Ibid.*
[174] Ott, "The Historical Jesus and the Ontology of History," 159.
[175] "Objectification and Existentialism," 333.
[176] "The Historical Jesus and the Ontology of History," 161.

"picture" would seem to be synonymous with the term "language," the Heideggerian counterpart.

This understanding of language and its relation to historical reality is further developed and affirmed by Ott in other writings.[177] On this view Ott seems to say that existence in history and therefore existence in faith are constituted linguistically. But existence in faith—to indicate how he squares Heidegger with Barth—was constituted linguistically with the creation of the canon of scripture, and it is within this linguistic "room" that faith has always resided and must continue to dwell.[178] Thus the *proseity* of God is secured historically by the witness of scripture.

Ott cannot allow Bultmann's coalescence of act and word on the grounds that the linguistic tradition of faith is *given:* it is "rather the historic, fate-laden medium in which God's word speaks to us."[179] For the same reason Ott cannot allow Bultmann's translation of the mythological language of the New Testament into existentialist language, for that would transpose the thought and language of the New Testament into an entirely different key.[180] Bultmann would agree, of course, that scripture is given and that the church must return to it again and again, but he is not willing to say that it is given in the sense the Barthian Ott claims. In fact, it is not clear that the Heideggerian Ott is willing to allow what the Barthian Ott seems to aver. Notice this formulation:

On the other hand, the peculiarity of systematic theology, its moving beyond the individual text, becomes understandable in view of the nature of language. The individual text, and even connected texts such as the theology of Paul, John, Matthew, Luke, Hebrews, etc., are as linguistic utterance not already the subject matter itself. Rather they point to the subject matter, witness to it, name it, reflect upon it, call upon it to become present.[181]

177 E.g., in an unpublished essay of 1960, "Language and Understanding as the Basic Problem of Contemporary Theology" (summarized by Robinson in *New Frontiers* I, 53); *Denken und Sein,* especially 190 ff.; "What Is Systematic Theology?" 77–111, especially 100 f., 106 ff.; "Das Problem des nicht-objectivierenden Denkens und Redens in der Theologie," 327–52.
178 Ott, "What Is Systematic Theology?"86.
179 Robinson, interpreting Ott, *New Frontiers* I, 55; cf. Ott, "Theologie als Gebet und als Wissenschaft," 132.
180 "Objectification and Existentialism," 322.
181 Ott, "What Is Systematic Theology?" 86.

And what is the subject matter itself? It is either "the Christ event, the reality of revelation and of believing," or it is the gospel of Christ which remains unspoken. This one gospel which remains unspoken "is heard through all gospels and witnesses, if understanding takes place at all."[182]

Bultmann, too, is concerned to hear the one gospel through the various scriptural witnesses. He merely wants it to be audible to modern man. It remains uncertain whether Ott proposes to go beyond Bultmann, or whether he has not yet come up to him.

If Ott is now asked what happens when the witness of scripture falls silent, when the language of the tradition is no longer audible, when theological statements cannot be "cashed," he is plainly at a disadvantage. To this question he is inclined to show a Barthian face, i.e., he resorts to the distinction between historical reality and language, in order to preserve the *proseity* of God.[183] He rightly avers that we cannot determine in advance what can be understood,[184] but he takes this to be the answer to the epochal failure of language as depicted by Heidegger.[185]

When, however, Ott takes faith as his starting point, as his presupposition—and that is clearly his intention throughout[186]—he can be Heideggerian "exhaustively and without remainder."

Similarly our answer to God's word is not abstract, prior to or apart from our words, as if they were some optional or dispensable, secondary or

---

[182] *Ibid.*, 86 f.

[183] The distinction between reality and language is maintained with respect to both the language of faith—that is, theology ("What Is Systematic Theology?" 86 f.)—and the language of poetry ("Das Problem des nicht-objektivierenden Denkens und Redens," 336 f.). If Ott is positing the "unspoken" as something "there," apart from the language which names it, calls it to be present, has he not fallen back into meta-physics? That is to say, what, on his own view, gives him the right to "conceptualize" or even "name" a "something" that precedes the picture, the word, to which the word refers? Cf. *supra*, 113 f.

[184] Heinrich Ott, *Dogmatik und Verkündigung* (Zürich und Zollikon: EVZ-Verlag, 1961), 10.

[185] In this connection, it should be noted that Ott rejects "the world come of age" as constitutive of Bonhoeffer's thought: *ibid.*, 11.

[186] Cf., e.g., "What Is Systematic Theology?" 93 n. 7, where Ott registers surprise at the thought that faith might come and go in theology; "Theologie als Gebet und als Wissenschaft," 124: "God is experienceable in prayer. That God is, is a fact of experience. And theology rests on this experience." Yet this experience is not experience of an object: "Prayer is that experience which is actually openness to the unexperienceable."

incomplete expression of a response already made. Rather existence is itself essentially linguistic, and faith takes place within our language, which is our answer—not just a secondary *expression* of our answer—to God. The inadequacy of our linguistic response is the inadequacy of our response as a whole, and it would be to ignore our historicness to assume that the "accidents" of linguistic formulation were somewhere transcended in a truer "essential" response. The limits of our language are limits of our historic existence as such—and all the more so when language is understood to mean not just our vocabulary, but the encompassing medium for under-standing and conveying meaning in which we exist.[187]

We need not allow for exaggeration on Robinson's part in formulating this summary; it is what Ott says because it is what Heidegger says. Ott wishes to model his work on Heidegger's primal thinking. Such thinking, according to Ott, "takes place insofar as what is to be thought unveils itself."[188] The essential thinker does not dispose of his subject matter from a distance, but lets it grow out of the occurrence that happens to him; primal thinking remains forever in the way because it is experience, encounter; it is response to a claim. Primal thinking does not overcome metaphysics by defining all thinking as objectifying and then distinguishing from it an act of authentic existence (Bultmann); rather, it understands thinking itself as *experiential* in character.[189]

The Heideggerian side of Ott manifests its own rather clear logic. Existence is essentially linguistic. Faith takes place within *our* language, as our answer to God's call; it is not just a secondary expression of our answer. The limitations of our response are imposed upon us by the language fund available to us. Since theology as primal thinking is also experiential in character, language is given a material relation to theology as well. Theology is no longer merely an inevitable, secondary, objectifying expression of a purer inner awareness.

It would seem to follow that the historic situation of modern man, as defined by his linguistic "room," is initially determinative with respect to the horizons of his faith, as well as with respect to the horizons of the theological language at his disposal for the articulation of that faith. On this view Ott would have to look not only in the direction of the traditional language of faith (following Barth), but also in the direction of the current language fund in relation to which prayer and

---

187 Robinson's summary, *New Frontiers* I, 55 (italics his).
188 "What Is Systematic Theology?" 108.
189 *Ibid.*, 108 f.

theology must be carried out. In his essay read at the Second Drew Consultation Ott gave some indication that he was willing to look in this direction. He stated, moreover, that the risk of contemporary theology is to find a means of stating the Christian message without taking faith as a presupposition.[190] So far as I can see, he will have to abandon his Barthian premise if he wishes to carry this program out.

The Heideggerian Ott's understanding of language was advanced in the paper referred to above.[191] It becomes especially clear in his analysis of the language of poetry, based, in this case, on a poem of von Eichendorff.[192]

The poem, according to Ott, conveys minimal information, but that information is of no importance; on the other hand, the poem is not empty talk, a phenomenon of pure subjective emotion. "Rather, it creates its own world—a world in which the individual elements are meaningfully ordered in relation to one another and refer to one another in a certain analogy to the 'real' world of things at hand."[193] But is this "world" of the poem an imaginary world in contrast to the "real" world? It is by no means evident that this is the case, since one must reckon with the effect of the world of the word on the "real" world, and there is no criterion at hand for distinguishing between the two. "Is man *as man* real in any other sense than that he finds his own abiding place in a world that is poetically created and established by the word?"[194]

If the rhythm of the poem is indispensable to it, it follows that the poem does not simply denote. Rather, it occurs as event. By it the hearer (or reader) is brought to a definite place. In this particular poem, he is brought neither to a particular forest nor to an idea of a forest, but to a place where the language world of the poem and the so-called external world are fused into a single continuum. The external world, the "real" world, is taken up into the word. Thus there is a new pattern: "the idea of the establishment of a new world."[195]

Speech, as a consequence, cannot be properly understood as something man invents as the occasion arises. The poet could not have

[190] Cf. my remarks in "Colloquium on Hermeneutics," *Theology Today* 21 (1964), 304 f.

[191] Published as "Das Problem des nicht-objectivierenden Denkens und Redens in der Theologie."

[192] The following five paragraphs have also appeared, in a slightly different form, in my article, *op. cit.*, 297 f.

[193] Ott, "Das Problem des nicht-objectivierenden Denkens und Redens," 332.

[194] *Ibid.*, 333 (italics his).

[195] *Ibid.*

spoken *of* the forest unless the forest had first spoken *to* him. Man is led by the word before the mystery of being, before reality itself as something veiled. Words bring man before the mystery, but the mystery does not permit dispensing with words. Man lives in and out of the words. The poem speaks out of the mystery of the forest and into the same mystery: it is thus a crossing over, a transition, and is maintained as such. It does not arrive, but must be accomplished ever anew.

Ott, like Heidegger, takes his clues for the nature of speech basically from poetry. From his analysis he draws two conclusions. First, the dualism of existing thing or condition and ideal denotation or designation is not adequate to express the phenomenon of the poetic word. Secondly, the poetic word is a way or occurrence which brings man before a reality no longer expressible in words. The words are not thereby rendered superfluous, since it is only by means of them that one is brought "there" in the first place. The poem serves just this occurrence. If one transforms the speaking "of something" of the poem into an "about something" of informational speech, one misses the very essence of poetry.[196]

Analogously, "theological thinking and speaking is also a way which conducts man to a definite place. I would like to describe this place as the place of freedom for the obedient hearing of the word of God."[197]

Theological language as the language which leads man to the place for obedient hearing of the word of God is, on Ott's own terms, not something which can be invented or just raked up from anywhere. Theology cannot speak until it is first spoken to. The word which leads before the mystery of God, to transpose his terms, must itself be called forth by the mystery of God. Is it then presumption on Ott's part to want to move beyond silence to nonmetaphysical talk about God, and by that means to authentic theological language?[198] One cannot answer for Ott, of course. It is appropriate to inquire, however, whether the time of silence has passed—that is, to ask after the time of the time.[199]

196 *Ibid.*, 336 f.
197 *Ibid.*, 349.
198 So Robinson, *New Frontiers* I, 37.
199 As a postscript to his Consultation paper Ott appends some further illuminating remarks (*ZThK* 61 [1964], 351 f.). He is clearly agitated by talk of "the end of the Constantinian Era," a symptom of which is the whole discussion over the authority of the Bible, but not to the point of distraction: "Nevertheless, the Gospel itself, the presence of Christ in human history, remains above such historical shift in the epochs" (*ibid.*, 352).

The Heideggerian correlative to language understood in this way is
the history of being. Since thinking and language are integral to each
other in Heidegger's view, the following pointed characterization of
the history of being by James Robinson is entirely to the point:

> Since the basic subject matter of thought is being, the history of thought
> is rooted in the history of being. Thinking takes place in the way being
> gives itself to be thought. Being, as the condition of the possibility of the
> history of thought, must itself have a history, must be historic. The epochs
> in the history of thought are basically epochs in the history of being. For
> being is not a static entity but an event.[200]

The history of thought is to be understood as the history of being "in
its self-manifestation," and the primal thinker, who holds himself into
the face of being, thinks what the time of the time gives him to think.
The primal thinker is at the mercy—deliberately so—of the history of
being.[201]

What in Ott's program corresponds to the history of being? Does the
theologian's relation to God in his self-manifestation correspond to
the primal thinker's relation to the history of being?[202] Ott's view of
language would seem to imply as much, but over against this is to be
set his doctrine of the *proseity* of God. Is not Ott's ambivalence the
result of his attempt to hold Barth and Heidegger together?[203]

That Ott is not willing to surrender the Barthian legacy is confirmed
in his discussion with John Cobb.[204] Cobb asserts that the identity of
the Christ event does not guarantee an identity of prehensions. Yet Ott
is committed to the view that the *proseity* of God is secured by the
witness of scripture, which testifies to the self-identity of God. The
theologian, furthermore, is bound to this witness as the linguistic room
in which faith dwells. When it is asked how the theologian may be
presumed to be thinking the self-same God, Ott's answer consists of
pointing to the *communio sanctorum*. Each witnesses his own witness,

---

[200] *New Frontiers* I, 25 f.; cf. the whole passage, 23–30. Also cf. Ott's discussion,
Denken und Sein, 105 ff.

[201] Cf. Hans Jonas, "Heidegger and Theology," *Review of Metaphysics* 18 (1964),
215 ff.

[202] Hans Jonas (*ibid.*, 212 f.) suggests that Ott draws precisely this correlation.

[203] Robinson also notes an ambivalence in pointing to the fact that Ott cannot make
up his mind whether being corresponds to creation or whether God is to be understood
as a being: *New Frontiers* I, 42 f.

[204] "Response to the American Discussion," *ibid.*, 202 ff.

yet together with the church he also witnesses the common witness.[205] As Cobb notices, the common witness is a Barthian rather than a Heideggerian point. Let Cobb summarize.

The Christ event is the self-presenting of God to man. The witness is one for whom personally this event constitutes such a self-presenting by God. Since the initiative here is with God, and since God's act is not conditioned by the personality or prior experience of the receiver, it must always be self-identical.[206]

Cobb's formulation makes it clear why Ott must reject Heidegger's history of being as relevant for theology, and why he cannot take the *Zeitgeist* of modern man seriously. But if Ott rejects both of these, what has Heidegger taught him about the nature of language and thinking?

The promise of Ott's work lies, in my judgment, in the contest going on between Barth and Heidegger. It is precisely the instability of his position that raises expectation. Like van Buren and Ogden, Ott is caught up in the struggle to be faithful to the Christian tradition, on the one hand, and to attend—on the other—to such a thinker as Heidegger, whose relevance to the time of the time is nothing if not uncanny.

Yet in Ott's case the struggle is proceeding at a rather theoretical level. This may be said in spite of the fact that Ott recommends a nonconceptual view of language. Those who advocate poetry are not necessarily given to the composition of poetry! The question to be asked of Ott, as well as of many of his European colleagues, is whether they consider it important, even necessary, to learn the language of the world in order to be able to do theology. That is to ask how seriously they take the disjunction between modern man's—and that includes the Christian's—understanding of himself and his world and the understanding for which faith calls. The decision not to contemplate this disjunction is tantamount to the decison to withdraw into a linguistic ghetto. It is very likely, in view of the tradition that shelters them, that many will remain disinclined to quit the cloistered precincts of the sacred language of the church. Ott and others will doubtless strive, with a diligence only European theologians seem able to command, to maintain commerce across the hiatus, if only to the extent that they can do so within the confines of a book-lined study.

---

[205] *Ibid.*, 204–206.
[206] *New Frontiers* I, 184.

PART TWO

Language as It Occurs in the New Testament: Parable

By his painting,
[Renoir] himself defined the conditions
under which he intended to be approved.
                            Maurice Merleau-Ponty,
                                        Signs

Introduction:
Parable and Letter

IN PARTS TWO AND THREE THE AIM IS TO HOLD FAST TO
particular language phenomena in the New Testament itself. Initially,
at least, that requires a certain narrowing of the range of phenomena
to be observed. Too much in the field of vision tends to obscure the
contours of the particular: gazing at a universe of discourse promotes
inattention to what actually occurs and prompts assimilation of the
phenomena to what one already "knows." In order not to blur the
discreteness and concreteness of phenomena, it is proposed to look
"long and softly" at two specific modes of language: the parable of
Jesus and the epistolary discourse of Paul.

Yet even these categories are too broad. A. T. Cadoux and A. N.
Wilder remind us that Jesus employed a variety of parables in a variety
of ways.[1] Attention, consequently, is restricted to specific parables, in
this case primarily to the Great Supper and the Good Samaritan. On
the basis of an extended consideration of the former an effort is made
to generate theses which may or may not refer to other parables. These
theses are tested, so to speak, in the analysis of the Good Samaritan
that follows, but without an explicit attempt to reduce the two parables
to a least common denominator. With respect to the preliminary analysis of the parable as metaphor which prefaces the individual studies,
the reader is advised that it is designed only to win the right to look
again and from a fresh perspective at the parables themselves; these
reflections do not constitute a compendium of fresh generalizations
which can then be used to interpret each parable. The movement—
from preliminary reflection to phenomenon to theses—is circular, to be
sure. But the end term is not identical with the initial term: having

[1] A. T. Cadoux, *The Parables of Jesus: Their Art and Use* (London: James Clarke &
Co., n.d. [1930]) 57 f.; Wilder, *Language of the Gospel* (see Abbreviations), 81.

won the right to a fresh examination of the parables by means of a critical review of the prevailing understanding of parable as such (chap. 5), the study proceeds to a detailed analysis of the Great Supper in particular (chap. 6) and to the construction of theses which rest on that analysis (chap. 7). The study of the Good Samaritan (chap. 8) attempts to broaden the range of particular phenomena by one. The treatment of the parables, therefore, is still under way: it remains to be seen where taking hold of the phenomenon in this way will lead.

The letters of Paul, similarly, should not be pressed conveniently and easily into one mold. They range from the stately Epistle to the Romans to the highly personal note to Philemon, from the tense and evocative Letter to the Galatians to the more sedate mood of Philippians. But these characterizations, like others which could be given, may not prove to be discriminating. How shall we seek to expose Paul's disposition to and use of language in his correspondence? The *how* is all-important for the reason that it must be congenial to the *what*. It seems advisable, then, to allow the *what* to teach us the *how*. In order to give the *what* of Paul's language a hearing, the effort is made here, as in the case of the parables, to reflect on the character of the language and the structure of the letter as such (chaps. 9, 10). In this instance, however, the question of the structure of the letter is opened up with special reference to Paul's understanding of language. I have done this for the parable in a rather different way. There follows a study of Paul's use of alien language in articulating the word of God, as exemplified in I Cor. 2:6–16 (chap. 11). Again, these studies can only be said to be under way.

Narrowing the focus to a few phenomena in this way does not necessarily mean taking a sharp or hard focus. That is to say, looking intently at a limited spectrum of samples does not imply that one is endeavoring to establish a tidy concept in relation to which all other similar or related phenomena can be ordered. On the contrary, looking at a restricted range may mean that one is attempting to catch sight of the particular phenomenon as a whole, including its penumbral field. For the latter a leisurely and nonaggressive focus is requisite.[2]

The parable, for example, will not be made to stand out from all other forms of language. This may cause some irritation to those who aspire to rigid definition with stable terms. In support of the course

---

2 "Soft" and "sharp" focus are used with the meanings developed by Philip Wheelwright, *The Burning Fountain: A Study in the Language of Symbolism* (Bloomington, Ind.: Indiana University Press, 1954), 52–75, especially 62–64.

taken, one might point to the ambiguity of the term itself. Wackernagel's investigation of the terms παϱαβολή, *parabola,* clearly demonstrates that we have to do with a very elastic term in the Hellenistic period.[3] The Greek word, through the Septuagint, took on the semantic range of *mšl,* which is very broad.[4] In this way, according to Wackernagel, the Greek term acquired the primary meaning of "word, saying" and passed thus understood into demotic Greek and Latin.[5] But literary Latin continued to use the term only in the sense of *"Gleichnis,* comparison." Those who start out from the literary usage and Aristotelian rhetoric will have difficulty accommodating the diversity of biblical and popular usage.

It is not only that the name is malleable, but the phenomenon itself does not appear to admit of reduction to hard and fast categories. Even if the term is confined to the parable as used by Jesus, and the Synoptic parables (i.e., leaving John out of account) reduced to a list universally agreed upon, it would still be difficult to bring all the parables under one formal definition. The parable, like other works of art, linguistic and visual, can be defined, but only with considerable loss. To grasp the parable in its fullness means to see what happens when parable occurs, to see what happens in the words themselves and to see what happens within the horizons circumscribed by the parable. To put it another way, parable-event involves what happens at the center in the words in relation to what transpires on the circumference in the speaker and hearers, and beyond that, what this does to "world" (i.e., con-text). By focusing softly on the center it is hoped that the structure and intention of the parable will bring the penumbral field into view as well.

The burden of my contention is that what one sees is determined to no small degree by how he looks. If there is some connection between the phenomenon to be observed and how one goes about bringing it into view, it follows that some correlation between subject matter and language used to bring it to expression is to be expected also for the

---

[3] J. Wackernagel, *Kleine Schriften,* Band 2 (Göttingen: Vandenhoeck & Ruprecht, n.d. [1953]), 1239–44.

[4] Cf. F. Hauck, *TWNT* V (1954), 744 f.

[5] Cf. Eberhard Jüngel, *Paulus und Jesus. Eine Untersuchung zur Präzisierung der Frage nach dem Ursprung der Christologie* (Tübingen: J. C. B. Mohr [Paul Siebeck], 1962), 107, who proposes to understand the parable "in the original sense of the word, 'word.' "

New Testament. The analysis sets out, as a consequence, with the view that form and content cannot finally be divorced.[6] Any disinclination to allow the subject matter to come up when form is under discussion, and the other way around, will make the following chapters hard to swallow. But no other option appears before us if we wish to bring the fullness of the phenomena into view in the way suggested.

The rationale for approaching the parable and the letter against the background of the modern consensus, the established views, is taken for granted.[7] Here it need only be said that he who ignores Jülicher and Deissmann deprives himself of the foundations upon which recent scholarship has built its rather formidable and impressive structures. If the interpreter chooses to work in a vacuum, he will very likely build on sand. Jülicher for the parable and Deissmann for the letter represent milestones which the hasty traveler overlooks to his peril.

It is assumed, perforce, that one cannot come to the subject *ab ovo.* That being the case, it is better to come with the best insights available. Jülicher and Deissmann have won their colors in a half-century of severe testing. Nevertheless, just as one is assisted in gaining access to the parable and the letter by means of a scholarly tradition of some depth, he should also come to them with at least a minimal premonition of the foibles of that tradition. Deissmann and Jülicher were working *out of* something *into* something. To what extent was that "into" determined by that "out of"? And is that "out of" any longer a real threat to understanding? Or, in the meantime, has their "into" settled and crystallized until it now constitutes the new obstruction that needs to be overcome, the new "out of" in relation to which it is necessary to think "into" something else? Thus, while recent scholarship and even the common understanding (which is where scholarship finally comes to rest) are indispensable to further reflection, they constitute at the same time a potential, if not real, constriction of the horizon. Out of and against them is all new interpretation to be won.

For the parables the works of C. H. Dodd[8] and Joachim Jeremias,[9]

---

[6] In agreement with Wilder, *Language of the Gospel,* 12 f., 33, 79; Jüngel, *op. cit.,* 135 ff., 291 ff.

[7] I have attempted to justify this assumption and set out some of its ramifications in "The Hermeneutical Problem and Historical Criticism," *New Frontiers* II, 164–97; "Creating an Opening: Biblical Criticism and the Theological Curriculum," *Interpretation* XVIII (1964), 387–406.

[8] *Parables* (see Abbreviations).

[9] *Parables* (see Abbreviations).

in addition to that of A. Jülicher,[10] are prerequisite to all further discussion. So substantial is their contribution, and so influential have their books become, that the study of the parable was conceived in conscious and overt dialogue with them. It will be evident, not alone from what is reiterated but also from what is assumed, that I am deeply indebted to them. I have occasionally fastened onto one of their statements and followed it up in a way or ways which they, perhaps, did not intend, but which seemed to me to be justified by what they implied. It may also strike the reader that I am looking through gaps in their respective treatments at some aspect or aspects of the parable which never quite came into view for them. It would be ungrateful of me, not to say deceptive, not to confess that they themselves helped call my attention to these fissures by their own painstaking analyses.

An interesting and, with respect to the current scholarly consensus, relatively unique effort of Birger Gerhardsson to interpret the parable of the Good Samaritan in a quasi-allegorical way[11] functions as the specific reference of the study of the same parable presented here (chap. 8). Out of deference to the Lucan context and because Gerhardsson contends that Jesus made use of well-known rabbinic techniques in this parable to interpret the law, my own study is aimed at Jesus' use of the parable as a means of interpreting the Old Testament. While I hold that Gerhardsson has misunderstood the parable as Jesus employs it, I am also of the opinion that he, along with a few other recent interpreters, is correct in challenging the prevailing view of the parable. My specific difference with them is that I do not think the challenge can be sustained on the basis of the parable understood as allegory.

Ernst Fuchs' effort to grasp the parables as language events is the underground spring which nourishes my own approach to the parables.[12] I say "underground" because I have kept him largely out of sight. In particular, he has called attention to the parables as media of Jesus' self-attestation, an emphasis which I do not seek to follow up, except obliquely. I am also warmly sympathetic with a provocative

---

[10] *Die Gleichnisreden Jesu,* I (Tübingen: J. C. B. Mohr, 1888; 2d ed., 1899); II (1899); I and II reprinted 1910; two parts reprinted as one (Darmstadt: Wissenschaftliche Buchgesellschaft, 1963).

[11] Birger Gerhardsson, *The Good Samaritan—The Good Shepherd? "Coniectanea Neotestamentica,"* XVI (Lund: C. W. K. Gleerup, 1958).

[12] *Hermeneutik,* 211–30; "The Parable of the Unmerciful Servant (Matt. 18, 23–25)," in *Studia Evangelica,* K. Aland *et al.,* eds. (Berlin: Akademie-Verlag, 1959), 487–94; Fuchs II, 136–42, 219–26 [32–38], 348 f. [141 ff.], 361–64 [153–56], 367–71 [158–62], 392–97 [179–84], etc.

study by Eberhard Jüngel, one of Fuchs' students.[13] His work parallels my own in many respects, though I have made no effort to bring my own line of thought, conceived prior to the appearance of his book, into conformity with his. It seems best to let them stand for the time being as two independent but converging approaches to the same problem.

Amos Wilder has included the parable among other forms of early Christian rhetoric in an illuminating study to which I am broadly indebted.[14] The contributions of Maurice Merleau-Ponty, Ray L. Hart, and especially Owen Barfield, have been no less decisive but more difficult to specify.

Some justification is to be expected for selecting the parable as a locus of inquiry. One might stipulate that with the parables we are in particularly close contact with the historical Jesus;[15] it was in this domain that the original quest of the historical Jesus is held to have been most successful, and that may be the reason the "new hermeneutic" has taken the parables as its point of departure.[16] But the interest of the new hermeneutic in the parables has, I think, other grounds.

Gerhard Ebeling has remarked, "The parable is the form of the language of Jesus which corresponds to the incarnation."[17] Eberhard Jüngel has attempted to work out an explication of this thesis in his recent book.[18] To put Jüngel's thesis briefly, the parable "collects" Jesus, his relation to God, his eschatology, his ethic, *and* the hearer into a language event which is the kingdom;[19] the kingdom comes to speech in the parable as parable.[20] The kingdom comes to speech as parable because it is in this way that the *nearness* of the kingdom as God's future can be brought into relation to man's present without the loss of the distinction, yet in parable the former can qualify the latter.[21] Günther Bornkamm, in an excellent brief sketch of the parable as used

[13] *Op. cit.*
[14] *Language of the Gospel*, 79–96.
[15] Jeremias, *Parables*, 12.
[16] J. M. Robinson, "The New Hermeneutic at Work," *Interpretation* XVIII (1964), 351 f.
[17] *Evangelische Evangelienauslegung: Eine Untersuchung zu Luthers Hermeneutik* (2d ed.; Darmstadt: Wissenschaftliche Buchgesellschaft, 1962), 108.
[18] *Op. cit.*, 87–174.
[19] Cf. his *Leitsätze, ibid.*, 173 f.
[20] *Ibid.*, 135.
[21] *Ibid.*, 159. The same point was made earlier by James M. Robinson in an essay entitled, "Jesus' Understanding of History" (*JBR* 23 [1955], 17–24, esp. 19 f.), which was already moving in the direction indicated here and in the following chapters.

by Jesus, puts the same point in a different way.[22] Bornkamm identifies the parable as a not fortuitous medium of giving expression to the
mystery of the kingdom. In the parable a mystery lies hidden, and that
mystery "is nothing but the hidden dawn of the kingdom of God itself
amidst a world which to human eyes gives no sign of it."[23] Hence,
"the parables are the preaching itself" and do not merely serve "the
purpose of a lesson which is quite independent of them."[24]

These formulations assert and attempt to justify the view that the
parable is the mode of language most appropriate to the incarnation.
One could even say they postulate that the parable is the linguistic
incarnation. If in the parable we encounter the logos incarnate, the
theological justification for extended reflection on the parable is that
theology is driven perennially back to its source and ground—presumably the incarnation—in order to refurbish its thought out of the litter
of the primordial event; the parable, it is held, is among the more
significant aspects of the incarnational linguistic litter preserved in the
New Testament.

The so-called kerygmatic theology, it may be recalled, looked to the
proclamation of the primitive church as its source and ground; the
"new hermeneutic" proposes to look to the linguistic modes of Jesus'
"history": this is the basis for its interest in the "historical" Jesus. The
underlying reasons for this shift are investigated in Part I. The divergence of the "new hermeneutic" from kerygmatic theology should not
be set down to a renewed concern for raw facts, but rather to the
notion that the language which bore the incarnation, i.e., which made
it eventful, must now be re-examined, in this time when theology
appears to be at sea, for the bearing it may have on theology's task
today. This calls for nothing less than a reassessment of what is "given"
to theology, a reassessment that may well have far-reaching consequences for the shape of theology itself.

The future of theology need not be made to bear the whole weight of
this attention to parable. There is a rising tide of interest in language
analysis in the theological disciplines, which has spilled over from
literary criticism and philosophy. One may, if he wishes, merely in-
dulge a fad. For those of less esoteric tastes, there is the interest which
accrues to a mode of language often imitated but rarely duplicated.

My discussion of the letter was determined to a much lesser extent

---

22 *Jesus of Nazareth*, Irene and Fraser McLuskey, with J. M. Robinson, trans. (New
York: Harper & Brothers, 1960), 69 ff.
23 *Ibid.*, 71.
24 *Ibid.*, 69.

than that of the parable by explict dialogical partners. Adolf Deissmann lurks, of course, behind the analysis of the form, structure, and
language of the letter, but only in a general way. The present effort to
break through the legacy Deissmann bequeathed to the prevailing
conception of the Pauline letter was aided and abetted from a distance
by one of his contemporaries, Johannes Weiss. The skepticism of Weiss
regarding the offhand character of Paul's letters as understood by
Deissmann is reflected in the work of Rudolf Bultmann and Martin
Dibelius. And it was also in the form-critical school that other and
significant contributions were made to the study of the letters, the
collective force of which, in my judgment, has not yet been made
evident. Chapter 10 attempts to focus the significance of that work and
then move beyond it.

Ulrich Wilckens becomes a more explicit dialogical partner in the
essay on I Corinthians 2:6–16 (chap. 11). Wilckens' brilliant study[25] of
the passage led to the hermeneutical problem of whether translation of
the gospel into new and alien language and categories can be legitimately carried out. Paul's use of Gnostic terminology in the passage in
question serves as the occasion for exploring this problem both in
particular and in principle.

These two studies are anticipated, and Parts Two and Three of the
whole work linked, by a provisional sketch of a phenomenological
approach to language (chap. 9). This sketch endeavors to articulate,
more formally and directly, the view of language which informs the
studies of both the parable and the letter. How the one informs the
other is indicated by a backward glance at the parable and a preview of
the letter. By "listening in" on the language of the letter, the ground is
laid for the analysis in chapter 10.

With respect to the language of the letters, the remarks of Amos
Wilder especially have again served as fresh stimulus.[26] And, as in the
case of the parable, I have worked against a constellation of other
figures who have not written on the epistle itself but who have contrib-
uted to my understanding of the phenomenon of language.

These studies of the letter, like those of the parable, are quite
fragmentary. In particular, the structure of the Pauline letter here being
set out calls for a more detailed analysis, yet to be published, of the
stylistic and form-critical data. In addition, the peculiarities of indi- .
vidual letters require more attention than could be afforded them. And

---

[25] Ulrich Wilckens, *Weisheit und Torheit: Eine exegetisch-religionsgeschichtliche
Untersuchung zu 1. Kor. 1 und 2* (Tübingen: J. C. B. Mohr [Paul Siebeck], 1959).
[26] *Language of the Gospel*, 22 f., 39–43, 91.

this is to say nothing of the movement and rationale of the integral components of the letter (e.g., thanksgiving, body, travelogue) in and of themselves. It is to be expected, finally, that such investigations will eventuate in a reassessment of Pauline theology. In the meantime a beginning, but only a beginning, has been made.

The selection of the Pauline letter as the second focal point of inquiry could be justified, perhaps, on the basis of the position Paul has occupied in the history of theology and especially in the history of the Protestant tradition. An understanding of what Paul was about can certainly illuminate certain peculiarities in the developments which stem from him. This general way of putting the matter can be sharpened. Gerhard Ebeling has written that Paul represents the beginning of Christian theology proper. According to Ebeling, the phenomenon of theology is characterized by this: "faith of itself insists upon understanding in a way which corresponds to the situation in which understanding is to take place."[27] When these two things are put together, it follows that Paul found it necessary to translate the gospel into theology in accordance with the requirements of the situation in which understanding was to take place. What happened in this process is of the utmost importance in understanding what the theological task is in its inner necessity.

For this reason, too, Paul serves as a critical point on the spectrum which runs from the parable to a full-blown systematic and philosophical theology. He marks the transition from a nondiscursive mode of speech to a highly sophisticated and refined language which came to be characteristic of the later church. But he also marks the juncture in the Christian language tradition which serves as the basis of the Jesus-Paul antithesis. It is not fair to compare Paul with Jesus, Wilder suggests, because Paul is discoursing in another vein. Indeed he is. But why he is discoursing in another vein becomes crucial for the reason that his relation to Jesus is at stake. By extension it could be said that this *why* is also determinative for the relation of all subsequent theology to Jesus.

It will not be possible in this context to carry the analysis of the parable and letter so far as to attempt resolutions of these far-reaching questions. Our task is first of all to catch sight of language as it occurs in these two modes, with the hope that direction may be found for further investigation and reflection.

---

[27] "Theologie I. Begriffsgeschichtlich," *RGG*, VI (1962), 760.

The Parable as Metaphor

ล 5 ฿ ─────────────────────────

C. H. Dodd has provided a classic definition of the parable.

> At its simplest the parable is a metaphor or simile drawn from nature or common life, arresting the hearer by its vividness or strangeness, and leaving the mind in sufficient doubt about its precise application to tease it into active thought.[1]

This definition provides four essential clues to the nature of the parable: (1) the parable is a metaphor or simile which may (*a*) remain simple, (*b*) be elaborated into a picture, or (*c*) be expanded into a story;[2] (2) the metaphor or simile is drawn from nature or common life; (3) the metaphor arrests the hearer by its vividness or strangeness; and (4) the application is left imprecise in order to tease the hearer into making his own application.

It will be profitable to pursue these clues, which Dodd has not always followed up, as a means of broaching the phenomenon. We may begin with the last, (4).

I

The parable, according to Dodd, leaves the mind "in sufficient doubt about its precise application to tease it into active thought." This may be taken to mean that the parable is not closed, so to speak, until the listener is drawn into it as a participant. The application is not specified until the hearer, led by the "logic" of the parable, specifies it for himself. This goes together with Dodd's further observation that the parable is argumentative, inducing the listener to make a judgment

---

[1] Dodd, *Parables*, 16.
[2] The bare definition is expanded as indicated, *ibid.*, 16–18.

upon the situation set out in the parable and to apply that judgment, either explicitly or implicitly, to the matter at hand.[3] The parable thus involves what Bultmann calls a transference of judgment.[4] This would not seem to be the case with the so-called "exemplary-stories," where the application is evident in the example.[5]

Few, if any, of the parables were originally given *applications* by Jesus.[6] This is not to say that Jesus did not sometimes call attention to the *point* of the parable by means of a question or some other device.[7] In any case, if Dodd is correct, a parable with an application affixed would be a contradiction in terms.[8] There is a strong tendency in the Synoptic tradition, however, to provide the parables with applications. In the process of handing the tradition around and on, the horizon of meaning tends to become fixed and is transmitted along with the parable. It may become fixed in relation to a particular situation in the life of the primitive church, or it may be crystallized in the form of a generalizing conclusion.[9] The parable may be given one or more conclusions to stabilize interpretation, or the application may be made apparent by a modification of the parable itself; in some instances both forms of stabilization are employed.[10] The hardening and crystallization of the tradition in this way produces what may be called the loss

---

[3] *Ibid.*, 22–24; cf. R. Bultmann, *History of the Synoptic Tradition*, 182 f., 191 f.; A .T. Cadoux, *The Parables of Jesus: Their Art and Use* (London: James Clarke & Co., n.d. [1930]), 45 ff., 56 ff., 118, 127, 139 f., 197.

[4] Bultmann, *History of the Synoptic Tradition*, 198.

[5] An "exemplary-story" (*Beispielerzählung*) is a parable involving no figurative element at all (Bultmann, *ibid.*, 178). According to Bultmann the Good Samaritan, the Rich Fool, the Rich Man and Lazarus, the Pharisee and the Publican are examples of this (*ibid.*, 178 f.). See further below, chap. 8, 211.

[6] Cadoux, *op. cit.*, 19 f., doubts that Jesus ever interpreted his parables. Jeremias (*Parables*, 105) is cautious: eight parables end abruptly without explicit application; originally the number must have been considerably greater, as is shown by the Gospel of Thomas, where only three parables are provided with an interpretation. Dodd (*Parables*, 27 f.) believes there were some applied parables in the traditions underlying the Gospels. But he draws back from attributing these to Jesus himself, while allowing that in some cases they reveal how the parable was understood "by those who stood near to the very situation which had called it forth" (29). Cf. Bultmann, *History of the Synoptic Tradition*, 182 ff., who also wants to reserve judgment in specific cases, but is willing to concede that the tendency of the tradition was to supply applications.

[7] Bultmann (*ibid.*, 182) distinguishes between point and application: the point is the *tertium comparationis*, the point at which the image touches the subject matter.

[8] The question of what constitutes an application is to be left open. A rule of thumb might be: must the listener make the transference of judgment for himself?

[9] Cf. Jeremias, *Parables*, 48 ff., 110 ff.

[10] Cf. N. A. Dahl, "Gleichnis und Parabel II. In der Bibel 3. Im NT," *RGG* II (1958), 1618.

of hermeneutical potential; i.e., the open end of the parable, which invites the listener to make his own application, is closed off.

What can be said of the disposition on the part of the primitive church to give applications to the parables? Scholars sometimes assume that, in identifying interpretive accretions as secondary, they are purging the dregs of early Christian interpretation from the pure nectar of the original utterance. In a sense they are justified in this attitude. It is always necessary to dismantle the tradition in order to reach its source, and reach its source we must if the parables are to be reinterpreted for another time and place. For this reason alone the critical historical work of Dodd and Jeremias is indispensable. For this reason, too, the fact that the church canonized its interpretations along with the parables is regrettable. At the same time, the parable invites application. In fact, it compels it. The proper question, therefore, is not whether the church was justified in interpreting the parables, but *how* in fact it did so, i.e., what specific application did it make of particular parables? A second legitimate question is whether this application was in harmony with the intent of the parable.[11] The resolution of the second question is more difficult than the first, for the reason that it requires reinterpretation of the parable in order to win its intent. In the end it may be possible to say only that the church interpreted the parables in such and such a way, while one application, in view of the contemporary situation, is . . . Nevertheless, it is both possible and necessary to risk normative judgments based on a critical grasp of the intent of each parable.

Taking Dodd's fourth clue in the strict sense, however, means that it is not possible to specify once and for all what the parables mean. For to do so would mean that the parable, once the application has been made and reduced to didactic language, is expendable. That Dodd's

[11] Jeremias' book unquestionably gives the impression that he wishes to set aside all accretions to the original parables as secondary; that these accretions more often than not obscure the real point of the parable in its original context. Whoever draws from this the conclusion that Jeremias regards the interpretive work of the tradition not only as obscuring the original context and point, but also as fundamentally misconceived, should ponder his remarks on p. 48: "Thus, by the hortatory application the parable [of the Unjust Steward] is not misinterpreted, but 'actualized'. . . . It is not a question of adding or taking away, but of a shift of emphasis resulting from a change of audience." It is consequently a question of whether the church at various points in its history *correctly* grasped the parable in relation to its own situation; this question cannot be determined merely by recovering the original context, though that is certainly the first step. On the other hand, it is more problematic whether the church was justified in canonizing particular applications along with the parable itself.

clue points to an essential characteristic of the parable is supported by the fact that the church preserved the parable along with the interpretation, in some cases even preserving the parable without appended interpretation. The parable, then, is not expendable. Why this is so, and why the application cannot be finally specified, impels a consideration of the nature of the parable as metaphor or simile.

II

Referring to point (1), above: the parable is a metaphor or simile.[12] Whether there is involved a simple metaphor, an elaborated or picture metaphor (similitude), or a metaphor expanded into a story (parable proper) is not immediately differentiating. The lines between the first and second and the second and third are, at all events, by no means easy to draw.[13] What is more significant is the nature of the metaphor or simile itself.

To say *A* is *like B* is a simile. The less known is clarified by the better known.[14] To say *A is B* is a metaphor, which, because of the juxtaposition of two discrete and not entirely comparable entities, produces an impact upon the imagination and induces a vision of that which cannot be conveyed by prosaic or discursive speech.[15] To go one step further, Owen Barfield suggests that in symbolic speech one speaks of *B* without referring to *A*, although it is supposed that *A*, or an *A*, is intended.[16] An element of comparison or analogy is thus common to all three, but the role which the comparison plays varies

---

[12] The difference between a metaphor and simile, as is often noted, is that in the latter the comparison is made explicit by *as* or *like*.

[13] Dodd, *Parables*, 18.

[14] Wilder, *Language of the Gospel*, 80.

[15] The formal distinction between a simile and metaphor is being raised to a substantive difference for the sake of convenience. The formal distinction, in fact, is not always discriminating, nor are simile and metaphor commonly restricted to the senses here indicated. The convention is introduced so as not to have to write each time, "metaphor understood as. . . ." Cf. Wilder, *ibid*.

Philip Wheelwright (*The Burning Fountain* [Bloomington, Ind.: Indiana University Press, 1954], 93 ff., 106 ff.; *Metaphor and Reality* [Bloomington, Ind.: Indiana University Press, 1962], 70 f.) enjoins us from making anything of the syntactical distinction between simile and metaphor. One can accept the points he is making, i.e., that the grammatical difference is not discriminating, that simile and metaphor belong to the same spectrum, without being deprived of the use of the terms in rather different senses. In fact, Wheelwright appears to give to the simple simile something like the meaning I have suggested (*The Burning Fountain*, 106 f.), while reserving the term metaphor for simile plus plurisignation (i.e., significative at more than one level).

[16] Owen Barfield, "Poetic Diction and Legal Fiction," in *The Importance of Language*, Max Black, ed. (Englewood Cliffs, N.J.: Prentice-Hall, 1962), 52.

decisively. In simile it is illustrative; in metaphorical language it is creative of meaning. In simile as illustration the point to be clarified or illuminated has already been made and can be assumed; in metaphor the point is discovered.[17] The critical line comes between simile and metaphor; symbolism is metaphor with the primary term suppressed.

The proposed distinction between simile as illustration and metaphor as the means by which meaning is discovered is comparable to C. S. Lewis' demarcation between a master's metaphor and a pupil's metaphor.[18] The "magistral" metaphor is one invented by the master to explain a point for which the pupil's thought is not yet adequate; it is therefore optional insofar as the teacher is able to entertain the same idea without the support of the image. On the other hand, understanding itself emerges with the "pupillary" metaphor, with which it is consequently bound up; the "pupillary" metaphor is indispensable to the extent that understanding could not and cannot be reached in any other way. This distinction is also paralleled by Ian Ramsey's differentiation between a picture model and a disclosure model.[19] Ramsey draws the parallel himself, in fact, by likening similes to picture models (similes have "a descriptive use in respect of some important and relevant feature of the object they model"[20]), and metaphors to disclosure models (metaphors "generate a disclosure," yield "many possibilities of articulation," are not descriptive, and do not invite explanation or paraphrase[21]).

Illuminating as it would be to follow up what has been written on simile, metaphor, and symbol, especially in literary criticism, it is more germane, in view of the dominant understanding of parable, to concentrate on the difference between metaphorical and discursive language, or between the "logic" of the metaphor and the logic of predication.

"The logical use of language," writes Barfield, "presupposes the meanings of the words it employs and presupposes them constant."[22] Logic is not normally employed in the creation of meaning, but in

---

[17] Metaphor, of course, may "rediscover" a point previously made but now lost, which is what makes it impossible to draw a hard and fast line between metaphor and simile.

[18] C. S. Lewis, "Bluspels and Flalansferes," in *The Importance of Language, op. cit.,* 36–50.

[19] *Models and Mystery* (London and New York: Oxford University Press, 1964), 9 ff.

[20] *Ibid.,* 48.

[21] *Ibid.,* 48 ff.

[22] "Poetic Diction and Legal Fiction," 66.

making it explicit. The propositions of logic are therefore tautologies.[23] The ideal of the logician is to evolve a language which is drained of recalcitrant elements, i.e., which perfectly obeys the laws of thought. Such a language would, of course, be captive to the knowledge already implicit in its terms.[24] This is what Philip Wheelwright calls steno-language by prescription.[25]

This understanding of logic is akin to what Heidegger analyzes as the logic of predication.[26] Predication focuses the seeing sharply,[27] narrows it by calling attention to this or that. The predicate allows that to be seen to which it directs attention. The attention thus restricted, the predicate can be abstracted from the primordial referential totality to which it belonged and handled in isolation. Logical language—to indicate now the extremity toward which this process gravitates—is a tissue of abstracted predicates which are manipulated by formal rules. For both Barfield and Heidegger the logic of prediction necessarily fragments the circumspective referential totality upon which language is founded.[28]

Metaphor, on the other hand, raises the potential for new meaning. Metaphor redirects attention, not to this or that attribute but, by means of imaginative shock, to a circumspective whole that presents itself as focalized in this or that thing or event. Metaphor involves a "soft," as opposed to a sharp, focus.[29] If imagination may be substituted for metaphor in this context (the justification is that imagination traffics in symbols[30]), then Ray Hart's delineation of the active imagination is apropos: "What active imagination sunders is the 'givenness' of the

---

[23] Owen Barfield, *Poetic Diction* (see Abbreviations), 16, referring to Ludwig Wittgenstein's *Tractatus Logico-Philosophicus.*

[24] Barfield, *ibid.,* 16 f., 113 n. 1, 131 n. 1; "Poetic Diction and Legal Fiction," 66 f.

[25] *Metaphor and Reality,* 37.

[26] *Being and Time,* sec. 33 (pp. 195–203).

[27] Cf. Wheelwright, *The Burning Fountain,* 63.

[28] Cf. the remarks of Ray L. Hart ("Imagination and the Scale of Mental Acts," *continuum* 3 [1965], 15): "All mental powers are tethered to the concrete event, for what is offered them, but reason has the longest stakeline. Its capacity for universality is its capacity for farthest removal. And reason removes from the concrete event, we said earlier, by means of cataleptic pauses or stations. Reason places the event under 'arrest.' Reason assumes that an event is a closed affair, a delimited base from which solid ideas may arise and to which they apply; that its significance is its closure, not the new field of potentiality it opens and opens upon. The concepts of reason are abstract just because they are abstracted from a stable referent."

[29] On the distinction between "sharp" and "soft" focus, see Wheelwright, *The Burning Fountain,* 62–64.

[30] Hart, *op. cit.,* 16.

delineated object with respect to the focalized limits of its allegedly self-presentation. It wrests the 'thing' out of its customary context, taken for granted by the perceiver or reasoner, and puts it into an alien (to the everyday mentality) context that is however its natural habitat, viz., the context of interaction-event."[31] That is to say, metaphor shatters the conventions of predication in the interests of a new vision, one which grasps the "thing" in relation to a new "field," and thus in relation to a fresh experience of reality.[32] Metaphor does not illustrate this or that idea; it abuses ideas with their propensity for censoring sight. To be sure, once a metaphor has passed into the language, it may become ossified and subsequently adapted to lexicons and logic, with the consequent loss of its hermeneutical potential--until rediscovered by some would-be poet.

"It is not surprising," Barfield muses, "that philologists should have had such a vivid hallucination of metaphor bending over the cradle of meaning."[33] The poetic predilection for metaphor and symbol is not at all arbitrary.[34] If *A* stands for the fresh insight that beckons the poet mutely, and *B* stands for the available language fund, a fund that has acquired conventions and is presided over by tradition, the poet must allow *A* to come to expression *through* and *out of B. A* is not "there" except as it enters language, but it cannot, because it is a fresh insight, be merely accommodated in conventional language. *A* is raised to cognitive status in language only as the linguistic tradition undergoes some modification. The metaphor is a means of modifying the tradition—it is talking "what is nonsense on the face of it"[35]—and as such is not expendable in the apprehension of *A*.

The latent cognitive outreach of *A,* on the other hand, is by no means exhausted in metaphor. Metaphor is only one of the modalities of cognition. A fresh apprehension of reality can, of course, be articulated in discursive speech—with some gain as well as some loss. But

[31] *Ibid.,* 20.
[32] "The world, like Dionysus, is torn to pieces by pure intellect; but the poet is Zeus; he has swallowed the heart of the world; and he can reproduce it as a living body" (Barfield, *Poetic Diction,* 88; cf. 115, 191).
[33] *Ibid.,* 88.
[34] It might be pointed out in this connection that even the poets, according to Cleanth Brooks, do not always understand the function of metaphor correctly. Some, e.g., A. E. Housman, hold that metaphor is a mere surrogate, a rhetorical gilding, an alternate way of saying something, and not the necessary and inevitable way ("Metaphor and the Function of Criticism," in *Spiritual Problems in Contemporary Literature,* S. R. Hopper, ed. [New York: Harper Torchbook, 1957], 133 f.).
[35] Barfield, "Poetic Diction and Legal Fiction," 67.

metaphor is the cognitive threshold of poetic intuition. As such it concentrates a circumspective whole, it embodies a "world" in a "soft" focus. For this reason the metaphor resists literal interpretation (the poetic metaphor is often a pretty tall story, taken literally[36]); it constitutes a gesture which points to but does not spell out the background and foreground, the penumbral field, of an entity or event. The poet summons and is summoned by metaphor in the travail of the birth of meaning.

Many a poet has summoned metaphor when it was on holiday. Fabricated figures are not up to the work of the genuine image. Yet the difference between true and false metaphor is not easy to specify. In general it may be said that "a true metaphor or symbol is more than a sign; it is a bearer of the reality to which it refers. The hearer not only learns about that reality, he participates in it. He is invaded by it."[37] The word gives presence to the referent in such a way that the listener is confronted by it; the auditor does not make a distinction between the vocables and the reality to which the vocables give presence. Word and reality are encountered in their inner unity. Language becomes event.

Going together with the eventfulness of metaphor is its translucency. As a rule of thumb, if it is transparent that when the poet says B he is really talking about A, if he is riding a figure as a literary means of transport, the metaphor is contrived. On the other hand, if the image is opaque, if the writer is giving vent to his fancy, it is equally contrived. True metaphor comes into being in that misty strait between transparent and opaque figurative speech, at the point where metaphor and reality are irrevocably wedded, so that one illuminates and gives life to the other. It is not too much to say that true metaphor reveals a mystery: the mystery of kaleidoscopic reality directly apprehended.

These considerations of the nature of metaphor have attempted to keep the previous questions regarding the parable in view. If the parable is metaphor, as Dodd maintains, the nature of metaphor will have some bearing on how the parable is to be understood. That bearing may now be pursued.

If B may now be allowed to stand for the parable and A for its putative meaning (we might say, application), it may be asked (1)

[36] Owen Barfield, "The Meaning of the Word 'Literal,'" in *Metaphor and Symbol*, L. C. Knights and Basil Cottle, eds. (London: Butterworth Scientific Publications, 1960), 49.

[37] Wilder, *Language of the Gospel*, 92. Cf. Paul Tillich, *The Protestant Era*, J. L. Adams, trans. (Chicago: University of Chicago Press, 1948), 107 f.; *Systematic Theology*, I (Chicago: University of Chicago Press, 1951), 122–26.

why is B indispensable as the means of access to A? And (2) why cannot the "meaning" of B, i.e., A, be finally specified?

1. A must be heard in language. The common, everyday understanding which inheres in language is the result of the process of the crystallization, of the stabilization, of tradition. Dictionary language is steno-language by habit.[88] Language acquires conventions which are further refined by means of logic. This shared understanding embodied in language is the stuff of which B is made.[39] Since the maker of metaphor must employ language, A must come to expression in B. But the maker of metaphor, like the maker of the parable, utilizes B in such a way as to (*a*) break the grip of tradition on the language, and (*b*) discover new meaning. The two are reciprocal: rupturing the tradition permits a glimpse of another world through the cracks; the discovery of new meaning fosters the penetration of the tradition. Unlike Athena, who sprang from the head of Zeus full grown, new meaning does not emerge in full bloom. The fact that language is historical thus imposes the link between A and B upon the maker of the metaphor, and hence the parable.

This way of putting the matter is one-sided owing to the fact that A and B have been represented as two discrete things. As the "meaning" the parable intends, A cannot be accommodated, to be sure, in language crystallized in its everydayness. There is thus a theoretical discrepancy between A and B. The metaphor or parable, however, in drawing upon the common language reservoir, delivers language from the tyranny of fossilized tradition, so that B undergoes a coherent deformation. B is thus accommodated to A in the process of discovery. But the matter can and must be put the other way around: the deformation of B is what leads to the discovery of A; A is not "there" prior to the language which "speaks" it, and in this sense, it is B, the language tradition, in evoking an unpredisposed view of itself, that leads the poet and parable-maker to descry A in the first place. The linguistic tradition delivers itself over to historicness in spite of the efforts of man, the maker of dictionaries and grammars, to hold it at bay. A is thus not superimposed on B, but B, language as it is known and used, invites its own deformation by refusing its total complicity to man, the manipulator of words. In order not to let the point fall prey to yet another form of one-sidedness, it should be added that it is the interplay be-

---

[88] Wheelwright, *Metaphor and Reality*, 37.
[39] Attention will be given subsequently to the "realism" of the parables.

tween the effort to create a fund of rational discourse with stable terms, and the deformation of that fund, that makes human knowledge move—i.e., gives it a history.

2. There is a second reason why B is indispensable to A, and with it we come to the reason why the "meaning" of the parable cannot be finally articulated. The crux of the matter lies in the temporal and existential horizons of metaphorical language.

The logic of predication, as noted earlier, is narrowing, restricting. It identifies an "attribute" of the phenomenon, isolates it, and then handles it as an abstraction. The metaphor, by contrast, inheres in a vibrant nexus which resists reduction by predication. It resists specificity. It intends more, much more, than it says. What it says is minimal; what it intends is maximal. Discursive speech reduces the intentionality of language as near to explicit reference as possible; metaphorical language conserves the implicit tentacles of its vision, inasmuch as it concentrates a "world" in its figure or narrative.

If predication disengages the attribute from the phenomenon and thus from the primordial referential totality to which it belonged, it also arrests the phenomenon. It lifts the thing or event out of the flux of time in order to have a fixed term with which to deal. It is rather like clipping a single frame out of a motion picture film and then, on the basis of the still picture, conceptualizing the various elements which appear in that frame in a way that is intended to do service for the whole show. Precisely because the predicate has a static picture as its object, it is taken to be "timeless"; it appears not to depend on any particular disposition to entities.[40] However little in fact this may be the case, the logical use of language, or steno-language by prescription, as a matter of course, has to resist the toll of time in order to preserve the constancy of its terms. Pure logic is purely abstract.

The metaphor, on the other hand, is open-ended temporally. It opens onto a vibrant nexus, whose movement it seeks to reflect in its "tensive" language.[41] That is, metaphor does not clip a single frame from the film, but seeks to concentrate the movement, the flow, in an image or constellation of images which gives presence to the movement. It must perforce resist rational fragmentation and refuse ideational crystallization. It endeavors to let the next one see what the previous one saw but to see it *in his own way*. As a result, it opens onto a plurality of situa-

[40] Cf. Heidegger, *Being and Time*, 199 ff.
[41] Wheelwright, *Metaphor and Reality*, 45–69, develops the notion of "tensive" language at length.

tions, a diversity of audiences, and the future. It does not foreclose but discloses the future; it invites but does not come to rest in eventful actualization. Metaphors may live on indefinitely, since the constellation of meaning which they conjure up depends both on their revelatory power *and* the perceptive power of the mind which encounters them. They are constantly being refracted in the changing light of the historical situation.[42]

Closely connected with the temporal horizon of the metaphor is its existential tenor; it may be said to have the one because of the other. In contrast to rational abstraction, which evidences the greatest cognitive distance from event, the metaphor belongs to that mode of cognition, the imagination, which stands closest to event. "Since non-discursive forms of articulation (to take an example other than poetry, the sacrament of the Eucharist) intend to embody an event 'on its own terms,' they sustain a more intimate connection with the imaginative perpetuation of it than do the discursive modes. . . ."[43] Imagination and its metaphorical vehicle give themselves to being in process, to unfinished reality, so to speak, which they do not merely report but actually participate in. "Imagination is both a cognitive and an ontic power, participating in the very being of the realities it opens upon."[44] The metaphor, like the parable, is incomplete until the hearer is drawn into it as participant; this is the reason the parables are said to be argumentative, calling for a transference of judgment. Metaphor and parable sustain their existential tenor because they participate in immediacy, and immediacy pertaining to the future as well as to the present and past.

Tentative consent was given, in the discussion of Dodd's fourth clue above, to the affirmation that the parables are "argumentative." It is important to understand precisely in what sense this is meant. A. T. Cadoux has argued that "almost all the parables, of whose occasion we are fairly sure, were spoken in attack or defense."[45] He therefore concludes that the parable is characteristically a "weapon of contro-

---

[42] The possibility of the death—and birth, rebirth—of metaphors and symbols qualifies these formulations. Insofar as theology is bound to the "language event" of its infancy, it cannot easily consign the revelatory images of its infancy to the flames. If it does, it may find that it has come unhooked from its own historical ground. On the other hand, it is a question whether theology can deliberately keep the historic images alive.

[43] Hart, *op. cit.*, 17.

[44] *Ibid.*, 6.

[45] Cadoux, *op. cit.*, 12.

versy."[46] Jeremias clearly draws on Cadoux at this point, for the similarity of formulation is unmistakable.[47] Yet when Cadoux invokes Bultmann in support of his view that the parables always seek to persuade (opponents),[48] he is not entirely correct. Bultmann nowhere limits the audience of the parable to critics, but assumes that diverse segments of the public constituted Jesus' listeners.[49] Nor does Dodd support Cadoux in this restriction. It would appear, then, that Cadoux and Jeremias have correlated the "argumentative" character of the parable with an alleged context of debate and controversy.

This correlation goes together with their view of the function of the parable: Cadoux holds that the parable persuades.

It will be noted that here too the parable is never merely illustrative: it is always something of an argument, with one or more of the characteristics already noted—emotional persuasion, argument from analogy, allurement of the hearer to self-conviction, the clothing of new or difficult thought in form more easy of assimilation than direct statement, expression of what is incapable of definition.[50]

Jeremias argues that it is always a defense of the gospel.[51] Cadoux and Jeremias thus link character ("argumentative"), function, and context together. The question is whether a particular understanding of the "argumentative" character of the parable has not in fact been determinative for the other two points.[52]

"Argumentative," on the other hand, may mean simply that the hearer's judgment is precipitated,[53] without the qualification that the hearer is hostile to or actively engaged in debate with Jesus. The auditor may, of course, be a critic or opponent, in which case he may well take the view of the parable that Cadoux and Jeremias hold. But he may also be friendly to Jesus, in which event he is likely to have a rather different disposition to the parable. The temporal and existential tenors of the parable as metaphor suggest that the hearer may be

[46] *Ibid.*, 13 f.
[47] See chap. 6, 175 f.
[48] Cadoux, *op. cit.*, 45.
[49] Cf., e.g., Rudolf Bultmann, *Jesus and the Word*, L. P. Smith and E. H. Lantero, trans. (New York: Charles Scribner's Sons, 1958), 31 ff.
[50] Cadoux, *op. cit.*, 197.
[51] *Parables*, 145.
[52] See further, chap. 6, 175–82 and notes.
[53] The formulation is Bultmann's (*History of the Synoptic Tradition*, 191 f.).

drawn into the parable, i.e., his judgment precipitated, now in this way, now in that. This I take to be the intention also of Dodd's fourth clue. On this view, the parable is not an argument in the strict sense, but rather a "revelation" which calls for response. Amos Wilder has it that the basic character of the gospel as a whole is revelation, not persuasion.[54]

The true metaphor, it was said, reveals a mystery. The parable, too, betokens a mystery, which it adumbrates in something very like a riddle or a picture puzzle.[55] Both function like Alice's looking glass, through which one peers upon a strangely familiar world, where strangeness is suggested by the dislocation or rearrangement of the familiar. If the logic of predication looks *at* the phenomenon, the logic of the metaphor looks *through* it. The one looks *toward* the phenomenon, the other looks *away from* or *around* it (circumspectively: Heidegger). The poet directs attention to B in order to allow A to come into view, for A is not there to be looked at directly. Again, the mystery is the mystery of being, in transit from the past to the future. Being presents itself in the moment of transition, permitting only a glimpse: out of the fissures wrought by metaphorical impact upon surface reality into a future that has not yet fallen out. The glimpse, as it were, is bodied forth in metaphor, which seeks to preserve its character as glimpse (mystery), while conjuring up the background and foreground, the past and future, concentrated in that glimpse.

Returning to Dodd's definition of the parable as simile or metaphor, I have distinguished somewhat arbitrarily between the two terms he uses interchangeably.[56] This appears to coincide with Dodd's meaning, for he, too, inveighs against the understanding of the parables as "forcible illustrations of eminently sound moral and religious principles. . . ."[57] If simile is understood as illustration, it is metaphor that characterizes the parable.

---

[54] *Language of the Gospel,* 29.

[55] On the parable as riddle, cf. Austin Farrar, *A Study in St. Mark* (London: Dacre Press, 1951), 241 f.; Martin Dibelius, *Die Formgeschichte des Evangeliums* (3d ed.; Tübingen: J. C. B. Mohr [Paul Siebeck], 1959), 256 f. = *From Tradition to Gospel,* B. L. Woolf, trans. (New York: Charles Scribner's Sons, 1935), 256; J. J. Vincent, "The Parables of Jesus as Self-Revelation," in *Studia Evangelica,* K. Aland *et al.,* eds. (Berlin: Akademie-Verlag, 1959), 84.

[56] Barfield ("Poetic Diction and Legal Fiction," 52 f.) also places simile on the same gamut to which metaphor and symbol belong.

[57] Dodd, *Parables,* 25. He is writing here of Jülicher's "broadest possible application." The effect of Jülicher's method of making the parables empty out into a general principle, he writes, is "rather flattening."

The preceding reflections on the parable as metaphor require further elucidation in relation to the history of the modern interpretation of the parables. In a limited but pointed way, we now propose to probe the dominant line of parable-interpretation, as represented by the Jülicher-Dodd-Jeremias axis, in an effort to expose the critical nerve of the prevailing view, with reference to the parable understood as metaphor.

The parables in the Synoptic tradition are of two formal types: those introduced with a comparative formula, and those begun simply with a noun.[58] It is possible that this difference indicates a difference also in the nature of the parable. Since, however, there is a tendency to prefix the comparative formula in the process of transmission,[59] it would be premature to rest a substantive distinction on the introductory phrase. On the other hand, the introduction may have no bearing at all on the nature of the parable. Amos Wilder is of the opinion that even the parables of the kingdom introduced by such a phrase as "The Kingdom of Heaven is like . . ." are not true similes.[60] According to Jeremias, the introductory phrase, in its simplest form the bare dative,[61] should not be translated "It is like . . ." but "It is the case with . . . as with. . . ."[62] These considerations support the view that the parables are metaphorical and should not be taken as similes.

The translation "It is like . . ." is often misleading, says Jeremias, for the point of comparison is not always the initial element in the figure, e.g., the kingdom is not like a merchant, but like a pearl (Mt. 13:45 f); it is not like a householder, but like the distribution of wages (Mt. 20:1–16).[63] Granted that the comparison does not turn on the initial element in the parable, it remains a moot question, it seems to me, whether it is possible, especially in the narrative parables, to identify the point of comparison with such precision as Jeremias thinks possible. The translation of the introductory phrase, "It is the case with . . . as with. . . ." rightly suggests that the parable has some, as yet unspecified, bearing on the subject at hand. While the introductory

[58] Jeremias, *Parables*, 100.

[59] *Ibid.*, 102.

[60] *Language of the Gospel*, 80, n. 2.

[61] Indicating comparison, which corresponds to Aramaic *1ᵉ*. For the various forms of this phrase in the New Testament and the rabbinic literature, see Jeremias, *Parables*, 100 f.

[62] *Ibid.*, 101.

[63] *Ibid.*; cf. Clayton R. Bowen, "The Kingdom and the Mustard Seed," *American Journal of Theology*, 22 (1918), 562–69.

formula sometimes identifies the topic, e.g., the kingdom, it does not provide any clues to the way in which the story relates to this subject matter. If the parable is a genuine metaphor, it is more likely that the parable *as a whole* is to be brought into relation to the subject. To say that the kingdom is like the pearl is not much better than to say the kingdom is like the merchant. The kingdom is likened to: the merchant in quest of fine pearls, who, in finding one of unusual quality, sells all he has and buys that one. Who can say which item in the figure represents the kingdom? Jeremias' inclination to pinpoint the comparison strikes one as the old allegorical method of interpretation narrowed to a single point: instead of the figure touching the subject matter at a number of points, it touches it at only one.

Cadoux was certainly correct in his view that the restriction of contact between subject matter and parable to a single point has unfortunate consequences. In the first instance, it renders everything in the parable unnecessary ornamentation, save for the single element which serves as the point of comparison. Beyond that, it induces one to miss the organic unity of the parable.

A parable is the work of a poor artist if the picture or story is a collection of items out of which we have to pick one and discard the rest. A good parable is an organic whole in which each part is vital to the rest; it is the story of a complex and sometimes unique situation or event, so told that the outstanding features of the story contribute to the indication and nature of its point.[64]

Cadoux, let it be said, also opposed the allegorical method of interpretation, but he did so in the interest of preserving the integrity of the parable.

In pursuing this point, it will be illuminating to go back to the beginning of modern research on the parable. The work of A. Jülicher[65] is usually identified as the turning point, for it was he who dispelled the centuries-long domination of allegorical interpretation.[66] Dodd and Jeremias, as well as other modern scholars, build directly on the conclusions of Jülicher. Nevertheless, Jülicher is regarded as

---

[64] Cadoux, *op. cit.*, 50 ff. (the quotation is found on p. 52).

[65] *Die Gleichnisreden Jesu,* I (Tübingen: J. C. B. Mohr, 1888; 2d ed , 1899), II (1899); I and II reprinted 1910; two parts reprinted as one (Darmstadt: Wissenschaftliche Buchgesellschaft, 1963).

[66] Cf. Dodd, *Parables,* 24; Jeremias, *Parables,* 18 f. Further, Bultmann, *History of the Synoptic Tradition,* 198 f.

having made one fundamental mistake: he took the parables to convey one point of the broadest possible application. Let Jeremias summarize.

His struggle to free the parables from the fantastic and arbitrary allegorical interpretations of every detail caused Jülicher to fall into a fatal error. In his view the surest safeguard against such arbitrary treatment lay in regarding the parables as a piece of real life and in drawing from each of them a single idea of the widest possible generality (here lay the error).[67]

For Jeremias, as for Dodd,[68] the parables are a piece of real life from which a single point or idea is to be drawn, but this point or idea is *not a general principle;* it is rather a point made with reference to a particular situation within the ministry of Jesus.[69] Jülicher's "broadest possible application" has been replaced by the particular historical application circumscribed by the conditions of the ministry. In other respects Jülicher's position is unmodified.

The advances made with Jülicher's rejection of the allegorical method of interpretation and with the attention of Dodd and Jeremias to the historical context of the parable are scarcely to be rejected. If Jülicher laid to rest the view that the details of the parable may be assigned independent significance, Dodd and Jeremias have made it impossible to regard the parable as illustrating a generalized moral maxim. Nevertheless, Dodd and Jeremias are as much exercised with the *content* Jülicher assigned to the parabolic teaching as they are with the nature of the parable. On Jülicher's view, they feel, the parables "are stripped of their eschatological import. Imperceptibly Jesus is transformed into an 'apostle of progress,' a teacher of wisdom who inculcates moral precepts and a simplified theology by means of striking metaphors and stories. But nothing could be less like him."[70] Jülicher did not appreciate the eschatological orientation of Jesus' message, but Dodd and Jeremias do, and so can make the consequent correction in his reading of the parables.

Jülicher's moral *point* of broadest possible application has become the eschatological *point* of particular historical application. The terms which have undergone modification in these formulations mark the advance; the term which has remained constant constitutes the prob-

[67] Jeremias, *Parables*, 19.
[68] *Parables*, 18 f., 24 ff.
[69] *Ibid.*, 26–33; Jeremias, *Parables*, 21 f. and *passim.*
[70] *Ibid.*, 19; cf. Dodd, *Parables*, 25 f.

lem. The parables of Jesus, concludes Jeremias, can be summed up in "a few simple essential ideas."[71] Each parable represents a single idea, and the synthesis of ideas conveyed by the parables affords "a comprehensive conception of the message of Jesus."[72] Like Jülicher, Dodd and Jeremias derive a set of ideas from the parables, a set historically oriented, to be sure, and not a set of general moral maxims, but nevertheless *a set of ideas*. The ideational *point* of Jülicher remains ideational.[73]

Is the parable as metaphor amenable to ideational reduction? Interpreted historically, i.e., in relation to a particular context, what a given parable meant to its various hearers or readers can probably be reconstructed with lesser or greater success, provided the context can be recovered. But the original meaning of many of the parables is beyond recovery owing to the fact that the situation in which they were uttered has been lost.[74] Insofar as the original setting can be reconstructed out of the tradition, Dodd and Jeremias may be said to have met with a degree of success in particularizing the original intent of the parables. It has to be kept in mind, however, that Jesus' audience was diverse, so that the single audience/single idea correlation is fallacious. Furthermore, the parable as metaphor is many-faceted, with the consequence that a "historical" interpretation in terms of the leading "idea" truncates the parable, even for those who originally heard it.[75] And

[71] *Parables*, 115.

[72] *Ibid*. Cf. Dodd, *Parables*, 197. Dodd guards himself more in this respect than does Jeremias.

[73] It is interesting to note that in the first English edition of Jeremias' work (New York: Charles Scribner's Sons, 1955 = 3d German ed., 1954), with respect to the parable of the Laborers in the Vineyard, Jeremias writes: ". . . the question arises whether our parable has teaching as its object. None of the detailed parables of Jesus consists of mere teaching" (p. 25). This point is missing from the revised edition (cf. p. 36). But even in the earlier formulation Jeremias has in the mind the contrast between "mere teaching" and the parable as "vindication of the Gospel" (1st Eng. ed., p. 27; cf. 2d ed., p. 38). He is thinking, of course, of the way in which the church converted the parables, which originally had a debate context, into devices for instruction. Such a shift was inevitable, given the change in context. While the proclivities of the church in handling the parables have emerged clearly enough in his study, Jeremias never, so far as I can see, challenges the view that the parables were ideational in Jesus' hands. He gives us the contrast between *ideas* formulated in debate and *ideas* drawn out of the parables for catechetical purposes.

[74] Bultmann, *History of the Synoptic Tradition*, 199.

[75] In support of the line being taken here, it could be pointed out that Jeremias has had difficulty with his "few simple essential ideas": between the third (1954) and sixth (1962) editions of his work he found it necessary to enlarge the number of interpretive categories (from eight to ten): in addition, he sometimes finds it necessary to list a particular parable under more than one rubric (suggesting that the single idea may not

finally, if the parable lays a burden on the future, as was indicated by
considerations relative to the metaphor, it would also have to be said
that the parable itself gives warrant for broaching the question of what
the parable *means* (as well as what it meant), a warrant which the
church claimed for its part from the earliest days. Ernst Fuchs has seen
the significance of this point.[76] Since the nonideational nature of the
parable as metaphor has not been taken sufficiently into account, a historical interpretation (what the parables meant) has tended to crystal-
lize the parable into a leading idea, to correlate this with a delimited
audience, and to foreclose the future. Jeremias in particular appears to
be content with the recovery of the "authentic voice" of Jesus,[77] by
which he means the idea Jesus had in mind in speaking any particular
parable to a specific group. But the "actual living voice of Jesus" must
be accorded the right to its own mode of discourse if that voice is to be
"actual" and "living."

It is to Dodd's credit that he has recognized the temporally restrictive
character of a purely historical interpretation of the parables. In the
preface to the third edition of his *Parables of the Kingdom,* he has
responded to criticism of just this order in the following way:

By all means draw from the parables any "lesson" they may suggest,
provided it is not incongruous with what we may learn of their original
intention. We shall not easily exhaust their meaning.[78]

This remark refers to a passage in his original text that is very
instructive:

The parables, however, have an imaginative and poetical quality. They are
works of art, and any serious work of art has significance beyond its
original occasion. No pedantry of exegesis could ever prevent those who
have "ears to hear," as Jesus said, from finding that the parables "speak to

---

be so single after all). It is not always easy, furthermore, to distinguish among his
categories. These observations are intended only to point to the difficulty of confining the
parable in the straitjacket of a single, simple idea.

James M. Robinson implies a similar criticism of Jeremias, *et al.,* when he states that,
"The parables will therefore by the very nature of the artistic form provide us with a
correct response to a situation whose historical pole is completely devoid of concrete
historical details" ("Jesus' Understanding of History," *JBR* 23 [1955], 20).

[76] E.g., Fuchs II, 141 f.
[77] *Parables,* e. g., 22, 114.
[78] Dodd, *Parables,* vi f.

their condition." Their teaching may be fruitfully applied and re-applied to all sorts of new situations which were never contemplated at the time when they were spoken. But a just understanding of their original import in relation to a particular situation in the past will put us on right lines in applying them to our own new situations.[79]

Dodd correctly emphasizes two points: (*a*) the meaning of the parables is not exhausted with their original import; (*b*) the original import, i.e., the historical interpretation, is controlling with respect to reinterpretation. The latter is not to be forgotten in pursuing the former.[80]

It is thus possible—I say "possible" to indicate that prudence is required—to affirm that the parable, as metaphor, has not one but many "points," as many points as there are situations into which it is spoken. And that applies to the original as well as subsequent audiences. The emphasis on one point over against the allegorization of the parables was a necessary corrective, but one point understood as an idea valid for all times is as erroneous as Jülicher's moral maxims, even if that idea is eschatological!

It should here be reaffirmed, in the interest of avoiding misunderstanding, that the details of the parable do not have independent

---

[79] *Ibid.*, 195.

[80] The significance of the critical historical method for determining the original import of the parable, and thus for providing a control over reinterpretation, must be emphasized, owing to the criticisms of Dodd and Jeremias being developed here. On the one hand, Dodd and especially Jeremias, in correcting Jülicher, have insisted on the crucial importance of the situation for parable interpretation. The direction in which Jesus aims the parable and the particular context in which it is heard have everything to do with its original meaning. James Robinson has summed the matter up well: "When . . . one disregarded the speaker's intention and provided only an aesthetic or literary interpretation, one did violence to the inherent nature of the subject matter under investigation and to this ˙extent failed in one's task as an interpreter. Interpretation has frequently taken its point of departure from the beginning or the end of the parable, looking upon it as a whole, undifferentiated along the way by a point of existential involvement on the part of the hearer. Thus a false perspective of continuity, of normal unbroken progression, of process under law as revealed by the world of nature, has been forced into the parable as a factor dominating the interpretation. This exegetical foreshortening is corrected when the parable is approached from the flank, i.e., from the position of the intended hearer and the point in the parable to which such a hearer is expected to attach himself" ("Jesus' Understanding of History," 18 f.). The original meaning of the parable is thus to be grasped in relation to the locus from which it is spoken and the locus from which it is heard. Without losing sight of this point, on the other hand, it is possible to claim (*a*) that the nature of the parable as metaphor has not been properly grasped, and (*b*) that the two loci have been too narrowly defined.

significance.[81] They are subordinated to the whole so as not to disturb
its unity.[82] In the allegory every detail or most details are conceptual
ciphers; the allegorization of the parables is therefore their rationalization.[83] The parable does not lend itself to allegorization because the
parable as metaphor is designed to retain its own authority; the
rationalization of its meaning tends to destroy its power as image. This
is the reason Fuchs insists that the parable is not meant to *be* interpret*ed*, but to interpret. The parable keeps the initiative in its own
hand. Therein lies its hermeneutical potential.

Reduction of the meaning of the parables to a single idea, be it
eschatological or christological, is only a restricted form of rationalization. As is the case with the allegory, theological reduction seeks to
control the metaphor. In the same way and for the same reason,
correlating the kingdom with the pearl maims the image. The strict
subordination of detail to the whole and the independent power of the
figure warns against such solitary reductions and correlations. The
metaphor must be left intact if it is to retain its interpretive power.

III

The consideration of the parable as metaphor has thus far skirted
Dodd's second and third clues, although we occasionally caught sight
of the realism of the parables and the element of vividness or strangeness. The parabolic metaphor, it will be recalled from above, (2) is
drawn from nature or the common life, and (3) arrests the hearer by
its vividness or strangeness.[84] It will be necessary to reflect upon these
two clues together, as the following questions suggest. Why should a
commonplace, even if fetchingly depicted or narrated, be vivid or
strange? Suppose it be allowed that a catch of fish or a wedding feast
can be vividly narrated. Why should that be arresting, if arresting is
taken to imply more than a pause to note with aesthetic pleasure? And
why should such a vivid vignette be argumentative, precipitating the

---

81 Dodd, *Parables*, 18–21, especially 19. Cf. Bultmann's analysis of the style of the
parable, *History of the Synoptic Tradition*, 187–92, for the laws of parsimony of
detail.

82 Dodd, *Parables*, 21.

83 Barfield, *Poetic Diction*, 201, suggests that allegory involves a more or less conscious hypostatization of *ideas*, followed by a synthesis of them. Allegory may, of course,
make use of previously created material, in which case allegory is a rationalization of
mythical or other language.

84 *Supra*, 133.

hearer's judgment? Why should it call for, even compel, decision? If these questions pose problems difficult of solution, it might be well to inquire why the parables are realistic in the first place.

Dodd has observed, with the backing of numerous other scholars, that the parables provide a reliable index to petit-bourgeois and peasant life in a provincial village in the Roman Levant.[85] The realism of the parables is so acute that, in the judgment of Jeremias, it is natural to suppose that some of them were suggested by actual events.[86] Wilder, too, can scarcely overemphasize how human and realistic the parables are.[87] They provide intimate and accurate observations on nature and life. What was once thought to be an inaccuracy, because it did not square with Western ways, has proved to be commonplace in the East.[88]

Perhaps more important than accuracy in detail is what Wilder calls the impact of their "immediate realistic authenticity."[89] Authenticity consists in the absence of romance, idealization, false mysticism, escapism, fantasy, miracles, sentimentality; in short, the parables are rooted in things as they are.[90] Jeremias has put the matter succinctly.

The hearers find themselves in a familiar scene where everything is so simple and clear that a child can understand, so plain that those who hear can say, "Yes, that's how it is."[91]

Jeremias, I fear, has quite another point in mind than the one I wish to make, but his characterization, so far as I can see, tallies with Wilder's use of the term authenticity.

Wilder ventures to speak of the secularity of the parables.[92] The

[85] Dodd, *Parables*, 21; cf. his *The Authority of the Bible* (rev. ed.; Glasgow: William Collins Sons [Fontana Books], 1960; reprinted 1962), 144–48.

[86] *Parables*, 23.

[87] *Language of the Gospel*, 81 ff.

[88] Jeremias, e.g., calls attention to the "bad farming" represented by the parable of the Sower: the farmer sows indiscriminately. Yet, because the farmer sows *before* he ploughs, he sows the entire field—the path, among the thorns, and on rocky ground, as well as on the good ground. The parable thus depicts a convention in Palestinian agriculture. Jeremias, *Parables*, 11 f. and n. 3.

[89] *Language of the Gospel*, 81.

[90] *Ibid.*, 82.

[91] Jeremias, *Parables*, 12, meaning that the parables give the appearance of being free from "problematic elements."

[92] *Language of the Gospel*, 81.

parables rarely take up explicitly "religious" themes. Is this because, in wishing to speak about *A* (religion), Jesus directs attention to *B* (a secular image), as is the case with metaphorical and symbolic language generally, in that they look away from the subject-matter? Or can one say that the really authentic world, the everyday world, is one in which God does not "appear"? In the latter case, the secularity of the parables is correlative with their realism. In the former, the secularity of the parables is bound up with the nature of metaphorical language. A third possibility presents itself, viz., the union of the two. The secularity of the parables may give expression to the only way of legitimately speaking of the incursion of the divine into history: metaphorical or symbolic language is proper to the subject matter because God remains hidden. In that case even "religious" themes may be presented in "secular" dress, i.e., "religious" subject matter is viewed merely as a part of the profane landscape. But this point, as others, must await further consideration of the element of realism.

Dodd offers a typically lucid explanation for the realism of the parables:

It [the realism] arises from a conviction that there is no mere analogy, but an inward affinity, between the natural order and the spiritual order; or as we might put it in the language of the parables themselves, the Kingdom of God is intrinsically like the processes of nature and of the daily life of men. . . . Since nature and supernature are one order, you can take any part of that order and find in it illumination for other parts. . . . This sense of the divineness of the natural order is the major premise of all the parables. . . .[93]

In this context Dodd denies any affinity between Jesus and the apocalyptists, who disparaged the present order. His accounting is the more surprising in view of the fact that, a few pages later, he describes the message of Jesus as related to a "tremendous crisis in which He is the principal figure and which indeed His appearance brought about."[94] To this he adds that the course of events, involving disasters upon the Jewish people, persecution of the disciples, and the suffering and death of Jesus himself, contains within itself the mystery of the kingdom, the *paradoxical* revelation of the glory of God. "Behind or within the

[93] Dodd, *Parables*, 22.
[94] *Ibid.*, 26.

paradoxical turn of events lies that timeless reality which is the kingdom, the power and the glory of the blessed God."[95]

In what sense can this "tremendous crisis," this paradoxical revelation, be illuminated out of the natural order? If we may assume a common-sense or everyday view of what the term "natural" denotes— which corresponds to the "immediate realistic authenticity" of the parables, to which everyone can say, "Yes, that's how it is"—then it may be said that this is precisely what the kingdom is *not* like. For the mystery or paradox of the kingdom upsets the conventions, the standards of the common judgment—in sum, the "natural" order. But then Dodd may have in mind "that timeless reality which is the kingdom" when he writes "natural"; in fact, it must be so if he can wed nature and supernature. In any case, by his own definition the coming of the kingdom is a paradox: it contradicts the common-sense opinions of men. To its manifestation not everyone is willing to say, "Yes, that's how it is."

It is not the mystery of the kingdom to which one promptly says, "Yes"; it is rather the everydayness embodied in the imagery of the parable. Mr. Everyman knows what it means to have lost a sheep or a coin, to sow a field, to have weeds grow in his field, to have a wayward son, to suffer injustice, to stand idle in the market place, to see an unscrupulous steward feather his own nest: these are things he knows and can affirm, "That's how it is."

But there is more to it than identification with the coarse realities of existence. Amos Wilder is on the mark when he writes, "Jesus, without saying so, by his very way of presenting man, shows that for him man's destiny is at stake in his ordinary creaturely existence, domestic, economic and social."[96] That is to say, the everydayness of the parables is translucent to the ground of man's existence. When Jesus speaks of a lost sheep, a mustard seed, a banquet, or some other commonplace, the auditor senses without prompting that more is involved than a pleasant or amusing anecdote, even one which relieves the coarseness of life by jesting. The parabolic imagery lays bare the structure of human existence that is masked by convention, custom, consensus. It exposes the "world" in which man is enmeshed and to which and for which he must give account. It is this element of ultimate seriousness that is implicit in the patent everydayness of the parable. The "field" which

[95] The quotation is found *ibid.*, p. 80. Cf. 71 ff.
[96] Wilder, *Language of the Gospel*, 82.

the parable thus conjures up is not merely this or that isolated piece of earthiness, but the very tissue of reality, the nexus of relations, which constitutes the arena of human existence where life is won or lost.[97]

If the parable cracks the shell of mundane temporality, it does so without an explicit call to ultimate seriousness. The listener is not overtly prompted. The parable simply and artfully calls up the "world" in such a way that "he who has ears" knows that more is at issue than a piece of change or a doting old father.

Taking Wilder's statement, quoted above, as axiomatic, it is nevertheless the case that *everydayness* is not merely incidental to the "field" intended by the parabolic image. Man's destiny is at stake *in his everyday creaturely existence*. The parable does not direct attention by its earthy imagery *away from* mundane existence, but *toward* it. The realism of the parable is not merely a device. Everydayness is ingredient in the parable because everydayness constitutes the locus of the parable's intentionality. In that case, however, why speak of metaphorical language at all? If the parable speaks directly about what it intends, in what sense is it metaphorical? The observation that everydayness is ingredient in the field intended by the parable because it constitutes the locus of the parable's intentionality, and the previous assertion that the parable conceals its call to ultimacy by looking out upon the mundane, appear to be contradictory.

This dilemma may be resolved by referring once again to the nature of metaphorical language. Barfield has observed that the literal and nonliteral meanings of a word or sentence can bear various relations to each other.[98] There is, first of all, the substituted meaning: a young Englishman announces to various persons outside an underground station, "There will be rain in Northumberland tomorrow," by which he means "Are you the person who advertised in the Personal Column . . . etc.?"[99] In the prearranged code one meaning is substituted for another. This is also the case, in a less categorical fashion, with the fossilized metaphor: there are very few oats left in the sentence "He is sowing his wild oats." In the second place, figures which convey a nonliteral meaning while retaining something of the literal force may

---

[97] Contrast the parables in the Gospel of Thomas, in which an earthy image looks not to the mundane but to an ethereal realm. This difference between the parables of Jesus and those in Thomas was called to my attention by James M. Robinson.

[98] "The Meaning of the Word 'Literal,' " 48 f.

[99] The illustration is drawn from P. G. Wodehouse, *Leave It to Psmith*.

be said, to use Barfield's designation, to have concomitant meanings.[100]
Concomitant meanings are characteristic of the poetic metaphor, as, for
example,

> She dwelt among the untrodden ways
>
> . . .
>
> A violet by a mossy stone . . .

where the metaphorical and literal meanings are obviously intertwined.
One might expect, Barfield suggests, that the retention of the literal
sense in the poetic metaphor would be dependent on its plausibility.
"But that is not in practice the case. The literal meaning of

> The moon is my eye,
> Smiling only at night. . . .

or

> There is a garden in her face

is a pretty tall story."[101] Literal plausibility, it would seem, often
permits the metaphorical meaning to be divorced from the image with
flattening results. With reference to Christina Rosetti's poem "Does the
road wind uphill all the way?" Barfield avers that the metaphorical
sense (A)

> detaches itself from B, like a soul leaving a body, and the road and the inn
> and the beds are not a real road and inn and beds, they look faintly
> heraldic—or as if portrayed in lacquer. They are not even poetically real.
> We never get a fair chance to accord to their existence that willing suspen-
> sion of disbelief which we are told constitutes "poetic faith."[102]

Such metaphorical language approaches the status of the prearranged
code. But where the literal meaning is not simply credible, attention is
called to it all the more. This line of Coleridge,

---

[100] I do not propose to explore the various ways in which concomitant meanings can
be related to each other, as, e.g., in allegory and symbolism, but to confine myself to
the concomitance of the poetic metaphor and the parable.

[101] Barfield, "The Meaning of the Word 'Literal,' " 49.

[102] Barfield, "Poetic Diction and Legal Fiction," 54.

As if this earth in fast thick pants were breathing

does not commend itself empirically, but one is inclined, as a consequence, to take a second look at this particular piece of ground.

The parable in which everydayness is ingredient would appear to be a special case of metaphorical language. Its initial plausibility, in the case of the nature parables and certain others drawn from the sphere of human life, tempts the hearer to substitute another meaning, i.e. to disregard the literal and thus to allegorize. The temptation is in force because the hearer or reader assumes that the literal subject matter could not possibly be the real subject matter. In the parable of the Sower, for example, the equations seed = word and soils = people can be made and the literal meaning quietly abandoned. Similarly, Matthew's allegorical code for the parable of the Weeds (13:36–43) invites the reader to disregard the imagery (B) and attend only to the meaning (A), in which case "meaning" rises from image "like a soul leaving a body." In the parables characterized as "exemplary-stories," on the other hand, the opposite temptation is in force: the reader is tempted to find the meaning in the literal sense. Classical examples are the Good Samaritan and the Pharisee and the Publican.

But to accede to either temptation is to overlook another characteristic of the metaphor and particularly the parable, viz., that it is not merely credible. Like the cleverly distorted picture puzzles children used to work, the parable is a picture puzzle which prompts the question, What's wrong with this picture? Distortions of everydayness, exaggerated realism, distended concreteness, incompatible elements—often subtly drawn—are what prohibit the parable from coming to rest in the literal sense; yet these very factors call attention to the literal all the more. Just as the literal imagery is not simply credible, so the parable points to a world where things run backward or counter to the mundane world. Yet that other world, like the literal sense, has a certain plausibility, a strange familiarity. It is the interplay between, or the concomitance of, the literal and the metaphorical that makes the two reciprocally revelatory. The literal and the metaphorical meanings of the parable have to be grasped concomitantly.

Metaphorical language, it was suggested, does not look *at* the phenomenon, but *through* it. Metaphor seeks to rupture the grip of tradition on man's apprehension of the world in order to permit a glimpse of another world, which is not really a different but a strangely familiar world. Metaphor, moreover, remains temporally open-ended, thus permitting the hermeneutical potential of the vision conjured up to make its own claim upon the future. It is in these senses that parabolic imagery is genuinely metaphorical. It does not look *at* everydayness, but *through* it. It fractures everydayness in the interest of a referential totality of a peculiar order. It does not pre-empt the world it opens onto, but allows that world to emerge in encounter with the hearer. The realism of parabolic imagery, consequently, is not, without qualification, simply the locus of the parable's intentionality; although the latter is rooted in everydayness, secularity, it is of a different order altogether. The parable induces an imaginative grasp of the one by the way in which it presents the other. And only in this way can the "world" of the parable be grasped at all.

In saying that parabolic metaphor induces an imaginative grasp of the "world" of the parable by the way in which the everyday world is presented, we are brought, finally, to the explicit consideration of what has been described as vividness or strangeness.

To be sure, vividness can be accounted for in part by virtue of the fact that the parables catch Mr. Everyman in the commonplace acts of daily living. More than that, they catch him at those junctures which he thinks of as *characteristic* of his existence. Not all sons are wayward, not every sheep or coin is lost, one is not awakened every night by a friend in need. Yet these sporadic, even rare, occurrences are taken to epitomize life. Concentration on a familiar thing, or a thing taken to be familiar, makes it stand out suddenly from its background. One notices the sower perhaps for the first time. But, as Owen Barfield says in observing the poetic use of this device, it is concentration on a familiar thing in making it stand out from an *unfamiliar* background.[108] That is to say, the familiar is brought into the context of the unfamiliar

---

[108] Barfield, *Poetic Diction*, 173 f. The metaphysical poets in particular use this device in a characteristic way. George Herbert, for example, is fond of importing a "plain, cold, manufactured" article into an alien context:

> When God at first made man,
> Having a *glass* of blessings standing by,
> "Let us," said He, "pour on him all we can. . . ."

(cited *ibid.*, 174). It is easy to see that *glass* in this context loses its manufactured character and takes on the incandescence of, let us say, the Holy Grail. On the other hand, the word *glass* lends immense concreteness to "standing by" and "pour" and the other, more ethereal language, to say nothing of the subject matter. This reciprocity is what Fraenkel, Riezler, and others have identified as characteristic of the Homeric metaphor (cf. Bruno Snell, *The Discovery of Mind*, T. G. Rosenmeyer, trans. [New York: Harper Torchbook, 1960], 200 f. and n. 20). Homer (Iliad 15.615) describes the Greek battle line enduring Hector's assaults as a rock in the sea endures, despite wind and waves. The inanimate object illuminates human behavior because it is viewed anthropomorphically, but that is possible only because the Greek battle line is viewed petromorphically at the same time (Snell, *op. cit.*, 201). The interplay between the two is revealing, and it is difficult to estimate whether the Greeks or the rock have gained the more.

and so is vivified. The familiar couched in the familiar is boring; the familiar and unfamiliar in juxtaposition are stimulating.

Parabolic imagery is vivid in just this way. Everydayness is framed by the ultimate. The commonplace is penetrated so that it becomes uncommonly significant. That which is taken to characterize the humdrum, fatigue, and irritation of experience is set in a context from which, in the opinion of Mr. Everyman, it is estranged. The superimposition of the two is revealing.

Vividness of this order, as Barfield also notes, requires that the strangeness produced by the superimposition shall have *interior* significance. It cannot be artificial, contrived, or merely eccentric. Vividness must inhere in the different thing that is said, not solely in the way that it is said. "It must be felt as arising from a different plane or mode of consciousness. . . . It must be a strangeness of *meaning*."[104] The everyday imagery of the parable is vivid fundamentally, then, because it juxtaposes the common and the uncommon, the everyday and the ultimate, but only so that each has interior significance for the other. The world of the parable is like Alice's looking-glass world: all is familiar, yet all is strange, and the one illuminates the other.

Closely related is what Dodd describes as the surprise element in many of the parables, i.e., an unusual action. If the development of the story is unnatural, Dodd apologizes, it is because the point of the parable is that such actions are surprising.[105] Jeremias, too, takes note of such unusual features, while adding that Jesus employs extravagant exaggerations which are characteristic of Oriental storytelling; both are intended either to call attention to the point or to impress it upon the hearers by means of "shock tactics."[106] The trait of hyperbole, according to Wilder, echoes Jesus' eschatological challenge, and is the only point at which the parables diverge from realism.[107]

The underlying assumption, it is worth noting, is that the surprising and hyperbolic aspects of the parables require justification over against the otherwise predominant realism. They are explained as indicating or emphasizing the point, or as an echo of the eschatological crisis. Bultmann, on the other hand, suggests that the "immense concreteness" of the language of Jesus can be *raised* to hyperbole, to which paradox is

104 Barfield, *Poetic Diction*, 171 (italics his).
105 *Parables*, 21.
106 Jeremias, *Parables*, 29 ff. He borrows the phrase "shock tactics" from J. J. Vincent, "The Parables of Jesus as Self-Revelation," 80.
107 *Language of the Gospel*, 85.

related.[108] I take this to mean that hyperbole is stepped-up realism, surrealism if you will. Paradox, as Bultmann illustrates it, is hyperbole raised to the level of the impossible (e.g., the Pharisees strain out gnats and swallow camels).[109] In that case, what may be conveniently embraced under the term hyperbole (i.e., all unrealistic elements) may not be the opposite of realism, but its intensification.

This line, however, promises to fall short of the goal, unless it is recalled once again that the realism—which I prefer to call everydayness—of the parable concentrates on the familiar in such a way that it is shattered: Mr. Everyman can affirm the everydayness of the parables, but he is rudely shocked at two points. He is startled when the parabolic narrative unfolds in such a way as to turn his everydayness inside out or upside down: it is simply not cricket for the employer to pay those who worked only one hour the same wage as those who worked the full day. He is shocked, too, at the so-called transference of judgment: a just God does not indiscriminately reward his children. Here, of course, it is necessary to distinguish among the hearers. If the auditor happens to have worked one hour, he may take a more congenial view of the proceedings. His everydayness is happily disrupted. For both, nevertheless, the everyday world is surprisingly and oddly disfigured.

Hyperbole and paradox, for this reason, are intrinsic to the parable.[110] They are one means, among others, of indicating the "gappiness" of conventional existence. If they do so more overtly, they may be regarded as helpful signs of what transpires in other parabolic metaphors more covertly.

In sum, the parables as pieces of everydayness have an unexpected "turn" in them which looks through the commonplace to a new view of reality. This "turn" may be overt in the form of a surprising development in the narrative, an extravagant exaggeration, a paradox; or it may lurk below the surface in the so-called transference of judgment for which the parable calls. In either case the listener is led through the parable into a strange world where everything is familiar yet radically different.

This characterization of the parable also explains their argumentative or provocative character, why they demand a decision. They

---

[108] Bultmann, *History of the Synoptic Tradition*, 166 f.

[109] *Ibid.*, 167 n. 1 gives this definition.

[110] J. A. Findlay, *Jesus and His Parables* (London: Epworth Press, 1950), 10 *et passim*, regards the "element of surprise" as of the essence of the parable.

present a world the listener recognizes, acknowledges. Then he is
caught up in the dilemma of the metaphor: it is not his world after all!
Should he proceed on this venture into strangeness or draw back? He
must choose to unfold with the story, be illuminated by the metaphor,
or reject the call and abide with the conventional. It is too little to call
the parables as metaphors teaching devices; they are that, but much
more. They are language events in which the hearer has to choose
between worlds. If he elects the parabolic world, he is invited to dispose
himself to concrete reality as it is ordered in the parable, and venture,
without benefit of landmark but on the parable's authority, into the
future.

The Parable of the Great Supper:
Text and Context

≯ 6 ⊀ _____

THE PARABLE OF THE GREAT SUPPER (δεῖπνον μέγα, Lκ.
14:16) has been preserved in the traditon in three versions: Mt.
22:2–10; Lk. 14:16–24; Gospel of Thomas, Logion 64. Although there
are significant differences among the three, there can be no doubt that
they represent a single tradition.[1]

I

Narrative content and structure. The anonymous man (ἄνθρωπός τις)
who gives a great supper and invites many in Luke's version (14:16) is,
in Matthew's account (22:2), a king who gives a marriage feast for his
son. The single servant of Luke (14:17, cf. 21 [twice], 22, 23) is a
plurality in Matthew (22:3, 4, 6, 8, 10),[2] which, moreover, is differenti-

---

[1] It is usually assumed that the parables of Jesus originally had only one form and
were spoken in one specific context. This assumption naturally precipitates the quest to
recover that one form and particular context. However legitimate this procedure may be
for other reasons, I wish to make a restrained protest against what seems to me to be
the improbability of the assumption. Is it not likely that Jesus spoke a given parable on
a number of occasions (this much is customarily granted) and in different contexts,
adapting it each time, perhaps, to the circumstances? This does not mean that the
parable was basically modified each time, but that it was directed now to this, now to
that group or person, with a consequent shift in nuance. The many-faceted character of
the parabolic metaphor, in fact, lends itself exceedingly well to such usage. While it
would seem feasible to seek to establish the structure of a particular parable, it would
probably be an error, for the reason given, to attempt to fix every detail. It is more
accurate, therefore, to speak of independent traditions rather than of an original parable
(hypothetical *Vorlage*) which was subsequently modified by the church. This, of course,
by no means relieves us of the necessity of tracing the tradition and of attempting to
distinguish between original and secondary elements. It only makes the task more
difficult, since it robs the effort of the prospect of a firm and uniform ground term.

[2] The shift from one to a number of servants may be explained on the basis that a
king might he expected to have more than one servant: Bultmann, *History of the
Synoptic Tradition*, 175.

ated (22:4 ἄλλους δούλους, other servants). The invitation delivered by
the first group is rejected (22:3), the second group is abused and even
killed (22:6), so that a third group,[3] or the first group, is again
dispatched to invite others to the feast (22:8, 10). In Luke, however, the
same servant functions throughout.

In both Matthew and Luke the invitation is issued three times, in
Matthew twice to the invited and once to the uninvited, in Luke once
to the invited and twice to the uninvited.[4] Matthew's invited guests
first indicate they do not propose to come (22:3) and then proceed to
make light of the whole affair, one going off to his plot of ground,
another to his place of business (22:5). In view of this drift in the
narrative, it is surprising to learn that some (οἱ δὲ λοιποί, the rest)
stay behind and collectively beat and kill the second group of servants
(22:6). The fact that this response breaks into the development of the
narrative and that it has an allegorizing ring to it brings v. 6 under

[3] Triadic repetition, often found in folk-narrative (*ibid.*, 191; Jeremias, *Parables*, 204;
Dodd, *Parables*, 129 n. 1), suggests that a third group may be intended here. This
view is supported by οἱ δοῦλοι ἐκεῖνοι in 22:10: "those servants," i.e., the ones just
addressed (22:8), presumably in distinction from the first two groups, although one
might have expected a second ἄλλοι. In any case, there is clearly a triple mission on
the part of the king's servants.

[4] Τοῖς κεκλημένοις (to those who have been invited), Lk. 14:17, reinforces the
notion, specified by ἐκάλεσεν πολλούς (he invited many) in 14:16, that the initial
invitation had already been made; the reminder at the time of the banquet is a special
courtesy (Jeremias, *Parables*, 176 and n. 16). Jeremias is of the opinion that τοὺς
κεκλημένους (Mt. 22:3) is a Semitism: the participle here has gerundive force, meaning "those to be invited" (68 n. 74). The invitation dispatched in v. 3 would therefore
be the initial invitation, and that given in v. 4 the courtesy reminder (*ibid.*, 68). The
narrative development, however, does not support this opinion: if those invited replied
to the first invitation that they would not come (v. 3b), why did the king prepare the
banquet and send word that it was ready? If it is supposed that the king was a stubborn monarch who would not take "No" to his preliminary summons for an answer
(which is possible), then it must be said that the first invitation and refusal do not
comport well with the eschatological crisis indicated by the parable. No, the parable
opens with the banquet prepared: the hour is at hand. Ἀπέστειλεν . . . (he sent
. . ., v. 3) πάλιν ἀπέστειλεν (again he sent . . . v. 4) are rapidly succeeding events.
Moreover, κεκλημένοι means "those invited" elsewhere in the parable (22:4, 8;
cf. Lk. 14:17, 24), as Jeremias recognizes, so that an exception must be made of 22:3
without sufficient basis in the text.

Jeremias has attempted to square v. 3 with Matthew's allegorization of the parable.
On the basis of the allegory (on which see *infra*), v. 3 represents the sending of the
prophets and their rejection. This took place long ago. It follows, so Jeremias must have
reasoned, that the invitation in v. 3 was the original one. The discovery of a Semitism is
a convenient means of resolving the problem left in the text by Matthew. That Matthew
has allegorized the parable there is no doubt, but it is too much to assume that Matthew
has made the parable conform to the allegory in every detail.

suspicion.[5] Luke's invitees, on the other hand, begin to make excuses. Three are given,[6] the first two of which correspond roughly to the first two responses given to the second invitation in Matthew's version (22:5b). The third excuse in the Lucan form has nothing in common with the third response in the Matthean account.[7] Nevertheless, the threefold response (in Luke to the first, in Matthew to the second, invitation) constitutes a parallelism in structure.

The king or host becomes wroth at the disregard for his carefully laid feast (Mt. 22:7; Lk. 14:21). In Matthew his wrath takes the form of a punitive expedition against those murderers and their city[8]—all while dinner is waiting on the table! Verse 7, like v. 6, scarcely fits the pace of the parable. The two verses must have been introduced into the narrative for ulterior reasons. Finally, however, the king, recalling that the feast is ready and waiting but that his original guests are unworthy (22:8; cf. Lk. 14:24), seeks to fill the hall indiscriminately by sending his servants to gather any they may meet in the way, both good and bad (22:8 ff.). The host's wrath, according to Luke, issues in the exclusion of those originally invited (14:24; cf. Mt. 22:8b), and gives rise to an invitation to the poor, maimed, blind, and lame. They, too, are herded in from the streets and alleys (14:21). Unlike Matthew's king, Luke's host senses the need for haste (ἔξελθε ταχέως, Go out quickly, 14:21). But a swing through the city does not fill the places set (14:22). The order is given for a second expedition into the country in order to fill the house (v. 23).

Reduced to its barest dimensions, the structure of the parable appears to be as follows:

I. Introduction
    a. A man
    b. gives a banquet
    c. invites those (socially) worthy
II. Development and Crisis
    a. banquet is ready
    b. sends servant for courtesy reminder (Lk. once, Mt. twice)

[5] Verse 22:7 goes with and is dependent upon 22:6. If the latter is suspect, the former is also.

[6] On the triadic repetition, see *supra,* n. 3.

[7] According to Cadoux (A. T. Cadoux, *The Parables of Jesus: Their Art and Use* [London: James Clarke & Co., n.d. (1930)], 62 f.) the third excuse introduces an unlikely element (the man knew he would be married) and reflects the attitude toward marriage given in I Cor. 7:32 f. He therefore takes it to be intrusive.

[8] On this motif, see Jeremias, *Parables,* 33, 68 and n. 75.

     c. guests refuse to come and/or offer excuses, go off on pretexts (Lk. three excuses, Mt. two pretexts and the response of "the rest")

III. Denouement

     a. man is wroth

     b. invites those (socially) unworthy (Mt. once, Lk. twice)

     c. table is filled

     d. judgment upon those originally invited[9]

Matthew's second sending of servants, as noted above, is contrived. Does this leave two sorties, or has Matthew made a substitution? Luke has three, the third of which may be his own invention to point up his interest in the mission to the Gentiles.[10] It is possible that only two invitations were involved, the courtesy reminder to the original guests and the summons of the uninvited. Analogously, Matthew offers two pretexts and a third response which is secondary. Does this leave two, or has Matthew made a substitution? Luke offers three excuses. These "symmetrically constructed excuses," according to Jeremias, show the marks of Lucan style.[11] Taken together, the two problems suggest that the two instances of triadic structure may be secondary.

For sheer simplicity of structure, aside from the elaboration of the excuses, the version in the Gospel of Thomas (Logion 64, 92.10–35)[12] is superior to the Synoptic tradition. Thomas has the introduction, although items *b* and *c* are abbreviated. Bultmann observes that conciseness of narrative and economy of detail are characteristic of the parable.[13] Items II *a, b, c* are also present, but Thomas has only one courtesy reminder (in contrast to Matthew). In Thomas, however, the reminder is reiterated for each guest (92. 13 ff.).[14] The third section is represented only by items III*b* and III*d*, the latter serving as a generalizing conclusion. The invitation to those (socially) unworthy is

---

    [9] The order of III*d* is indeterminate: it comes as III*b* in Matthew's sequence. It may be said to be a floating item, which raises a question about its authenticity.

    [10] Jeremias, *Parables*, 64 and many commentators; or is the second Luke's invention? The formulation, Lk. 14:21, certainly is (Cadoux, *op. cit.*, 63).

    [11] *Parables*, 72 n. 84.

    [12] Plate and line are cited according to the edition of A. Guillaumont *et al.*, *The Gospel According to Thomas* (New York: Harper & Brothers, 1959).

    [13] Bultmann, *History of the Synoptic Tradition*, 188, 190.

    [14] Cf. Hugh Montefiore, "A Comparison of the Parables of the Gospel According to Thomas and of the Synoptic Gospels," in H. E. W. Turner and H. Montefiore, *Thomas and the Evangelists*, "Studies in Biblical Theology," 35 (London: SCM Press, 1962), 58, who thinks this feature goes with Gnostic emphasis on the individual.

given only once (in contrast to Luke). Nothing is said about the wrath of the host or the table being filled. Thomas thus has an abbreviated introduction, an abbreviated denouement, and only two invitations. Only at the point of excuses (Thomas gives four) is the version in Thomas more elaborate than the Synoptic account. Moreover, Thomas does not support the triadic repetition in either instance.[15]

In other respects, too, Thomas manifests greater simplicity, is more in line with parabolic style. In Thomas, as in Luke, the host is anonymous and there is only one servant who functions throughout. The original guests are allowed to make their excuses in direct discourse, again as in Luke.[16] Direct discourse and soliloquy are characteristic of the parable and popular narrative.[17] Like Matthew, Thomas' invitation to the uninvited is to those whom the servant may find (Mt. 22:9 f.; Thomas 92. 32 f.), whereas Luke has specified the unworthy in accordance with a previous logion (14:21; 14:13).[18] Whether the wrath of the host and the filling of the table are incidental to the parable, and hence whether Thomas simply reflects a greater economy of detail or has intentionally abbreviated, cannot be easily resolved on the basis of style.

II

Synoptic context. As a consequence of form-critical analysis, which has shown that the framework of the Synoptic accounts has been furnished largely by the Evangelists, it is necessary to investigate the particular setting given to individual elements in the tradition. The presumption is that the parables, too, have been assigned to contexts by the redactors on the basis of their interpretation of them.[19] It is possible that in some cases an interpretation which had already been attached to the parable in the tradition influenced the redactor's placement. It is noteworthy that the Gospel of Thomas transmits the parables without

[15] E. Haenchen (*Die Botschaft des Thomas-Evangeliums,* "Theologische Bibliothek Töpelmann," 6 [Berlin: Töpelmann, 1961], 56 n. 68) suggests that the parable in Thomas looks "genuine" in the historical-critical sense because it is not interested in those touches which Matthew and Luke utilize to relate the parable to the history of the church and its mission.

[16] Cf. Montefiore, *op. cit.,* 61.

[17] Bultmann, *History of the Synoptic Tradition,* 190 f.; Cadoux, *op. cit.,* 62.

[18] Cf. Montefiore, *op. cit.,* 62.

[19] Jeremias, *Parables,* 96 f.; cf. Bornkamm in G. Bornkamm, G. Barth, and H. J. Held, *Tradition and Interpretation in Matthew* (Philadelphia: Westminster Press, 1963), 11.

setting.[20] In any case, it is certain that the body of the parables was handed on with greater fidelity than the context and interpretation.[21] A consideration of the contexts to which the Great Supper is assigned opens the way for the reconstruction of the history of the tradition.

Matthew introduces the parable of the Great Supper into a Marcan setting, viz., the Passion Week controversies.[22] With respect to his own framework, the Wedding Feast (22:1-14) falls within the "fifth book," in the narrative and debate material (19:2—22:46) which leads up to the final discourse (23:1—25:46).[23] More particularly, it is assigned to the second day of Passion Week, into which Matthew, like Mark, collects debate material. The first part (21:18—22:22) of this section may be divided into three units:

1. the fig tree (21:18-22)
2. the question of authority and the three appended parables (21:23—22:14)
3. the question concerning tribute (22:15-22)[24]

The question concerning authority is posed by the religious authorities (chief priests and elders: 21:23). The first parable (the Two Sons, 21:28-32) is presumably addressed to them, with the conclusion, "The tax collectors and harlots go into the kingdom but you do not" (21:31).[25] The second parable (the Wicked Tenants) is transparently a continuation of the same theme: in 21:45 f. the chief priests, to whom

[20] Jeremias, *Parables*, 97.

[21] Cf. N. A. Dahl, "Gleichnis und Parabel II. In der Bibel 3. Im NT," *RGG* II (1958), 1618.

[22] Matthew expands the Marcan section containing (1) the question about authority, (2) the parable of the Wicked Tenants, with (1) the parable of the Two Sons, (2) the parable of the Wedding Feast (= the Great Supper). The Wedding Feast is the third in Matthew's trilogy of parables.

[23] K. Stendahl, *The School of St. Matthew and Its Use of the Old Testament,* "Acta Seminarii Neotestamentici Upsaliensis," XX (Uppsala, C. W. K. Gleerup, Lund, 1954), 25.

[24] The second part, like Mark, contains three conflict dialogues.
1. The question concerning the resurrection (22:23-33)
2. The question concerning the great commandment (22:34-40)
3. The question about David's son (22:41-46)
These in turn are followed by the woes against the Pharisees (23:1-39) and the eschatological discourse (24:1—25:46), with its triology of parables (25:1-46). E. Lohmeyer and W. Schmauch, *Das Evangelium des Matthäus* (2d ed.; Göttingen: Vandenhoeck & Ruprecht, 1958), 302.

[25] On the exclusive sense of προάγουσιν (precede) see F. Blass and A. Debrunner, *A Greek Grammar of the New Testament and Other Early Christian Literature,* Robert W. Funk, trans. and rev. (Chicago: University of Chicago Press, 1961), sec. 245a (3); Jeremias, *Parables*, 125 n. 48.

are joined the Pharisees, perceive that he is speaking about them. Then follows the Wedding Feast.

The theme, conflict with religious authorities, their rejection of the kingdom and consequent exclusion from it, at hand in Mark, is developed and heightened by Matthew by means of the two parables (the Two Sons, peculiar to him, and the Wedding Feast, from Q [?]) which he inserts into this context.

A second motif, identified by Günther Bornkamm as characteristic of Matthew,[26] is superimposed upon two of the parables. This note, that the coming judgment applies also to the members of the congregation since they are a mixture of good and bad, comes to expression in 21:43 and 22:10, 11-13, 14. Furthermore, Matthew has amplified what Jeremias calls the soteriological motif[27] in the interests of hortatory preaching, i.e., the situation in the later church. These two motifs require further specification.

The notion that the church is a mixed body, requiring separation between the good and evil at the final judgment, is suggested at the outset by Matthew's construction of the discourse of John (3:1-12),[28] and is elaborated in the collection of parables in chapter 13.[29] In addition to the contextual motif that the judgment has fallen on the Pharisees, Matthew makes it clear in the parable of the Wicked Tenants, by formulations peculiar to him, that the disciples, too, must produce good fruits or forfeit the kingdom (21:41, reiterated as a conclusion in 21:43). This is the norm of the judgment, and hence the means by which Matthew brings his eschatology into relation to his ecclesiology.[30]

The same emphasis is achieved in the parable of the Wedding Feast by the appearance of three elements also peculiar to Matthew: (1) the generalizing logion in 22:14; (2) the addition (or fusion[31]) of the second parable, of the Guest Without a Wedding Garment (22:11-13); (3) the anticipation of the final separation by the phrase πονηρούς τε καὶ ἀγαθούς, in 22:10. Whether the phrase "both bad and good" (cf. Mt. 5:45) in 22:10 is original with the parable need not, and perhaps cannot, be determined; it emphasizes the indiscriminateness of the call

[26] *Op. cit.*, 20 f.
[27] *Parables*, 69, 76 f., 80, 89.
[28] Bornkamm, *op. cit.*, 15 f.
[29] *Ibid.*, 19.
[30] The juxtaposition of end-expectation and church is the theme of Bornkamm's essay.
[31] Jeremias, *Parables*, 65 f., 67 f., 94 and n. 16 (further references).

into the kingdom which is characteristic of this and other parables.[82] Nevertheless, when applied to the situation in the later church, such indiscriminateness constituted a special problem: was baptism a door which admitted all and sundry alike into the kingdom? The extension of the Wedding Feast in the parable of the Guest Without a Wedding Garment introduces the principle of merit,[33] and the generalizing logion in 22:14 ("Many are called, but few are chosen"), which does not comport with either the Wedding Feast or the Guest Without Proper Garment,[34] makes this principle acute by reversing the ratio of called to chosen: in the Wedding Feast few are "called" but many are "chosen."[35] Matthew has thus "corrected" the parable in view of the situation in the church of his time.

The soteriological motif, by which Jeremias means the refraction of the material in the direction of the history of salvation,[36] is developed in this context (1) by the connection of the parable of the Two Sons with John the Baptist (21:32),[37] and hence with the previous question concerning authority (21:25 f.); (2) by the further allegorization of the parable of the Wicked Tenants;[38] and (3) by the allegorization of the parable of the Wedding Feast. The last two Matthew has turned into allegories of the history of salvation. If, in the first instance, the Baptist is assigned his place in the history of salvation, in the last two a fully developed allegorical scheme emerges.

Confining our attention to the Wedding Feast, it would seem that

---

[32] Ibid., 65 and n. 67.

[33] Ibid., 66. The figure of the wedding garment is not sufficient in itself, perhaps, to substantiate the notion of merit. When taken in conjunction with 22:10 and 21:41, 43, however, this meaning seems beyond dispute.

[34] Admission in the parable of the Wedding Feast is indiscriminate, as has been noted, and in the second parable only one guest is turned out. Cf. Jeremias, Parables, 106.

[35] It should be emphasized that we are not here considering whether these elements are authentic tradition going back to Jesus or not, but only their function in this context. Jeremias (Parables, 227 n. 90) attributes the motif of the final separation of the disciples to Jesus, while Bornkamm (op. cit.) finds it to be characteristic of Matthew. There is not necessarily a conflict between these two opinions.

[36] Supra, n. 27.

[37] The connection of 21:32 with 21:28–31, according to Jeremias (Parables, 80 f.), is probably pre-Matthean, for John (cf. 21:32 with 21:25!) is the catchword which led Matthew to insert the parable in this position. In that case, the catch-phrase οἱ τελῶναι καὶ αἱ πόρναι (the tax-collectors and the prostitutes) probably precipitated joining v. 32 to the parable in the pre-Matthean tradition. However that may be, v. 32 is secondary to 21:28–31, and the juxtaposition of the parable of the Two Sons and the pericope on authority is certainly to be attributed to Matthew.

[38] See Jeremias, Parables, 70–77 for details. In Matthew's version the parable covers the history of redemption from Sinai to the last judgment (ibid., 77).

Matthew intends the first mission of the servants (22:3) to suggest the prophets and the rejection of their message, the second (22:4) to denote the apostles dispatched to the city (22:7b), i.e., Jerusalem, i.e., Israel; the latter underwent suffering and martyrdom (22:6), as a consequence of which the holy city was destroyed (22:7). The mission into the streets to collect every chance person (22:9 f.) would then reflect the mission to the Gentiles, and the entry into the hall (22:10b) might be an allusion to baptism. This nuptial feast, which is spurned by the invited but received by the uninvited, can only be the feast of salvation. However, only he who has a wedding garment is finally welcome (22:11 ff.). The survey of the guests (22:11) points to the last judgment, and the "outer darkness" (22:13) is obviously hell. If Jeremias is correct in this interpretation, Matthew's parable depicts the history of salvation from the appearance of the prophets to the last judgment.[39] That it has been allegorized is supported by its literal dependence at certain points on the parable of the Wicked Tenants, which immediately precedes.[40] On this view, Matthew justifies the mission to the Gentiles on the basis of Israel's rejection of the kingdom, but he also issues a warning to the church: "many are invited, but few are allowed to remain." Matthew has thus conceived the parable as a piece of apologetic and exhortation suitable to his own milieu.

It has been observed that Matthew has (1) expanded and intensified the controversy with the religious authorities which he took over from the Marcan context; (2) introduced the motif of the final discrimination among disciples; and (3) allegorized the parable as the history of salvation in order to undergird the mission to the Gentiles. Jeremias takes (1), viz., controversy with the Pharisees, to be the original context of the parable.[41] If this view is sound, Matthew has reintroduced the parable into an appropriate context.[42] On the other hand, Jeremias assigns the interpretation of the parable as a missionary

---

[39] *Ibid.*, 67–69.

[40] Cf. 22:3 ἀπέστειλεν τοὺς δούλους αὐτοῦ (he sent his servants) with 21:34 (identical; Lk. 14:17 has τὸν δοῦλον, his servant); 22:4 πάλιν ἀπέστειλεν ἄλλους δούλους (Again he sent other servants) with 21:36 (identical); the beating and killing of the servants in 21:35 f. is paralleled by 22:6; cf. 22:7 ἀπώλεσεν τοὺς φονεῖς ἐκείνους (destroyed those murderers) with 21:41 ἀπολέσει αὐτούς (will destroy them); the inexplicable treatment of the servants in 22:6 is explained by 21:35 f.: they had come to collect the rent! Jeremias, *Parables*, 69 n. 77 and p. 95.

[41] *Ibid.*, 44 f., 63.

[42] It is difficult to see why Jeremias regards Luke's context (table sayings) as apparently appropriate (97). A parable about a feast in a collection of table sayings does not seem to be sufficient warrant for saying the setting is appropriate.

command to the primitive church—i.e., (3) in part.[43] In that case Matthew has preserved and enhanced an interpretive nuance already attached to the parable. So far as can be determined, Matthew alone is responsible for (2), which justifies Bornkamm's view that this particular feature betrays Matthew's own interests. At all events, Matthew was sufficiently flexible to carry the tradition forward, retaining and developing certain elements he found in the tradition while adding another. In this process, however, the original thrust of the parable seems to have been lost, since the second and third have vitiated the force of the first, if indeed the first is of any assistance in recovering the original meaning of the parable.

The Great Supper occurs in Luke within the long and diverse "travel narrative" (9:51—19:27), as a part of a well-defined section consisting of table-talk in the house of a Pharisee (14:1):

1. healing of the man with dropsy—controversy over the sabbath (14:1-6)
2. etiquette of guests at banquets (14:7-11)
3. etiquette of hosts (14:12-14)
4. the Great Supper (14:15-24)

These materials appear to be linked together on the basis of their external relation to a feast.[44]

Formal linkage is provided by the phrase φαγεῖν ἄρτον, to eat bread, (14:1) which is taken up by 14:15 (in the exclamation of the guest). Again, δεῖπνον μέγα, a great banquet, (14:16) reflects 14:12 (ὅταν ποιῇς ἄριστον ἢ δεῖπνον, when you give a dinner or a banquet) and 14:8 ὅταν κληθῇς ὑπό τινος εἰς γάμους! When you are invited by anyone to a marriage feast; cf. Mt. 22:2, 3). The catchword in 14:7-24 is καλεῖν, to invite: 14:7, 8 (twice), 9, 10 (twice), 12, 13, 16, 17, 24. Jesus addresses: (1) the lawyers and Pharisees (14:3) at table (14:1); (2) those invited to a feast (14:7); (3) the host (14:12); and finally (4) a guest at the dinner (14:15 f.). As in Matthew, it is the Pharisees and lawyers who are the object of this discourse (cf. 15:2).

The parable is apparently taken by Luke to be a hortatory illustration of the point made more directly in 14:12-14: Luke has the servant go out and collect the poor, the crippled, the blind, and the lame (14:21).[45] Luke has therefore applied the parable to the community,

[43] Ibid., 64.
[44] Bultmann, History of the Synoptic Tradition, 325 f.
[45] Jeremias, Parables, 44 f., 64.

via the saying in 14:12 f., by making it turn on the distinction between friends, kinsmen, and rich, on the one hand, and the poor and disabled, on the other. This theme dominates the parable to an even greater extent in Thomas (Logion 64, Pl. 92. 34 f.), where for the first group is substituted tradesmen and merchants, while the second group is not specified at all.[46] Luke has thus linked the parable with the second half of the teachings given in 14:7-14, i.e., with the teaching on the etiquette of hosts (vv. 12-14).

Jeremias takes the second invitation to the uninvited (14:22 f.), as we have noted, to be an expansion of the original parable: Matthew and Thomas refer only to one invitation to the uninvited. Jeremias attributes this expansion to Luke's source.[47] But he thinks Luke may have read more into the double invitation than that the host wanted to have the banquet hall filled at all costs. In that case, Luke may have taken the first invitation to the uninvited to refer to publicans and sinners in Israel,[48] the second to refer to the Gentiles, which was a matter of great importance to him. Jeremias is of the opinion that the church had already interpreted the parable as a missionary charge,[49] but this emphasis comes to the surface only in Luke (14:23).[50]

"For I tell you, none of those men who were invited shall taste my banquet" (14:24) is problematic. The sentence sounds like Jesus' conclusion to the parable, introduced as it is by the formula, "For I tell you," "you" here being plural.[51] Taken together with the introductory exclamation (14:15), "my banquet" would then refer to the Messianic banquet (Lk. 22:30). So Luke understood it,[52] and the conclusion to the parable in Thomas appears to agree with this reading (Pl. 92. 34 f.).

---

[46] It should be noted, however, that in both Matthew (22:9) and Thomas (Pl. 92. 32 f.) the invitation to the uninvited is indiscriminate, while Luke has specified the second group in accordance with 14:12 f. B. Gärtner (*The Theology of the Gospel According to Thomas* [New York: Harper & Brothers, 1961], 47) is therefore mistaken in saying that the motif of the underprivileged has disappeared from Thomas' version, since the contrast is implied quite apart from Luke's particular formulation.

[47] *Parables*, 64; cf. 69.

[48] Equals city (πόλις): *ibid.*, 64, 69 (but cf. *infra*, 184 f. on Mt. 22:7b).

[49] *Ibid.*, 64.

[50] ἀνάγκασον εἰσελθεῖν, compel to come in.

[51] It is often noted that ὑμῖν does not agree with the single servant of the parable. For the introductory formula, cf. 11:8, 15:7, 10, 16:9, 18:8, 14, 19:26. Jeremias, *Parables*, 177 (cf. 45 and n. 80); Bultmann, *History of the Synoptic Tradition*, 184.

[52] On p. 69 Jeremias (*Parables*) affirms this view, but on p. 177 he appears to equivocate.

It is possible, however, that 14:24 was originally spoken by the host: γὰϱ connects 14:24 with the command in v. 23, and "my banquet" (v. 24) corresponds to "my house" (v. 23). How is one to understand κύϱιος (RSV "master") in v. 23? Is it to be held to the "literal meaning, i.e. "host," which derives from the narrative context? Has it acquired concomitant meanings (both "host" and "Jesus")? Or has a new "literal" meaning displaced the old one, i.e., has the meaning "lord" = "Jesus" = "the Christ" come to dominate the term?[53] Speaking for Luke, it is difficult to think that Luke did not at least have concomitant meanings in view.[54] In that case, Luke connected v. 23 with the conclusion to the parable as *he* understood it. This view is correlative with the tendency to allegorize the parable. If, on the other hand, the first "literal" meaning is original to the parable, how did Jesus understand the reference? Jeremias answers: "the earthly setting of the story forbids the supposition that Jesus himself could have uttered it as an allegory of the feast of salvation, but he may well have had this in mind, as well as the rejection of the invitation by Israel."[55] If he had this in mind, he must also have had in mind a nonliteral or metaphorical meaning of κύϱιος. Are we then to distinguish between what Jesus had in mind and what his hearers understood him to mean?[56] If so, the significance of the parable depends on grasping the concomitant meanings, whereas those who miss the point will be those who take it "literally."[57]

To return to the question regarding v. 24, its present form appears to be the result of an effort to raise the nonliteral meaning of the parable to the surface, to make sure that it is not missed. For this reason v. 24 is taken by some to be secondary.[58] On the supposition that it originally

---

[53] On the use of the word "literal" and the history of words, see Owen Barfield, "The Meaning of the Word 'Literal,'" in *Metaphor and Symbol,* L. C. Knights and B. Cottle, eds. (London: Butterworth Scientific Publications, 1960), 48–57.

[54] Cf. Jeremias, *Parables,* 45, where κύϱιος in the Gospel of Luke is taken predominantly to refer either to God or to Jesus.

[55] *Ibid.,* 69.

[56] Jeremias (*ibid.,* 72 f.) advocates just this distinction.

[57] On the other hand, those who take it "figuratively" would also miss the point, would they not, since the "point" (not application!) is made by the narrative and not by the "figurative" meaning. This might lead to the generalization, which requires development, that there are two types of "literal" interpretation: that which holds to the surface, i.e., earthly, meaning, and that which opts for the "figurative" meaning. The latter is, of course, allegory. It is for this reason that I put it pointedly: the significance of the parable depends on grasping the concomitant meanings.

[58] E.g. Bultmann, *History of the Synoptic Tradition,* 175.

had, in a slightly altered form, a literal meaning in the first sense, what is its relation to the parable? Jeremias again answers: even so, it breaks through the pattern of the narrative and "it is only a real threat if it refers to the Messianic banquet."[59] In short, it has no point (in the narrative) if it is restricted to its "literal" sense. Nevertheless, as the parallelism with Matthew (22:8b) shows, the host probably did make such a threat (cf. Thomas Pl. 92. 34 f.), although in Matthew it is not utilized as the conclusion. As was suggested, it is a floating item in the structure of the parable. Bultmann thinks Matthew may be more original at this point.[60] Granting that such a threat was made, Luke has placed it at the conclusion of the parable owing to *his* introduction (14:15): the two together provide a context of the Messianic banquet which was intended to interpret the parable.

The Lucan version of the parable reflects, as does the Matthean recension, various levels of tradition and interpretation. These may be set out in summary form:

1. By linking the parable with 14:12–14, Luke gives the impression that the parable is a hortatory illustration of the previous saying;

2. The second invitation to the uninvited, if an expansion, suggests that the parable has been partially developed as a history of salvation (cf. Matthew), involving the mission to the Gentiles;

3. The immediate setting—introduction (14:15) and conclusion (14:24)—leads one to read the parable as an allegory of the heavenly banquet. Jeremias attributes (1) to Luke himself, and (2) and (3) to his source.[61] As in the case of Matthew, he takes none of these to be original. Luke's source, and hence Luke, and Matthew apparently agree on one thing: the parable vindicates the mission to the Gentiles.[62]

III

Original context. Jeremias takes the original form of the parable to be a vindication of the gospel directed to Jesus' critics and opponents: to

[59] *Parables*, 178. Jeremias notes (178 n. 23) that E. Linnemann attempts to overcome this difficulty by suggesting that the original guests did not mean to decline the invitation, but only to say that they would be late (*Gleichnisse Jesu* [Göttingen: Vandenhoeck & Ruprecht, 1961], 95; cf. 3d ed. [1964], 95 f. and n. 161–64). I agree with Jeremias that this is a severe solution to the problem and, I think, overlooks the real issue.

[60] *History of the Synoptic Tradition*, 175.

[61] *Parables*: (1) 97; (2) 64; (3) 69, 177. Jeremias takes as evidence that (2) and (3) belong to Luke's source the fact that both developments are also reflected in Matthew.

[62] Cf. Jeremias, *Parables*, 64, 69.

them he says, you, like the guests, have slighted the invitation; hence God has called the publicans and sinners in your stead.[63]

Like A. T. Cadoux and C. H. Dodd before him, Jeremias rightly insists that an understanding of the parable depends upon identifying the situation into which it was originally spoken.[64] There undoubtedly was a tendency to transform parables (and other elements in the sayings tradition) spoken to Pharisees, scribes, Sadducees, and the crowd into words serviceable to the Christian community. In the process of transmission and interpretation, consequently, the church would have felt the need to readdress the parables, i.e., direct them to the church rather than to opponents and the public.[65] In seeking the original meaning, one must therefore ask: into what particular context was this parable originally spoken, i.e., was it addressed to the religious authorities (scribes and Pharisees, priests), the crowd (Israel), the disciples, or was it aimed into a context of which all these groups were constituent elements?

Now if the context provided by the Gospels is secondary, as has been rightly urged, and cannot furnish us with the original setting, how are we to discover the latter? The answer must be that we must look primarily to the parable itself, take up such clues as can be had from the history of tradition, and refer them both to what is otherwise known of the ministry of Jesus. There are various difficulties in the way of this process, which lead in the end, as it seems to me, to more weight being placed on the first than the last two. Nevertheless, it will be prudent to take as broad a view as possible.

Jeremias avers that the Gospel parables were addressed to Jesus' critics and not to sinners. "All the Gospel parables are a defense of the Good News."[66] The actual message of Jesus was couched in the direct offer of forgiveness, the explicit welcome to the guilty, the open call to follow him. The announcement that salvation is here is restricted to similes (not parables).[67] To be sure, Jeremias contradicts his own assertion, for example, when he concludes that certain parables were

---

[63] *Ibid.*, e.g. 45, 63 f.; here Jeremias is following the line developed by Cadoux, *op. cit.*, e.g. 12–14, 56, 59, 116, 138, etc.

[64] Dodd, *Parables*, 26, 31 f.; Jeremias *Parables*, 21 f.

[65] Jeremias' understanding of the primary function of the parable as employed by Jesus rests in part on this law of transformation, as we shall see. Cf. his remarks: *Parables*, 38, 42 (with a list of examples), and 113 (laws 5 through 10).

[66] *Ibid.*, 145.

[67] *Ibid.*, 123.

originally addressed to disciples,[68] the possibility of which he never denies, and when he states that certain parables were used to illustrate Jesus' teaching.[69] While at an earlier point he guards against a sweeping assertion,[70] the presumption always is that parable has the critic, the opponent in view.

It will be noticed that Jeremias is inferring from the direction in which the tradition developed that the original audience must have been predominantly Jesus' opponents.[71] He is supported, of course, by the presence of a considerable amount of debate material in the Gospels, as well as by the analogy of the rabbinic parables. On the other hand, I suspect Jeremias, like Cadoux before him, is confusing the argumentative character of the parable with a debate and controversy context; the two are by no means correlative.[72] It will be helpful, in any case, to inquire why Jeremias is so restrictive in his definition of the audience to which the parable was directed, and consequently of its primary function.

Jeremias conceives of the historical setting of the parable as comprised of a single, definite situation,[73] with a well-defined group as audience.[74] That the situation was concrete and definite we may grant; that it was single or that the audience was homogeneous is dubious.

A number of considerations prompt us to qualify Jeremias' assumptions, with the consequence that the question of the original setting of the parable has to be reopened, at least in certain respects. Other aspects of the recent historical work done on the parables are not necessarily affected.

Two considerations may be stated as historical probabilities. It is very likely that Jesus' audience was composed of a single, homogeneous group only rarely. Jesus may have spoken to a particular segment of his audience on any given occasion, of course, but it is by no means clear that the parabolic form as such requires us to understand that Jesus

[68] *Ibid.*, 160.

[69] *Ibid.*, 123.

[70] *Ibid.*, 21: "Moreover, as we shall see, they [the parables] were *preponderantly* concerned with a situation of conflict. They correct, reprove, attack. *For the greater part, though not exclusively,* the parables were weapons of warfare" (italics mine).

[71] I.e., extrapolating from the direction to a hypothetical zero point.

[72] See chap. 5, *supra*, 143 ff.

[73] *Parables*, 113.

[74] *Ibid.*, 40 ff.; cf. 22, 38, 166 ff., 169, etc. It is not altogether clear whether Jeremias wishes to distinguish three basic groups (religious authorities, crowd, disciples), or just two (those "outside," disciples). He sometimes distinguishes among the opponents as well.

had his critics, the religious authorities, primarily in view. Is it possible that the parable is designed to be spoken to a diversity of audiences simultaneously?

The second probability is that the parables were spoken on more than one occasion. Just as the proverb, the aphorism, the arresting simile bear repetition, the parable by its very nature is open to reiteration. The fact that many of the parables were transmitted in the first stages without context suggests that they were associated with no one particular situation, but rather were employed in a number of particular situations, which may not have been identical.

Neither the first nor the second of these probabilities, nor the two taken together, affords a sufficient basis for definitive conclusions. Their force is simply to put a question mark against Jeremias' thesis that the situation was singular and the audience homogeneous.

Two further considerations may take the form of questions of clarification. Does Jeremias mean by the vindication of the good news to opponents and critics, its vindication to those who were hostile to the content of the message? That is to say, is it hostility that defines an opponent or critic? If this may be presumed to be the case, it should be remarked that an audience can be hostile for various reasons, and it is wholly possible that the crowd (the sinners) and the disciples were also hostile upon occasion. Was it the presumption of nonhostility on its own part that led the later church to readdress the parables?

It has been noted, though not often enough, that the parables do not presuppose faith, i.e., a positive identification with Jesus, on the part of the hearers. Has Jeremias taken the absence of such a pervasive "Christian" milieu as evidence that the audience was regularly unfriendly? In the subsequent life of the church, the parables were more and more taken up into a context in which faith could be and was presupposed. It was inevitable, under the circumstances, that they should be understood differently. With the change of audience, however, was the church led to a presumption which had fatal consequences for the proper understanding of the parable, and hence the essential content of Jesus' message? To put it acutely, did the church have the right to assume that it was no longer offended, provoked at Jesus' claim? Did it achieve this right precisely by interpreting the parables as spoken into a situation in which faith was presupposed and hence as spoken without offense to the hearers?

These two questions are intended merely to point up the fact that the critics and opponents, taking Jeremias' own view as the point of departure, need by no means be confined to a specific social or religious group, and that they can even be understood as the community of faith where that community has domesticated the parable.

And finally, it is appropriate to add two reflections on the relation of Jesus himself to the parable. If Jesus spoke his parables primarily to adversaries, what is to be made of his proclivity to move to the side of his auditors? By this is meant his disposition to stand where they stand, to risk, as it were, the outcome of the parable with them.

In the first place, the parable as metaphor is open-ended, which means that Jesus is willing to confirm his hearers in their right to make a choice, to "hear" in their own way. Since the parable does not stipulate its terms in advance, it allows them to be discovered by everyone who attends to the narrative. Although the parable does not open, to be sure, onto just any world, it is nevertheless the case—and this is the point to be made here—that Jesus disposes himself to the parable as one who, like his hearers, is "listening" to what transpires in the narrative. That this is the case is demonstrated by the fact that Jesus does not preside over how the parable is heard. If he had wanted to control the "message" of the parable, he could have spoken in some more discursive mode of discourse. He thus accords the parable a certain measure of independence over against himself and, in so doing, moves to the side of his auditors vis-à-vis the parable.

Jesus also moves, in the parable, to the side of his auditors in looking out upon the everyday world. With them he affirms, "That's how it is." The parable confirms that Jesus sees the same mundane world as his hearers. If he then sees *through* the mundane world, he nevertheless sees through *what his hearers see*. He is initially one with them within the workaday world in which they both dwell.

Jesus takes up a position on the side of his hearers in yet another respect. Having projected the parable as that to which he himself is also listening, and having affirmed his own proximity to the everyday world, he "responds" to the parable by entering in upon the world to which the parable points. The parable, it could even be said, is an implicit invitation to follow him. The call to follow is possible only on the basis of the proximity of the one calling to those who are called. Now, of course, not everyone who is listening will be disposed to take the lead of the parable, to enter in upon its world. Jesus' position beside his hearers is circumscribed by his "response" to the parable: he is identified with tax collectors and sinners because they respond to the parable as he does, whereas the Pharisees and publicans draw back.

Nevertheless, Jesus' relationship to his hearers is not predetermined. It is they, by their response, who determine that relationship; not he. For his own part, he makes no conditions; the parable sets the conditions, and he must take his chances along with other hearers.

The last point has been formulated somewhat unguardedly and without attempting to demonstrate its validity. It may be corrected by noticing that Jesus' "response" is given, so to speak, with the enunciation of the parable itself. Response does not follow upon but accompanies the parable: the parable opens onto the world in which Jesus dwells, the world to which he gives himself, as it were, in the parable. As call to follow, the parable indicates that Jesus has already set out upon the way.

The point is confirmed, provisionally, by noting that Jesus is grouped with tax collectors and sinners. What the parables imply, the logia state (e.g., Mt. 21:31), and the Evangelists assume (e.g., Lk. 15:2). Doubtless Pharisees and others agreed. What this association of Jesus with tax collectors and sinners signifies is not merely that he took up the cause of those who needed a friend, but that the proper response to the parable is to hear it as a sinner, i.e., as one who is open to grace. He who hears it as a sinner hears it as a word of grace; others may indeed hear it as blasphemy. That Jesus moves to the side of sinners and "hears" the parable with them as a word of grace goes together with the absence of any claim for himself in the parable.

Thus if Jesus, on Jeremias' view, spoke his parables primarily to adversaries, it is difficult to make anything of his proclivity to stand with his hearers—unless, of course, one is to reckon Jesus himself among the critics and opponents. Before determining whether there is any sense in so bold a proposal, it is necessary to inquire, as a corollary, whether Jeremias has kept in view that Jesus is a part of the situation into which the parables were addressed. It is clear that Jeremias affirms this point in principle,[75] but the question is whether it marks the setting of the parables as Jeremias conceives it. We may put it this way: the parables, on Jeremias' view, are spoken from here (Jesus' situation) to there (the situation of critics, opponents, and the like). The question then becomes, to what extent did Jesus' situation enter into and qualify the situation of his audience (to use a less precise term)? To what extent does the correct understanding of the parables, on the part of both his original auditors and later interpreters, depend upon a grasp of

[75] Ibid., e.g., 228 f., 230 and especially 230 n. 1, where Jeremias affirms Fuchs' view that in the parables Jesus hides his own self-attestation.

the stage which was set by Jesus' own appearance upon it? In this respect, it would appear that Jeremias' view is a fragment: everyone simply becomes an opponent and critic.

It may be inferred from the preceding remarks that Jeremias' view of the parable as addressed to critics and opponents is to be affirmed, provided "critic" and "opponent" are understood generically. Jeremias does not apparently so understand them, but identifies them with particular religious groups (as is the case with the Evangelists writing from the standpoint of the later church). In the generic sense Jesus himself is a critic and opponent in that he is "offended" by the parable in his solidarity with his hearers. At the same time, Jesus can scarcely have opponents if he moves to the side of his hearers and identifies himself with them. What is being urged, to put it simply, is the metaphorical range of the terms "opponent," "critic," "Pharisee," etc., i.e., the literal and nonliteral meanings grasped concomitantly, and the expansive horizon of the parable as a mode of language, as opposed to an understanding of parable as a technique of debate.

These considerations lead to two further observations. In the first place, Jeremias fails to recognize that the vindication of the gospel is also its proclamation. What from one standpoint is a defense of the gospel, is from another point of view its affirmation. The parable is often a call to repentance, as Jeremias emphasizes,[76] a call to decision,[77] and is addressed as such to all "opponents and critics" who stand in need of such a call.

The church, in the second place, failed to notice that parables of this order, i.e., addressed presumably to those "outside," could be applied directly to itself. The church assumed a fundamental distinction between itself (those "inside") and those "outside." It was thus forced to reinterpret the parables in relation to its own self-determined situation. By so doing, it tended to take the edge off them.

We may therefore anticipate that the parables will identify their own audiences, not particular historical or sociological groups, to be sure, but the generic classes, those who heard him gladly and those who murmured, within a given audience. The historical probabilities are that any given parable was spoken on a number of occasions, with now this, now that group in view, or with a collage of groups in the forefront. The parable cuts across economic, social, and religious classes in the interest of its own basis of discrimination, i.e., the good news. It

[76] *Ibid.,* 169.
[77] *Ibid.,* 230; cf. 132.

is not that Jesus' audiences were not actual, or were not made up of more or less well-defined groups; but they were not monolithic with respect to the way they heard his parables.

We may also anticipate that those "inside," i.e., the church, tended to take the initiative away from the parable and "apply" it, in the process of transmission and interpretation, to its own self-determined situation.

IV

Original content and structure. Considerations respecting the original content and structure of the parable, like those with reference to the original context, will be correlative with how one understands the parable as a mode of language and what is taken to be its intentionality in a given case. This is only to say that it is finally necessary to look at the parable itself in resolving such questions, although what is known of the form and style of the parable from parallels, especially Old Testament and rabbinic, and from the history of the tradition provides valuable clues. Jeremias has demonstrated how important this procedure is in the case of original context, and a similar process is to be followed in the case of original content and structure.

The following brief remarks are restricted to problematical points. There is no intention of attempting to fix a single, original form, at least not in detail.[78] It is rather a matter of grasping the parable as a whole, with a view to determining what is constitutive and what is not.

1. *Introduction.* The introductions to the parable in both canonical versions (Mt. 22:1–2a; Lk. 14:15) are to be regarded as secondary. The Gospel of Thomas has none. The comparative formula in Matthew ("The kingdom of heaven may be compared to. . . .") is a favorite of Matthew and may well be his own invention.[79] Luke's introduction

---

[78] In accordance with n. 1 above.

[79] Dodd (*Parables*, 121), does not think the two canonical versions come from a single proximate source; he therefore hesitates to decide whether the parable was originally a kingdom parable. He notes (p. 32), however, that Matthew has not introduced the formula indiscriminately. Since Thomas shows a preference for the same formula but does not introduce it in this case, and since Luke does not use it, Jeremias (*Parables*, 102) grants the possibility that it may be secondary in Matthew. Jeremias further suggests that the parable of the Guest Without a Wedding Garment (22:11–13), fused with the Great Supper in Matthew, may have its introduction in 22:2, which would account for the change from a banquet given by a private individual (Luke, Thomas) to a royal feast (65, 67 f.; but on 94 Jeremias does not follow his earlier suggestion). If this view is adopted, the comparative formula may have gone with the Guest Without a Wedding Garment and not the Great Supper.

(14:15), which goes together with his conclusion (14:24), belongs, as we have seen,[80] to the later tradition which sought to interpret the parable as an allegory of the heavenly banquet.

2. *Number of invitations and to whom sent.* Matthew has turned the triple invitation in the direction of an allegory of the history of salvation.[81] It has been noted that the bulk of vv. 6, 7 represent an allegorizing expansion of the parable.[82] For these reasons, the double invitation to the invited guests would appear to be a rearrangement in dependence on the allegory, and the second invitation in particular would appear to have been reconceived with this in mind. If the second invitation gains its significance in the Matthean account from its contribution to the history of salvation, which is to be regarded as secondary, the double invitation to the original guests loses its force; there seems to be no reason for sending the servants twice.[83] Luke and Thomas both presuppose the original invitation, and the law of economy of detail precludes a pointless reiteration.

On the other hand, Luke's third invitation—the second to the uninvited—may also involve allegorical interests.[84] It is by no means clear why commentators should have fixed on the third invitation as Luke's invention, since the second is palpably Luke's own formulation in dependence on 14:12 ff. If one follows the principle of reduction to the least common denominator, one of Luke's invitations is surely contrived, for both Matthew and Thomas report only one invitation to the uninvited.[85] But is this principle sound? Thomas omits the wrath of the host (found in both Matthew and Luke), the filling of the banquet hall (also found in both), and elevates the excuses to absolute status: merchants and traders are excluded (his conclusion). Thomas has no interest, therefore, in who is to be included, but only in who is to be left out. Hence, for his understanding of the parable, the repetition of the second invitation would not fit, i.e., would be meaningless.[86] The interest of its own special point. It would therefore be hazardous to Thomas tradition may thus have omitted the third invitation in the

[80] *Supra,* 173–75.
[81] *Supra,* 170 f.
[82] *Supra,* 165, 171.
[83] Jeremias, it will be recalled, attempts to justify the double invitation by regarding the first as the original one, and the second as the courtesy reminder. I found difficulties with this view: *supra,* 164 f. and n. 4.
[84] *Supra,* 166 and n. 10; 173.
[85] Jeremias (*Parables,* 64) assumes this principle.
[86] Cf. Montefiore, *op. cit.,* 78.

forge an alliance between Matthew and Thomas, each of whom manipulates the invitations for different reasons. Beyond that, it should be recalled that Matthew, as Luke, does have *three* invitations, although they are arranged differently. This parallelism in triadic structure is characteristic of the popular narrative,[87] and constitutes an alliance of Matthew and Luke against Thomas.

In pursuing the question of the triple invitation, it is illuminating to scrutinize the evidence for the allegorization of the third invitation in the Lucan tradition. According to W. Michaelis,[88] "Go out into the highways and hedges" (Lk. 14:23) denotes the country lanes and hedges (enclosing vineyards) where the servant is likely to find rural idlers, some of whom have perhaps stopped to rest in the shade. The places where this group is to be found, so he argues, are clearly distinguished from "the streets and lanes of the city" (14:21). The hearer or reader would therefore think of two distinct groups, the second of which would be the more remote. Quite literally, he would think of tax collectors and sinners on the one hand, and the heathen on the other. But does the shift in place require, or even suggest, that two distinct groups are involved? After all, more of the same kind of people are to be collected from the country, the supply in the city having been exhausted. Whence do the equivalences, city = Israel, country = Gentiles, arise?

Jeremias thinks Luke took "city" (πόλις) in 14:21 to refer to Israel,[89] for which he adduces Mt. 22:7 (a reference to the destruction of Jerusalem) and 21:43 (as the previous parable shows, Matthew understood the invitation to the uninvited to mean the mission to the Gentiles) as evidence.[90] The fact that both Matthew and Luke know this allegorical significance of "city" proves, in his judgment, that it belongs to the tradition which underlies both of them. There does not seem to be evidence, however, that city = Israel was an established allegorical convention prior to its development in the parable of the Great Supper. The equivalence, "country" = Gentiles, furthermore, does not stand on its own, but depends on reading the first invitation as one directed exclusively to Israel.

The evidence for Luke's allegorization of the double invitation rests, as a consequence, solely on the interpretation which Matthew (or the

[87] *Supra*, n. 3.
[88] *TWNT* V (1954), 69. 8 ff.
[89] Jeremias, *Parables*, 64, 69.
[90] *Ibid.*, 68.

tradition before him) has read into the parable. The allegorical meanings of "city" and "country" are derived from Matthew, the first
directly, the second indirectly.[91] The first derives from Mt. 22:7, which,
as we have seen, is part of an allegorizing expansion of the parable
having to do with the outcome of his second invitation to the invited.
Matthew's third invitation and the only one to the uninvited does not
appear to reflect the distinction between city and country.[92] The distinction must therefore be Luke's invention, provided the equation city
= Israel came down to him in the tradition. But the evidence for this is
based on Matthew alone, since Luke has not read this interpretation
explicitly into the parable. Given the wide divergence between the two
canonical forms of the parable and the allegorical proclivities of
Matthew, it is too much to adduce Matthew's interpretation as evidence that an allegorical interpretation came with the tradition to
Luke.

It does not require much imagination to suppose, however, that
Luke may have *understood* the double invitation in an allegorical
sense. It accords well with his understanding of the history of salvation.
But there is an important difference between allegorical interpretation
and the creation of allegory.[93] It is the latter that must be demonstrated in the case of Luke's third invitation, and it is just this
demonstration that falls short.

The question whether a third invitation, as in Luke's version,
belongs to the original form of the parable does not, perhaps, admit of
final resolution. In addition to the considerations already adduced,
however, there are other factors which suggest that it may be original.
It heightens the conflict critically, pointing as it does to the motif of the
full banquet hall (Mt. 22:10, Lk. 14:23).[94] Moreover, it introduces the

---

91 I.e., the second emerges in Luke after the first has been borrowed from Matthew.

92 Matthew does not know of missions into the city and country, only of a mission
ἐπὶ τὰς διεξόδους τῶν ὁδῶν (into the main thoroughfares) (22:9; simply εἰς τὰς
ὁδούς, into the streets, in 22:10). If διέξοδοι τῶν ὁδῶν means the place where the
streets of the city emerge into the country, is Matthew conflating Luke's two missions, as
Michaelis (TWNT V [1954] 112. 18 ff.) suggests, or has he made it impossible to speak
any longer of a mission into the streets and lanes of the city (= Lk. 14:21) since he has
had the king destroy the city in 22:7?

93 The parable of the Wicked Tenants is an illustration of the point: Jülicher (*Die
Gleichnisreden Jesu* II [Tübingen: J. C. B. Mohr, 1899], 385–406) and Bultmann
(*History of the Synoptic Tradition*, 177) regard the parable as created allegory. Dodd
(*Parables*, 124–32) and Jeremias (*Parables*, 70–77) demur on the ground that not
everything amenable to allegorical interpretation must be regarded as created allegory.

94 The motif of the full house is overshadowed in Matthew, lacking, as he does, the
second invitation.

note of comic relief, which I take to be characteristic of Jesus' parables. These two elements contribute materially to the artistry and subtlety of the parable, on the one hand, and to the narrative image and hence the "message," on the other.[95]

3. *Number of excuses and content.* There is a certain disjunction in Matthew's version between the response to the first invitation (they do not intend to come) and the second; the two excuses (pretexts) offered have a certain parallelism with the first two excuses in Luke; the third response in Matthew is clearly an allegorizing creation.[96] Granted the discrepancies between Matthew and Luke,[97] there is still the correspondence in triadic structure.

In Thomas, on the other hand, there are four excuses. All of them concern preoccupation with commercial interests. There is thus an affinity with Luke's indirect attack on the affluent.[98] While they echo themes in Matthew and Luke, they are related more vividly and the context seems to be urban rather than rural.[99] Their apparent elaboration and extension indicate that the excuses themselves are of primary interest to Thomas.[100]

Luke's excuses reflect a rural setting and are three in number. Both elements accord well with what is known of the original milieu[101] and form of the parable.

The number, as it seems to me, is not especially significant, nor is the specific content, except that the excuses must be recognizable, viz., pieces of everydayness. The hearer must be able to agree, "this is the world in which I live." Although recognizable and cogent to the everyday mentality, the excuses in the end will appear trite.[102] In this respect, Luke's excuses fit, as do the first two in Matthew and the four in Thomas. Only the threefold structure weighs in favor of Luke.

4. *Conclusion.* Of the conclusion little further need be said. Thomas' ending (Pl. 92. 34 f.) is unique and clearly secondary. There are diffi-

---

[95] These points are developed in the reading of the parable, chap. 7.

[96] *Supra,* 164 f.

[97] In addition to the differences in content, there is also the fact that in Matthew they are attached to the second, in Luke to the first, invitation.

[98] Jeremias, *Parables,* 44.

[99] *Ibid.,* 28; Gärtner, *op. cit.,* 47 f.; R. M. Grant, *The Secret Sayings of Jesus* (Garden City, N.Y.: Doubleday & Co., 1960), 170 f.; Montefiore, *op. cit.,* 48, 56 f.; R. M. Wilson *Studies in the Gospel of Thomas* (London: A. R. Mowbray & Co., 1960), 100 f.; Haenchen, *op. cit.,* 56.

[100] *Supra,* 166 f., 173, 183 f.

[101] Chap. 5, 153.

[102] Cf. chap. 5, 153 ff.

culties, as has been observed,[103] in the way of accepting Luke's conclusion as original. The pronouncement of the host over the excluded guests comes in Matthew in a more natural position, with the result that the denouement is climaxed by the house being filled. The parable had no application.[104]

---

[103] *Supra,* 173 f.
[104] Cf. chap. 5, 133–36.

The Parable of the Great Supper:
A Reading and Theses

≥ 7 ≤

I

A CERTAIN MAN—IT DOESN'T MATTER WHO—GIVES A
banquet. To it he invites the elite of the community, those in the social
register.[1] But when the time of the banquet arrives, and they are extended a courtesy reminder of the engagement, they begin to make
excuses. It is clear they do not intend to show up. The host is understandably miffed, and in his anger instructs his servants to go into the
streets and alleys of the city, there to gather such riffraff as he may
find to take the places of his erstwhile invited guests. Although the
city is presently cleared of tramps and beggars, the table is by no means
full, so the host orders the servant to canvass the suburbs for others
of the same order. The great hall is taxed to capacity at last.

We ponder the scene.

Invitations have been issued, the great banquet hall is prepared for
the feast, the table is laden with sumptuous food and drink. The
servant is dispatched to inform the guests that everything is ready. But
they refuse to come. And why do they refuse? Various reasons are
given, but it is clear that, for one and all, more important matters
clamor for attention, or at least matters accorded greater weight in the
circumstances.

Already, as the story takes shape, we surmise that something is
amiss. Is it not wholly unusual that every single guest should refuse in
turn and at the last minute? Having scarcely begun, the parable puts a
strain on our credulity.[2] The picture, to be sure, has a common enough

---

[1] For internal evidence that the invited guests were of the aristocracy, see Jeremias,
Parables, 177, and cf. his remarks on the rabbinic parallel, 179.

[2] Jeremias (*ibid.,* 30) holds that such "extravagant exaggerations" are simply "characteristic of the oriental way of telling a story," but also useful in impressing the point

frame: a man gives a dinner and invites various guests. There is nothing unusual in that. But these guests all decline, and for what appear to be the most trifling excuses. Not that the excuses are not valid in themselves—the pressure of business, the claims of a new wife[3]—but in relation to the occasion, which we gather is to be something of a social splash, they pale into pretexts. The affair may even be a command performance (as Matthew has it, the host is a king). And so we grope vaguely toward the clue that this is no ordinary banquet.[4] Nevertheless, the gravity of the invitation has only begun to dawn: at first blush it is only a commonplace; whatever it is that lurks ahead has put in its appearance in a completely unostentatious and unheralded way.

All the more reason to inquire, we reason, why the affluent should not be able to arrange their affairs so as to attend this social event. Perhaps the host set it for the wrong day. But that is unlikely in view of the excuses. Could it be that the host himself is socially in disrepute and that the nobles of the community intend deliberately to insult him?[5] That is a possibility we should perhaps entertain. Of course, it may be that the story itself is simply unlikely, in which case the guests are made to behave like puppets. But it is also possible that those invited, like ourselves, do not at first grasp the importance of the occasion (Mt. 22:5: "they made light of it and went off. . . ."). But we are not given the circumstances surrounding the host and his friends; he remains an anonymous "certain man," and his guests are faceless, save for their station and their excuses.

Looking back on it, it seems important that the precise reference remain in obscurity. We could of course say that the certain man was Jesus, and that this is the way his invitations are treated. But Jesus does not make this connection. In fact, the situation does not fit Jesus. Jesus

---

upon the hearers. He allows, nevertheless, that "occasionally Jesus seems to have allowed the meaning of a parable to influence its text, thus introducing paradoxical elements into an otherwise realistic story." It is just these paradoxical elements, deliberately introduced into the narrative, which are to be regarded as significant clues. Cf. chap. 5, *supra,* 160 ff.

[3] Cf. Deuteronomy 24:5.

[4] Dodd believes that the audience would not have missed the allusion to the heavenly banquet, a symbol of the coming bliss (*Parables,* 121; cf. 55 f. for references to Mt. 8:11/Lk. 13:28–29; Mk. 14:25/Mt. 26:29/Lk. 22:18, 15–16). Assuming the possibility, such an understanding would have been, in its own way, a misunderstanding of the parable, involving a literal nonliteral reading. On this use of literal, see *infra* n. 9.

[5] The rabbinic counterpart to the Great Supper, cited by Jeremias (*Parables,* 178 f.), identifies the host as a tax collector and hence as one held in contempt by the aristocracy.

does not first invite the affluent to his party and only later turn to the outcasts when he is refused. He is not therefore thinking of himself in the third person. It is for this reason that we are right in resisting the temptation to allegorize. We must try to take the story as it is. Jesus appears to leave the matter dark so that his hearers are drawn into the story and invited to draw their own conclusions. In truth, the parable is an invitation to draw a conclusion.

Meanwhile, the banquet hall stands empty, except for servants.

Now comes a turn in the story which we do not quite anticipate. Quite naturally and understandably the host is angry. We expect him to say that he will never invite these particular people again—which in fact he does say. He may even venture a stronger remark with reference to their character. Be that as it may, he dispatches his servants with the admonition to go into the streets and alleys to gather in social outcasts of every order. "Bring along everyone you meet," are his orders. This indeed is a drastic measure. It is all the more surprising since the host is obviously a man with connections, with friends in high places. Now he turns to the lowly, to the beggars and tramps, to the socially odious. And he doesn't merely invite, he sweeps them into the hall (Lk. 14:23: compels).

After collecting the rabble from the city (as Luke has it), he turns to the country, and the crowd becomes a horde. The story takes on proportions of the ridiculous. Having crossed once into the land of make-believe, we have no difficulty in negotiating it a second time. Still, the incongruity is grotesque. While it was to have been a great banquet and many were invited, one servant appears to have been sufficient to make the round of houses, and we hear of only three excuses. Its greatness only now becomes evident. What was set out as a sedate dinner party for the aristocracy has turned into a festival for everyone abroad in the streets and meadows, and the capacity of the hall appears to be infinite. What will the poor man do, pray tell, for china? But all this introduces a touch of humor into the proceedings, which evokes a chuckle, or perhaps a grumble.

And we have a second, composite clue: the original guests have the door shut in their faces (the blush of belated discovery is there!), whereas those who might never have expected to be embraced are drawn onto the stage in indiscriminate numbers. This never-never-land banquet has quite turned things upside down.

To our surprise, the story is at an end. As abruptly it began, so boldly it ends. It does not draw to a close; it vanishes. In our imagination we may hear the massive door of the hall creaking shut, and the loud voices of merry-making and reveling within. But that is all. We cannot supply a conclusion, for there is none.

II

Now what does the parable say? We may presume that persons of both types represented in the parable, i.e., the affluent and the lowly, were in the audience. On the one hand, there are those who know that they would go to a banquet of this type—if the occasion were sufficiently auspicious, if they were invited, and if the social standing of the host were above reproach. They can see no reason why *they* would not come. But the story will not have it so. They decline, and for reasons which they recognize, which they have perhaps advanced before, but which they do not care to have exposed to public view. And so they resent being shunted aside. They are offended because the story is unbelievable. They do not want to be put down in this peremptory fashion, to be ridiculed without recourse. They want to know the circumstances, so that they can determine for themselves whether or not they will attend!

There are those, on the other hand, whose mouths water at the thought of so sumptuous a repast. They secretly aspire to be of sufficient social standing and affluence to be the recipients of invitations. But *they* know they will not be asked. By what stroke of fate, short of a Cinderella transformation, could they hope to be included in this elegant company? Only in fairy tales do beggars sit at the tables of aristocrats, to say nothing of kings' tables.

The story thus vibrates in the minds of those who hear for different reasons. A degree of anticipation is evoked in every heart. The listeners themselves run ahead to the outcome, though the destiny toward which they severally rush is shattered on the narrative; neither group is able to negotiate the abrupt corners. The story has no surprise ending, indeed it has no ending at all, and that's the rub. The ending is incorporated into the parable from the beginning, only it doesn't announce itself. Those who hear stand by dumfounded. The pause, however, is only momentary. The first group now *knows* it has been excluded; the second group *knows* it has been embraced. But not a word of application has been spoken!

On the one side, the parable is a parable of judgment. It sets in bold relief the trifling excuses which are conjured up as the basis for refusing the invitation. Again, we must resist the temptation to raise these particular excuses to the level of principles: it is not the call of business or the rights of a new wife, in themselves, that frustrate dinner parties, even messianic banquets.[6] These excuses gain their bite here because the refusal of the affluent was founded on just such excuses. What the excuses were does not greatly matter. The point is that the invitation was not heeded. The aristocrats are those who cling to the conventions of the world; this is what makes it impossible for them to perceive the gravity of the invitation. By what stretch of the imagination could they be expected to grasp the character of the invitation? By none at all. There's the razor's edge. The call came to them disguised, shrouded as a commonplace.

On the other side, the parable is a parable of grace. It has the host cast his cloak around those who did not expect, could not have expected, an invitation. And they are not merely invited—they, too, might have drawn back, much as one retreats before the unsolicited offer of a silver dollar[7]—but are swept into the hall. The social outcasts have nothing to cling to; this is what makes it impossible for them to anticipate the invitation, and to be open to it as a free gift when it comes. The call comes to them shrouded in the miraculous.

It is important to notice that judgment and grace are not spoken of directly. The audience is not alerted in advance that there are two groups. No one is identified. Rather, as the story opens, each hearer is drawn into the tale as he wills. He is allowed to take his place on one side or the other. As the story unfolds, he must make up his mind whether he can unfold with it, i.e., whether he is congenial to its development. If, as the story reaches its turning point, this one or that draws back, we know who he is! If, as the story comes to its climax, we see a smile pass these lips or those, we have identified him, too! The parable identifies each member of the audience, tells each one who he is, and with that the group is split in two.

Not only are the hearers divided, but those who have received the blunt end of the stick know they have stood in the dock. They may not care for the judge, or even condescend to acknowledge him, but they have heard the sentence. And those who find themselves unexpectedly favored have at the same time received their invitation. They know themselves to have been invited, indeed compelled. They understand

---

[6] The Gospel of Thomas does raise the excuses to principles and thus obscures the parable at its foundation.

[7] Beggars, out of Oriental courtesy, modestly resist until forced into the house: Jeremias, *Parables*, 177, citing F. Hauck, *Das Evangelium des Lukas* (Leipzig: Deichert, 1934), 192.

the invitation. They also perceive who it is that gives it. The situation has been qualified, willing or not, by the parable and him who speaks it, although the latter has not appeared for an instant in the picture he is sketching.

III

It is now time to come full circle: we proceeded from reflections on the nature of the parable as currently understood to a consideration of the parable of the Great Supper in particular and in detail. These in turn led to a reading which referred to and was founded (however obliquely) upon the former. It is now appropriate to elicit from the resultant interpretation of the parable such theses as illuminate its structure and intentionality. It should be borne in mind that these theses are constructed with a single parable in view; whether or not any, all, or none of them can be referred to other parables is left open.

The theses are accompanied, where appropriate, by commentary. It is hoped that the individual theses will illuminate one another, and that they hang together in a way which gives expression to the parable as a unitary field.

I. We may begin with the language and form of the parable.

1. The language of the parable is fundamentally *neutral* with respect to the prior question for both speaker and hearers.

The parable does not talk about what the speaker has *in mind* or what the audience *expects* him to talk about. The parable shifts attention away from the subject clamoring for attention. Its language is therefore disarming (what is the subject under discussion?). The subject matter does not come explicitly to expression in the words.

It may therefore be said that the language of the parable is metaphorical, in the sense that it talks about B when A is intended, as well as in the sense that it seeks to redirect attention, by means of imaginative shock, to a previously unapprehended whole of reality, and thus to evoke a new vision of what is really "there."

2. The parable is a (double) *paradigm of reality*.

The parable is narrative in form (parable = expanded metaphor), but it is not merely an account of a connected series of events which makes a point by analogy; it is not merely a story, real or fictitious, with a moral. It is a paradigm (model or declension) of reality.

The paradigm is double in that it juxtaposes (compares, but not overtly, and hence in the metaphorical sense) two "logics," two ways of viewing, of comporting oneself with, reality:[8] the one resides in everydayness, in the conventions of predication, and is therefore "literal";[9] the other roots in imagination, in revelation, and thus by the nature of the case, i.e., because it is nonliteral, is metaphorical.

3. The parable as a paradigm of reality unfolds the "logic" of the everyday world in such a way that it is (a) brought to the surface, and (b) shattered.

The parable exposes, brings to recognition, the way in which man comports himself with the world in his everydayness, and it breaks this "logic" upon a new and radically different "logic."

4. The function of the parable as a paradigm of the "logic" of everydayness is (a) to expose this "logic" from a neutral basis so that it is self-evident and self-validating.

The parable does not admit of debate; it is unassailably anchored in everydayness.

5. Further, the parable as a paradigm of the "logic" of everydayness functions (b) to draw the hearer into this "logic," so that he first recognizes it as his own, and—second—is forced to submit to or resist the new "logic" that contradicts the old.

The hearer, without prompting, affirms, "This is in the world in which I live," but his world is then ruptured by an alien "logic" which leaves him no choice but to confirm or deny: having been directed to a well-trodden path, he hastens unwittingly along it, not suspecting that a concealed chasm lies immediately ahead. Cf., for example, Nathan's parable addressed to David (II Sam. 12:1-6).

6. And finally, the parable functions (c) to expose a fundamental disposition to things at hand based on the new "logic."

The parable evokes a radically new relation to reality *in its everydayness*. The parable does not turn the auditor away from the mundane, but toward it. He discovers that his destiny is at stake precisely in

---

8 If the introductory formula, "The kingdom of heaven is like . . ." is indeed original with the parable of the Great Supper, it does not refer to any particular point or element in the narrative; but rather to the way in which the metaphorical language fractures the literal language. The comparison is not between the kingdom and a banquet, but between two ways of comporting oneself in the world. The comparison, if it is proper to use the term at all, depends on the figure as a whole.

9 I realize I am using the word "literal" in a way which requires that the sense vary from age to age. Owen Barfield restricts the term to the cast of mind endemic to the age shaped by the scientific revolution (e.g., *Saving the Appearances,* 83, 92, 135, 159, 162 f.; cf. his essay, "The Meaning of the Word 'Literal,'" in *Metaphor and Symbol,* L. C. Knights and B. Cottle, eds. [London: Butterworth Scientific Publications, 1960], 48–57). What I have in mind is the literalness exemplified by Nicodemus in John 3.

his ordinary creaturely existence. By means of metaphor, the parable "cracks" the shroud of everydayness lying over mundane reality in order to grant a radically new vision of mundane reality.

7. The narrative or pictorial (metaphorical) language of the parable, as a consequence (theses 1–6), is not merely incidental to its point.

It is indispensable, in the first place because the new "logic" must be "heard" in the language of the old "logic," as a consequence of which the language of the old "logic" must undergo a coherent deformation, by means of metaphor, in favor of the new "logic." The parable cannot be accommodated in the "logic" of everydayness, but neither can it dispense with language attuned to the mundane world; the metaphorical language brings the familiar into an unfamiliar context and distorts it, in order to call attention to it anew, i.e., to bring it into a new frame of reference, a new referential totality.

The parable's field of intentionality is thus none other than the mundane world. The new "logic" turns out to be, not an isolated entity alongside of or over against the world in its everydayness, but the mundane world transmuted.

In the second place, the metaphorical language of the parable is indispensable because it does not specify, but allows to be specified. While it keeps the initiative in its own hands, it is passive initiative. For this reason the parable can be launched upon a diversity of audiences, each segment of which will hear it in its own way.[10]

8. The narrative is marked by an element of comic criticism: it exaggerates the situation critically and thus exposes the nerve of the two "logics."

9. The function of comic criticism is (*a*) to debunk the "going" understanding of the everyday situation.

It exposes the pretensions of the prevailing way of comporting oneself with reality. In so doing it challenges the authority of the anonymous "they" by ridiculing it. (The invited aristocracy refuse an attractive invitation; the social outcasts are constrained to enter in hordes.)

10. The function of comic criticism is (*b*) to open the way for a

---

[10] This is not to say that each segment will hear it "correctly." In fact, it may be presumed that most audiences will grasp it in terms of established conventions and thus miss the point. Of the parable of the Sower Barfield writes: "And one can well imagine the reluctance with which Christ launched it on the ocean of idolatrous misunderstanding, where we still mostly find it today" (*Saving the Appearances,* 180). There is a sense, of course, in which the misunderstanding of the parable allows the point to be made.

radically new disposition to reality, a disposition that is marked by the tragicomical.

The breach of the old "logic" amounts to an invitation and so beckons the hearer to embark upon the new. At the same time, the invitation is extended with comic relief: it makes no pretension, but recognizes how ridiculous it appears, both to the anonymous "they," i.e., to the going view, and to itself.

11. The parable does not have a conclusion.

12. The parable does not require interpretation or application; it *is* interpretation in that it interprets its hearers.

The parable is a narrative (a paradigm of reality, marked by comic criticism) which shifts the outcome of the story to the audience: the auditors are split into two groups, those who resist the new "logic" and those who enter upon it, who accept the invitation. The choice is made inevitable by the way in which the story unfolds.

II. We may now turn to the con-text.[11]

1. The parable is message (not: has a message) in the con-text of the ministry of Jesus.

Strictly speaking, the parable does not say something else, i.e., something which can be articulated in nonparabolic language. A distinction between metaphor and meaning is alien to it. The parable does not teach something, but gestures toward. Interpretation of parables should take place, therefore, in parables.

The parable as message is the linguistic aperture onto a world qualified by something other than the anonymous "they." This x-factor, which shatters the old world, does not appear in the field of the parable (the parable opens onto mundane reality); its nonappearance does not signify, however, that it is extraneous to the new world—it is in and with the world brought into view by the parable: the parable does not require, or even permit, that the hearer look around to see what new factor has transformed the con-text. Nevertheless, Jesus "appears" in the penumbral field of the parable as the one who speaks it: in the parable he raises a new world into being, so to speak, out of the linguistic debris of the old. Jesus belongs to the parable, not as a

[11] Con-text is hyphenated in order to call attention to the ontological horizons of the referential totality within which the ministry of Jesus takes place. The parable "concentrates" a world in its narrative picture which relocates the aristocrats, servants, tramps, etc., who people it. This is another way of saying that the so-called historical (as naïvely understood) context is not adequate for discussing context because it assumes the identity of all worlds, i.e., con-texts. Cf. chap. 5, *supra*, 138 f., 142 f.

figure in it, but as author of the situation depicted by the parable. This one-sided way of putting it is to be corrected by saying also that the new world impresses itself upon the language of Jesus because it presents (both presents' and pre'sents) itself to him. In parable Jesus both witnesses to the dawn of the kingdom and brings it near. Jesus and con-text go together: he belongs to the world of the parable, and the world of the parable belongs to him. Jesus and his world are "spoken" in the language of the parable.

Insofar as message can be discussed at all, it must be discussed as con-text.

2. In the con-text of the ministry of Jesus, the parable is to be understood as a mode of language which gives concrete expression to his appearance as the word.[12]

3. Although, in this regard, the parable may be considered the self-attestation of Jesus, i.e., as the inverbalization of Jesus as the word, it nevertheless shifts attention away from God and from Jesus himself, i.e., from the religious question, to a specific way of comporting oneself with reality. God and Jesus remain hidden.

4. The parable is an oblique invitation on the part of Jesus to follow him.

Since Jesus belongs to the situation figured in the parable, it is he who has embarked upon this way, who lives out of the new "logic."

5. The invitation is not only a provocation; it is also permission.

The parable gives the right to follow. It does so by conjuring up a world which is "there" as con-text for those who care to dwell in it; the parable is not verified by reality, but verifies reality. Neither does the parable exact a price, except insofar as it offers a world which can be received only on its own terms.

6. The parable is an offense to the religiously disposed ("the Pharisees"[13]), but a joyous surprise to the religiously disinherited (the "tax collectors and sinners").

The parable, like the comportment of Jesus (he eats with tax collectors and sinners), is an affront to the "logic" of piety, but good news to the dispossessed because they have no basis for a claim on God. The latter but not the former can accept the "logic" of grace (both understand it, the former only too well). "The tax collectors and sinners go

---

[12] Cf. *supra,* Introduction, 129 f.

[13] It should be clear by now that this term, as well as "tax collectors and sinners," is also metaphorical.

into the kingdom of God but you [the Pharisees] do not" (Mt. 21:31). The parable therefore grants permission on the basis of grace.

7. The grace which is mediated in the parable and deed appears to be wholly indiscriminate: it embraces all who live solely on the basis of grace. Yet it equally radically rejects those who reject it, but does so only by offering itself for what it is.

8. Such grace is grounded only in parable: the parable offers no means of attesting grace—i.e., the new "logic"—other than the language event which gives presence to the world that is under the aegis of the new "logic." The new world is not just "there" for any and all to enter apart from language event. He who does not make the journey by parable has no means for travel.

9. The parable, on the other hand, is not a language event mediating grace apart from the new "world" which invokes the parable as parable. The parable is not raked up from just anywhere. Insofar as it is called forth by and opens onto the "really real," it need not argue the point, give reasons, or refer itself to some other criterion more dependable than itself. To do so would be to betray itself as true parable. As true parable it cannot fail and will always find faith. Grace is thus self-authenticating.

10. The parable must therefore be its own criterion. The only means of testing faith is to attend to the parable: if the hearer is not offended, if he willingly and joyfully enters in upon the "logic" of grace, there is true faith.

The Old Testament in Parable:
The Good Samaritan

⤜ 8 ⤛

THE OLD TESTAMENT IS POSED AS A PROBLEM INITIALLY
for the church by its own constitution of the canon: it embraced the
two Testaments in a single canon, but drew a line between them and
marked the discontinuity by designating one the *Old* in contrast to
the *New*. The Old Testament is also a problem by virtue of the conflict between Jewish and Christian interpretation. This tension has
been heightened, furthermore, by the rise of the critical historical
method. This method, which endeavors to let the Old Testament
speak for itself, points back to but is not identical with Jewish interpretation. How the Old Testament may be appropriated by the Christian faith was consequently a problem for the church from the beginning, and has reappeared, under the impact of the historical method,
as a theological problem of the first magnitude in recent times.[1]

Apparently from the very first, perhaps in the wake of the precedent
of Jesus, the church undertook its own interpretation of scripture (i.e.,
the Old Testament) in support of its claim to the Old Testament as its
own book.[2] In claiming the Old Testament as its own, the church was

---

[1] Cf., e.g., B. W. Anderson, ed., *The Old Testament and Christian Faith* (New York:
Harper & Row, 1963); C. Westermann, ed., *Essays on Old Testament Hermeneutics*
(Richmond, Va.: John Knox Press, 1963).

[2] According to H. Conzelmann, *The Theology of St. Luke,* G. Buswell, trans. (New
York: Harper & Brothers, 1960), 162, it is a special theme of Luke that scripture
belongs to the church by virtue of the fact that it has the "correct" interpretation, a view
that plays its role in Luke's argument that the church is the legitimate heir of Israel.

It is instructive to notice that both Roman Catholicism and Judaism have understood
this point in one way, Protestantism in another. For the former, what is revealed in
scripture cannot be properly understood apart from tradition which correctly interprets
scripture. Valid tradition and possession of scripture therefore go together. Tradition,
moreover, is understood as the solution to the hermeneutical problem. Protestantism, on
the other hand, so far as it remains under the influence of the Reformation, rejects this

obliged to distinguish its interpretation from that of Judaism, and thus
in the end to distinguish its understanding of scripture as scripture
from that of Judaism. For an understanding of the scripture principle
is contingent upon, or correlative with, a hermeneutic.[3] If the church
subsequently set its interpretation of the Old Testament alongside that
of Judaism, as a rival interpretation resting upon the same understanding of the scripture principle, it did so at the peril of losing its claim
upon the Old Testament. And the rise of historical criticism has tended
to heighten the peril and make the claim more tenuous. In short, the
church's right to embrace the Old Testament in its canon cannot be
justified merely on the ground that the church, like Judaism, acknowledges sacred scripture.

The canonical status of the Old Testament was never actually a
central issue in the church, except in those heretical movements, e.g.,
Marcionism, which felt that the Old Testament could not be appropriated "on its own terms." It was what the Old Testament had to say for
itself, assessed in the light of his own understanding of the Christian
message, that led Marcion to reject it. But the unwillingness to appropriate the Old Testament "on its own terms" is reflected also by
Christian orthodoxy, which sought to buttress its claim by applying a
new hermeneutic. If, in retrospect, it looks as if the church read its own
faith back into the Old Testament by means of allegory, typology, and
the like, it should be recalled that this solution proved more viable than
rejecting the Old Testament outright. That is to say, orthodoxy chose
to do battle over the correct interpretation of the Old Testament rather
than relinquish its claim to the scriptures of Israel.

Now that historical criticism has once again brought into the foreground the tension between the Old Testament understood "on its own
terms" and Christian interpretation of it—that is, broadly speaking,
between Jewish and Christian claims to the Old Testament—it is not
surprising that, as an option to ignoring the Old Testament or rejecting it altogether, attempts are being renewed to interpret the Old
Testament in a specifically Christian, or christological, sense.[4] Nor is it
surprising that a strict historical interpretation of the Old Testament

---

understanding of tradition, and thus this means of laying claim to scripture. It has to
devise other means of validating its claim, with the consequence that hermeneutic
remains a perennial problem in Protestantism. Cf. Gerhard Ebeling's lucid discussion in
Word and Faith, 305 ff.

[3] Cf. Ebeling, *ibid.*

[4] See *infra,* n. 31.

almost always has a Marcionite tinge to it when viewed theologically. To the extent that historical interpretation tends to coincide with Jewish interpretation, attempts to construct a specifically Christian interpretation gain urgency and vindicate themselves as efforts to save the Old Testament for the church.

Efforts to salvage the Old Testament for the church by means of christological interpretation, by whatever hermeneutical device, are bound to fail unless it is seen that hermeneutic is correlative with an understanding of scripture as scripture. If one chooses to contest Jewish or critical historical interpretation, he must also be prepared to contest the understanding of the scripture principle upon which they rest. For what scripture is cannot be divorced from how it is to be interpreted. The fact that the *what* of scripture is taken for granted makes the hermeneutical problem impossible of solution along any but traditional lines. And these lines have reached an impasse, with the weight falling on the Jewish side by virtue of the historical method.

The following essay is a preliminary attempt to approach the question from a New Testament perspective, without losing sight entirely of the theological problem. Specifically, it approaches the problem from the standpoint of Jesus' use of scripture in parable. Needless to say, the following study is based on previous considerations of the parable. However, taking up the problem of Old Testament interpretation from a New Testament perspective is not thereby justified. It has been said that critical historical interpretation tends to converge with Jewish interpretation on the assumption that the Old Testament was[5] a Jewish book. But historical interpretation cannot draw a line across history at the turn of the ages and insist that all historical interpretation of the Old Testament must draw on data from prior to that juncture as its basis. How Jesus and the primitive church interpreted the Old Testament also provides us with historical data—and Jewish data at that! These data must also be taken into account in historical interpretation.

From this it is not to be inferred that the hermeneutical methods of Jesus and various segments of the early church should automatically commend themselves to the church as viable solutions to the problem of Old Testament interpretation. Understanding of these methods is,

---

[5] The tense is important: it is only the fact that the Old Testament *was* a Jewish book before the rise of the church that promotes this alliance. That the Old Testament is still a Jewish book is not relevant to historical criticism; it is now also, by the claim of the church, a Christian book, which is equally irrelevant.

of course, prerequisite to assessment. And understanding requires that hermeneutic and what is concomitant therewith, understanding of scripture as scripture, be brought into view. It is possible that by grasping the way in which Jesus interpreted scripture we shall come upon his hermeneutic and his understanding of scripture as such, which in turn may open the way to a reconsideration of how the church both understood and misunderstood Jesus' use of scripture. It is quite possible that the locus of the problem, when grasped in this way, will undergo a radical shift. The question may not turn so much on how Jesus or the church or Israel manipulated scripture, as on how scripture manipulated Jesus, the church, and Israel when brought into the context of the appearance of Israel's Messiah. In that case, understanding of the Old Testament does indeed turn on whether the Messiah has come, as the early church thought. An attempt to open the problem up from the side of Jesus' use of scripture in parable, if successful, may illuminate the contemporary theological problem as well.

The isolation of the parable within the Jesus tradition, in view of the preceding chapters, does not require further justification.[6] But the relation of scripture to parable is problematical, and it is to that connection that attention must first be given.

I

Scripture may be said to function in relation to the parable (including the rabbinic parables) in three ways: (1) as the text for which the parable is exposition; (2) as the source of the basic image or figure utilized in the construction of the parable; or (3) as the means of elucidating or enlivening the parable.

According to Jeremias, the primitive church introduced scriptural references and allusions into the parables of Jesus, usually in support of allegorizing tendencies (e.g., the parable of the Wicked Tenants), but there is scant evidence that Jesus cited scripture explicitly to any significant degree in the body of his parables. Hence, if only for the reason that the parable makes little or no overt and explicit use of of scripture and scriptural allusion in the narrative body of the parable.[7]

It is a different matter to assert that Jesus drew upon Old Testament

---

[6] Cf. *supra*, Introduction, 129 f.

[7] In his survey of the influence of the Old Testament on the parables, Jeremias (*Parables*, 31 f.) notes that there is a remarkably small number of references to

imagery in the construction of his parables, for in this case it is not a matter of scriptural quotation or allusion, but of dependence upon a common reservoir of images, of reference to a system of interlocking images and figures, known and meaningful in and of themselves to the hearer. The parable would then depend for its significance on the ability of the hearer to catch the overtones, to supply, as it were, out of his own heritage, the body of the image, which alone has the power to let the parable speak. Harald Riesenfeld has argued that the parables make use of a repertory of Old Testament images and motifs in a quasi-allegorical way,[8] with the consequence that the parables of Jesus are not really intelligible to someone not immersed in Old Testament lore. Riesenfeld's student, Birger Gerhardsson, has attempted to make the case for the parable of the Good Samaritan in particular, not only that Jesus draws upon Old Testament imagery, but that he employs well-known rabbinic techniques of interpretation.[9] It is my intention to examine this effort more closely in due course.

It should be noted that the view advocated by Riesenfeld and Gerhardsson apparently runs counter to the widely held view that the parables are realistic in essence, that they reflect the everyday world. C. H. Dodd has put the matter well.

---

scripture. Luke 13:24–30 is a mosaic: the conclusion of one parable (Mt. 25:10–12) is merged with three related similes (Mt. 7:13 f., 22 f., 8:11 f.), two of which involve scriptural references (Lk. 13:27/Mt. 7:23 = Ps. 6:8; Lk. 13:29/Mt. 8:11 = Ps. 107:3) (Jeremias, 95 f.). Mt. 25:31, 46 may be editorial (Jeremias, 31 n. 27; 84 n. 83; 206). The allusions to Isa. 5:1 ff. and Ps. 118:22 f. in the parable of the Wicked Tenants (Mk. 12:1–12 and parallels) are seen to be secondary by a comparison of the three Synoptic versions and Thomas (Logion 65): Luke and Thomas lack the former, and Thomas reports the latter as an independent logion (66) (Jeremias, 31). Mark 4:32 and parallels (the Mustard Seed), Mt. 13:33 and parallel (the Leaven), and Mk. 4:29 (Seed Growing Secretly) may contain original scriptural allusions; in the first two instances, however, Jesus employs the Old Testament images in their opposite sense (Jeremias, 31 f., 149)! In addition, Jeremias thinks the publican's prayer in Lk. 18:13 may reflect the opening words of Ps. 51 (Jeremias, 144). While there appears to have been a tendency in the tradition to elucidate the parables by means of scripture, the instances in which scripture was utilized by Jesus in the elaboration of the parable seem to have been small indeed (*ibid.*, 32).

[8] "The Parables in the Synoptic and the Johannine Traditions," *Svensk Exegetisk Årsbok* 25 (1960), 37–61, cited by Wilder (*Language of the Gospel,* 81); cf. E. Hoskyns and N. Davey, *The Riddle of the New Testament* (London: Faber & Faber, 1931), 182–88.

[9] Birger Gerhardsson, *The Good Samaritan—The Good Shepherd?* "Coniectanea Neotestamentica" XVI (Lund: C. W. K. Gleerup, 1958).

Each similitude or story is a perfect picture of something that can be observed in the world of our experience. The processes of nature are accurately observed and recorded; the actions of persons in the stories are in character; they are either such as anyone would recognize as natural in the circumstances, or, if they are surprising, the point of the parable is that such actions *are* surprising.[10]

Neither Dodd[11] nor Amos Wilder[12] wishes to press this characteristic too far: it is possible, both would allow, that now and then there are allegorical overtones in what is otherwise a completely human and realistic picture or narrative. Nevertheless, Wilder insists, "the impact of the parables lay in their immediate realistic authenticity," and to press the concrete, realistic images in the direction of allegorical ciphers "is to pull the stories out of shape and to weaken their thrust."[13]

If realism and allegory are occasionally compatible (extended allegory tends, as a rule, to weaken realism[14]), it is to be wondered whether secularity and allegory dependent upon the Old Testament stock of images can be reconciled, even occasionally. Lucetta Mowry has noted that the subject matter of the parables, with four exceptions, is secular,[15] and Wilder suggests that the naturalness and secularity of the parables points to something very significant about Jesus and the gospel, viz., that for Jesus man's destiny is at stake precisely in "his ordinary creaturely existence."[16] Ernst Fuchs puts it pointedly: "Jesus does not use the details of this world only as a kind of 'point of contact'; instead, *he has in mind precisely this 'world.'* "[17] If the secular world is the "field" intended by the parable, does the Old Testament stock of images belong to this world as part of its secular landscape? If so, what are the consequences for Jesus' use of the Old Testament?

10 Dodd, *Parables*, 20 f. (italics his). Cf. chap. 5, *supra*, 152–60.

11 *Op. cit.*, 21; cf. his remarks on the symbol of the heavenly banquet (p. 121), which Jesus alludes to merely as a banquet.

12 *Language of the Gospel*, 81 f.

13 *Ibid.*, 81. Cf. his further remark on the same page: "In the parable of the Lost Sheep the shepherd is an actual shepherd and not a flash-back to God as the Shepherd of Israel or to the hoped-for Messiah who will shepherd Israel."

14 Dodd, *Parables*, 19 f.

15 "Parable," in *The Interpreter's Dictionary of the Bible*, III (Nashville, Tenn.: Abingdon Press, 1962), 650. The exceptions are: the Rich Fool, the Rich Man and Lazarus, the Publican and the Pharisee, and the Good Samaritan. It might be inquired whether the "religious" content of these four parables is really religious, or whether it is religion viewed as a secular phenomenon.

16 Wilder, *Language of the Gospel*, 82.

17 "The New Testament and the Hermeneutical Problem," in *New Frontiers* II, 126 (italics his).

This matter can be viewed from still another perspective. Assuming that Jesus is drawing upon a repertory of images belonging to the common Jewish heritage, is there anything determinative in this fact for his relation to the Old Testament? Could Jesus, for example, have drawn upon the Homeric metaphors with equal effectiveness, had his audiences been steeped in the Iliad and Odyssey? Or is the Old Testament the necessary linguistic school for the Christian faith? We are here touching upon the root problem of the relation of the New Testament to the Old Testament, which could be specified, to take one example, as the problem of typology. Even if it were established that there is *some* inner relation between the Old Testament images and the parable, it would still be necessary to inquire *what* this relation is.

This line of reflections may be arbitrarily terminated in order to note the first way, mentioned above, in which scripture may be related to the parable. The rabbinic parables are characteristically used in the exposition of scripture.[18] Gerhardsson is certainly justified in saying that one might antecedently expect Jesus to use the parable for this purpose also.[19] This is not often assumed to be the case, and indeed there is little evidence to indicate that Jesus did employ the parable in the exposition of scripture. One ostensible exception is the parable of the Good Samaritan in its Lucan context (Lk. 10:25–37). It is just this point that is felt to provide the sharpest contrast between the rabbinic and Jesus' use of parables. Let Bornkamm summarize:

The rabbis also relate parables in abundance, to clarify a point in their teaching and explain the sense of a written passage, but always as an aid to the teaching and an instrument in the exegesis of an authoritatively prescribed text. But this is just what they are not in the mouth of Jesus, although they often come very close to those of the Jewish teachers in their content, and though Jesus makes free use of traditional and familiar topics.[20]

---

[18] P. Fiebig, *Die Gleichnisreden Jesu im Lichte der rabbinischen Gleichnisse* (Tübingen: J. C. B. Mohr, 1912), 239 f.; L. Mowry, *op. cit.*, 652; Gerhardsson, *op. cit.*, 25; Eberhard Jüngel, *Paulus und Jesus. Eine Untersuchung zur Präzisierung der Frage nach dem Ursprung der Christologie*, "Hermeneutische Untersuchungen zur Theologie," 2 (Tübingen: J. C. B. Mohr [Paul Siebeck], 1962), 166. Amos Wilder (*Language of the Gospel*, 81 n. 1) rightly warns against overemphasizing this point: the rabbinic parables are occasionally prophetic and noncasuistic in character; cf. Berakoth 28b, Pirke Aboth 3.17, Shabbath 153a.

[19] *Op. cit.*, 25.

[20] Günther Bornkamm, *Jesus of Nazareth*, Irene and Fraser McLuskey, with J. M. Robinson, trans. (New York: Harper & Brothers, 1960), 69. Cf. P. Fiebig, *op. cit.*, 239 f., 260.

It will now be clear that the relation of the parables to scripture in Jesus' usage is entirely problematic. Were it not for the position which the parables occupy in the tradition and the importance they are accorded by those of varying persuasions, one would be inclined to look elsewhere for light on Jesus' relation to the Old Testament. It would be possible, of course, to proceed *via negativa* and eliminate all possible contact between the parable and scripture. A detailed demonstration of this order would only be a tour de force, were it successful. It remains to examine with care those cases where the tradition has reported a connection between scripture and the parable, or where there is reason to suspect a connection not explicitly recorded. Attention will be devoted here exclusively to the parable of the Good Samaritan.

The reasons for selecting the parable of the Good Samaritan are two. In the first place, the Lucan context connects the parable with the lawyer's question about eternal life (Lk. 10:25–28), which is initially answered out of the law. The parable would appear to be a midrash on the second part of the commandment. In the second place, starting out from the patristic tradition that the parable is a christological allegory, Gerhardsson has argued that Jesus draws upon the Old Testament imagery of the good shepherd (with its constellation of meaning), and employs well-known rabbinic techniques in debating the interpretation of the commandment with the lawyer in question. Together or singly, these could afford valuable clues to Jesus' use of the Old Testament and specifically to his hermeneutic. The balance of this chapter will in effect be a study of the parable and of Gerhardsson's interpretation of it.

II

Gerhardsson first considers the parable of the Good Samaritan apart from its context.[21] The parable is not concerned with the injured man, but with the three persons who come across him, as the concluding question (Lk. 10:36) shows. The challenge to the hearer is to identify the true neighbor: he is, of course, the Samaritan.[22] Adopting Jeremias' view that the parables of Jesus are marked by a polemic directed against the Jews, particularly the Pharisees and their scribes,[23] Ger-

---

[21] I.e., omitting Lk. 10:25–28, 37b (the imperative), but including vv. 29, 36–37a (Gerhardsson, *op. cit.,* 9 f.).
[22] *Ibid.,* 10.
[23] Jeremias, *Parables,* 21 f., 123, 145 f., 166 f., 169, *et passim.*

hardsson reasons that the parable is intended as a criticism of the Jewish leaders.[24] It cannot be accidental, furthermore, that the parable exhibits such striking affinities with the shepherd motif found in the Old Testament, particularly in Ezekiel 34. The elements are the same: "The defenseless flock, abandoned by the false shepherds, given over to wild beasts, receiving the promise of the true shepherd."[25] The interpretation which suggests itself is therefore the following: the injured man represents Israel, the priest and Levite the religious leaders, and the Samaritan is the true shepherd ($r'h$ ysr').[26]

Is there any other support for this understanding of the parable? Indeed there is. It is to be found in the significance of the name Samaritan (the significance of names is utilized in patristic exegesis as well as in the Jewish, including Old Testament, and early Christian tradition),[27] and in the double meaning of the root of the word for shepherd, r' or $r'h$.[28] Σαμαρίτης represents *šmrwny*, derived from *šmr*, which means both to "watch over" and "to keep, observe." The intransitive verb can mean "to be a shepherd" (e.g., Hos. 12:12), the present active participle "shepherd" (e.g., I Sam. 17:20). Like *rō'eh*, *šōmēr* is used to designate God and his anointed. The Samaritan in the parable thus stands for the true shepherd, who is also the true keeper of the law.[29] In patristic exegesis it was a commonplace, beginning with Origen, to note that Samaritan meant *watchman*.[30] The patristic tradition, then, which universally interpreted the parable christologically,[31] has preserved under its "florid allegorizing" the original sense

[24] The priest and the Levite do not represent a Jewish party, but the religious leaders as a whole (*op. cit.*, 11 n. 2); cf. chap. 5, *supra*, 143–45, 161 f.; chap. 6, 176–82.

[25] Gerhardsson, *op. cit.*, 14. On pp. 11–14 he analyzes Jn. 10:1–16 and Ezek. 34 as a basis of these judgments; he concludes that Ezek. 34 lies behind Jn. 10.

[26] *Ibid.*, 14 f.

[27] *Ibid.*, 15–18.

[28] *Ibid.*, 19–21, 25–29.

[29] *Ibid.*, 17.

[30] *Ibid.*, 15.

[31] *Ibid.*, 3–5. Gerhardsson summarizes, p. 5: *"The 20th century exegetes seem as united in their opposition to a christological interpretation as the early fathers in their support of it."* Italics his.

Twentieth century-exegetes are not quite as united as Gerhardsson seems to think. Cf. Paul Fiebig's early attack upon Jülicher's strong opposition to allegory (*op. cit.*; also *Altjüdische Gleichnisse und die Gleichnisse Jesus* [Tübingen und Leipzig: J. C. B. Mohr (Paul Siebeck) 1904]; and Bultmann's remarks, *History of the Synoptic Tradition*, 197 ff.). This was followed up by Gerhard Kittel, *Jesus und die Rabbinen* (Berlin: E. Runge, 1914), p. 7; F. Hauck, *TWNT* V (1954), 747, 750; and J. J. Vincent, "The Parables of Jesus as Self-Revelation," in *Studia Evangelica*, K. Aland *et al.*, eds. (Berlin: Akademie-Verlag, 1959), 79–99, especially 81. Among the list of those either attacking

of the parable, viz., that the subject was Christ himself.[32]

Similarly, the Greek word πλησίον, "neighbor," represents the Hebrew word $re^{a'}$. The Hebrew word for shepherd is $ro'eh$. These words are graphically quite similar, and even their phonetic difference is slight in many forms; moreover, they derive from a single verb, $ra'ah$.[33] "It is not too rash to suggest," says Gerhardsson, "that this parable did not originally deal with who is the *true neighbor, re^{a'} (rē'eh)*, but who is the *true shepherd, ro'eh.*"[34] Such an interpretation is possible on the basis of the rabbinic rule that a word may be interpreted in its double significance.[35] The lawyer asked a question concerning the commandment (Who is my neighbor?) and received an answer about the true shepherd.[36] Such wordplay strikes the modern reader as grotesque, but it is quite in accord with the techniques of Jewish midrash, as exemplified, for example, at Qumran.[37]

The shift in meaning must have taken place before the parable took its canonical form, for the Greek word πλησίον preserves the secondary interpretation, which accords with the proclivity of the church for transforming the parables into didactic and paraenetical vehicles for its own situation;[38] the church would not need reminding of who the true shepherd was, but they would be interested in the lawyer's question! The secondary meaning was secured by the final imperative: "Go and do likewise."[39]

The Lucan context, in Gerhardsson's judgment, supports his analysis

---

Jülicher or attempting to re-establish an allegorical method of interpretation, in addition to Gerhardsson should be numbered J. Daniélou (*infra,* n. 45); Raymond E. Brown, "Parable and Allegory Reconsidered," *NT* 5 (1962), 36–45; J. Arthur Baird, "A Pragmatic Approach to Parable Exegesis: Some New Evidence on Mark 4:11, 33–34," *JbL* 76 (1957), 201–207; E. J. Tinsley, "Parable, Allegory and Mysticism," in *Vindications: Essays on the Historical Basis of Christianity,* Anthony Hanson, ed. (London: SCM Press, 1966) 153–192.

[32] Gerhardsson, *op. cit.,* 18.

[33] *Ibid.,* 19 f.

[34] *Ibid.,* 20.

[35] *Ibid.,* 27.

[36] *Ibid.,* 29.

[37] *Ibid.,* 26–28. Cf. K. Stendahl, *The School of St. Matthew and Its Use of the Old Testament,* "Acta Seminarii Neotestamentici Upsaliensis," XX (Uppsala: C. W. K. Gleerup, Lund, 1954), 185 ff.; W. H. Brownlee, "Biblical Interpretation Among the Sectaries of the Dead Sea Scrolls," *Biblical Archaeologist* 14 (1951), 54–76.

[38] Cf. Jeremias, *Parables,* 33–66.

[39] Gerhardsson, *op. cit.,* 21. Gerhardsson thinks this injunction, however, may not be wholly secondary (21 n. 4); it is a set phrase from the language of the Jewish schools (10 and n. 1), and is suitable to the Lucan context (23 f.).

of the parable.[40] There is depicted a learned discussion of the law between Jesus (a διδάσκαλος, [teacher] *rby*) and a lawyer (a νομικός [rabbi]).[41] The discussion proceeds according to custom, including the use of rabbinic formulae and Hebrew. Since the rabbis were fond of the parable in the exposition of scripture, it is not surprising that the lawyer's question, which has to do with an *exegetical* point (what is the meaning of *re'ᵃkha* in the text?), evokes a parable as a midrash on the text. The transcript abbreviates the discussion (customary in the rabbinic literature), but the parable gives evidence that Jesus knew and used rabbinic techniques of interpretation (see above). The conclusion is that the pericope, Lk. 10:25-37, was a unity from the first.

The original significance of the parable, Gerhardsson believes, accords with the meaning of the pericope of the rich young man (Mk. 10:17-21 and parallels), with which it has certain formal parallelisms:[42] the answer of the law as traditionally expounded is not sufficient; Jesus refers to scripture as the Messiah, i. e., gives his own interpretation, which means in the end that he interprets scripture messianically or christologically.[43] It is by no means clear how Gerhardsson gets from the former to the latter; does the authority of the Messiah to reinterpret scripture imply that such reinterpretation, *eo ipso,* will be christological interpretation?

The formal affinity of Gerhardsson's view with that of Ernst Fuchs, who regards the parables as (veiled) self-attestations of Jesus himself,[44] and with the patristic view,[45] requires that these tendencies in contem-

----

[40] Gerhardsson (*ibid.,* 22-29) makes the following points.

[41] It does not matter that a precise Hebrew equivalent for νομικός cannot be established; the lawyer in any case was a learned student of the law (*ibid.,* 23). Cf. T. W. Manson, *The Sayings of Jesus* (London: SCM Press, 1949 [1961]), 260, who surmises that Luke uses "lawyer" rather than "scribe" because the latter would be misunderstood by Gentile readers. Cf. W. Gutbrod, *TWNT* IV (1942), 1081.

[42] The two are introduced with the same initial question, which is answered out of the law.

[43] Gerhardsson, *op. cit.,* 29. One might have expected him to draw a parallel also between the Good Samaritan and the parable of the Lost Sheep (Lk. 15:4-7/Mt. 18:12-13), but he does not seem to notice this possibility.

[44] *Hermeneutik,* 223 ff.; "Bermerkungen zur Gleichnisauslegung," Fuchs II, 136-42; cf. Jüngel, *op. cit.,* 87, 87 f. n. 3; Jeremias, *Parables,* 230.

[45] Gerhardsson wants to distinguish his understanding of the parable as an *allegoric parable* from the patristic understanding of it as a *timeless allegory* (*op. cit.,* 22). Here he parts company with J. Daniélou, "Le Bon Samaritain," in *Mélanges Bibliques rédigés en l'honneur d'André Robert* (Paris: Bloud & Gay [1957]), 457 ff., who wants to reinstate the patristic allegory (Gerhardsson, *op. cit.,* 31 additional note). If the patristic

porary scholarship be carefully distinguished from each other and from the patristic tradition. The differences are correlative with how one understands Jesus' understanding and use of scripture. It is not possible here to embark upon a systematic examination. It will be necessary, as a consequence, to restrict ourselves to a re-examination of the parable of the Good Samaritan with the problem of scripture in view.

III

The discrepancy between the formulation of the question ("Who is my neighbor?" Lk. 10:29) and the question answered by the parable ("Which of these three proved neighbor?" Lk. 10:36) is regularly noted. The disjunction may be epitomized as *"Quis diligendus?"* (the lawyer's question) and *"Quis diligens?"* (the question answered by the parable).[46] This hiatus has been advanced as an argument for divorcing the parable from its Lucan context,[47] but it has also been explained or minimized.[48] What is not often noticed is that the prevailing modern interpretation of the parable, i.e., that the parable defines neighbor as he who needs my help, is as much in conflict with the parable as is the lawyer's question.[49] The lawyer's question still tends to dominate the parable! Jesus' question, "Which of these proved neighbor . . .?" turns the lawyer's question around, if indeed the range to which "neighbor" is applicable is any longer the question at all.

Without a reformulation of the leading question or a recasting of the parable, the incongruity stands. It could even be said that the discrepancy is not alleviated by disengaging the parable from the lawyer's question. For his question continues to be the hearer's question. It should be asked, furthermore, whether the parable really deals with the subject of love as opposed to the object of love. Or are these options—subject or object—simply misleading?

---

view is that the parable is a timeless allegory of the history of the human race or soul, Gerhardsson's view is that it contains a timeless christological didache; in his own judgment it is a difference between two types of universality and timelessness.

[46] A. Jülicher, *Die Gleichnisreden Jesu* I and II (Tübingen: J. C. B. Mohr, 1910; two parts reprinted as one, Darmstadt: Wissenschaftliche Buchgesellschaft, 1963), II, 596; Gerhardsson, *op. cit.*, 6; Jeremias, *Parables*, 205.

[47] E.g., Jülicher, *op. cit.*; R. Bultmann, *History of the Synoptic Tradition*, 178; Jüngel, *op. cit.*, 169 f., decides that vv. 25–28 are secondary, but leaves the question open whether vv. 29, 36 f. are also.

[48] E.g., by T. W. Manson, *The Teachings of Jesus* (Cambridge, Eng.: The University Press, 1951), 301; Jeremias, *Parables*, 205; Gerhardsson, *op. cit.*, 28 f.

[49] Gerhardsson (*op. cit.*, 19) correctly emphasizes this point. T. W. Manson (*Sayings of Jesus*, 261) does not follow the dominant view, but holds that the parable does not define neighbor at all.

It is methodologically sound to follow Gerhardsson in considering the parable initially in and of itself.[50] Quite apart from the Lucan framework it appears that the parable is devoted to the question of neighbor.[51] On the other hand, it is doubtful whether a moralistic interpretation does more than reflect the later interest of the church, which happens in this case to coincide with modern interests.[52] Jeremias has demonstrated the pronounced tendency of the tradition to convert parables with eschatological horizons into hortatory material.[53] Going together with a moralizing interpretation is the definition of the Good Samaritan as a *Beispielerzählung* (exemplary story). An exemplary story does not draw its pictorial element from a sphere other than the one to which its *Sache* belongs; it has no figurative element at all. "The 'exemplary stories' [Beispielerzählungen] offer examples = models of right behavior."[54] The exemplary story does not, therefore, call for a transference of judgment as do the parables proper.[55] The Samaritan is just an example of a true neighbor (or, to follow the prevailing view, of the true love of one's neighbor), nothing more. Gerhardsson, in my judgment, has rightly challenged the validity of this designation,[56] although for what strike me as the wrong reasons.[57]

In comprehending the parable it is important to grasp how the

---

[50] Gerhardsson, *op. cit.*, 9; cf. Jüngel, *op. cit.*, 170.

[51] W. Michaelis, *Die Gleichnisse Jesu. Eine Einführung* (3d ed.; Hamburg: Furche, 1956), 205; R. Bultmann, *Jesus and the Word*, L. P. Smith and E. H. Lantero, trans. (New York: Charles Scribner's Sons, 1958 [1934]), 96; Jüngel, *op. cit.*, 170.

[52] Gerhardsson (*op. cit.*, 8 f.) notes that the situation with respect to the message of Jesus has changed materially since Jülicher formulated his views. It is strange that Jülicher's reading of the Good Samaritan as a *Beispielerzählung* has gone virtually unchallenged. The Lucan tradition has given support, however, to a moralistic reading, terminating as it does with the exhortation, "Go and do likewise."

[53] Jeremias, *Parables*, 42–48 *et passim*.

[54] Bultmann, *History of the Synoptic Tradition*, 178 n. 1; cf. 177 f.; Jülicher, *op. cit.*, I, 112; II, 585; E. Linnemann, *Gleichnisse Jesu. Einführung und Auslegung* (2d ed.; Göttingen: Vandenhoeck & Ruprecht, 1962), 55; Jüngel, *op. cit.*, 170 f.

[55] Bultmann, *History of the Synoptic Tradition*, 198.

[56] *Op. cit.*, 5 and n. 6; p. 9.

[57] The other parables identified as exemplary stories are: the Rich Fool, the Pharisee and the Publican, the Rich Man and Lazarus, (the Wedding Guest [Lk. 14:7–11], the Proper Guests [Lk. 14:12–14]): Jülicher, *op. cit.*, I, 112; II, 585–641; Bultmann, *History of the Synoptic Tradition*, 178 f. Naturally we are not considering here whether the designation is appropriate in these other cases, but it is interesting to note that the exemplary stories are also those identified as having religious content (see n. 15), except for the two Lucan examples added by Bultmann.

hearer is drawn into the story. From what perspective is the parable told?[58] Initially at least, the account compels the hearer to put himself in the place of that nameless fellow jogging along the wild and dangerous road.[59] Straightway he finds himself the object of a murderous attack which leaves him stripped, beaten, and half-dead. While lying helpless in the ditch, he is aware that the priest and Levite pass by with only an apprehensive glance. It does not matter to him whether their callousness can be excused or justified, and if the hearer (as victim) is a layman, his secret anticlericalism is confirmed. The priest or Levite as hearer will, of course, be incensed. At this juncture the lay hearer will anticipate the arrival of a benign layman on the scene;[60] the ecclesiastical listener, muttering under his breath, will expect no less. In the teeth of just such anticipations, to the utter amazement and chagrin of every listener as Jew[61] (the previous dichotomy is bridged in an instant), a hated enemy, a half-breed, a perverter of true religion comes into view and ministers to the helpless victim when he is powerless to prevent him.[62] While still in inner turmoil over this unexpected turn of events, the hearer is brought up short with the question: "Which of these three, do you think, proved neighbor . . . ?" It is a question on which the Jew chokes. The lawyer in the Lucan account cannot bring himself to pronounce the name of that hated "neighbor," but he can hardly avoid the answer which the parable demands.

The Samaritan is undoubtedly the primary shock, although the behavior of the priest and Levite will raise preliminary resistance in certain quarters, nodding approval in others. The first sentences of the story evoke a silent "Yes, that's how it is" from everyone, but the clerics will already have begun their retreat with their own appearance. Nevertheless, the subsequent development overwhelms first reactions

[58] Bornkamm, op. cit., 112 f., thinks this point is crucial and I agree.

[59] Ibid.; Jeremias, Parables, 205.

[60] Jeremias, op. cit., 204.

[61] T. W. Manson, Sayings of Jesus, 263: we may suppose that the man who fell among thieves was a Jew. According to rabbinic teaching, an Israelite was not to accept alms or a work of love from a non-Jew, since Israel's redemption is thereby delayed: Jüngel, op. cit., 172, quoting W. Grundmann, Die Geschichte Jesu Christi (2d ed.; Berlin: Evangelische Verlagsanstalt, 1959), 90; cf. H. L. Strack and P. Billerbeck, Kommentar zum Neuen Testament aus Talmud und Midrash IV (2d ed.; München: C. H. Beck'sche Verlagsbuchhandlung, 1956), 538 f., 543 f.

[62] Jeremias, Parables, 204.

and brings the Jewish audience together again in a common crisis. Only the destitute and outcasts weather the second onslaught; they alone are untouched by the attack.[63]

When it is asked why Jesus chose the Samaritan as the central figure in the parable, it is simply not satisfactory to answer that the Samaritan is merely a model of neighborliness. For in that case the parable is reduced to a commonplace[64] and its bite completely vitiated. Rather, the Samaritan is he whom the victim does not, could not expect would help, indeed does not want help from. The literal, i.e., historical, significance of the Samaritan is what gives the parable its edge. In this respect the Samaritan is a *secular* figure; he functions not as an esoteric cipher for a religious factor as Gerhardsson thinks, but in his concrete, everyday significance. On the other hand, the Samaritan is brought into a constellation in which he cannot be anticipated. It is this surprising, odd turn which shatters the realism, the everydayness of the story. A narrative begun with all the traits of an experience about which everyone knows, or thinks he knows, is ruptured at the crucial juncture by a factor which does not square with everyday experience. The "logic" of everydayness is broken upon the "logic" of the parable. It is the juxtaposition of the two logics that turns the Samaritan, and hence the parable, into a metaphor.

Metaphor directs the hearer's attention, not to this or that, but to the whole background and foreground of the event by means of imaginative shock; it does so by virtue of the fact that it does not allow the figure or narrative picture to come to rest in the literal meaning. Metaphor seizes a focal actuality which it loosens from its moorings in everydayness in order to descry its penumbral actuality or field;[65] the latter is disclosed to the imagination by means of metaphor. If it is the literal meaning of Samaritan that provides the initial jolt to the everyday mentality embodied in the story, it is the nonliteral meaning that triggers, through the parable, a whole new vista—i.e., the penumbral

---

[63] The Pharisees excluded non-Pharisees from their definition of neighbor, the Essenes were to hate all sons of darkness, and a rabbinical saying ruled that heretics, informers, and renegades should be pushed (into the ditch) and not pulled out. Personal enemies were also excluded from the circle (Mt. 5:43): Jeremias, *Parables*, 202 f. The victim in the ditch could also belong to one of these categories; every listener bcomes victim. The parable would not have been offensive to listeners of this type.

[64] Dodd, *Parables*, 24 ff.

[65] I am indebted to Ray L. Hart ("Imagination and the Scale of Mental Acts," *continuum* 3 [1965], 3–21, esp. 19 f.) for the elements of this formulation.

field. In sum, comprehending the figure and the parable depends upon grasping the literal and nonliteral meanings concomitantly.[66]

The nonliteral or metaphorical horizon of the figure of the Samaritan and of the parable is suggested by the literal meaning and depends upon it. In this case, the Samaritan is both just a Samaritan and he whom the hearers could not expect and do not wish to see on that road. The parable is both just a story of a good Samaritan and a parabolic metaphor opening onto a referential totality which is informed by a new vision of reality that shatters the everyday view.

Since the metaphor gives itself existentially to unfinished reality, so that the narrative is not complete until the hearer is drawn into it as participant, the hearer is confronted with a situation in relation to which he must decide how to comport himself: is he willing to allow himself to be the victim, to smile at the affront to the priest and Levite, to be served by an enemy? The parable invites, nay, compels him to make some response. And it is this response that is decisive for him. Furthermore, since the parable is temporally open-ended, it is cast onto a plurality of situations, a diversity of audiences, with the consequence that it refuses ideational crystallization.[67] Every hearer has to hear it in *his* own way. The future which the parable discloses is the future of every hearer who grasps and is grasped by his position in the ditch.

These considerations have prepared the way for a brief characterization of the other figures in the narrative. The victim is faceless and nameless, perhaps intentionally so, since every listener finds himself in the ditch. The poor traveler is literally the victim of a ruthless robber. So were the poor, the lame, the blind, and the others whom Jesus drew to his side. In fact, one has to understand himself as the victim in order to be eligible. Furthermore, the victim is given his true identity in relation to the three figures who come along the road. *How* he views them determines who he is! The priest and the Levite, on the other hand, are those from whom the victim might have expected more. But they should also be considered from their own point of view. The priests and Levites in the audience can almost be heard, either protest-

[66] Cf. chap. 5, *supra,* 136–52, and a recent article by H. Jack Forstman, "Samuel Taylor Coleridge's Notes Toward the Understanding of Doctrine," *JR* 44 (1964), 310–27, especially 319 ff.

[67] It is for this reason that the parables should not be allegorized (allegory: reduction to a congeries of ideas or concepts, for which the narrative elements are ciphers), but it is also the reason why the parables cannot be reduced to a leading idea (Jeremias, *Parables,* 115) or understood to teach "spiritual truths." Rationalization in any form maims the parabolic image.

ing that they want to review the situation as the narrative pushes them by, or justifying or excusing themselves. They have the option, of course, of moving to the place of the victim or the Samaritan! In both cases the literal and metaphorical meanings must again be grasped concomitantly.

The parable has been considered thus far without raising the christological question. Gerhardsson's thesis compels us to ask whether Jesus appears in the narrative picture. Certainly not explicitly. The question can be rephrased: does Jesus appear in the *field* of the narrative picture? It would be a mistake to hasten to a positive answer. It should first be noticed that the question is restricted to Jesus, i.e., without reference to his messiahship. One is led to think, as Gerhardsson does, of Jesus as the physician, healer, shepherd who moves to the side of the destitute, tax collectors, prostitutes, sinners. The Samaritan is one who does not consider whether he has any business helping an enemy (it cuts both ways!); he does not cast an apprehensive glance around for the robbers; he does not calculate the cost or the consequences, anticipate a reward, or contemplate a result. To this extent Jesus stands behind the Samaritan. He is there in the Samaritan not as a messianic figure, but as one who lives in the "world," or under the "logic," drawn by the parable. It can of course be said that in this Jesus moves to God's side in relation to mundane reality, that he acts out of the vision of a world under "the jurisdiction of God's righteousness."[68] But to do so is to affirm that Jesus is declaring who God is, and that he is looking at the in-breaking of a kingdom nobody else sees.

If the latter is allowed to stand, then it could also be said that Jesus hovers behind the Samaritan also in the sense that he is the one whom his hearers could not expect and from whom they wanted no help, that is, so long as they refuse to be victims or to allow themselves to be helped by the alien. In that case the parable is christological, but not in the sense Gerhardsson takes it to be.

It should be recalled at this point that the parable ends by calling upon the hearer to pass judgment on the performance. He is no longer victim, priest, or Levite, or even Samaritan, but judge. From the point of view of the conclusion, the parable invites the auditor to take up a new position, this time in relation to the three named actors. He knows the answer to the question posed and suspects that he has walked into

[68] Cf. Ernst Käsemann, "Gottesgerechtigkeit bei Paulus," *ZThK* 58 (1961), 377 f. ("God's Righteousness in Paul," *JThC* 1 [1965], 109 f.), who uses the phrase in a formulation from the Pauline perspective.

the trap. Indeed he has. The parable is an invitation to comport oneself with reality in the way the Samaritan does. This should not be understood exclusively or even primarily as a moral demand to love neighbor; it is more a boon than a demand, more a grant that entitles the hearer to stake out his existence in the "world" of the parable, a "world" under the jurisdiction of God's righteousness. The right is granted by virtue of the language event which verifies the reality of that world. If, then, the hearer is invited to "see" what the Samaritan "sees" and embark upon his "way," he is also invited to follow Jesus, for Jesus, as we saw, "appears" in the penumbral field of the parable as one who has embarked upon this way. Indeed, the parable bodies forth Jesus' "world," opening metaphorically as it does onto a "world" under the aegis of love. To put it succinctly, the parable is permission on the part of Jesus to follow him, to launch out into a future that he announces as God's own. In this sense, too, it is christological.

A final observation is necessary, for on it depends the "logic" set out in the preceding. The hearer is able to affirm the Samaritan and enter into his "world" only because he has first been victim: "We love, because he first loved us" (I John 4:19).

IV

It is evident from the foregoing analysis that the parable cannot be rightly understood as a punning exegesis[69] of the Old Testament text as Gerhardsson proposes. While I would concur in his intuition that the parable requires a more adequate interpretation than modern exegetes generally have given it, and that the patristic tradition preserves, albeit in distorted form, its correct horizon, his own thesis is too ingenious, not to say palpably in contradiction to the mode of language of the parable as Jesus employs it. The real question is not the extent to which Jesus was influenced by his time and age,[70] but whether the language of Jesus, and hence his hermeneutic, is amenable to or shatters rabbinic categories.[71] The answer does depend, of course, on how one understands Jesus of Nazareth.[72]

---

[69] Gerhardsson, op. cit., 27.

[70] Ibid., 31.

[71] That is to say, one cannot allow the common tradition to dominate the question of Jesus' own mode of discourse. That the latter is to be determined in relation to the former is true enough, but the particularity of the historical relativizes the significance of correlative modes and structures. The crucial item is what Jesus does with the common tradition.

[72] Cf. Amos Wilder, "Eschatology and the Speech-Modes of the Gospel," *Zeit und Geschichte. Dankesgabe an Rudolf Bultmann zum 80. Geburtstag,* E. Dinkler, ed.

More specifically, the everydayness (or realism) of the parable inveighs against Gerhardsson's view. On his view the narrative elements are merely ciphers. To the contrary, the metaphorical value of the narrative elements depends, paradoxically, on their everyday meaning for cogency. Gerhardsson is simply unable to cope with this aspect of the parable.

It is still possible, nevertheless, to inquire whether the parable is an interpretation of the Old Testament text (as in the Lucan context). In seeking an answer, it is necessary to begin again with the parable itself.

What is the prior question to which the parable addresses itself? Even without Lk. 10:29, 36 f., I have noted, modern interpreters agree that the parable is devoted to the question of neighbor.[73] According to Bultmann, the point of the story lies in the contrast between the loveless Jew and the loving Samaritan.[74] Jüngel rightly points out that this contrast by itself does not yield the point, but rather the relation of the two to the anonymous man in need of compassion.[75] The priest and Levite represent the Jew who interprets the law correctly,[76] the Samaritan the unexpected one who misunderstands (*sic*) the law but understands the call of love. The parable therefore presents itself as a reinterpretation of the law on the authority of him who speaks the parable (cf. the "But I say to you" "I tell you" of the Great Sermon). The Lucan context is consequently not inappropriate to the parable.[77]

We may now consider the Lucan context. In contrast to Matthew

---

(Tübingen: J. C. B. Mohr, 1964), 27. Amos Wilder's criticisms in this article and another ("Form-History and the Oldest Tradition," *Neotestamentica et Patristica*, W. C. van Unnik, ed. [Leiden: E. J. Brill, 1962], 3–13) of Gerhardsson's broader thesis with respect to tradition and interpretation in the early church, fully articulated in *Memory and Manuscript: Oral Tradition and Written Transmission in Rabbinic Judaism and Early Christianity*, Eric J. Sharpe, trans., "Acta Seminarii Neotestamentici Upsaliensis," XXII (Uppsala, 1961), serve as background for my criticisms of Gerhardsson's treatment of the parable of the Good Samaritan in particular.

[73] *Supra*, n. 51.

[74] *History of the Synoptic Tradition*, 178.

[75] *Op. cit.*, 171.

[76] Jeremias (*Parables*, 203 f.) carefully considers this point and finds it dubious on two grounds: (1) Did the priest and Levite consider the man to be dead (v. 30, ἡμιθανῆ, half-dead)? (2) Was the Levite governed by ritual considerations? It is perhaps the ambiguity of the situation that gives the parable its pinch: the priest and Levite wanted to debate the issue.

[77] Bultmann, *Jesus and the Word*, 96; G. Bornkamm, "Das Doppelgebot der Liebe," *Neutestamentliche Studien für Rudolf Bultmann*, Beihefte zur ZNW, 21 (2d ed.; Berlin: Töpelmann, 1957), 85; Jüngel, *op. cit.*, 172.

(22:34–40) and Mark (12:28–31), who have Jesus answer the question of the first commandment, Luke puts the summary of the law in the mouth of the lawyer. Bornkamm thinks that such a summary of the essence of the law is alien to the rabbinic understanding of the law.[78] However that may be, the reduction of the law to the double commandment (cf. Mt. 22:40) may well derive from Jesus. By attributing the summary to the lawyer, however, the possibility of relating the parable of the Good Samaritan to the commandment is opened up.[79] Whether or not the Lucan complex is original, the combination "brings the original sense of the double commandment of Jesus and thereby his understanding of what 'neighbor' means to expression in an incomparable way."[80] The question of the authenticity of the Lucan context is thus not decisive for a correct understanding of Jesus' intention with respect to the interrelation of commandment and parable. Luke or the tradition before him holds fast to the thrust of the parable by providing this context.[81]

It is appropriate, consequently, to consider the parable as an interpretation of an Old Testament text; specifically, of the double commandment. As an interpretation, the parable must be grasped with respect to its metaphorical field. The love of God or God's love (subjective or objective genitive) do not figure explicitly in the picture. The Samaritan does not love with side glances at God.[82] The need of neighbor

---

[78] Bornkamm, "Das Doppelgebot . . .," 86. The rabbis of course occasionally gave brief synopses of the law, but would have been opposed to a reduction in principle.

[79] Ibid., 92. Bornkamm thinks Matthew and Luke had variants of the Marcan text before them; Manson (Sayings of Jesus, 259) thinks the Lucan story is independent of Mark.

[80] Bornkamm, "Das Doppelgebot . . .," 93.

[81] Manson (Sayings of Jesus, 260) suggests that the Lucan account presupposes, so to speak, the Marcan account in that the lawyer gives what he knows to be Jesus' answer in order to raise the further question. The Lucan version begins in earnest where the Marcan account leaves off. One can reach this conclusion by inference from the parable itself rather than by attempting to establish first the authenticity of the Lucan context as Manson does.

[82] Bornkamm, Jesus of Nazareth, 110; cf. the remarks of Ebeling, "Die Evidenz des Ethischen und die Theologie," ZThK 57 (1960), 337 n. 3 (= "Theology and the Evidentness of the Ethical," JThC 2 [1965], 112 f. and n. 18), e.g., "The 'blessed of the Father' [Mt. 25:40] have as little idea of having done something to Jesus as those who are 'cursed' for their failure have any idea that they have been guilty of failing Jesus. Those who took the part of the hungry, homeless, sick, and lonely had done so simply because they saw the need as a plain opportunity to intervene remedially. They did what impressed itself on them in this case as reasonable, because necessary. The interpolation of the idea that it was to be done for Jesus' sake would threaten to ruin the whole." Ebeling also quotes some cutting remarks of Wilhelm Herrmann.

alone is made self-evident, and the Samaritan responds without other motivation. At the same time, the narrative picture forces the hearer to take up the position of one in need of compassion. In so doing he learns what "as thyself" means.[83] The hearer himself becomes the object of unconstrained, unmotivated mercy, at the point where he could not expect and perhaps was not willing to accept it. The narrative picture is therefore secular; God does not "appear."

While the need of neighbor is self-evident, the priest and Levite, as custodians of the law, pass by. Only the Samaritan answers the call of neighbor's need. What frees him to do so, while the other two are constrained to look away? It would be admissible to reply that the Samaritan simply saw and responded to the self-evident need of the victim in the ditch, were it not also the case that a Samaritan could not be expected to react in this way, and were it not also the case that the priest and Levite were confronted by the same pressing need. Manifest need does not of itself lay a claim on just any chance passer-by. The Samaritan, moreover, belongs to the parable (whether the narrative refers to an actual incident or not is beside the point), which means, to proceed from a trite point, that the Samaritan is there and behaves as he does by virtue of the parable. The triteness of the point should not be allowed to force the conclusion that Jesus is therefore merely telling a story. On the contrary, if the parable metaphorically discloses Jesus' world—the one he sees being invaded by love—then the Samaritan is there and behaves as he does by virtue of the parabolic world in which selfless response to neighbor's need is the thing to do, is taken for granted. The Samaritan in the narrative picture has this freedom, the freedom to risk all, to proceed with his love unhurried, deliberately. The parable itself gives him this freedom.

To say that the parable grants the Samaritan the freedom to act out of love is to shift the question to another sphere, viz., the sphere of language, and to direct attention away from the Samaritan to those who are listening to the story. The parable is indeed language and it has to do not with a Samaritan, but with Jesus' auditors. The parable as word leads, according to the Lucan context, to the call for action: "Go and do likewise" (Lk. 10:37). However misleading the moralistic interpretation of the parable may be, it has the virtue of calling attention to the event-character of what transpires in the parable and, as a consequence, of what is intended to transpire in the listeners. The

[83] Bornkamm, *Jesus of Nazareth*, 113.

deficiency of the moralistic view is that it does not grasp the primal word-character of the event. Remarkably enough, the Samaritan goes about his compassion wordlessly. For all that his act is no less language event. It is language event in that it "bespeaks" that which precedes, evokes, permits love. The Samaritan discloses in wordless deeds the world in which love as event is indigenous, a world that is made present, to those attending, in the deedful words of the parable. Ebeling puts the word-character of deeds succinctly:

Man's deeds have word-character. It can be learned from them whether he has understood something of the situation in which he finds himself, or whether he completely misunderstands it. It can become plain from a man's deeds—more clearly and more convincingly than by words—what is in the man. A very ordinary deed can be uncommonly eloquent and significant. It can awaken hope and plunge into despair, it can—not in its immediate effect as a deed, but in its effect on the understanding, and thus in its word-effect—open up a whole world, but also destroy a world.[84]

Insofar as the Samaritan's deeds "communicate" his world to those attending the parable, i.e., insofar as his world arrives for them and they are led to it, the parable is a language event that shapes their future decisively. It is precisely its word-character that makes it an event of radical significance. As Jüngel puts the announcement of the parable, "The reign of God is as near you as the Samaritan to the one threatened by death."[85] The reign of God is as near as the parable, in which it may provisionally arrive. The parable thus forges an eschatological unity of promise and demand.[86]

It was remarked earlier that the parable draws a narrative picture that is wholly secular: neither God nor his Messiah "appear," and the Samaritan responds to the need of neighbor without ulterior reasons. Nevertheless, it must now also be said that the reign of love—to use a "secular" term—has drawn near for the Samaritan too, as it were. He has taken up his abode in a world where the plight of neighbor, in and out of itself, draws a net of love around the co-humanity of the two. Love's drawing near for him is thus language event. The con-text for co-humanity is established as love, not by virtue of any necessity attaching to neighbor's need, arising out of natural law, or attendant

84 "Die Evidenz des Ethischen," 344 ("Theology and the Evidentness of the Ethical," 119).
85 Jüngel, op. cit., 173.
86 Ibid.

upon his own religious or moral drives, but merely on the basis that the man in the ditch becomes the occasion for love to come into play. The language event which grounds the Samaritan's action precedes the language event which the parable may become for its hearers. Only when language event has taken place, can language event take place. That Jesus belongs to the penumbral field of the parable as the one who lurks behind the Samaritan and dwells in his world provides the justification for reading the parable christologically: in Jesus God has drawn near as love, which gives Jesus the right to pronounce that drawing near upon the world in parable.

With respect to the Lucan context, it follows that Jesus does not allow the lawyer's question (and ours) to dominate the parable, for the lawyer's question is an effort to hold the question of neighbor at arm's length, and hence the force of the commandment. From the perspective of the parable the question "Who is my neighbor?" is an impossible question.[87] The disjunction between question and answer, considered so grievous by Jülicher and those who have followed him, far from being inimical to the parable, is necessary to the point.[88] This means also that Jesus does not allow the law to dominate love as God's drawing near. Rather, Jesus proclaims the law in a context qualified by the event of divine love and interprets it with the help of the concrete instance of love's needfulness.[89] Jesus thus brings the question of neighbor near in its own right, i.e., as a self-evident question,[90] but makes it impossible to give the right answer except out of the event of grace in his own person and word. "The law now says [in the proclamation of Jesus], with your permission, look, I stand on the side of *love!* I allow you *your* righteousness. That is the sense, e.g., of the double commandment of love of God and neighbor (Mk. 12:28–34 and parallel)."[91]

For Jesus the law labored under severe handicaps. It had been confined to a field in which God was ostensibly present but from which he was actually remote. The scribes and Pharisees sought to relate it to everyday existence in countless ways, but it grew less

[87] Bornkamm, *Jesus of Nazareth*, 113.

[88] *Contra* Jeremias, *Parables*, 205: "The alteration in the form of the question hardly conceals a deeper meaning."

[89] Fuchs I, 286 f., 290.

[90] Cf. Ebeling, "Die Evidenz des Ethischen," 336 ff. ("Theology and the Evidentness of the Ethical," 112 f.).

[91] Fuchs I, 287 (italics his).

relevant with each step. Rabbinic interpretation of the law sought to engage the Jew, but ended by disengaging him from reality. Jesus attempted nothing less than to shatter the whole tradition that had obscured the law. To put it in a way that is still enigmatic, but in the way the parable suggests, Jesus had to interpret the law in parable.[92]

---

[92] The reader may wish to compare my earlier reading of the parable in "How Do You Read?" *Interpretation* XVIII (1964), 56–61.

PART THREE

Language as It Occurs in the New Testament: Letter

Speaking of itself is a hearing.
It is attending to the language which we speak.
Speaking is therefore not a simultaneous hearing but a
    prior hearing.
We not only speak language, we speak out of it.

Martin Heidegger,
Unterwegs zur Sprache

The Phenomenology of
Language and Form and Literary
Criticism: Parable and Letter

≯ 9 ⩔ ────────────────────────────────

THE DISCUSSION OF THE PARABLE HAS BEEN COVERTLY
carried on as a phenomenology of parabolic language in relation to
form and literary criticism. The phenomenology of language has not
itself been given thematic status. That deficiency should now perhaps
be rectified. It is not possible, of course, to allow it anything approxi-
mating adequate treatment. It is appropriate, nevertheless, to delineate
more explicitly than has been done thus far the contours of a phenomenological approach to the New Testament.

The thematic remarks that follow should be taken as wholly provisional. They are designed to indicate the horizons of a phenomenology
of New Testament language, without focusing the foreground too
sharply. They provide, so to speak, a phenomenological approach to
phenomenology. The thematic discussion is then addressed, in the
same chapter, to the parable and to the letter. The one is a backward
glance over terrain already traversed, and for that reason, perhaps, a
revealing postscript. The other serves as a means of reopening the
question of the nature of the Pauline letter. The treatment of the letter
in this chapter (chap. 9) should be considered in closest connection
with the form, style, and literary criticism of the letter that is sketched
in chapter 10.

A preliminary move is made in chapter 10 toward establishing the
form and structure of the Pauline letter as a basis for resolving the
stalemate that characterizes the literary analysis of the epistles. The
proposals made there draw upon form-critical and stylistic data. Phenomenological reflections on the Pauline letter have been projected

onto this sketch, inasmuch as such reflections "listen in" on the movement of Paul's language and the structure of the letter as a whole. Yet the form-critical and stylistic analysis will hardly be intelligible, at least in the sense intended, apart from phenomenological considerations. The two chapters thus anticipate each other.

I

In speaking of the power of man's imagination to alter those appearances of nature with which his figuration, i.e., his organization of sense data into things, supplies him, Owen Barfield has written:

> We should remember this, when appraising the aberrations of the formally representational arts. Of course, in so far as these are due to affectation, they are of no importance. But in so far as they are genuine, they are genuine because the artist has in some way or other experienced the world he represents. And in so far as they are appreciated, they are appreciated by those who are themselves willing to make a move towards seeing the world in that way, and, ultimately therefore, seeing that kind of world. We should remember this, when we see pictures of a dog with six legs emerging from a vegetable marrow or a woman with a motor-bicycle substituted for her left breast.[1]

We should remember this, too, when arbitrating between classical and modern painting. If classical painting is thought of as the representation of nature and modern painting as the expression of the subjective, the observation of Merleau-Ponty is apropos: "The classical perspective is only one of the ways that man has invented for projecting the perceived world before him, and not the copy of that world."[2] It is therefore an optional interpretation of a spontaneous vision. This is not because the perceived world contradicts the laws of classical perspective, but because the perceived world does not insist on any one perspective.[3]

Modern painting in that case need not be understood as the exchange of an objectivist perspective in favor of a subjective experience, but as a fundamental protest against the tyranny of a single perspective.[4]

The relation of the perceiver to the perceived world is enormously complicated by the presence of language. It is not merely a case of

---

[1] Owen Barfield, *Saving the Appearances,* 146.
[2] Maurice Merleau-Ponty, *Signs,* Richard C. McCleary, trans. (Evanston, Ill.: Northwestern University Press, 1964), 48.
[3] *Ibid.,* 48 f.
[4] Cf. *ibid.,* 47, 52.

seeing but of saying as well. Seeing and saying were perhaps originally related, as the common expression "Now I see"—i.e., understand—in response to a statement seems to indicate. What is to be seen is granted by the saying which names it, gives it presence.[5] With respect to the power of language to bestow and delimit sight—the limits of which are unknown—Erich Heller gives this sound advice to his students: "Be careful how you interpret the world, it *is* like that."[6]

Language, like painting, is subject to domination by a classical perspective. It is not that the perceived world insists on a single linguistic perspective, but that the perceived world falls under the sway of the perspective embedded in language as commonly understood: saying presides over seeing. So long as a single linguistic perspective dominates, not only is the world seen that way, but language itself is held captive by the same perspective. The captor is also led captive.

The recent and current protest, primarily on the part of littérateurs, phenomenologists, and existentialists, against the prevailing understanding of language, roots in the view that world and language have fallen into the bondage of a single perspective. This is exemplified by the point of view of linguistic analysis. Although ostensibly engaged in the common task of language analysis, philosophical linguistic analysis, at least in the form of verificational analysis, operates with the law of the single perspective, while the phenomenology of language takes the view that language participates in the creation, preservation, and modification of the appearances. The one wants to clean up a single perspective, the other to enlarge upon it. Heidegger thus places himself and Carnap at opposite ends of the spectrum.[7] If we are inclined to the view that language, like painting, permits us to see the world in a particular way, phenomenology has the better of the argument.

Phenomenology, then, wants to enlarge upon that single perspective which appears to dominate the current understanding of language and with which certain linguistic analysts work. How does it propose to do this? Not, in the first instance, by investigating other, nonempirical

---

[5] Cf. Remy C. Kwant, *Phenomenology of Language* (Pittsburgh: Duquesne University Press, 1965), 145: "It is correct to say that we speak from our 'seeing.' . . . Right now we want to complement that assertion by adding that language makes us see."

[6] Erich Heller, *The Disinherited Mind: Essays in Modern German Literature and Thought* (New York: Farrar, Straus, & Cudahy, 1957), 26 f. (italics his).

[7] Martin Heidegger, "Some Suggestions Concerning Principal Perspectives for the Theological Consultation on 'The Problem of a Non-objectifying Thinking and Speaking in Contemporary Theology.'" Mimeographed address read to the Second Drew Consultation on Hermeneutics, April, 1964 (p. 4 of text).

uses of language as, e.g., Frederick Ferré very ably does in *Language, Logic, and God,*[8] although such functional analyses of language serve to challenge the hegemony of verificational analysis in the linguistic domain. This observation is merely in the interest of avoiding the misunderstanding which the preceding formulation may suggest: phenomenology of language is not a kind of linguistic analysis. The *how* can best be specified, perhaps, by characterizing the aim of phenomenology in general and then specifying it in relation to language.[9]

According to James M. Edie, "Phenomenology is neither a science of objects nor a science of the subject; it is a science of *experience.*"[10] Phenomenology does not concern itself primarily with the discrete object nor with the discrete subject, but with the conjunction of the two: it seeks to investigate how in fact the selfhood of the self and the worldhood of the world arise. Its field is therefore the *Lebenswelt,* the experienced world.[11]

If Husserl, as some hold, confined himself up to his final period to the analysis of the fully reflexive consciousness, i.e., "pure" consciousness, Heidegger, Sartre, and Merleau-Ponty shifted the phenomenological program to the preconceptual, prereflexive substructures of consciousness, and thus to the *reflecting* consciousness which is the basis of the *reflexive* consciousness. Only because the self is *re-flecting* can it become aware of itself, *reflexively,* in the act of *reflection.*[12] Selfhood is constituted initially by reflecting or mirroring the world, and secondarily by reflection upon its reflecting. The first may be called the *reflective* self, the second the *reflexive* self.

The subject (self) and the object (world) are taken to be coconstitutive of each other: the self is intentional, i.e., is directed toward objects, and thus reflects an intentionally constituted world; an intentionally constituted world is a world comprised of objects held in view. But the world presents itself to the prereflexive consciousness in such a way that it is re-flected rather than reflected upon.

Now the self as fully reflexive consciousness utilizes language in a correlative mode. That is to say, language to the reflexive self is language which is reflected upon. But to the re-flective, prereflexive,

---

[8] New York: Harper & Row, 1961.

[9] In what follows I am drawing heavily on James M. Edie's "Introduction" to *What Is Phenomenology?* by Pierre Thevanaz, J. M. Edie *et al.* ed. and trans. (Chicago: Quadrangle Books, 1962), 13–36.

[10] *Ibid.,* 19.

[11] *Ibid.,* 22.

[12] *Ibid.,* 24.

preconceptual self, language is *re-flective:* it re-flects the intentionally constituted world.

The phenomenology of language proposes to investigate the latter, just as phenomenology—as practiced by the early Heidegger, Sartre, and Merleau-Ponty, for example—proposes to analyze the structure of the prereflexive, preconceptual self in general.

Desirable as it would be to elaborate what this means for the phenomenological orientation to language, we must content ourselves with some hints. I draw chiefly on Merleau-Ponty's work.[13]

As a point of departure, however, we may take these statements of Heidegger:

In language, as a way things have been expressed or spoken out, there is hidden a way in which the understanding of Dasein has been interpreted.

The dominance of the public way in which things have been interpreted has already been decisive even for the possibilities of having a mood—that is, for the basic way in which Dasein lets the world "matter" to it. The "they" prescribes one's state-of-mind and determines what and how one "sees."[14]

Because language permits, even fosters, sedimentation (Merleau-Ponty[15]), because language houses collective representations (Barfield[16]), phenomenology must reckon with language as tradition, as convention, as the custodian of average intelligibility (Heidegger[17]), for language gives even to the prereflexive self what is to be seen. These sedimentations both provide the conditions for understanding and obstruct it (H.-G. Gadamer[18]).

The problem which presents itself and to which a phenomenological analysis is addressed, is the problem of the field or horizon within which, in a given period or epoch, understanding takes place, in relation to the penumbra of that field and in relation to the manifold possibilities which fall outside that field. What is viewed directly is

---

13 Particularly the two essays, "Indirect Language and the Voices of Silence," and "On the Phenomenology of Language," in *Signs*, 39–83, 84–97, respectively.

14 Heidegger, *Being and Time*, 211, 213.

15 *Signs*, 92.

16 *Saving the Appearances*, e.g., 97, 105, 127.

17 *Being and Time*, 212.

18 Hans-Georg Gadamer, *Wahrheit und Methode. Grundzüge einer philosophischen Hermeneutik* (Tübingen: J. C. B. Mohr, 1960), 279.

investigated with respect to what is caught only in the corner of the eye and with respect to what falls outside the field of vision altogether. Such investigation may proceed both historically and theoretically. Heidegger, for example, conceived as his first task the investigation of the language tradition of the West: the immediate foreground of this tradition is comprised of the everyday parlance of Mr. Everyman, but in order to bring the field of the foreground into view, Heidegger found it necessary to go as far "afield" as the pre-Socratics. His phenomenological analysis constitutes a kind of history of the tradition as well as a theoretical analysis.[19]

Sedimentation occurs also at a higher level in the empirical (Merleau-Ponty[20]) or logical (Barfield) use of language, in which significations are pre-established. "The logical use of language presupposes the meanings of the words it employs and presupposes them constant."[21] The logical use of language is founded on sedimentation and traffics in tautologies.

If phenomenology works against the background of language as the shelter of average intelligibility and pre-established significations, it brings into the foreground language as the medium of discovery. "For the speaking subject, to express is to become aware of; he does not express just for others, but also to know himself what he intends," writes Merleau-Ponty.[22] Language discovers the world to the eye, and thought to the mind. It hovers about the significative intention, waiting to give birth to sight and thought. Articulation, consequently, is as important for the one speaking as for the one listening: the problem for the poet, novelist, or philosopher is to learn to speak with his own voice, and to do so he must engage in the "coherent deformation" (Malraux[23]) of the available fund of significations, which takes both him and the hearer across the threshold of discovery.

It follows that all language is indirect or allusive. Speech never comes to rest in itself, as though there were nothing left to be said; it is

[19] Cf. the remarks of Heidegger, e.g., *An Introduction to Metaphysics*, Ralph Manheim, trans. (New Haven: Yale University Press, 1959), 44 f., 83, 92; *Essays in Metaphysics: Identity and Difference*, Kurt F. Leidecker, trans. (New York: Philosophical Library, 1960), 41 f. Also cf. John B. Cobb, Jr., *Living Options in Protestant Theology* (Philadelphia: Westminster Press, 1962), 213.

[20] *Signs*, 44.

[21] Owen Barfield, "Poetic Diction and Legal Fiction," in *The Importance of Language*, Max Black, ed. (Englewood Cliffs, N.J.: Prentice-Hall, 1962), 66.

[22] *Signs*, 90.

[23] Cited by Merleau-Ponty, *ibid.*, 91.

bounded only by more speech. There is never the one-to-one correlation between word and thing, or word and thought, which would be characteristic of finished language.[24] Rather, language remains unfinished because signifying is always surpassed by the signified. Just as unspoken language, primordial discourse, precedes articulation, so it follows articulation: articulation is bounded by the silent word, from which it proceeds and to which it returns.[25]

As phenomenology is concerned with the silence that surrounds language, it attends to the silence which permeates language. Merleau-Ponty asks, "What if language expresses as much by what is between words as by the words themselves? By that which it does not 'say' as by what it 'says'?"[26] A painter hesitates before the manifold possibilities open to him in executing a canvas, in order to allow his *intention* to govern the creation of the painting which does not yet exist. In that act he selects out of a myriad of possibilities one set of lines, one congeries of colors to express his intention. The specific selection, if the artist is successful, will strike us as inevitable, once we grasp that line and color have been wedded with intention. It is the marriage of the two that transfuses the work with silence, that makes it "gappy" (Ray L. Hart's term), inasmuch as line and color do not convey the artist's intention explicitly, but permit the viewer to discover it in an act of "answering imagination."

So it is with the writer who hesitates before the page in endeavoring to give expression to the as yet unsaid. The marriage of words, syntax, style, form with intention leaves traces of what the author is hearing, but never brings it exhaustively to expression. One may read a poem or an essay a hundred times before its meaning explodes between the lines. Only then does the movement or the gesture which the whole is break in upon one out of and between the words. Then we feel something has been said.[27]

It is this silence that phenomenology pursues because it is correlative with creative speech. It is not by accident that Heidegger identifies primordial discourse as the foundation of articulation,[28] and hearing, hearkening, and keeping silent as constituent elements in the structure

---

[24] Cf. *ibid.*, 42 f.

[25] Cf. Wilder, *Language of the Gospel*, 24 f., citing Ignatius and Rilke.

[26] *Signs*, 45.

[27] *Ibid.*, 45 ff. It is invariably frustrating in this context to try to document **that** something; we end by having to give expression to it ourselves in our own way.

[28] *Being and Time*, 204.

of discourse.[29] To broach the phenomenon of language it is necessary to broach the penumbral field of articulation, to attune the ear to the silence which surrounds and permeates speech. When this occurs, the way is opened into that intentionally constituted world of the pre-reflexive, preconceptual self which is re-flected in language and pre-interpreted in primordial discourse.

II

Linguistic analysis of the functional variety seeks to discriminate among the manifold ways in which language is actually used.[30] The phenomenology of language, on the other hand, attempts to press language for its ontological bearings. A preliminary step is to analyze the modes of language, formally conceived, in relation to their proximity to or distance from primordial discourse, the silence which surrounds language.

In a section of *Being and Time* especially significant for our theme,[31] Heidegger has analyzed the assertion as a derived mode of discourse. Primordial interpretation, according to Heidegger, grasps things in a totality of reference-relations, it reaches out into a totality of involvements, without fragmenting that totality in discrete or isolable points. Things understood in this structure are understood *as* something only in relation to this circumspective totality. This "as" Heidegger calls the existential-hermeneutical "as."[32] The assertion, however, points out, predicates, communicates: it narrows the seeing down from the circumspective whole to the thing itself, allows the thing to be given a definite character, and thus lets someone see the thing with us.[33] The "as" of the assertion is an apophantical (letting the entity be seen) "as." The apophantical "as" is founded upon the existential-hermeneutical "as."

The route by which discursive speech arises is thus evident. The assertion, by means of predication, isolates entities, phenomena, from their referential totality and allows them to be seen in themselves, but in a certain way predetermined, so to speak, by their position within the referential nexus. These predicates may then be abstracted from the entities and passed around as predicates attached to no particular

29 *Ibid.*, 206 ff.
30 Informative, imperative, performative, interrogative: Ferré, *op. cit.*, 55 f.
31 Sec. 33, 195–203.
32 *Ibid.*, 189.
33 *Ibid.*, 196 f.

entities. And finally, systems of logic are invented to manage abstracted predicates.

In Heidegger's judgment, logic makes thought the bar to which language must give account of itself. In so doing, logic loses sight of its own origin in primordial discourse. This is not to say that logic no longer has a utilitarian function, or that it does not refer to the "real" world. It is only to say that the "world" to which logic refers is the "world" which has become the object of scientific-technological thinking, and thus subject to control and manipulation.[34]

If this route from primordial language to logic may be thought of as a spectrum, it is possible to give a formal account of the modes of discourse by placing them in their relative positions on such a spectrum.[35] The following outline is confined to three cardinal points, which are determined by the disposition of language (*a*) to language, and (*b*) to the *Lebenswelt*.

At the end of the spectrum at farthest remove from primordial discourse, attention is directed to linguistic formulations themselves; language itself is the object of reflection. Because this reflection is reflection upon the language deposit left by previous reflection, it may be termed secondary reflectivity. This mode of language is characteristic of contempory linguistic analysis, as it is of theological discourse in many of its periods.[36]

At the end of the spectrum closest to primordial discourse, language is characterized by directness, immediacy, spontaneity, nondiscursiveness, to use Wilder's terms.[37] Here language re-flects, without reflecting upon, the world. Heidegger identifies this as the "poetical" mode:[38] language which aims to communicate the existential possibilities of one's state of mind and thus disclose existence as such. This mode may be termed re-flective, owing to its proximity to the circumspective "as" and primordial discourse.

In between falls what may be called language in the mode of

[34] Heidegger, "Some Suggestions Concerning Principal Perspectives," 11 (see n. 7).

[35] Cf. Heinrich Ott ("Theologie als Gebet und als Wissenschaft," *ThZ* 14 (1958), 131) who regards the problem of the relation between original saying and secondary reflection as not yet sufficiently clarified for the understanding of theology as science. These remarks may be regarded as a contribution to that end.

[36] John Dillenberger, "On Broadening the New Hermeneutic," *New Frontiers* II, 155 ff.

[37] "Form-History and the Oldest Tradition," *Neotestamentica et Patristica,* W. C. van Unnik, ed. (Leiden: E. J. Brill, 1962), 8.

[38] *Being and Time,* 205.

primary reflectivity. This mode of language does not reflect upon language as such, but upon the fate of re-flective language in the face of a concrete but competitive *Lebenswelt*. That is to say, it holds re-flective language up to that which it *intends* (its object in the phenomenological sense), in view of the way in which it is heard, by the speaker and others. It is therefore a re-seeing or re-hearing in view of a diverging visual and auditory context.

This distinction seems necessary for the reason that secondary reflectivity feeds on primary reflectivity and not on re-flective language. It is notably difficult to raise poetry, for example, into discursive language, i.e., into language in the mode of secondary reflectivity, without first reflecting on the "world" of the poem in the primary mode. For the same reason, a theology of the parables is a highly artificial product, while a theology can be constructed out of Paul's language with rather satisfactory results.

These suggestions anticipate the discussion of parable and letter. In this context it need only be observed that the sharp difference between parable and letter is a difference relative to the history of the linguistic tradition. The parable is creating a tradition, founding a "world"; the letter is reviewing the destiny of that foundational language in relation to other "worlds," the world of the apostle, the worlds of his readers. The epistle breaks through a concrete *Lebenswelt,* or attempts to, in an effort to bring the world of the parable, the kingdom, to stand. The parable juxtaposes one world with another with a view to a "coherent deformation" of the available significative fund of the hearer.

These modes of language as formally conceived require more explicit thematic treatment than it is possible to give them here.[39] Our concern has been to catch sight of the formal relation of various modes of language to the *Lebenswelt* and to language itself.

It should be said that the characterization of language as belonging to one or another of these modes is by no means pejorative; it is purely descriptive. While these formal modes indicate the horizon of language in that mode, they do not tell us how the user is disposed to the language he is using. Language ostensibly in the mode of re-flectivity may in fact be pure ornamentation, ostentation, or deliberate obscurantism. Language in the mode of secondary reflectivity, on the other hand, may be entirely necessary to the recovery of language in its concreteness and authenticity, to the rediscovery of its primordial roots.

[39] Cf. Ray L. Hart's forthcoming work, tentatively titled "Revelation, Unfinished Manhood, and the Imagination."

With reference to idle, i.e., public language which has lost its existential-hermeneutical reference, Heidegger has said, "In it, out of it,
and against it, all genuine understanding, interpreting, and communi-
cating, all re-discovering and appropriating anew are performed."[40]
If idle talk offers the raw materials, secondary reflection is indispensable to overcoming the prescriptive power of "they say," if for no other
reason than that it is able to discern the problem in the first place.

The phenomenology of language, by holding this spectrum in view,
and by attending to the silence which surrounds language, endeavors to
refer language to what it intends and thus to discover the phenomena
anew. In this process it uncovers the ontological bearings of language
itself.[41]

III

Of the painting as a work of art Merleau-Ponty writes:

> The accomplished work is thus not the work which exists in itself like a
> thing, but the work which reaches its viewer and invites him to take up the
> gesture which created it and, skipping the intermediaries, to rejoin, without
> any guide other than a movement of the invented line (an almost incor-
> poreal trace), the silent world of the painter, henceforth uttered and
> accessible.[42]

This may be taken as an illuminating delineation of the verbal picture
we call parable, with reference of course to the parables of Jesus.

Such a characterization draws attention, in my judgment, to the
essential features of the parable, while explaining why even modern
interpreters overlook its heart.

When Merleau-Ponty depicts the work as something "which reaches
its viewer and invites him to take up the gesture which created it," here
and in what follows he is describing what has been set out above as the
metaphorical character of the parable. Metaphor directs attention not
to this or that, but to the whole background and foreground of
an entity or event by means of imaginative shock or surprise. Metaphor
seizes a focal actuality which it loosens from its moorings in everydayness (the "received" world) in order to descry its penumbral field. The
latter is the silent world of the parable, the preconceptual totality of

[40] *Being and Time*, 213.
[41] Merleau-Ponty, *Signs*, 86 ff.
[42] *Ibid.*, 51.

significations that goes with primordial discourse. The parable, furthermore, gives itself to unfinished reality, so to speak, in that it is not complete until the hearer is drawn into it as participant. The gesture which the parable is, to use Merleau-Ponty's term, is an invitation: it invites the hearer to follow the "almost incorporeal" traces of the verbal picture into the referential totality to which it points but which it does not spell out.

The language of the parable may be termed *re-flective,* owing to the fact that it re-flects the intentionally constituted world of the preconceptual self. Jesus speaks, according to Whitehead, "in the lowest abstractions that language is capable of, if it is to be language at all and not the fact itself."[43] The parable stands on the frontier of language and mirrors without conceptualizing the kingdom of God.

The preconceptual totality of significations which the parable reflects has been termed "world." This use of the word is likely to be misleading for one for whom "world" denotes an aggregation of discrete objects. Heidegger has shown that things are in the world primordially in the sense of being within the horizon of someone's *existentiell* projects: things are in the whole "workshop" within which circumspective concern already dwells.[44] "The world-structure within which the various objects in the world find their places is ontologically prior to the objects themselves."[45] This structure called "world" is "there" before anyone has observed or ascertained it, i.e., it is "there" primordially. The worldhood of the world announces or discloses itself when the referential totality within which circumspective concern already dwells is disturbed, when some tool or equipment is found to be unusable, un-ready-to-hand, or obtrusive. Such a disturbance calls attention both to the worldhood of the world and to things in themselves.[46]

This analysis need be pursued only in one connection: assertions or "is-statements" refer to the objects themselves, either in their particularity or in a generalizing way, or to the worldhood of the world itself. The assertion is therefore founded upon, and is derivative in relation to, the preconceptual world that is ontologically prior. The parable as

[43] A. N. Whitehead, *Religion in the Making* (New York: Meridian Books, 1960), 56.

[44] *Being and Time,* 105; these remarks refer to the whole section, 95–122.

[45] Schubert Ogden's formulation, *Christ Without Myth,* 48.

[46] "If it is to be possible for the ready-to-hand not to emerge from its inconspicuousness [i.e., from its place within the totality of significations], the world *must not announce itself*" (Heidegger, *Being and Time,* 106).

metaphor, on the other hand, intends the primordial world-structure with its various objects "in place" within a totality of significations.

In reflecting on the parable as metaphor, it was suggested that the parable does not merely descry the "received" world, but another world. Since the world it descries deforms the "received" world, it constitutes nothing less than an invitation to live in that world, to see the world in that way, to take up one's abode within a totality of significations that is different from the everyday world.

It was Adolf Jülicher who taught us the illegitimacy of allegorical interpretations of the parables, and in this he was surely right, for allegorization, for the modern period at least, is a form of rationalization. Nevertheless, Jülicher's maxim of broadest possible application is no less rationalistic, and when Dodd and Jeremias seek now to refer the maxims of Jülicher to a specific historical situation, they have not drawn essentially closer to the character of the parable. Jülicher reduced the plurality of allegorical ciphers to single abstract maxims, and Dodd and Jeremias want to refurbish these *ideas* with concreteness by referring them to the historical situation. But the parables do not transmit ideas. The way to refurbish the parables with concreteness is to allow them to become parables again, and that means to take them as metaphorical: only so will the almost imperceptible lines in the verbal picture adumbrate the referential totality, the kingdom of God, which they seek to disclose.

Nor is Bultmann exempt from the temptation to take the parables as illustrations of thoughts which could be expressed in other and more direct language, as his treatment in *The History of the Synoptic Tradition* shows. In treating the logia Bultmann distinguishes constitutive from ornamental motifs; to the latter belong simile, metaphor, paradox, and the like.[47] Even though he gives a lucid analysis of the style of the parable,[48] he is simply unable to cope with the mode of the parable's language in relation to its content: the parable remains an ornamentation of thought. On the other hand, Ernst Fuchs[49] and

---

[47] *History of the Synoptic Tradition,* 69 f.

[48] *Ibid.,* 179–205.

[49] E.g., *Hermeneutik,* 211–30; "The Parable of the Unmerciful Servant (Mt. 18: 23–35)," in *Studia Evangelica,* K. Aland *et al.,* eds. (Berlin: Akademie-Verlag, 1959), 487–94; Fuchs II, 136–42, 219–26 [32–38], 348 f. [141 ff.], 361–64 [153–56], 367–71 [158–62], 392–97 [179–84], etc. Cf. further the work of Fuchs' student, Eberhard Jüngel: *Paulus und Jesus. Eine Untersuchung zur Präzisierung der Frage nach dem Ursprung der Christologie,* "Hermeneutische Untersuchungen zur Theologie," 2 (Tübingen: J. C. B. Mohr [Paul Siebeck], 1962).

Amos Wilder[50] have led the way in rehabilitating the parable as parable.

It is no accident that the parables are often taken to be the most authentic material we have from the lips of Jesus. Authentic may be understood here as *ipsissima verba*, of course, but it may also be taken in the sense of fundamentally illuminating. At least this much can be said: if the parables are re-flective in the sense indicated, they tell us how Jesus was disposed to language, and indicate, by their metaphorical gesture, the "world in which Jesus lived." They also invite the hearer to pass through the "looking glass" into the domain of God's love. Jesus could not, in that case, merely hand the tradition on, even after correcting it at this point or that, but had to allow language to collect creatively on his significative intention, by a "coherent deformation" of the available language fund.

If Gerhard Ebeling is correct in asserting that "the parable is the form of the language of Jesus which corresponds to the incarnation,"[51] a new approach to the parables of Jesus is required, one which allows the parable to assert itself as the language event which brings the kingdom of God near. Phenomenology of language will play a major role in this, since it is prepared to attend to what the parable intends, seeking, as it does, to follow out the almost incorporeal traces leading to the silent world re-flected in the parable as metaphor.

IV

The language and form of the Pauline letters likewise evidence traces of the silence which surrounds language. As in the case of the parable, these traces are to be taken as clues to the nature of the language-gesture that the letter is. Taken together with more overt features of language and form, such clues indicate that the letter is a more complex language-gesture than the parable.[52] It is necessary to grasp the complexity of the letter in order to bring its intentionality[53] into view.

---

[50] *Language of the Gospel,* 79–96.

[51] *Evangelische Evangelienauslegung: Eine Untersuchung zu Luthers Hermeneutik* (2d ed.; Darmstadt: Wissenschaftliche Buchgesellschaft, 1962), 108.

[52] I owe this observation to Amos Wilder.

[53] Intentionality, needless to say, is to be distinguished from purpose or aim as generally understood. In the context of the discussion, intentionality refers to the "world" held in view by the writer or speaker, but it should also be taken to imply a locus from which that "world" is seen. Paul says, "You *there,* behold the *world* in which faith dwells." The letter gestures toward that world from a locus defined by the reader.

Our attempt to listen in on the letter is provisional. It is confined, moreover, to two clues: the movement of Paul's language within smaller units of language, and the structure of the letter form as such.

If the language of the parable can be characterized as re-flective, the Pauline letter can be characterized as language in the mode of primary reflectivity.[54] The letters presuppose the proclamation (kerygma)— whether Paul's own or that which came to him out of the tradition— and refer to it, in that Paul is reflecting upon the fate of that proclamation among his readers.[55] In this mode of reflection he moves between two poles: (a) what the proclamation intends, i.e., the focal actuality it holds in view or, to put it now in "deformed" common parlance, the "subject matter" of the proclamation; and (b) the way in which that proclamation is being heard, i.e., its fate among his hearers in view of their situation, their expectations. Paul thus attempts to juxtapose what is to be heard and the hearing within a language that brings each to bear on the other.

The movement between these two poles is evident, for example, in Romans 8:31-39. In this passage what is to be heard and the hearing are inextricably intertwined. The question in 8:35a ("Who shall separate us from the love of Christ?") refers, on the one hand, to the conditions of existence under which hearing must take place: "Shall tribulation, or distress, or persecution, or famine, or nakedness, or peril, or sword?" (8:35b; cf. 8:33a, 36, 38 f. and 8:3 ff.). It refers also to what is to be heard: Christ's obedience in death, his resurrection and intercession (8:34), which in turn is interpreted as God's deed (8:32a), which brings justification (8:33b, 34a).[56] Christ's love is therefore

---

[54] See *supra* for definitions of these modes.

[55] This is not to imply that Paul's oral announcement of the kerygma differed essentially from his written recapitulation. The movement of Paul's language in the letters appears to correspond to the movement of the kerygma: the kerygma is an abbreviated language-gesture of which the letter is an expansion (with "coherent deformations"). To say that Paul presupposes the proclamation is to say that he ultimately presupposes the presence of the true word in the world, to which the kerygmatic tradition in the Hellenistic church before him had already given expression; it is on the latter that Paul is immediately dependent (Bultmann, *Theology of the New Testament* I, 187).

[56] The justification for reading the sequence of this passage in reverse order is that the kerygmatic tradition apparently is expanded from a soteriological or christological nucleus (e.g., I Cor. 15:3 ff.) to a form containing a first article which referred to God and a second article which referred to Christ (e.g., Rom. 4:24 f., I Cor. 8:6). The development of the kerygmatic tradition is not without interest for the questions being considered here. The movement of Paul's language between two poles does not, however, depend on a resolution of the problem of the development of the kerygma.

God's love (cf. 8:35a with 8:39b; cf. Rom. 5:8), love which issued in the salvation event, which is grace (Rom. 5:1 f., 20 f.). Through this event man is made conqueror of all powers including death (8:37: "through him who loved us"). There is therefore nothing that can "separate us from the love of God in Christ" (8:39), nothing that can finally frustrate that love. With this Paul returns to the affirmation, implied in his rhetorical question, with which he began: "If God is for us, who is against us?" (answer: "nobody," 8:31; cf. the affirmation which stands at the head of the chapter: "there is therefore now no condemnation for those who are in Christ Jesus," 8:1).

The same movement or polarity can be traced in other and longer passages, e.g., I Corinthians 1:10—3:23, Galatians 1:6—2:21. Reference may be made, however, to one other shorter unit. In II Corinthians 8:9 Paul invokes what appears to be a kerygmatic summary of what is to be heard, the Christ-event: "For you know the grace of our Lord Jesus Christ, that though he was rich, yet for your sake he became poor, so that by his poverty you might become rich." The wealth and poverty of Christ are predicates which bear on the hearing, viz., on the wealth and poverty of the Corinthians: his grace is that, though rich, he became poor, that through his poverty the Corinthians might become rich.[57] This formulation, moreover, is set in the context of an appeal for the relief offering. The relief offering is connected, on the one hand, with the proof or manifestation (ἔνδειξις) of their love (8:24), and test (δοκιμή) of their service, which attests their obedience in confessing (ὁμολογία) the gospel of Christ (9:13), and, on the other, with Paul's characterization of his own ministry (6:10). What is heard, i. e., confessed, is bound up for both Paul and the Corinthians with the hearing, i.e., with the "world" invoked by what is heard.

This movement or sequence makes it clear that an affirmation about either God or Christ is at the same time an affirmation about oneself, about one's "world." But the reverse is also true: to say that in faith man does not fall into condemnation is to affirm God's saving act in Christ. Theological affirmations for Paul, therefore, are *reciprocally reflexive* with respect to the two poles. Bultmann has long since noticed this reciprocity and takes it as a theological axiom.[58]

The reciprocal reflexivity of Paul's theological statements means, as Bultmann rightly points out, that Paul's theology is not theoretical.

---

[57] The kerygma in I Cor. 15:3 ff. also announces that *Christ* died for *our* sins.
[58] *Theology of the New Testament* I, 190 f.; II, 128 ff.; *Jesus Christ and Mythology*, 68 ff.

Paul does not derive God from a rational analysis of the cosmos, nor does he attempt to erect a speculative *Weltanschauung*. Neither does Paul theologize on the basis of an anthropological or psychological analysis of man. In short, Paul's theology was developed neither deductively from axiomatic prepositions nor inductively from observations on the nature of man and the world.

Paul thus has no doctrine of God as he is in himself, or of man as he is in himself, or of the world as it is in itself; he does not take the spectator's view (the view that goes under the name of philosophy). Paul knows God only as God-for-us (Bultmann's characteristic phrase), the world and man only in relation to God. His theology, consequently, issues from the matrix of faith: "Paul's theological thinking only lifts the knowledge inherent in faith itself into the clarity of conscious knowing."[59]

Taken strictly, Bultmann's analysis of Paul's language means that every theo-logical statement is to be taken at the same time as an anthropo-logical statement, since statements about God have to do also with man's status before God. One can also turn this around and say that every anthropo-logical statement of Paul is at once a theo-logical statement, since Paul does not make observations about man as such, but only about man before God. A similar insight into Pauline anthropology is the basis of Karl Barth's assertion that true humanity is known only through Jesus Christ: knowledge of true man is knowledge of man-before-God, which includes knowledge of man's alienation from God as well as knowledge of the possibility of reconciliation.

As God and man are never considered in isolation, in the abstract, neither are they considered exclusively in their inner relationship: it is always God-for-man-in-the-world, and man-before-God-in-the-world. "World" is always implied in Paul's theological talk about God and man.

Furthermore, just as theology and anthropology are reciprocal, so are christology and soteriology. Paul does not speculate about the Christ; he knows him only with respect to his benefits, i.e., soteriologically. Paul therefore speaks only about the saving event which God wrought in Jesus Christ; this is the meaning of Paul's statement in II Cor. 5:19: "God was in Christ reconciling the world to himself. . . ." Since this saving event is significant only insofar as it happens to and for man,

---

[59] *Theology of the New Testament* I, 190.

Paul's soteriology is also developed out of his man-before-God perspective, i.e., it is the knowledge inherent in faith lifted to the level of conscious knowing. But soteriology is also christology, if we take Bultmann strictly. Every soteriological statement must also be a statement about the Christ, since it is man-redeemed-by-Christ about whom Paul is speaking.

The logic of Bultmann's view accords full reciprocity to the polar pairs, theology-anthropology and christology-soteriology. In actual theological practice, however, Bultmann denies that this reciprocity can be carried through. The reason for this is that one pole must be demythologized. Language about God and Christ, by the nature of the case must be mythological, i.e., it must speak of the transcendent in this-worldly terms.[60] Since such mythological language is bound to be misleading, Bultmann insists that theology can legitimately develop only one side of each pair, viz., the side that has man as its head term. This means that theology must be presented as anthropology, and christology as soteriology; but anthropology and soteriology can only be presented for what they are, with the qualification, of course, that they are not descriptive—i.e., neutral—with respect to man's situation. This position accords with Bultmann's definition of theology; it is faith giving account of *itself*.

What is meant by "head term" should be made clear. If theology is doctrine of the-for-man-God, then the correlative term is doctrine of the-before-God-man. God is the head term in the first instance; man is the head term in the second. In the first, "for-man" is a qualifier of the primary term, God. In the second, "before-God" is a qualifier of the primary term, man. Bultmann's point is that we know God and Christ

---

[60] Schubert Ogden denies, I know, that Bultmann has ever taken a monolithic view concerning God-language (*Christ Without Myth*, 146–53). This is doubtless the case, and Bultmann's lack of clarity reflects a certain ambivalence on his part, which Ogden notes (*ibid.*, 147 ff.). Nevertheless, Bultmann characteristically lumps more sophisticated God-language with mythology and regards them both as an element of unfaith within faith. The strongest evidence I can adduce for this interpretation is the structure of Bultmann's presentation of the Pauline and Johannine theologies in his *Theology of the New Testament*. In neither case does he ever employ God or Christ as head terms for his presentation. Cf. J. M. Robinson, *New Frontiers* II, 33 f. The resolution of the final enigmatic statement in Bultmann's article, "What Sense Is There To Speak of God?" (*Christian Scholar* 43 [1960], 222), is found in *Kerygma und Mythos*, III, H. W. Bartsch, ed. (Hamburg: Herbert Reich-Evangelischer Verlag, 1954), 58 (Schubert Ogden, trans., *New Frontiers* I, 160): The paradox of theology is that "like all science, theology can speak of faith only by objectifying it, and yet does so in the knowledge that all such speaking finds its meaning only in a transcendence [*Aufhebung*] of objectification," i. e., only when objectification is overcome.

only in faith; the primary term, therefore, is always man-under-faith, or man-before-God. For this reason Bultmann proposes to do theology exclusively in anthropological (and soteriological) terms.

It may be argued that the logic of the two forms is actually identical. If we say that we know God only as God-for-us, and man only as man-before-God, what difference does it make whether man or God is the head term? If it is held that God is the x-factor, does it make any difference whether man is qualified by this x-factor or this x-factor qualified by man? Furthermore, on Bultmann's terms, man too is an x-factor apart from God. In that case, it is a matter of two x-factors receiving their definitions from each other. To put the question differently, can the logic of one form be utilized without calling upon the logic of the other?

Bultmann's reticence in according full reciprocity to theological language has good grounds. In the first place, Bultmann is unequivocal that man-under-faith is the primary term in all theological work, and that means that theology arises out of and returns to existence in faith. Theology is therefore a kind of phenomenology of faith. In the second place, the structure of the term, the-before-God-man, is one in which "God" may remain hidden; as that which qualifies man, God reveals himself in hiddenness. This doctrine is near to Bultmann's heart, as to the heart of the Lutheran tradition.[61] It may be noted, furthermore, that the structure with man as the head term is also the structure of the parable. If the parable is subject to rational extrication, the form with God as the head term may be derived from it, but assertions with God as the head term remain derivative in relation to parabolic language. Bultmann has correctly discerned that God-for-man and man-before God are the two foci of an ellipse, the latter of which is the beginning and terminus of the movement. The movement of Paul's language, then, is anchored on the manward side.

We may conclude that the logic of the two forms is not identical.

In the discussion of the two forms of theological statement, involving the two terms, God and man, a third term is rarely noticed. It has repeatedly figured in my own discussion, and Bultmann acknowledges it as well. I refer to the term "world." In speaking of God and man in their relationship, Bultmann stipulates that this relationship is qualified by "in-the-world." It is always God-for-man-in-the-world and man-before-God-in-the-world. What is the significance of "world"?

[61] Cf. John Dillenberger, *God Hidden and Revealed* (Philadelphia: Muhlenberg Press, 1953).

The problem which immediately arises is whether in-the-world qualifies God in either of these hyphenated terms. In holding firmly to the transcendence of God, Bultmann appears to answer negatively. He would be constrained, in that case, to bracket God out of the formulation, once it is noticed that in-the-world belongs integrally to it. But he can think of God as the *x*-factor (God in brackets); a similar solution is proposed by Paul van Buren, who conceals God in the passive voice, thus bracketing him out.[62] Yet it is quite possible that Bultmann wishes to conceive transcendence in such a way that it can be qualified by in-the-world; in that case he must find the corresponding language in which to speak of God.

On the other hand, it is possible that the phrase can be reformulated so as to make it possible to qualify God with in-the-world. If the reformulation runs, God-in-Christ-for-man-in-the-world, has the addition, in-Christ, altered the conditions under which the term God may be used? Bultmann would again appear to reply negatively, since Christ is taken to refer to the heavenly Christ, at least in the theological language of Paul. Nevertheless, this question must be pressed, if indeed the phrase in-Christ adds anything to the formulation, and thus to the Christian proclamation. Bultmann would allow, of course, that God-for-us is fully known only through Christ-for-us. It appears that the primitive church did not scruple to allow God to be qualified by in-the-world, so long as God was understood as God-in-Christ.

The juxtaposition of the term God and the qualifying phrase in-the-world constitutes a problem for Bultmann and the modern mind generally where it passes without notice in the New Testament. It is not for that difference less real to the modern mentality. So long as theology continues to be understood as the extrication of knowledge inherent in faith, the qualification in-the-world is indispensable. This means that the problem for contemporary theology cannot be shifted away from the term God.

Heidegger's analysis of the term world reveals that "world" is ontologically prior to the objects that furnish the world. "World" is "there" before it is noticed. It consitutes the horizon within which objects have their place and within which man acts out his existence. World in this sense is not a formal definition of a spatial-temporal continuum, but an intentionally constituted field upon which individual and collective existence is projected.

[62] See *supra,* chap. 4.

Insofar as faith concerns existence, it must be something that belongs within the horizon denoted by world. And insofar as it concerns the existence of particular men, it must belong to their intentionally constituted fields, either as an "upon which" or as an "out of which" of their projections.

That Pauline theology is anchored on the manward side, and that the qualification in-the-world is indispensable, signify that Pauline theology intends a "world" in which faith is ingredient.

It was said that the parable reflects without conceptualizing a "world" under the aegis of God's love. It mirrors this world without discoursing about it because it is foundational language. That is to say, this is the world it sees as the really real; it is a linguistic gesture pointing to something "there." It names that something, giving it a presence. As such, it is an invitation to project one's existence upon that world rather than some other.

If the parable is that mode of language which founds a world, and that particular world under the domain of God's grace, all other language in the Christian tradition is derivative in relation to it. It is out of this "poetic" medium that the tradition springs, however far in fact it may subsequently wander from it. Paul's language, as well as other languages in the New Testament and early church, presupposes such a foundational language tradition.[63]

[63] There is no reason to qualify the general assertion on the grounds that there are forms of language other than the parable which found linguistic traditions and thus worlds. The point of the analysis of the parable as metaphor (chap. 5) was to show, in agreement with Owen Barfield, that "world" is discovered by means of metaphor. All language which comes under this definition is metaphorical or parabolic. This does not mean, of course, that it has to take the particular form of the parables, which are in some respects unique.

The ultimate dependence of New Testament language on parabolic language may be taken to be problematic for other, more cogent reasons: (a) the kerygma as the linguistic substratum of the church's tradition does not appear to be dependent upon the language of Jesus or derivative in relation to it; (b) the language of Paul, as well as that of other New Testament writers, does not grow for the most part directly out of the language of Jesus, to say nothing of the parables. While these problems require a more extensive analysis than can be given here, two observations may be made. First, to say that a language tradition is dependent upon, or derivative in relation to, a foundational language does not mean that the connection can be traced in words, grammar, style, or mode of speech. Dependence refers to the world invoked by the one as it is presupposed by the other. A phenomenology of language is thus required as a means of exposing the internal history of a tradition. In the second place, it is necessary to inquire what transpires when the transition is made from foundational language to other modes of discourse, e.g., from parable to kerygma. Foundational language, if it is to be conserved as discourse that intends a particular world, has to be buttressed by modes of language other than its own. The phenomenon to be analyzed is thus the transition from

The field of the parable is the everyday world, which undergoes a mute deformation as the parable unfolds. That mute deformation is precipitated by "something" in the penumbral field of the parable, something that does not necessarily come to attention at all. It was suggested that Jesus is that something as the one who *speaks* the parable; it is he who *names* the world, who *invokes* its presence. The precipitant is therefore the word itself, the parable that is spoken, out of the mouth of Jesus.

Insofar as in-the-world is taken to qualify God or God-in-Christ in the formulation given above, the qualification applies to the word or

---

foundational language to tradition. Those modes of language which foster the sedimentation of tradition bring some loss as well as some gain: more discursive modes of language identify and tend to isolate various elements within the referential totality, say, of the parable, thus narrowing down the open end and reducing the existential tenor or metaphorical language. At the same time, the particular world intended by the parable is set off from other particular worlds with which it is competing. The loss is inherent in the gain.

Since derivative modes of discourse tend to move away (i.e., to abstract) from the foundational language on which they depend, it is necessary for them to be thrown back now and again upon their source. In this sense theology, as a discursive mode of discourse, must take its bearings in each new period from foundational discourse, and it is for this reason that the "new hermeneutic" has directed attention anew to the language of Jesus, particularly the parable.

The question of the relation of parable to kerygma is thus another way of posing the question of the relation of Jesus to the primitive church, or of asking why the New Testament contains both Gospels (words of Jesus) and letters, along with other literary modes (words of the apostles and others). The disjunction between Jesus and the church is also, or perhaps fundamentally, linguistic: the apostles do not merely or even primarily repeat Jesus' words. The linguistic disjunction is to be expected and respected rather than overcome. But what has to be asked is whether derivative language preserves the intentionality of foundational language. Insofar as the language of Paul, for example, intends the world established by the parable, his language can be said to be dependent in relation to the parable.

The relation between the language of Jesus and the language of the church is enormously complicated by the fact that the church preserved the language of Jesus as a part of its tradition. The existence of the Jesus tradition was not unambiguous: how it was transmitted and interpreted affected its relation to various other traditions in the church, and its relation to various other traditions in the church affected how it was transmitted and interpreted. The language of Jesus could not be preserved purely as foundational language: the process of transmission itself involved interpretation—witness the Gospels. The intricacies of the development are illustrated in a very suggestive essay by J. M. Robinson, "Kerygma and History in the New Testament," in *The Bible in Modern Scholarship*, J. P. Hyatt, ed. (Nashville, Tenn.: Abingdon Press, 1966), 114–50. Robinson shows that the language of Jesus became problematic in various instances in the early church precisely because it was viewed as one part among others of the total tradition of the church. Yet the presence of the Gospels in the canon witnesses to the intention of the church to hold the language of Jesus up against itself as foundational language.

parable which founds the realm of God's grace (it is a human, oral word, such as passes between man and man: Ebeling). By extension it applies also to the speaker, Jesus (he who was fully man).

Nevertheless, Jesus avers that he does not speak on his own authority, and faith, as Bultmann claims, insists that it cannot attribute itself to itself, nor is it willing to rest with the explanation that it derives from Jesus of Nazareth. Jesus and faith refer themselves to something which does not "appear" at all in the "world" intended by the parable. Since that something does not "appear," it can only be referred to the source of the speaking and the source of the seeing. Jesus calls for faith while God remains hidden.

It now becomes possible to account for the reciprocal reflexivity of Paul's theological statements and the movement of his language on the basis of the development of the linguistic tradition in relation to its ground.

In theological language of Paul's type, the penumbral, or more accurately, perhaps, the umbral, field of the parable is brought explicitly into view.[64] There are at least two reasons for this development. In the first place, Paul, like the church generally, had to give account of its faith to those whose world was populated with many gods and lords. It was inevitable, if not necessary, that Paul should bring his own "Lord" into view. Competitive worlds beget competitive world views. Secondly, Paul was endeavoring to make the world under the jurisdiction of grace stand up for his readers. He could do this, by way of rational extrication, only by predicating of his Lord (or God) what he wanted to bring to stand in the world. Such predicates pull a world in their wake. Rational extrication of this order is a device the function of which is to lead back to foundational language and the world it intends. Such reflective language, moreover, provides the means of considering the destiny of foundational language under new and altered circumstances. After all, Jesus was straightway understood in a variety of competing ways! If Bultmann is correct, the Pauline theology has this virtue: it mapped out the horizons of the foundational tradition for the first time in a way that was faithful to the intention of that tradition. Although such theological work has to be done again and again in every new epoch, Paul's language provides a relatively fixed point in the history of the tradition.

---

[64] Strictly speaking, Jesus belongs to the penumbral field (the zone of partial illumination, that which is caught out of the corner of the eye), while God and Christ belong to the umbral field (the zone of perfect shadow).

While Paul brings the umbral field of the parable into view (in concert with the kerygmatic tradition before him), he does not make it the object of reflection in and of itself. The object or objects in that field are not subjected to what Heidegger defines as the logic of the assertion. The umbral field is still held, so to speak, in solution with the visible field, the everyday world. This is the significance of the reciprocal reflexivity of Paul's theological language.

The transition from re-flective language to language in the mode of primary reflectivity brought with it certain dangers. By bringing the penumbral and umbral fields of parabolic language into the visible field, the way is opened for the consideration of various objects within those fields in and of themselves. The totality of significations is fragmented, with the result that God and Christ are on their way to becoming entities, and the various objects in the mundane field are also subject to consideration in isolation (Who is my neighbor?). The fragmentation of the circumspective totality intended by the parable begets loss of its "world," and the various objects which become conspicuous for the first time can be redistributed and incorporated into alien worlds. That Paul did not take these steps himself attests his acute sensitivity to the call of the word: he steadfastly endeavors to throw his hearers back upon that word, and thus, so to speak, upon parable.

The inner movement of the Pauline theology can be put differently. Paul is trying to let what the proclamation intends, i.e., the Crucified, give him what is to be said in view of the hearer. On the ground that the letters indicate that the message has suffered distortion or non-understanding, Paul is in the mode of recapitulation, attempting to hear again himself, and at the same time to hear with ears attuned to the auditory range of his readers. When Paul specifically takes up the language of those who misunderstand, as e.g., in I Corinthians 2:6-16, he throws their fund of established significations up against the intended "subject," Christ crucified (I Cor. 2:2), in order to shatter the language which presides over their hearing.[65] Such efforts as these are subject to misinterpretation so long as one attends only to the words: *one must attend the "unspoken" in order to understand the spoken,* for the spoken as convention is being distorted in juxtaposing it with the "unspoken." Only in this way—by the juxtaposition of the expectations of the hearers and what is to be heard, which results in a mute

[65] This point is made the explicit theme of chap. 11.

deformation of the fund of expectations—are the conditions for under-standing created at all. Paul may not always be successful, of course, and his failures account for those "other voices" in his letters, but he should be read, in any case, not only word by word but sentence by sentence and section by section, with attention to the movement of the whole. And the movement of the whole refers also to the letter form as such, provided Paul has permitted his intention to effect a correspond-ing silent modification of the epistolary conventions of his time.

V

The suggestion that the Pauline letter is to be read with attention to the structure and movement of the letter as such calls for some preliminary remarks. These remarks anticipate the more extended analysis to be carried out in chapter 10.

The letter form as such, Wilder observes, "is almost as flexible as oral speech itself,"[66] and the style of Paul betrays on every page the marks of oral expression: imagined dialogue, accusation and defense, queries, exclamations, oaths, and the challenge "not so much to understand the written words but to listen and behold."[67] The letter, consequently, is an appropriate substitute for oral word—it is as near oral speech as possible—yet it provides a certain distance on the proclamation as event. If the parable is a gesture pointing the way into the kingdom of God, the letter is only one step removed: it wonders why the gesture has been missed.

The desire to keep the letter as near to oral speech as possible is inherent in the silent coercion to give presence to the Christ-event.[68] The written word tends to degenerate into meaning which can be isolated from its intentionality; the oral word retains its character as eventful speech when it is understood as free, untrammeled, spontane-ous word.[69] Oral word opens onto its "subject," while written word closes in on itself in thought. "Written" and "oral" are to be understood in these contexts, of course, metaphorically.

In this light it is possible to account for the "travelogue," as that which announces his imminent presence, as a constituent element in

[66] *Language of the Gospel,* 39.

[67] *Ibid.,* 23.

[68] That is to say, the fact that Paul dictated his letters is not sufficient explanation of their oral character.

[69] Wilder, *Language of the Gospel,* 20 ff. and "Form-History and the Oldest Tradi-tion," 8 f.; Ebeling, *Word and Faith,* 312 f., n. 1.

the Pauline letter. Paul resists the written word, the crystallization of speech, which tends to bring the proclamation to rest in creed. Owing to his longing to keep it in motion ("My little children, with whom I am again in travail until Christ be formed in you!" [Gal. 4:19]), he leaves traces of its oral character in form, style, and in the travelogue, which implies the promise of oral word. If the body of the letter is in danger of falling into written word, the travelogue announces the necessary correction.

The opening thanksgiving, a convention taken over by Paul and then Christianized and historicized, assembles the same elements, explicitly or implicitly, noticed in connection with the polarity of his language. It thus reflects a similar movement of language under the aspect of prayer. Here Paul assembles himself, his readers, Christ and God: himself and his readers implicitly before Christ, the ground of faith, and explicitly in the presence of God, to whom thanks are due. The thanksgiving looks back, so to speak, on the effects of grace already experienced, just as the body of the letter calls the readers again into the presence of Christ, that the word of the cross may take effect anew as grace. Thus it could be said that as the present flows out of the past, the body of the letter flows out of the thanksgiving. The thanksgiving gives the basis for the renewal of the word in the mode of recapitulation.

And finally, it may be suggested that the eschatological climax which rounds off the thanksgiving, though often in diminished form, holds the future open. While grace has been made effective in the past, its full effect is still outstanding, and always so, for grace gives itself to unfinished history, the future which is yet to be disclosed. It was this movement, perhaps, which led Paul also to round off the body of the letter with an "eschatological climax," at least in certain instances. The future does not actualize itself exhaustively in either past or present, but stands perpetually at the threshold, waiting to be appropriated in every tomorrow.

The Letter: Form and Style

————————————————————

I

THE EXTENT TO WHICH THE ADVENT OF FORM CRITICISM, when coupled with the history of religions approach and fresh theological perspectives, gave new life to the study of the Synoptic Gospels is nothing short of remarkable. Literary, particularly source, criticism had arrived at an impasse. The new development made it possible for the first time to push with some confidence back behind written sources into the oral period, during which the Jesus tradition was taking shape. By virtue of the obvious success enjoyed by form criticism, other avenues inviting pursuit emerged. The recognition that the Synoptics are built up out of traditions which once circulated as more or less self-contained units opened the way for the development of redaction criticism, so recently come of age. At the other end of the line, the question has been raised whether form criticism must not be pressed beyond the methodological barriers erected by itself with respect to the *Sitz im Leben* of the primitive community, viz., whether we must not seek form-critical access to the preaching of the historical Jesus itself. At all events, it is no longer in doubt that form criticism opened a new era in Synoptic studies with its appearance nearly fifty years ago.

In an analogous but by no means identical way, the situation with respect to Acts was transformed, at least potentially, when Dibelius conceived the notion of applying form criticism to Acts. Being unable to utilize the same techniques he had employed on the Synoptics, he developed, in his epoch-making essay of 1923, a technique he called style criticism as a means of determining whether and to what extent the author of Acts had a fund of tradition, comparable to that which lay behind the Gospels, at his disposal. If Dibelius' initial direction has now been vigorously challenged, especially by Ernst Haenchen, it is not less clear that he put Haenchen, Conzelmann, and others on the right track: the quest for written sources and interest in the historical reliability of the material were sidetracked in favor of an investigation of the author of Acts as historiographer, theologian, and maker of books. Style criticism has been succeeded by composition analysis, to use Haenchen's own designation.

This sweeping sketch, all too briefly drawn and without explicit justification, permits us, nevertheless, to come to the problem of the letters against the background of conspicuous, not to say spectacular, progress, in the study of the Synoptics and Acts. It is surprising, to say the least, that the epistles, which comprise twenty-one of the twenty-seven New Testament documents, have not attracted comparable attention and evoked corresponding advances in literary analysis. Are the epistles, by the nature of the case, not amenable to the techniques developed in connection with form and tradition criticism? Have the epistles simply gone wanting because energies were concentrated elsewhere? Or has work on the epistles been arrested by other factors which have not yet come to light?

Minimally, it may be said that the literary analysis of the epistles, particularly with respect to the epistle taken as a whole, has not advanced materially beyond what it was, say, half a century ago.[1] If, during this period, New Testament studies have reached important new achievements in understanding the theology of Paul, in describing the history of religions background of Paul's thought and that of his opponents, in reconstructing the history and chronology of his career (thanks in large part to the work on Acts), and in letting Paul emerge again in his own right—not that he does not always stand somewhere close to the front in traditions influenced by the Reformation!—nevertheless, with respect to critical literary questions the situation is far from satisfactory. A breakthrough is urgently needed in this sphere, if for no other reason than that the discussion tends to stall always at the same points and wear itself out on the same insoluble issues.

This judgment by no means blinks the fact that much work has been done on the letters, mainly in bits and pieces, in which use has been

---

[1] R. H. Fuller in his recent survey merely notes by way of appendix, after treating "Pauline Studies" under the rubrics of "theology" and "opponents," that certain partition theories have been revived (*The New Testament in Current Study* [New York: Charles Scribner's Sons, 1962], 68 f.). W. G. Kümmel is likewise unable to point to substantive gains regarding the letter as a literary form, see P. Feine, J. Behm, and W. G. Kümmel, *Einleitung in Das Neue Testament* (13th ed.; Heidelberg: Quelle & Meyer, 1964), 173 ff.

252 LANGUAGE, HERMENEUTIC, AND WORD OF GOD

made of style, form, and tradition criticism. The collective force of
these diverse endeavors, in my opinion, has not yet been made apparent. We will return to this point in due course. Furthermore—and
this goes together with the first—the letter form has not come into
view as a whole, I think, primarily because Deissmann is still too much
with us, in spite of the repeated qualifications of his thesis.[2] J. Weiss
once remarked: "The thesis of Deissmann in his *Bibelstudien* concerning the purely letter-character of the Pauline epistles can only be taken
as correct *cum grano salis.*"[3] Deissmann bequeathed to us the picture
of Paul dashing off notes to this or that congregation, sandwiched in
between travels, sermons, conferences, conflicts, and the like, for which
there are perfect parallels in the Egyptian nonliterary papyri. So long as
this picture prevails, the Pauline letter at least will continue to be
conceived as salutation, thanksgiving, and closing, with virtually anything in any order thrown in between.[4]

Günther Bornkamm, however, has presented the first viable proposal aimed at explaining and thus overcoming the chaos represented
by one Pauline letter, canonical II Corinthians.[5] He asks: is there any
explanation for the collection and arrangement of letters which II
Corinthians presents?[6] His thesis may be sketched in brief: (1) the
editor of the collection, in placing chapters 10–13 last, was following a
basic rule of early Christian edificatory literature, viz., the warning
against heresy and false teachers very often comes at the *end* of

[2] E.g., Kümmel, *op. cit.,* 174; E. Fascher, "Briefliteratur, urchristliche, formgeschichtlich," *RGG* I, 1412; C. F. D. Moule, *The Birth of the New Testament* (New
York: Harper & Row, 1962), 8.

[3] J. Weiss "Beiträge zur paulinischen Rhetorik," in *Theologische Studien, B. Weiss
dargebracht* (Göttingen: Vandenhoeck & Ruprecht, 1897), 210 n. 1.

[4] A. Deissmann, *Bible Studies,* A. Grieve, trans. (Edinburgh: T & T. Clark, 1901),
3–59. Take as illustrative of Deissmann's position this remark (p. 57): "The criticism of
the Letters of Paul must always leave room for the probability that their alleged
contradictions and impossibilities, from which reasons against their authenticity and
integrity have been deduced, are really evidences to the contrary, being but the natural
concomitants of letter-writing." Beside this may be set another remark (p. 47): "How
much more distinctly do the Letters to the Corinthians bear the stamp of the true letter!
The second of them in particular, reveals its true character in every line; in the author's
opinion, it is the most letter-like of all the letters of Paul. . . ." Cf. also *Licht vom
Osten* (4th ed.; Tübingen: J. C. B. Mohr [Paul Siebeck], 1923), 116 ff., 193 ff.

[5] Günther Bornkamm, *Die Vorgeschichte des sogenannten Zweiten Korintherbriefes,*
Sitzungsberichte der Heidelberger Akademie der Wissenschaften, Philosophisch-
historische Klasse, Jahrgang 1961, 2. Abhandlung (Heidelberg: Carl Winter, 1961);
English summary in *NTS* 8 (1962), 258–64. The following references are to the
German text, with corresponding English pages in brackets.

[6] *Ibid.,* 24 [261].

documents and sections, inasmuch as the appearance of false teachers and prophets was a sign of the last days. Evidence for this rule is found in the New Testament itself, e.g., I Cor. 16:22, Gal. 6:11 ff., Rom. 16:17-20, Jude 17 ff., II Pet. 3:2 ff., Rev. 22:11, 15, 18 f., as well as in Didache 16. Matthew 7:15 (close of the Great Sermon) and Didache 16 show that the rule was followed in secondary compositions.[7] It can be argued, of course, that Paul was himself following this rule in composing II Corinthians. However, chapters 10–13 do not reflect apocalyptic language and the opponents are not characterized as the fiends of the end-time, as one would expect if the canonical arrangement were original.[8] Beyond that—and here we return to Deissmann—one must be persuaded that II Corinthians as it stands makes no sense *as a letter.* (2) Paul's account of his anxious journey from Asia to Troas to Macedonia is interrupted at 2:14 with a remarkable paean of thanksgiving, which is followed by the long apologetic in respect of the apostolic office (2:14—7:4 [omitting 6:14—7:1]); only in 7:5 does he return to his journey and meeting with Titus. Bornkamm has postulated that the editor has inserted the apologetic into the correspondence at this point because of a formal connection: 2:12 f.—arrival in Troas, preaching, hastening on to Macedonia; this suggests the triumphal procession of the conquering apostle (2:14 ff. misunderstood!), viewed, of course, from a much later and idealized perspective.[9] Catchword or topical association can serve editors as well as original authors. And finally, (3) the editor inserted two collection fragments (8, 9), as a topical unit, before the "letter of tears."[10]

Bornkamm is rightly attempting to meet the deficiency of most literary analyses of II Corinthians (and other letters): "Yet it is clear that every literary analysis remains a vague attempt so long as the reasons may not be advanced or convincingly stated why a later collator came to compose the letter as a whole."[11] He seeks, therefore, to establish rules by which such secondary compositions were ordered. We could, perhaps, go a step further and ask whether it is possible to establish the *form*—with a reasonable degree of latitude—of the Pauline letter itself. If this be possible, then a double check would be

[7] *Ibid.,* 25 ff. [261 f.].

[8] *Ibid.,* 27.

[9] *Ibid.,* 21, 29 ff. [259 f., 262 f.].

[10] *Ibid.,* 17, 31 f. [260 f., 262 f.]. Bornkamm's reconstruction of the correspondence and his supporting exegetical arguments are not included in this sketch. The summary thus hardly does justice to his case, but our interest here is in the form of the letter.

[11] *Ibid.,* [261]; cf. 24.

provided for literary analyses: one in relation to Paul's own predilec-
tions, and one in relation to the letter form as it was adopted, crystallized, and developed in the subsequent church. It should not be
forgotten that the letter was widely adopted as a literary medium in the
primitive church and that Paul in particular was often imitated. These
two factors have conspired to make it difficult to sort Paul out from his
imitators, and to distinguish original from secondary and composite
epistles. It seems that only a close analysis of *form*, together with *style*
and *sequence* analysis, promises to bring further progress. Such analysis
would begin with Paul, who stands at the head of the Christian
epistolary tradition, and then trace the letter form through its various
stages in the primitive and early church. It would also be necessary to
compare and contrast the Christian epistle with its Hellenistic
counterpart.

II

Does the program suggested above have any prospects of success?
An estimate of its potential depends in part, of course, on whether one
thinks suitable ground has been laid. So long as the collective force of
the work on the epistles, inspired by form and style criticism—referred
to earlier—goes unnoticed, it is likely that such an estimate will be low.
In the interest of rectifying this deficiency, it is proposed to review this
work. The review, of necessity, must be extremely sketchy.

1. *Paraenesis.* In characterizing the style of the epistles of James,
Dibelius observes that James 1, 3:13 ff., 4, and 5 contain sayings and
groups of sayings of manifold content, in varied arrangement, and
without emphasis on any special point that relates to a particular
situation.[12] James is therefore to be characterized as *paraenetic* in style,
i.e., stringing together general moral maxims, sometimes without
connective, sometimes with catchword association or the use of an
identical or cognate word (verging on topical association); the function of such connectives is obviously mnemonic, hence they do not
provide continuity in thought but occasionally even thwart it.[13]

The closest parallels to the style of James in the New Testament are
certain sections in the Pauline letters, and these are precisely the

[12] Martin Dibelius, *Der Brief des Jakobus,* herausgegeben und ergänzt von Heinrich
Greeven, *Meyers Kommentar* XV (11th ed.; Göttingen: Vandenhoeck & Ruprecht,
1964), 15 f.; cf. "Zur Formgeschichte des Neuen Testaments (ausserhalb der Evange-
lien)," *ThR,* N.F. 3 (1931), 212–19.

[13] *Ibid.,* 16–23.

passages which are apparently not epistolary in character, i.e., which do not seem to have a specific situation in view. Dibelius cites I Thess. 4:1–12, 5:1–22, Gal. 5:13—6:10, Rom. 12 and 13, Col. 3 and 4 as examples.[14] These passages are not only distinctive in style, but apparently draw on a tradition the formation of which lies behind Paul.

As elements of the paraenetic tradition but not always occurring in paraenetic passages are, first, the *Haustafeln*, tables of household duties (e.g., Col. 3:18 ff., Eph. 5:22 ff., I Pet. 2:18 ff.), investigated by K. Weidinger[15] and established as emanating from a Hellenistic context;[16] second, the *catalogues of virtues and vices* (e.g., Rom. 1:29–31, Gal. 5:19–21, 22 f., Eph. 5:3–5, etc.), recently restudied by S. Wibbing[17] and found to rest on both Hellenistic and late Jewish traditions.[18] The latter are more loosely constructed and are scattered throughout the epistles.[19] To these David Bradley proposes adding the *topos*, which apparently belongs exclusively to paraenetic sections of the epistles.[20] A *topos* is a self-contained unit in paraenetic style which treats a topic of proper thought or action, a virtue or vice. Examples abound in Pseudo-Isocrates, Marcus Aurelius, Sirach, the Testaments of the Twelve Patriarchs. The *topos* is a moral essay in miniature, which may or may not derive from tradition, but which in any case reflects teaching that has become stereotyped in form. Thus, whether or not the *topos* is

---

[14] *Ibid.*, 15; Martin Dibelius, *Die Formgeschichte des Evangeliums,* Dritte, durchgesehene Auflage mit einem Nachtrag von Gerhard Iber, herausgegeben von Günther Bornkamm (Tübingen: J. C. B. Mohr [Paul Siebeck], 1959), 239 f. Cf. David G. Bradley, "The *Topos* as a Form in the Pauline Paraenesis," *JBL* 72 (1953), 240.

[15] *Die Haustafeln: Ein Stück urchristlicher Paränese,* "Untersuchungen zum Neuen Testament," H. Windisch, ed., Heft 14 (Leipzig: J. C. Hinrichs, 1928).

[16] F. W. Beare, *The Interpreter's Bible,* 11 (Nashville, Tenn.: Abingdon Press, 1955), 226, observes that these tables occur only in the sub-Pauline epistles.

[17] *Die Tugend- und Lasterkataloge im Neuen Testament, und ihre Traditionsgeschichte unter besonderer Berücksichtigung der Qumran-Texte,* Beihefte zur Zeitschrift für die Neutestamentliche Wissenschaft und die Kunde der älteren Kirche, W. Eltester, ed., 25 (Berlin: Töpelmann, 1959); cf. the earlier work of A. Vögtle, *Die Tugend- und Lasterkataloge im Neuen Testament. Exegetisch, Religions- und Formgeschichtlich Untersucht,* "Neutestamentliche Abhandlungen," XVI, 4/5 (Münster: Aschendorffschen Verlagsbuchhandlung, 1936). Another work in this vein has recently appeared: Ehrhard Kamlah, *Die Form der katalogischen Paränese im Neuen Testament* (Tübingen: J. C. B. Mohr [Paul Siebeck], 1964).

[18] Cf. Wibbing, *op. cit.*, 77, for a summary statement.

[19] Further examples: I Cor. 5:10–11, 6:9–10, II Cor. 6:6, 12:20–21, Phil. 4:8 (Wibbing, *op. cit.*, 78).

[20] Bradley, *op. cit.*, 238–46.

situational must be determined from context.[21] Günther Bornkamm points also to stereotyped figures current at the time (e.g., the athletic contest, I Cor. 9:24–27), the teaching of the two ways (Didache, Barnabas) taken over from Jewish tradition, and the development of community regulations (e. g., Pastorals) as elments belonging to the paraenetic tradition and subject to form-critical analysis.[22]

The paraenetic material in the epistles is thus subject to form-critical analysis, and in two respects: (1) with respect to individual forms and traditions incorporated into the letters in various contexts in connection with the development of other points, and (2) with respect to the paraenetic section as a convention in the epistle. Two things are striking with regard to paraenesis in the New Testament letters: (1) in the Pauline corpus only Romans, Galatians, and I Thessalonians exhibit paraenetic sections, which stand in each case near the close of the letter; (2) the presence of the paraenesis in the letter suggests that the Christian letter writer stood nearer the literary than the popular mode of epistolary conventions. The paraenesis, to be sure, is not strictly speaking a literary form, but roots in oral instruction in wisdom, the sermon, the homily, the "lecture" of the philosophical schools, the diatribe.[23] While marked by the rhetorical style, in which mnemonic devices, for example, play a major role, it is nevertheless taken up not by the common letter but by the formal letter.[24]

2. Opening Thanksgiving (eulogy). A second element in the letters which has been subjected to form-critical analysis is the opening thanksgiving (*hodaya*) or, as an alternative, benediction (*beracha*), which regularly follows upon the salutation (all Pauline letters except Galatians; all deutero-Pauline letters except Titus). In his extensive analysis, Paul Schubert found that the εὐχαριστῶ (thanksgiving) periods exhibited two clearly discernible forms, although they are occasionally mixed.[25] While Schubert demonstrated that these periods

21 Bradley (*ibid.*, 240) holds that by adding the *topos* to the *Haustafeln* and the catalogues of virtues and vices, and by the recognition of one other form, which he does not treat in this article, one is able to analyze *all* the material in the Pauline paraenesis in relation to forms current in the Hellenistic world. His published study is based on an unpublished Yale dissertation.

22 G. Bornkamm, "Formen und Gattungen im NT," *RGG* II, 1004 f.

23 H. Thyen, *Der Stil der Jüdisch-Hellenistischen Homilie*, "Forschungen zur Religion und Literatur des Alten und Neuen Testaments," 47 (Göttingen: Vandenhoeck & Ruprecht, 1955), 85; Dibelius, *Der Brief des Jakobus*, 17 f.

24 Cf., for example, Hebrews, the letters of Seneca (first century A.D.).

25 Paul Schubert, *Form and Function of the Pauline Thanksgivings*, Beihefte *ZNW* 20 (Berlin: Töpelmann, 1939), 35 f.

reflect Hellenistic epistolary style, James M. Robinson has shown that they also mirror primitive Christian liturgical style, and are related to the *hodaya* and *beracha* respectively.[26] Jack T. Sanders has further developed Schubert's analysis of the thanksgiving period proper, particularly with respect to its "eschatological climax" and close, and has then proceeded to analyze the formula used to introduce the body of the letter.[27] He has noted further that this formula, both in full and in abbreviated forms, is utilized in the body of the letter to indicate a transition in the argument or to introduce a new topic. In so doing he has moved over to style criticism and his observations link up with others made from the latter perspective.

It has long been noted that these thanksgivings or benedictions are "historicized" or adapted to the situation to which the letter is addressed. Robinson has drawn attention to "the non-liturgical, autobiographical *beracha* in II Corinthians 1:3 ff.,"[28] and E. Fascher notes that the thanksgivings in II Cor. 1:4–7 and Phil. 1:3–11 "correspond to the situation."[29] It can be shown, in my judgment, that the opening prayers tend to "telegraph" the content of the letter.

3. *Salutation and closing.* In his salutations (inside address and greeting) and closings (doxology, greetings, benediction), Paul makes use of epistolary conventions, which he Christianizes.[30] The three elements of the prescript (sender, addressee, salutation) are varied from instance to instance,[31] as are the three elements of the closing.[32]

4. *Other traditional material.* The form-critical indentification and isolation of hymns, kerygmatic formulae, confessions, and the like is

---

[26] "The Historicality of Biblical Language," in *The Old Testament and Christian Faith*, B. W. Anderson, ed. (New York: Harper & Row, 1963), 132, 146, 149 n. 29; these remarks are amplified in "Die Hodajot-Formel in Gebet und Hymnus des Frühchristentums," in *Apophoreta. Festschrift für Ernst Haenchen*, W. Eltester, ed. (Berlin: Töpelmann, 1964), 194–235.

[27] "The Transition from Opening Epistolary Thanksgiving to Body in the Letters of the Pauline Corpus," *JBL* 81 (1962), 348–62.

[28] "Historicality of Biblical Language," 146.

[29] "Briefliteratur, urchristliche, formgeschichtlich," *RGG* I, 1413.

[30] P. Wendland, *Die urchristlichen Literaturformen, im Handbuch zum Neuen Testament* I, 3 (Tübingen: J. C. B. Mohr [Paul Siebeck], 1912), 278.

[31] *Ibid.*, 340 f.; cf. E. Lohmeyer, "Probleme paulinischer Theologie I: Die brieflichen Grussüberschriften," *ZNW* 26 (1927), 158–73, reprinted in *Probleme paulinisher Theologie* (Stuttgart: W. Kohlhammer Verlag, n.d.), 9–29; cf. O. Michel, "Der Brief an die Römer," in H. A. W. Meyer's *Kritisch-exegetischer Kommentar über das Neue Testament* (11th ed.; Göttingen: Vandenhoeck & Ruprecht, 1957), 25 f., 337 ff.

[32] Wendland, *op. cit.*, 342 ff.

too well known to require review.[83] Special mention should perhaps be made of doxologies and benedictions found elsewhere than in the opening and closing of the letters,[84] exegetical and midrashic traditions,[85] and possibly traditional homiletical material.[86] Kendrick Grobel has recently identified an old Jewish chiastic retribution formula in Rom. 2:6–11.[87] The recognition of texts of this type in the letters does not help us materially, for the most part, in analyzing the letter as a form, however indispensable such analyses may be to exegesis. Nevertheless, they do contribute directly to our growing sensitivity to form and style.

III

The second ingredient that can contribute to the analysis of the form of the letters is style criticism.

It was Johannes Weiss who more than fifty years ago set out as one of the significant unfinished tasks of New Testament scholarship the investigation of the sentence structure, style, and rhetoric of the Pauline epistles.[88] Weiss had already made a beginning in this direction himself,[89] one that is reflected in his classic commentary on I Corinthians.[40] In typical German fashion, he mediated this interest to one of his pupils, Rudolf Bultmann, who shortly thereafter published a monograph on the style of the Pauline preaching and the Cynic-Stoic diatribe.[41] It was Weiss's conviction, substantiated by Bultmann, that

[83] Surveys are to be found in Dibelius, *ThR*, N. F. 3 (1931), 219–33; Dibelius, *A Fresh Approach to the New Testament and Early Christian Literature* (London: Ivor Nicholson & Watson, 1937), 143 f., 146 f.; Fascher, *op. cit.*, 1413 ff.; and especially Bornkamm, *RGG* II, 1002 f.

[84] L. G. Champion, *Benedictions and Doxologies in the Epistles of Paul* (Oxford: Kemp Hall Press, 1934); Fascher, *op. cit.*, 1415.

[85] Dibelius, *ThR*, N.F. 3 (1931), 227 ff. (e.g., Rom. 10); Fascher, *op. cit.*, 1413 f. (e.g., Rom. 4:1–25).

[86] E.g., Rom. 1:18–32; Dibelius *ThR*, N.F. 3 (1931), 230 f.; Fascher, *op. cit.*, 1414; Michel, *op. cit.*, 51 f.

[87] "A Chiastic Retribution-Formula in Romans 2," in *Zeit und Geschichte: Dankesgabe an Rudolf Bultmann zum 80. Geburtstag*, E. Dinkler, ed. (Tübingen: J. C. B. Mohr [Paul Siebeck], 1964), 255–61.

[88] Johannes Weiss, *Die Aufgaben der neutestamentlichen Wissenschaft in der Gegenwart* (Göttingen: Vandenhoeck & Ruprecht, 1908), 10 ff.

[89] "Beiträge zur paulinischen Rhetorik," in *Theologische Studien, B. Weiss dargebracht* (Göttingen: Vandenhoeck & Ruprecht, 1897), 165–247 (on which see A. Deissmann, *ThR* 5 [1902], 65 f.).

[40] *Der erste Korintherbrief* (9th ed.; Göttingen: Vandenhoeck & Ruprecht, 1910).

[41] *Der Stil der paulinischen Predigt und die kynisch-stoische Diatribe*, "Forschungen zur Religion und Literatur des Alten und Neuen Testaments," 13 (Göttingen: Vandenhoeck & Ruprecht, 1910).

the Pauline style is more akin to popular philosophy, as exemplified in the diatribe, than to the language of the common Egyptian letters as Deissmann thought. Weiss wrote in 1908: "On the whole I do not doubt that the judgment regarding Pauline diction will shift more in the course of time in a direction which will make it necessary to attribute to him a higher level of literary and cultural achievement."[42] His opinion with respect to diction he attempted to demonstrate with respect to style.

There has been a long, relatively dry spell since Bultmann published his study in 1910, relieved to my knowledge only by sporadic and to a certain extent tangential efforts: in 1955, Hartwig Thyen, a pupil of Bultmann, attempted to follow up the lines laid down by his teacher in an investigation of the Jewish-Hellenistic homily, and Terence Y. Mullins, in addition to his own contributions, calls attention to the monograph of F. Exler.[43]

Style analysis in the first instance is concerned to identify characteristic words and phrases, individual literary or rhetorical devices, and eccentricities of expression which betray an author's affinity with a certain tradition or traditions, or reveal his own distinctive use of language. The rhetorical question, τί οὖν ἐροῦμεν (what shall we say

[42] Weiss, *Die Aufgaben der neutestamentlichen Wissenschaft*, 11.

[43] Hartwig Thyen, *Der Stil der Jüdisch-Hellenistischen Homilie*, "Forschungen zur Religion und Literature des Alten und Neuen Testaments," 47 (Göttingen: Vandenhoeck & Ruprecht, 1955); F. Exler, *The Form of the Ancient Greek Letter: A Study in Greek Epistolography* (Washington, D.C.: Catholic University of America, 1923); Terence Y. Mullins, "Petition as a Literary Form," *NT* 5 (1962), 46–54, and "Disclosure: A Literary Form in the New Testament," *NT* 7 (1964), 44–60. One should, of course, also mention works closely related but not devoted exclusively to the style of the letters: E. Norden, *Agnostos Theos. Untersuchungen zur Formengeschichte Religiöser Rede* (Leipzig: Teubner, 1898; reprinted, 5th ed., Stuttgart: B. G. Teubner, 1958); W. Bousset, *Jüdisch-christlicher Schulbetrieb in Alexandria und Rom*, "Forschungen zur Religions des AT und NT," 6 (Göttingen: Vandenhoeck & Ruprecht, 1915); W. Bacher, *Die Proömien der alten jüdischen Homilie*, "Beiträge zur Wissenschaft vom AT," Heft 12, G. Kittel, ed. (Leipzig: J. C. Hinrichs, 1913); G. Klein, *Der älteste christliche Katechismus und die jüdische Propaganda Literatur* (Berlin: Reimer, 1909); S. Maybaum, *Die ältesten Phasen in der Entwicklung der jüdischen Predigt* (Berlin, 1901); Th. Schermann, *Griechische Zauberpapyri und das Gemeinde- und Dankgebet im ersten Clemensbriefe*, "Texte und Untersuchungen," 3. Reihe, 4. Bd., Heft 2b (Leipzig: J. C. Hinrichs, 1909); E. Stein, *Die homiletische Peroratio im Midrasch* (Hebrew Union College Annual 1931/32, 353 ff.); P. Wendland, "Philo und die kynisch-stoische Diatribe," in P. Wendland and O. Kern, *Beiträge zur Geschichte der griechischen Philosophie und Religion* (Berlin: G. Reimer, 1895). This list could be extended considerably. Among the more recent literature, note C. F. D. Moule, *An Idiom-Book of New Testament Greek* (Cambridge, Eng.: The University Press, 1953), 193–201, with further references.

then), for example, shows Paul's acquaintance with the dialogical style
of the diatribe, yet he uses it in Rom. 4:1 to introduce his theme;[44] the
latter goes together with the tendency for dialogue to retreat in the
Jewish-Hellenistic homily.[45] In the second place, style analysis attempts
to discern sentence and period structure. Parallelisms, for example,
have often been noted in the letters of Paul, of which I Cor. 1:25 is a
model example:

ὅτι τὸ μωρὸν τοῦ θεοῦ
σοφώτερον τῶν ἀνθρώπων ἐστίν,
καὶ τὸ ἀσθενὲς τοῦ θεοῦ
ἰσχυρότερον τῶν ἀνθρώπων.

For, the foolishness of God
is wiser than men,
And the weakness of God
is stronger than men.   —RSV

Weiss and others have provided extensive analyses of such periods.
Paul Schubert's work on the Pauline thanksgivings is an effort to
establish the construction of a period. And finally, style analysis may be
taken in the broad sense to mean the investigation of the form and
function of constituent elements within the whole, or of the form and
function of the literary form *as a whole*. Of the former the paraenesis
would be an example, and constitutes, at the same time, an element
which must be taken into account in analyzing the Pauline letter as a
whole. The construction of these more or less arbitrary categories
within style criticism is determined by the movement from minutiae to
the whole.

While progress on the lower end of the spectrum has been considerable, it is by no means at an end. Nevertheless, a sufficient basis has
been laid to enable style criticism to concern itself in a preliminary way
with larger units and with the letter as a whole.

It is appropriate at this juncture to offer a few random observations
with respect to the analysis of the larger unit, and thus approach the
whole via the part. The following is limited largely to formal observations (i.e., the question of function is not considered).

[44] Michel, *op. cit.*, 99, cf. 129. F. Blass and A. Debrunner, *A Greek Grammar of the
New Testament and Other Early Christian Literature*, Robert W. Funk, trans. and rev.
(Chicago: University of Chicago Press, 1961), sec. 496.
[45] Thyen, *op. cit.*, 41 f.

Joachim Jeremias, among others, has noticed that Paul makes frequent use of the schema *a b / b a,* i.e., chiastic structure.[46] Paul employs the chiastic inversion of parts of sentences for purely rhetorical reasons, the chiastic inversion of contrasting pairs of words and statements (not merely for rhetorical reasons, but also to make sequence more obvious), and the chiastic development of two or more concepts introduced thematically. The first two types of chiasm are amply illustrated by Jeremias, although his examples could be extended. With respect to the third—the chiastic development of concepts thematically presented—Jeremias cites I Cor. 1:24 f. as a case in miniature, but he also notes that this pattern prevails for longer passages, e.g., I Cor. 15:35-57 (rhetorical questions in 15:35 are answered in reverse order), I Cor. 9:1-27 (the questions in 9:1a are dealt with in reverse order; also noted by H. Leitzmann), and Gal. 1:10—6:10 (the whole letter! Paul answers the two objections to his gospel in reverse order). Bultmann has made a similar claim for Romans 5—8: the two great themes of 5:1—7:6 are dealt with in chapter 8 in a new way and in reverse order: 8:1-11 is concerned with freedom from sin(5), and 8:12-29 with freedom from death (6:1—7:6).[47] Among other examples, mention may be made of one not noted by Jeremias. In I Cor. 1:13 Paul introduces his discussion of internal strife at Corinth with three rhetorical questions:

μεμέρισται ὁ Χριστός;
μὴ Παῦλος ἐσταυρώθη ὑπὲρ ὑμῶν;
ἢ εἰς τὸ ὄνομα Παύλου ἐβαπτίσθητε;

Is Christ divided?
Was Paul crucified for you?
Or were you baptized into the name of Paul? —RSV

The first is the overarching question. The last, concerning baptism, is treated in 1:14-16. Then in 1:17 Paul makes the transition back to the theme of the cross, which prevails from 1:18 through 2:16. Verses

[46] Jeremias ("Chiasmus in den Paulusbriefen," *ZNW* 49 [1958] 145-156) takes this position in spite of the largely negative review of Nils Wilhelm Lund, *Chiasmus in the New Testament: A Study in Formgeschichte* (Chapel Hill, N.C.: University of North Carolina Press, 1942); reviewed by Grobel, *ThR* 17 (1948), 146; cf. Blass and Debrunner, sec. 477 (2).
[47] *Existence and Faith,* 152 f.

3:1 ff., especially 3:4 f., show that Paul is again or still occupied with
factions based on men, and 3:5–25 intends to show that all apostles and
evangelists are subordinate to Christ (climax in 3:21 ff.). The three
questions (1:13), designated by *a b c* are answered in the order *c b a*.
These observations support the judgment of Wilckens that 1:10–4:21
is a tightly written unity.[48]

Apropos of style criticism of this order may be mentioned another
pattern discernible in I Cor. 11:2–34: Paul introduces the whole in
11:2 with a formula, Ἐπαινῶ δὲ ὑμᾶς ὅτι κτλ. (I commend you because), which is renewed in 11:17 with a change in topic (οὐκ ἐπαινῶ
ὅτι κτλ., I do not commend you because).[49] The general theme
παραδόσεις (traditions, 11:2), furthermore, is reiterated specifically
when he comes to the heart of the second discussion, and in such a
way that Paul recalls the whole of the introductory formula (cf. 11:23
with 11:2). It is to be noted further that Paul employs a second
formula in introducing the first subtheme in 11:3 (θέλω δὲ ὑμᾶς
εἰδέναι ὅτι κτλ., I want you to understand that). If *a* stands for the
general theme, *b* for the first subtheme (11:3–16), and *c* the second
subtheme (11:17–34), the following pattern emerges: *a b a c*.[50]

Patterns of the types noted are not necessarily helpful in determining
the form of the letter, but they do carry us in the direction of establishing Pauline style. Furthermore, they tend to confirm the tight internal
coherence and structure of certain sections in the Pauline letters. Such
coherence and structure can also be established by close sequence
analysis. Galatians 1:1—5:26, for example, is a tightly conceived unity;
Jeremias' stylistic observations only confirm this judgment and lend
weight to it. Wilckens has exposed the internal logic and coherence of
I Cor. 1:10—4:21; stylistic observations support that judgment. The unity
of Romans 1—8, especially 5—8, is supported by Bultmann's remarks.
It should be said in this connection that sequence analysis, no less than
style analysis, is a much-neglected aspect of Pauline criticism. Bultmann's analysis of the great defense of the apostolic ministry in II Cor.

---

48 Ulrich Wilckens, *Weisheit und Torheit: Eine exegetisch-religionsgeschichtliche
Untersuchung zu 1. Kor. 1 und 2* (Tübingen: J. C. B. Mohr [Paul Siebeck], 1959),
5–11.

49 Verses 11:3 ff. are positive: he does commend them; while in 11:17 ff. Paul is
negative: he cannot praise them.

50 One might point to Gal. 5:1–26 as another example, but without introductory
formulae: 5:1 general theme (= *a*), 5:2–12 first subtheme (circumcision, = *b*), 5:13a
reiteration of general theme (*a*), 5:13b–26 second subtheme (= *c*).

2:14—6:10 is a model of sequence analysis,[51] and style analysis supports his view that this passage is closely articulated.[52] The opinion, emanating from Deissmann, that the letters were struck off in a casual way and amidst the turmoil surrounding Paul's ministry is perhaps what has crippled sensitivities to Paul's style and logic. One is too much inclined to expect the letters to be chaotic because Deissmann thought that was the way letters are written!

These laconic remarks on the subject of style and sequence analysis may serve to suggest the basic disposition in respect to which the letter as a whole is to be approached. It is entirely possible that a great deal more can be learned about the constituent elements and construction of the letters than has heretofore been thought possible, for the reason that style and sequence analysis show that Paul may not have been so undisciplined after all. We may turn, then, to the subject of constituent elements and the form of the letter as a whole.

IV

The form of the letter, according to Wendland,[53] whose discussion is still normative,[54] is comprised of salutation (sender, addressee, greeting) and opening thanksgiving at the head; doxology, personal greetings, and benediction at the close. In addition to these formalities, Dibelius has identified the paraenesis as a distinctive section in some of the epistles,[55] and Schubert,[56] followed by Sanders,[57] has extended the formal analysis of the opening *hodaya* (or *beracha*), including the formulá which introduces the body of the letter. Can we go further? I would suggest that we may now speak in a preliminary way of the theological body of the letter, but not merely for the reason that it is

---

[51] *Exegetische Probleme des zweiten Korintherbriefes,* "Symbolae Biblicae Upsaliensés," Supplementhäfaten till Svensk Exegetisk Årsbok 9 (Uppsala, 1947; reprinted Darmstadt: Wissenschaftliche Buchgesellschaft, 1963).

[52] As illustrative of the point, one may point to the use of ἔχω (with οὗτος, τοιοῦτος, αὐτός) at 3:4, 12; 4:1, 7, 13 to renew the basic theme in a new way.

[53] P. Wendland, *Die urchistlichen Literaturformen,* 339–45. Cf. Béda Rigaux, *Paulus und seine Briefe: Der Stand der Forschung,* "Biblische Handbibliothek" II, August Berz, trans. (Munich: Rösel-Verlag, 1964), 167 ff.; pp. 164–203 of this work contain a summary of the form-critical investigation of the Pauline letters. Unfortunately, it came into my hands too late to be utilized in writing my own summary.

[54] Cf. Dibelius, *A Fresh Approach,* 142 ff.; Kümmel, *Einleitung,* 174.

[55] *ThR,* N.F. 3 (1931), 212 ff.; *A Fresh Approach,* 143 f.; *Die Formgeschichte des Evangeliums,* 3d ed., 239 ff. (*From Tradition to Gospel,* B. L. Woolf, trans. [New York: Charles Scribner's Sons, 1935], 238 ff.)

[56] *Op. cit.*

[57] *Op. cit.*

what is left after opening, closing, and paraenesis are subtracted. Style and sequence analyses have enabled us to identify tight, closely argued sections, which regularly manifest the closest interrelation of theological and practical concerns,[58] and which customarily form the body of the letter. We are in a position, consequently, to look at these sections with a different eye. We may provisionally identify the following: Romans 1:13—8:39,[59]: I Cor. 1:10—4:21; II Cor. 1:8—2:13, 7:5—16,[60] 2:14—7:4, 10:1—13:14; Gal. 1:6—5:26 (6:17?); Phil. 1:12—2:30; I Thess. 2:1—3:13; Philemon 8–22.

Taking I Cor. 1:10—4:21 as a point of departure, it is worth noting that the skillfully framed argument of 1:10—3:23 is climaxed in 3:18–23 by a recapitulation of the essence of the argument (vv. 18–20, introduced by the formula μηδεὶς ἑαυτὸν ἐξαπατάτω, let no one deceive himself[61]) and its resolution (vv. 21–23, introduced by ὥστε, so).[62] We thus have a formal conclusion to the argument. Nevertheless, Paul appears to go on with the same theme in 4:1–21, drawing specific consequences from the ground he has laid.[63] Paul allows that judgment belongs to the Lord and will come with the eschaton (4:1–5), and that the Corinthians have misunderstood σοφία (wisdom) because they have forgotten that the eschaton is still outstanding (4:6–13). One might suggest that here Paul provides a kind of eschatological conclusion which corresponds to the eschatological climax rounding off the *hodaya* or *beracha* (Schubert, Sanders), but which is directed to the issue under discussion. Paul turns, finally, to his apostolic relation to the congregation, which issues in a review of past and future personal contacts with the congregation (4:14–21). This last section might be termed the promise of *oral* apostolic word (in contrast to the written), or, to use a more descriptive but less precise label, travel projections.

Does this structure assist us in reading the body of the Pauline letter elsewhere? In the short and highly personal letter to Philemon, Paul climaxes his appeal in vv. 20 f. and then turns abruptly, as though it

[58] Cf. Dibelius, *A Fresh Approach*, 148 ff., where he suggests that Paul looks at everything from a higher level.
[59] It is uncertain where the thanksgiving ends and the body of the letter begins (Schubert, *op. cit.*, 5), but an introductory formula occurs at 1:13 (Sanders, *op. cit.*, 360). The question of the disposition of Rom. 9—11 is left open.
[60] The introductory formula occurs at 1:8, but the opening *beracha* appears to extend to 1:11 (Sanders, *op. cit.*, 360 f.).
[61] On the significance of this formula, see Wilckens, *op. cit.*, 8.
[62] Wilckens gives a close analysis of 1:10—4:21 (*ibid.*, 5–11), which I have elaborated and modified in chap. 11.
[63] Cf. Wilckens, *op. cit.*, 10 f.

were inevitable, to his anticipated visit (v. 22): he adds to the written word, so to speak, the promise of an oral word. There is no eschatological conclusion to the body of the letter. One could say, of course, that it is natural for Paul to take up the subject of anticipated visits at the conclusion of his letters, just as we do in writing to friends or relatives whom we hope to see. However, these travel notes do not necessarily occur at the end of the letters, as appended personal information, but can be joined to the body of the letter, even taken up into it as a part of its argument. This is clearly the case with the "travel section" in II Cor. 10—13, which begins in 12:14 and continues through 13:10! That his oral word shall match his written word is a matter of great moment to Paul in his conflict with the Corinthian troublemakers. Furthermore, the "travel section," as it might be termed, serves as the *body* of the letter of reconciliation found in II Cor. 1:8—2:13, 7:5-16, if Bornkamm's analysis stands: the substance of the letter turns on Paul's steadfastness in travel plans and his anxious movement to meet Titus. The travel section occurs in Philippians at 2:19-30, and is preceded, interestingly enough, by an eschatological conclusion in 2:14-18. In I Thessalonians the travel notes run from 2:17 through 3:8 and again are preceded by an eschatological climax (2:13-16)[64] to the main argument (2:1-12). The eschatological climax is missing from II Cor. 10—13 and the letter of reconciliation, I think, because there the travel projections are wholly integral to the argument; the travelogue is taken up into the body of the letter.[65] In I Corinthians 4, Philippians, and I Thessalonians the travelogue forms a distinct but closely related unit, which appears to permit, or even to demand, a conclusion that embraces an eschatological motif.

The situation is somewhat different with respect to Romans.[66] A

[64] This eschatological climax may go with the second thanksgiving period (Sanders, *op. cit.*, 356).

[65] It is possible that the eschatological climax is also missing because this theme is taken up in the body of the letter. Cf. James M. Robinson, "Kerygma and History in the New Testament," in *The Bible in Modern Scholarship*, J. P. Hyatt, ed. (Nashville, Tenn.: Abingdon Press, 1966), p. 143.

[66] These remarks are based on the canonical form of Romans, leaving chap. 16 out of account. It is possible, even likely, however, that one has to reckon with more than one form of this letter.

As is well known, the designation of Rome as the place to which this letter was sent is omitted at 1:7, 15 in some manuscript traditions. There is evidence, furthermore, that one recension of Romans ended at 14:23, another at 15:33 (based on the placement of the long doxology, found in the canonical form at 16:25-27, and certain patristic evidence). For a summary statement see John Knox, *The Interpreter's Bible*, 9 (Nashville, Tenn.: Abingdon Press, 1954), 363 ff. Knox also calls attention to the striking fact

travel section is found at 15:14–33, as though it were an appendix to the letter. Yet its contents reveal the reasons Paul is writing, viz., to anticipate the oral with a written word, necessitated, on the one hand, by his commission to fulfill his ministry in the east (15:18 ff.) before moving to the west, and, on the other, by his charge to carry the gospel to those who have not heard it (15:21, 28). This section, moreover, corresponds precisely to the opening of the letter (1:8–17). Michel[67] has observed that 15:14–33 "corresponds to 1:8–17 point for point"; 1:8–17 and 15:14–33 serve, consequently, as the brackets which enclose and justify the body of the letter, and this justification is anticipated, furthermore, by the salutation (1:5 ff.).[68]

---

that Paul does not mention his intention to go to Spain in chap. 1, nor does he actually promise to visit Rome. All that a Roman reader would have learned from chap. 1 is that Paul wanted to come, while in chap. 15 this desire becomes a promise, buttressed by his decision to extend his work to Spain (John Knox, "A Note on the Text of Romans," *NTS* 2 (1956), 191–93). M. Jack Suggs (by letter) points, in addition, to the "near-epistolary" style of Romans (a characterization which he attributes, in turn, to Kendrick Grobel). From this battery of observations, Suggs concludes that Romans should be regarded (a) as a circular letter, (b) as a presentation of the current Pauline line on issues raised by the "Judaizing controversy," which (c) relied heavily on earlier written and oral models composed by Paul himself (he calls attention to the parallels between Rom. 12 and I Cor. 11—13, and the peculiar use of the diatribe form in Rom. 10).

The conclusion to be drawn is, perhaps, that the short recension (without chap. 15) was a circular or catholic letter, used by Paul "to establish himself as the accredited apostle to the Gentiles" (Knox, "A Note on the Text of Romans," 193) among churches he had not founded. This would account for the character of 1:1–15, the "near-epistolary" style, and the absence of chap. 15. The long recension (with chap. 15) served the same purpose with respect to the church at Rome.

N. A. Dahl, "The Particularity of the Pauline Epistles as a Problem in the Ancient Church," *Neotestamentica et Patristica* (Leiden: E. J. Brill, 1962), 261–71, especially 267–69, attempts to account for the same phenomena on the basis that a later "catholicizing" editor omitted what was too specific in the interest of giving this epistle, as others, a more general reference. Dahl does not account, however, for the peculiar character of 1:1–15 or for the style of the body.

So far as I can see, these possibilities do not threaten my analysis of the canonical form of Romans; in fact, they may provide the means of explaining why the "travelogue" in Romans is divided as it is, thus serving as brackets to enclose the whole. The short or circular form of the letter, on the other hand, would serve as eloquent testimony to Paul's consciousness of the significance of his personal presence among the churches, even those he had not founded (see especially Rom. 1:11–13). And it is this consciousness which accounts, in my judgment, for the "travelogue" as a constituent element in the Pauline letter. In short, Rom. 1:10–15, on this view, is a travelogue-surrogate for a circular letter, which has been worked into the thanksgiving!

Just as Rom. 15:14–32 particularizes this travelogue-surrogate for the Roman church, is it possible that Paul added other particularizations for other destinations?

[67] *Op. cit.,* 325.

[68] First Corinthians 16, on the other hand, may well be composite (J. Weiss, W. Schmithals). In any case, travel projections which appear there (16:5–12) occur in

The travelogue would be difficult to imitate in an epistle conceived as a literary convention, viz., apart from a living situation, and especially when produced by an author not moved by Paul's strong consciousness of the significance of his personal presence to his congregations. In those epistles where the letter form has been adopted merely as a literary vehicle the written word is understood as the essential medium. Nevertheless, the travelogue of the Pauline letters is imitated in the subsequent epistolary tradition. That it was felt to be required is indicated by II Tim. 4:6–18 (greetings in vv. 19–21), Titus 3:12‚14 (greetings in v. 15), Hebrews 13:18 f., 22 f. (greetings in v. 24, doxology in vv. 20 f.), II John 12 (greetings in v. 13), III John 13 f. (benediction and greetings in v. 15). There is nothing corresponding, so far as I can see, in James, I and II Peter, I John, Jude; these epistles have apparently abandoned the Pauline tradition.

In addition to these instances, all of which place the travelogue at the close of the letter just before the greetings, I Timothy 3:14 f. exhibits an abbreviated travel section in the body of the letter. It is not, however, integral to its context; Conzelmann describes it as a piece coming in pause,[69] Fred Gealy—rightly I think—as a literary fiction.[70] But it is a fiction, however wooden, created by someone who knew the Pauline letters intimately. Colossians and Ephesians do not have travelogues in the Pauline sense, although both letters have passages (Col. 1:24—2:6; Eph. 3:1–3) which correspond in function: they attempt to justify and commend the mission and message of Paul as apostle to the Gentiles, and thus deal with his "movement" in a broad sense. Colossians 4:7 ff. and Ephesians 6:21 f., on the other hand, while not travelogues, announce the arrival (epistolary aorist) of Tychicus, who will tell them of Paul and at the same time serve as his ambassador.

It seems likely that Col. 1:24—2:6, Eph. 3:1–3, I Tim. 3:14 f. are attempts to imitate the Pauline travelogue, while the other examples adopted it as a convention, and because it was no longer thought of in

---

conjunction with directions for the collection. With these may be compared the travel items in II Cor. 8 and 9 (8:16–24; 9:1–4), which are also joined to instructions regarding the collection. In these instances the travelogue is more or less integrally related to the arrangements for gathering and delivering the offering. Have we to reckon with a "collection letter" as an independent type?

[69] M. Dibelius, *Die Pastoralbriefe,* neu bearbeitet von H. Conzelmann, *Handbuch zum Neuen Testament,* 13 (Tübingen: J. C. B. Mohr [Paul Siebeck], 1955), *ad loc.*

[70] Fred D. Gealy, *The Interpreter's Bible,* 11 (Nashville, Tenn.: Abingdon Press, 1955), *ad. loc.*

relation to the oral word it was given a place among other sundry concluding items.

No mention has yet been made of Galatians. Since the integrity of Galatians has never been in serious doubt, one might expect the ground plan of the Pauline letter to be intact there. On the other hand, in view of the fact that Galatians has no opening thanksgiving, it may also be unique in other formal respects as well. It is striking, nevertheless, that Galatians lacks the customary Pauline travelogue. John Knox feels the weight of this omission:

One might have expected some reference to a later visit when Paul would personally confront his opponents. . . . Indeed, in view of the desperate importance of the issue in Galatia, one cannot help wondering why Paul is not going instead of writing.[71]

In view of the importance Paul attaches to the oral word, it is strange, perhaps incredible, that Paul did not make some mention of any intention to follow up the letter with a personal visit—unless, of course, he was writing at a time when a return to Galatia was out of the question, not just for the present (cf. Philippians) but for the foreseeable future. If the travelogue can be established as integral to the Pauline letter, the debate over an early or late date for Galatians is also settled. Knox's intuition was sound, as the structure of the Pauline letter proves: Paul wrote Galatians at a time when he had no intention of ever returning to Galatia, i. e., at a relatively late date.

If the customary Pauline travelogue is lacking, its surrogate is not. In 4:12-20 Paul reviews the circumstances of his coming to Galatia and his reception there, and concludes with the wish that he might be present again with them. This is a "travelogue" in a situation where travel in that direction is out of the question, i.e., in a situation where Paul cannot add the promise of an oral word to the written word, he recalls the previous oral word and wishes he might renew it. Its position within the body of the letter is possibly also explained by this fact.

Second Thessalonians, to come to the final example, presents something of a puzzle. Minimally the absence of a travelogue requires explanation, and there are several which could be given. The explanation may prove decisive for the question of authenticity.

The elements of the Pauline letter thus far identified and isolated are

---

[71] John Knox, "Galatians," *Interpreter's Dictionary of the Bible,* II (Nashville, Tenn.: Abingdon Press, 1962), 343.

subject, of course, to variation in and among themselves in the constitution of any particular letter. This variation raises the question of their relation to each other and to the letter as a whole. The question is important not only for the analysis of the formal structure of the letter but also for any assessment of its significance. Consideration must be restricted to suggestions concerning the travelogue and thanksgiving.

It has already been suggested that the travelogue is related to the body in the same way that the promise (or threat) of oral word is related to the written word in Paul's disposition toward language. In I Cor. 4:20 Paul writes that "the kingdom of God does not consist in talk (ἐν λόγῳ) but in power (ἐν δυνάμει)"; what immediately follows —"shall I come to you with a rod?"—suggests that Paul regards the oral word as a rod (or as a manifestation of love, as the case may be) and the letter as a poor substitute for either. This view is supported by II Cor. 12:14—13:10, Gal. 4:12-20, although in the former, to be sure, Paul defends the congruity of his written and his spoken word (II Cor. 10:10 f.). The letter was especially suited as a medium of bridging the gap between oral and written speech, combining as it does aspects of each.[72] It would appear, nevertheless, that Paul wrote reluctantly.[73] His reluctance is manifested in the structure of the letter, in his instinct to join a "travelogue" to the body of each letter.

The thanksgiving is a conflation of an epistolary convention with a liturgical tradition.[74] On the one hand, it is reminiscent of corporate life in worship, and on the other it functions as an epistolary vehicle for expressing Paul's immediate concerns. Paul constructs his thanksgivings with the specific situation in mind, as is evidenced by Rom. 1:8 ff., II Cor. 1:3 ff., Phil. 1:3 ff. In I Thessalonians, moreover, the thanksgiving is made to serve as the body of the letter, occurring first in the customary position (1:2 ff.), then being renewed at 2:13 ff. and 3:9 ff. In spite of this feature we find all the elements of the Pauline letter body present: body with formulary opening, 2:1-12; eschatological climax, 2:13-16; travelogue, 2:17—3:8. Hence the thanksgiving was not an element whose form and content had already been crystallized. As a consequence, these prayers tend to telegraph the content of the letter, and are developed in such a way that they normally lead up to the opening theme.

[72] Wilder, *Language of the Gospel*, 22 f., 39.
[73] *Ibid.*, 22, citing E. Fuchs.
[74] Sanders, *op. cit.*, 358, 362, following Robinson, "Historicality of Biblical Language," and "Die Hodajot-Formel in Gebet und Hymnus."

The observation could be made that even the elements of the
salutation and closing are subject to the duress of special circumstances.[75] Whether the paraenetic sections permit only general rather
than specific reference, as Dibelius thought,[76] requires re-examination
in my opinion. At all events, these elements, particularly the paraenesis,
must be considered with respect to the movement of the letter as a
whole.

V

The preceding observations permit us to posit the following working
hypothesis concerning the substructure of the Pauline letter form: (1)
salutation (sender, addressee, greeting); (2) thanksgiving; (3) body,
with its formal opening, connective and transitional formulas, concluding "eschatological climax" and travelogue; (4) paraenesis; (5) closing
elements (greetings, doxology, benediction). It should be emphasized
that these elements are subject to variation in both content and order,
and that some items are optional, although the omission of any one
calls for explanation. It is put this way around on the view that Paul is
not rigidly following an established pattern, but is creating his own
letter form—in relation, of course, to the letter as a literary convention.
If he has molded this particular pattern out of the circumstances of his
apostolic ministry and on the basis of his theological understanding, he
seems to follow it without conscious regard to its structure. It is just
the way he writes letters. It is only in this sense that we can legitimately speak of "form."

[75] Especially evident in Gal. 1:1 ff. and 6:11 ff., but also discernible in Rom. 1:1 ff.,
15:30 ff., perhaps in I Cor. 1:1 f., II Cor. 1:1, not to mention II Thess. 3:14–17.

[76] *Die Formgeschichte des Evangeliums,* 3d ed., 239; *A Fresh Approach,* 143 f.
Dibelius was of the opinion that the paraenetic sections of the Pauline letters contained
general rather than specific applicability. He regarded it as an error to attribute all the
sins enumerated in such passages to the church in question, for the reason that Paul was
drawing on tradition not formulated by himself. Dibelius may have overstated his case,
though he is undoubtedly correct in asserting that the paraenetic material was not the
spiritual and theological property of Paul to the same degree as the body of letters. The
same could be said of salutation, thanksgiving, and the like. If the latter were adapted,
however modestly, to the specific situation in most cases, we would expect such adapta-
tion to apply also to the paraenesis. This particular aspect of the letters, as it appears to
me, requires rethinking in two respects. (1) Are the ethical sections framed by and
referred to the theological sections? If so, how? (2) Are the paraeneses constructed with
the particular situation in mind? How can we determine what has specific reference and
what not? What is required in resolving these questions is more than the customary
exegesis can provide, for it is necessary to attend to the way in which the paraeneses are
set in the letter as a whole, and the way in which the traditional material is framed in
its own immediate context, in addition to which one must be alert to Paul's disposition
to conventional language. These factors may drastically affect the understanding of the
paraenesis which takes the items *seriatim* and refers them to tradition.

Taking this hypothetical substructure as the basis, we may take a cursory look at the Pauline corpus with a view to ascertaining whether and to what extent Paul follows his own norm. This procedure is not so strange as it sounds when one considers that a number of the Pauline letters may be composite. In this connection we can do no more than acknowledge that the nature of the argument is circular: the pattern of the letter has to be established out of the letters in the New Testament, and that may mean out of letters some of which may be the result of secondary composition. That some of the letters are in fact secondary compositions can be settled finally, in my judgment, only in relation to the consideration of the form of the letter. The following remarks should be considered no more than an effort to project lines which are just beginning to emerge and have yet to be substantiated by detailed analysis and comparison.

It is striking, in view of the recent discussion of the integrity of the Thessalonian letters, that I Thessalonians matches the proposed structure point for point and in the proper order. As a matter of fact, it stands alone in this regard. Philemon is also a model epistle with only eschatological climax to the body and paraenesis missing. One could perhaps account for these omissions in so brief a personal letter. All the elements are present in Galatians save for the thanksgiving, which, as nearly all commentators agree, has its special explanation; the greeting in Galatians, on the other hand, is combined with a doxology, perhaps as a substitute for the customary thanksgiving. The order is somewhat modified: the travelogue-surrogate falls within the body of the letter (4:12–20), and the eschatological climax, if it be such, comes at the end of the paraenesis (6:7–10). As in Galatians, all the elements are present in Romans but in modified order. The travelogue, as was noticed, serves as brackets to enclose the whole, and there appear to be two eschatological climaxes, one at 8:31–39, and one at 11:25–36. Chapter 16, of course, is left out of account.

Turning next to I Corinthians and Philippians, we may consider them together. First Corinthians 1:1—4:21 and Philippians 1:1—2:30, as indicated, manifest the same structure up to the point of the paraenesis; paraenesis and closing are thus missing. It may legitimately be asked what might have been expected to follow in each case.

It was observed that the body of the letter is rounded off by an eschatological period and a travelogue. Can it be established that in the Pauline letter only paraenesis and closing may follow? Such a rule manifestly cannot be applied rigidly, since Galatians is an apparent exception, though there Paul does not employ the travelogue in the usual manner, i.e., as the promise of oral word to follow upon written word. In Romans the travelogue stands even after the paraenesis. Nevertheless, there may be justification for holding to the view that the travelogue normally closes the body of the letter, especially when it is recalled that in the deutero-Pauline letter the travelogue is regularly given *end* position, i.e., just before the closing matter (Eph. 6:21–22; Col. 4:7–9; II Tim. 4:6–18; Tit. 3:12–14; cf. Heb. 13:18 f., 22 f.; II Jn. 12; III Jn. 13 f.). That is to say, the travelogue was felt to *close* the letter.[77]

In the case of Philippians, it has often been asserted that 3:1—4:1 gives the appearance of an independent letter, or at least the body of one; it is certainly not the expected paraenetical section. Verses 4:10–20, furthermore, introduce a new subject; they appear to combine an informal "thank you" (thanksgiving?) with a kind of travelogue (review of their relationship); this may therefore be an independent letter, now truncated. These considerations support the view that Philippians is composite.

First Corinthians 5—15, on the other hand, could be taken as an extended paraenesis appended to the body of the letter. In fact, it is comprised of brief essays on numerous specific problems, seemingly topically arranged and without strong connectives between several of the parts. However, it is not paraenetic in style, nor does it draw upon the paraenetic tradition as do the sections identified by Dibelius as paraeneses. In these respects I Cor. 5—15 is unique in the Pauline corpus.

It can be viewed in one of two ways.

a. It can be taken as a group of essays on specific problems, loosely strung together in the manner of the paraenesis, and thus understood as a substitute for paraenesis, felt by Paul to be required by the situation in this case; or

b. It can be conceived as a compilation of diverse Pauline materials put together by a redactor (J. Weiss, W. Schmithals). The redactor may have had the paraenesis in mind as a model, or he may have been creating a primitive *Kirchenordnung* (church order). I have advanced the latter thesis in an unpublished paper on the basis that the structure of I Cor. 5—15 corresponds section for section to the Didache.[78]

[77] One may add, with respect to Galatians and Romans, that in Galatians the whole letter is body, or so it could be argued, with the consequence that the formal structure is swallowed up in Paul's passion, without, however, the loss of the structural items; in Romans the travelogue serves a special function, thus accounting for its position.

[78] Didache 1–6, manual of Christian morals; 7–15, church order, including liturgical matters as well as discipline; 16, warning against false prophets and corrupters, set in an

On any view II Corinthians is composite. We have, it seems, the body of three letters: 1:8—2:13 + 7:5–16; 2:14—7:4; 10:1—13:10.

It is just possible that 2:14 ff., which begins τῷ δὲ θεῷ χάρις . . . (Thanks be to God . . .), is an unusual thanksgiving period which leads directly into the body of the letter without opening formula.[79] In that case only the salutation is missing.[80]

Second Corthinthians 10:1 begins with a broken form of the introductory formula, and, since the situation which called it forth is so very much like the crisis in Galatia in intensity, one might assume that Paul began this letter with abbreviated preliminary matters and came directly to his subject. In fact, II Cor. 10:1 ff. is quite analogous to Gal. 1:6 ff.

Putting these two observations together, it could be said that the redactor in compiling II Corinthians has omitted only the salutations in order to camouflage the seams. He was obviously less interested in the form of the Pauline letter.

Attractive as is Bornkamm's thesis respecting the composition of II Corinthians, it has to be said that the great apology, 2:14—7:4, is only a letter fragment. Even if 6:1 ff. can be construed as the eschatological climax, the travelogue is still missing. Under the circumstances, it is incredible that Paul would not have thought of encountering the Corinthians face to face, or at least of sending an emissary. This is particularly so if one regards the great apology as the first of three letters dealing with the crisis in Corinth, as Bornkamm does. If one regards it as having been written during the period when Paul had determined not to pay them "another painful visit" (2:1), there seems to be no good reason to distinguish it from the letter of reconciliation (1:1—2:13, 7:5–16).

Something may have dropped out, of course, in the redaction of II Corinthians.[81] If the great apology is complete, some account must be given of the missing travelogue. A second glance suggests that the

---

apocalyptic context. I Cor. 5–15: 5:1–7:40 and 8:1–11:1 = first division, on the ground that association with idols corrupts morals (cf. Did. 6:3); 11:2—14:40 = second division; 15 = third division (i.e., warning against false teaching set in an apocalyptic context).

[79] Χάρις τῷ θεῷ is employed by Paul elsewhere in outbursts of praise in the midst of letters: Rom. 6:17, 7:25; I Cor. 15:57; II Cor. 8:16, 9:15.

[80] Or it may be a renewal of the opening thanksgiving, in which case the thanksgiving is missing also.

[81] Cf. C. L. Mitton, *The Formation of the Pauline Corpus of Letters* (London: Epworth Press, 1955), 25 ff., for interesting remarks concerning the formation of the Pauline corpus and questions of integrity. One's disposition to the latter is not a little

letter of reconciliation may be a travelogue without a body. Is it possible that chapters 1—7 are a unity after all, with a travelogue enclosing the body of the letter precisely as is the case with Romans? Or are Weiss and Bultmann right in thinking that the great apology goes with the "tearful letter" (10:1—13:10), in which case, too, it gets a travelogue? So far as form is concerned, the former of these alternatives is the more cogent, in spite of the difficulty in transition from 2:12 f. to 2:14.[82]

Second Thessalonians so closely parallels the structure of I Thessalonians that premature conclusions based on form should be studiously avoided. The three thanksgiving formulae of I Thessalonians (1:2 ff., 2:13, 3:9 f.) are paralleled by three in II Thessalonians (1:3, 1:11 f., 2:13); the second thanksgiving in I Thessalonians has a double liturgical closing (3:11, 12) as does the second in II Thessalonians (2:16 f., 3:5),[83] to give two examples. However, there is at least one crucial difference already noticed: II Thessalonians does not have a travelogue.[84]

---

dependent on his disposition also to the former. If the Pauline letters fell into obscurity for a time, as Goodspeed and Knox hold, the possibilities of loss and disarrangement are proportionately increased.

[82] The transition from 7:4 to 7:5 is not so difficult, in my judgment. Verse 7:4 sounds very much as if Paul anticipated a reconciliation.

[83] Sanders, op. cit., 359.

[84] M. Jack Suggs has argued cogently for dating II Thessalonians, if genuine, about 42 A.D. ("Concerning the Date of Paul's Macedonian Ministry," NT 4 [1960] 60–68). He further remarks (by letter) that the absence of the travelogue from II Thessalonians does not constitute an argument against its authenticity, since Paul had no intention of returning to Macedonia in the near future. Would this argument not also apply to I Thessalonians? There, however, we do find a "travelogue," written at a time when Paul presumably did not intend to return immediately. The term "travelogue" may not be a suitable designation for the phenomenon under discussion. The "travelogue" is an expression of Paul's promise or desire of adding an oral word to his written word. It is in this sense that we have contended that it is a constituent element in the genuine Pauline letter.

Postscript. Since this essay was written further reflection upon the "travelogue" has made it clear that Paul regards his presence to the congregations under three different but related aspects at once: the aspect of the letter, the apostolic emissary, and Paul's own person. All of these are media by which Paul makes his apostolic authority effective in the churches. The underlying theme is therefore the apostolic parousia (cf. I Cor. 5:3–5), which appears to be a more suitable designation for the phenomenon in question. Detailed analysis reveals that all three motifs are normally present in the section on apostolic parousia, though one or the other may be suppressed for particular reasons. These sections, moreover, exhibit a fairly consistent pattern of articulation, i.e., they can be analyzed structurally and formally. A further analysis is required, of course, to support these assertions.

Word and Word in
I Corinthians 2:6–16

⅗ 11 ⅙ ────────────────

ERNST KÄSEMANN HAS SUGGESTED THAT σοφία IN THIS
text should be translated "theology."[1] Such a translation is only appropriate if one is aware that theology does not, in this context, denote a science in the modern sense, but refers to teaching or doctrine
which leads to salvation. Sophia was so understood in the Hellenistic world. Sophia in the Gnosticizing sense, as propounded by the
Corinthian schismatics, does not stand in the tradition of classical Greek
philosophy, but belongs broadly to the circle of the Hellenistic mystery
religions and popular philosophy. Within this frame of reference
Gnostic sophia refers to esoteric knowledge which in and of itself
effects redemption. Quite literally, it is saving knowledge.

Yet, as Paul takes the term up from the Corinthians for criticism,
it is not to contrast one doctrinal system with another, although that,
to be sure, is obliquely involved. It is striking that Paul nowhere in
this context (1:10—4:21) takes up the various points of the Corinthian
doctrine and refutes them as such.[2] He does indeed begin at the point
of strife among the members of the congregation (1:10 ff.), but this
is only the symptom of a deeper malady (cf. 3:1 ff.). His concern is
rather to set σοφία over against ὁ λόγος τοῦ σταυροῦ (the word of the
cross). The fundamental contrast for Paul is between σοφία λόγου (wisdom of word) and λόγος σταυροῦ (word of the cross) (1:17 f.; cf.
2:1 ff.), and thus a contrast between two words, two languages.

Käsemann's suggestion, then, is not without its point, provided

---

[1] Ernst Käsemann, *Exegetische Versuche und Besinnungen*, Erster Band (Göttingen:
Vandenhoeck & Ruprecht, 1960), 268.

[2] It is a different matter, e.g., in I Cor. 8:1 ff. and 15:12 ff., though even here one
has to infer the opponent's position and reckon with the possibility that Paul may have
misunderstood.

theology is understood as theo-logos, i.e., as word of God. It may be objected that the use of theology in this sense involves an unjustifiable narrowing of the term and a collapsing of theology and proclamation into one. However that may be, for Paul the issue was whether God was coming to speech, and coming to speech specifically through the medium of the Crucified. If theology may be defined in its root sense as God entering language, then the debate with the Corinthians was a theo-logical debate. In any case, Paul was forced to raise the question with reference both to the proclamation of the Corinthian parties and to his own proclamation, to the former because it was questionable whether the Crucified was really coming to speech and to the latter because it was evident that the Crucified had not really come to speech. For the epistle itself was occasioned by the partial failure of Paul's own language. The question whether the God of Jesus Christ was being given a presence in language therefore leads to reflection upon the intentionality and destiny of language. Theology in its specifically Christian sense is thereby conceived.[3]

Insofar as we restrict ourselves to the text itself, we would have to say that it is theology in the latter sense that is under consideration. But theology in the sense of reflection upon the intentionality and destiny of the language of the proclamation does not yet overtly intend a doctrinal system, or even specific doctrines. It holds fast to the subject which is struggling to come to speech, in this case the Crucified. It does so by attending anew to the Crucified within the horizons of concrete historical existence. If, then, we wish to probe the intentionality of the text, we are bound to attend to that which is striving to come to speech and attend to it within the language horizons of the auditors for whom it is destined.

It may be inferred from what has been said that a tabulation of the doctrinal assertions of Paul will not suffice, for this is precisely what shifts our attention away from the proper subject. Theology in the sense of doctrinal assertions or systems is what is *not* under consideration in the text. On the contrary, since Paul is laboring to hear the word anew for himself and for the Corinthians, we must observe his effort to wrest the Christ from his partial or total eclipse in and by the Corinthians, and that means in and by their language. Only by so doing can the intentionality of the text come to light at all.

---

[3] E. Fuchs, *Hermeneutik*, 182; G. Ebeling, "Der Grund christlicher Theologie," *ZThK* 58 (1961) 228; "Theologie I. Begriffsgeschichtlich," *RGG* VI, 759 ff.

I

The problem of factions (σχίσματα 1:10, ἔριδες 1:11; cf. 3:3 ff.) Paul immediately grounds in Christ: Is Christ divided? The question is interpreted to refer to the crucifixion (Paul was not crucified for you, was he? [certainly not!]) and to baptism in a secondary but related way (you were not baptized into the name of Paul, were you? [certainly not!]). These questions are developed in reverse order, that of baptism in 1:14 ff. and that of crucifixion in 1:17 ff. The former is a peripheral concern to which he does not return after 1:16, while the latter, though he does not take it up in the form suggested by the rhetorical question in 1:13, dominates the remainder of the discussion (through 4:21).

The formulation of 1:17 affords a transition back to the theme of the cross: οὐ . . . βαπτίζειν ἀλλὰ εὐαγγελίζεσθαι, οὐκ ἐν σοφίᾳ λόγου, ἵνα μὴ κενωθῇ ὁ σταυρὸς τοῦ Χριστοῦ (not . . . to baptize but to preach the gospel, and that not in a sophistry of language, lest the Cross of Christ be rendered void). The theme word, σταυρός (cross), is picked up in 1:18 in the phrase ὁ λόγος τοῦ σταυροῦ (the word of the cross), and the latter elaborated as a thesis. The sudden shift from the problem of factions to an extended discussion of sophia (1:18–2:16) creates an abrupt transition, the significance of which has often been lost to view. Ulrich Wilckens has grasped this transition as a signal point in the whole discourse (1:10–4:21) and has rendered it intelligible by showing that the theme of sophia is internally related to Corinthian factiousness. He is thus able to fathom the inner unity of Paul's train of thought, a train which is virtually unbroken from 1:10 through 4:21.[4]

Verses 3:18-23 occupy a special place, according to Wilckens, in

---

[4] Ulrich Wilckens, *Weisheit und Torheit: Eine exegetisch-religionsgeschichtliche Untersuchung zu 1. Kor. 1 und 2* (Tübingen: J. C. B. Mohr [Paul Siebeck], 1959). The present essay has been written with Wilckens' study primarily in view. While Wilckens' work is a model of exegesis combined with the history of religions methodology, his reading of I Cor. 1 and 2 suffers in the end from myopia. He has been trapped in part by the terminological battle (cf. the biting remarks of James Barr, *The Semantics of Biblical Language* [London and New York: Oxford University Press, 1962]), and in part by what Samuel Sandmel has called parallelomania ("Parallelomania," *JBL* 81 [1962], 1–13). We would do well not to disparage either lexical or comparative investigations out of hand (Barr, in particular, tends to belittle the former as they are currently pursued). Nevertheless, both lexicography and the use of comparative materials can obscure the integrity of a document rather than illuminate it. If Wilckens had not been so concerned to expunge the Gnostic taint from Paul's language and conceptualities, he might have attended more closely to the intention of Paul's discourse.

unfolding the interrelation of the two themes: in 3:18–20 Paul sum-marizes the previous section on sophia, on the basis of which he resolves the question of factions (3:21–23; note ὥστε in 3:21).[5] Sophia, then, is the basis of strife and rivalries in the church. The bearing of 3:18–23 on the unity of the entire section is supported by the way in which Paul resumes the theme of factionalism, ostensibly dropped with the formulation of 1:17, in 3:1 ff. The two themes are visibly connected here for the first time: Paul cannot address them as pneu-matics because they are still σαρχικοί (worldly men—cf. 2:10 ff., where πνευματικός [spiritual] and ψυχικός [unspiritual] are set off against each other); they are the latter because there is envy and strife among them and because they claim allegiance to particular apostles (3:3 ff.; cf. 1:11 ff.).[6] Since they are not pneumatics, they cannot possess the sophia they claim to possess, for such sophia is accessible only to those who possess the spirit (2:10 ff.). Their claim to sophia is in fact based on a misunderstanding of what sophia is (1:18 ff.).

In 4:1–21, on Wilckens' view, Paul draws further consequences for his strained relation to the church at Corinth, especially to the groups which opposed him.[7] (1) Paul and the other apostles are servants of Christ and therefore have independent status vis-à-vis the congregation (4:1–5; cf. 2:15). (2) Since Paul and Apollos stand in complete unity, there is no basis for rivalries in the church (4:6; cf. 3:5 ff.). (3) The basis of factions in Corinth lies in the fact that some of the Corinthians have forgotten that the eschaton still lies before them and so under-stand their freedom as absolute. But the apostles are bound over against God as the giver, and over against the entire congregation as those addressed by their proclamation, the expression of which is their weakness in and against all worldly limitation (4:7–13; cf. 2:1 ff.). (4) And finally, Paul announces his imminent arrival since he, as father of the congregation, has the responsibility for settling the problems which have arisen (4:14–21; cf. the appeal in 1:10 to which 4:14 returns). Although Wilckens has indicated the connection with the preceding, he has overlooked substantive matters and, above all, missed the way in which the basic theme is carried through to the conclusion.

---

[5] *Ibid.*, 7.

[6] In 3:5 ff. Paul interprets his and Apollos' work: both build on the only foundation, which is Christ, and thus are coequal in their subservience to God. The relation to the preceding is self-evident.

[7] Wilckens, *op. cit.*, 10 f. One gets the impression that Wilckens regards chap. 4 as something of an appendix to the discussion.

The thesis of 1:18 is explicated, according to Wilckens,[8] first of all in its basic sense over against both Jews and Greeks (1:19–25).[9] It is then elaborated, in two parallel sections, with respect to the manner of God's election in the founding of the congregation (1:26–31), and with respect to the manner of the apostle's preaching, by means of which the congregation was constituted (2:1–5). His analysis again grasps the integrity of the passage, but does not, in my view, bring its underlying theme adequately to the surface.

Wilckens wants to set 2:6–16 off from the preceding.[10] While 2:6–16 is a legitimate paragraph, σοφίαν δὲ λαλοῦμεν (but we do speak a wisdom) in 2:6 is set in contrast to σοφία ἀνθρώπων (human wisdom) in 2:5 and λαλοῦμεν (we speak) in 2:6 resumes κηρύσσομεν (we proclaim) in 1:23, as Wilckens notes.[11] In 2:6 δέ (but) indicates, moreover, that the following is a qualification of what has been said.[12] From a literary point of view the connection is evident if not close. There is a terminological shift, however, which troubles Wilckens and causes him to pose the question: Has Paul carried through the basic antithesis set out in 1:18 ff.?[13] Owing to the Gnostic terminology which dominates the passage and the alleged assimilation of Paul's thought to Gnostic categories, he is driven to answer the question negatively and so to embark on *Sachkritik*.[14] The legitimacy of his program can scarcely be contested in principle, but it may be asked whether he has not been misled by terminological parallels and presuppositions regarding the conceptualities in which the word may come to expression, and thus ultimately led to obscure the integrity of 2:6–16 in its context.

Wilckens' analysis of 1:10—4:21, and 2:6–16 in particular, goes to-

---

[8] *Ibid.*, 6.

[9] The emphasis on signs as what the Jews require, left unexplained by Wilckens, is brought into relation to sophia by J. M. Robinson via the Q material in the Synoptic tradition ("Basic Shifts in German Theology," *Interpretation* 16 [1962], 82 ff., especially 86 and n. 38). Only in Q and I Cor. is sophia connected with the rejection of signs. Cf. his further remarks in "History and Kerygma in the New Testament," in *The Bible in Modern Scholarship*, J. P. Hyatt, ed. (Nashville, Tenn.: Abingdon Press, 1966), pp. 128 f., 139 f., where he suggests that this constellation may reflect a tradition stemming ultimately from Jewish wisdom and leading to second-century Gnosticism.

[10] *Op. cit.*, 6, 52–96.

[11] *Ibid.*, 52 and n. 1.

[12] Used to introduce an explanation: F. Blass and A. Debrunner, *A Greek Grammar of the New Testament and Other Early Christian Literature*, Robert Funk, trans. and rev. (Chicago: University of Chicago Press, 1961), sec. 447 (8).

[13] *Op. cit.*, 52.

[14] *Ibid.*, 52 f., 60, 67 f., n. 2, 68, 73, 74 f., 85, 87, 88, 93, 98, etc.

gether with the substantive issues he identifies. The concept of sophia
entertained by the Corinthians is to be correlated with their trans-
eschatological comportment (note the ironic attributions of 4:8).[15]
Such sophia does not therefore consist merely of knowledge of the
counsels of God, of the plan of salvation, but of the content of salvation. The same conception is found, to be sure, in Jewish apocalyptic
thought, but there it is determined basically by its eschatological
temporal sense, i.e., it is prepared for the elect but meantime hidden
before the world until the time of the eschatological revelation.[16] It is
precisely I Cor. 2:10 ff. that reveals the basic Gnostic orientation of the
pericope: in the apocalyptic tradition the revelation of the hidden
mysteries of wisdom is conceived as a future eschatological event, as
the formulations in 2:7, 9 show, while Paul here has in view the
present-eschatological pneumatic revelation of salvation, which has
already taken place for ἡμῖν (you) as πνευματικοί (pneumatics).[17]
Thus, according to Wilckens, Paul's capitulation in 2:6 ff. before the
position he is fighting reveals all the more clearly the contours of the
heresy. The Gnostic myth of the redeemer that lies behind 2:8 determines the course of the entire section: the process of revelation and
the reception of salvation is to be understood in connection with the
myth of the descent of the redeemer and salvation itself as the "person"
of the redeemer, who gathers all those who recognize him through
gnosis (sophia) into their primordial unity. So the apocalyptic concept of the sophia of God as the substance of salvation becomes a
christological title in the Gnostic sense.[18] If Paul has opposed this
understanding in the preceding section with the word of the cross,
it can be inferred that the controversy turns on christology: a σοφία
christology over against a σταυρός christology.[19]

Aside from the question whether the identification of σοφία with
the exalted Christ and the resulting developed christology is defen-
sible from a history of religions point of view,[20] this reading of the
issue gives some exegetical difficulties,[21] and, above all, misconstrues
the central problem. For it is more than doubtful that Paul is oppos-

---

[15] *Ibid.*, 20.
[16] *Ibid.*, 64 ff., especially 70 n. 1.
[17] *Ibid.*, 67 f. n. 2.
[18] *Ibid.*, 73.
[19] *Ibid.*, 25.
[20] Cf. the critical remarks of H. Köster in *Gnomon* 33 (1961), 593 ff.
[21] Several noted by Köster, *ibid.*, 591 f. (cited in n. 62 below).

ing one christology with another, if by that is meant that Paul is seeking to impose his own christological categories upon the Corinthian schismatics. The text nowhere supports such an understanding. On the other hand, that Paul is seeking to confront them with the ground of faith, the crucified Christ, is obvious. But the latter is not the same as the former. Were the two held to be the same, Wilckens would be guilty of the same error he attributes indirectly to Paul, namely, positing an anthropological correlate for the σοφία θεοῦ (divine wisdom), a sophia which, as he correctly urges, is reserved only for God.[22] Even the cross when taken up into a christology can become σοφία, if it is divorced from its ground.

II

What is at issue in Paul's discussion of σοφία in 1:10—4:21 (1:17—2:16)? Christ did not send Paul to baptize but εὐαγγελίζεσθαι (to preach), and this not in σοφία λόγου (sophistry of language). If he employed the latter, the cross would be vacated of its power (1:17).[23] In 1:18 he resumes εὐαγγελίζεσθαι with ὁ λόγος (the word)—the one determined by the cross—in contrast to σοφία λόγου.

It is this word (λόγος) which is variously characterized as μωρία (foolishness)/δύναμις (power) in the following discussion. From the point of view of those being saved[24] this word is δύναμις (1:18, inferred from σῶσαι [to save] in 1:21, and again in 1:24). Δύναμις apparently corresponds to what the Corinthians regard as σοφία λόγου. Paul therefore wishes to show that the λόγος which is δύναμις is the word of the cross and no other, the word which makes present (gives a presence to) the crucified Christ (1:24, 2:2). It is this word that has redemptive power. However, from the point of view of those on the way to perdition,[25] the word of the cross is μωρία. And because it is μωρία, it also τὸ ἀσθενές (weakness, 1:25), one could even say ignoble

[22] *Op. cit.,* 39 and 52 f.

[23] κενόω = to render powerless, ineffective. Wilckens, *op. cit.,* 20 and n. 1. Thus the catchword δύναμις (1:18 and following) is anticipated already in the verb.

[24] τοῖς σωζομένοις (1:18) is resumed by τοὺς πιστεύοντας (those believing, 1:21), κλητοῖς (called, 1:24), τὰ μωρά, τὰ ἀσθενῆ (the foolish, the weak, 1:27), τὰ ἀγενῆ, τὰ ἐξουθενημένα, τὰ μὴ ὄντα (the ignoble, the despised, what does not exist, 1:28) and ὑμεῖς (you, 1:30). On the neuter plural used to denote persons, see Blass and Debrunner, *op. cit.,* sec. 138 (1); Wilckens, *op. cit.,* 41.

[25] τοῖς ἀπολλυμένοις is resumed by σοφός, γραμματεύς, συζητητὴς τοῦ αἰῶνος τούτου (the wise, the scribe, the sophist of this age, 1:20), Ἰουδαῖοι, Ἕλληνες (ἔθνεσιν) (Jews, Greeks, Gentiles, 1:22, 23) σοφοὶ κατὰ σάρκα, δυνατοί (τὰ ἰσχυρά), εὐγενεῖς (worldly wise, powerful, noble, 1:26, 27), τὰ ὄντα (what exists, 1:28).

(ἀγενής 1:28), despised (ἐξουθενημένος 1:28), that which does not exist (τὸ μὴ ὄν 1:28).[26]

Ὁ λόγος in 1:18 is taken up by διὰ τῆς μωρίας τοῦ κηρύγματος (through the foolishness of preaching) in 1:21[27] and by κηρύσσομεν (we preach) in 1:23, which emerges as δύναμις and σοφία of God (1:24). This proclaimed word is the basis of their election (1:24, 26) and precisely so in order that God may bring to naught the things that raise their boast against him (1:26-31; cf., e.g., II Cor. 10:5, Rom. 3:19, 27). The underlying theme reappears explicitly in 2:1: ἦλθον οὐ καθ' ὑπεροχὴν λόγου ἢ σοφίας καταγγέλλων . . . (I did not come ... proclaiming as one superior in the maniuplation of words or wisdom ...), a formulation which betrays the juxtaposition of word and sophia in the apostle's mind (cf. 2:4, 1:17).[28] In 2:2 is set out what is constitutive of the true word (reiteration of 1:18, 23). The critical-eschatological power of the word is given expression in 2:3,[29] and again in 2:4 Paul refers to ὁ λόγος μου καὶ τὸ κήρυγμά μου (my language and my gospel), which was not and is not vested ἐν πειθοῖς σοφίας λόγοις (in persuasive language of sophia)[30] but in the demonstration of the spirit and power. The weaknesses (foolishness) of the proclaimer (2:3; cf. 4:9-13) correspond to both the mode of his speech (2:1, 4a: vis-à-vis human sophia) and its content, i.e., the Christ (2:2). The contrast of 2:4 is not between πειθός (persuasion)

26 The justification for correlating these predicates lies in the train of thought: the word of the cross is commensurate with that to which it refers (Christ crucified) and with those in whom it invokes faith (cf. n. 24).

27 It is unnecessary to distinguish in this analysis between proclamation as content and as act, for, as 2:1-5 shows, at bottom they are one. Cf. J. M. Robinson, A New Quest of the Historical Jesus, "Studies in Biblical Theology," 25 [London: SCM Press, 1959], 41 and n. 2; and the remarks of G. Ebeling, Theologie und Verkündigung, 34 ff., especially 37. To distinguish between act and content is just what obscures the hermeneutical problem, i.e., divorces the content from the language context to which the proclamation is addressed, and thus thwarts proclamation as event.

28 ἢ is used also to link terms which are related or similar, in some cases where one can substitute for the other. See Bauer on this word (W. Bauer, A Greek-English Lexicon of the New Testament, W. F. Arndt and F. W. Gingrich, trans. and adapt. [Chicago: University of Chicago Press, 1957]).

29 Note the catchword ἀσθένεια (weakness). The formula ἐν φόβῳ καὶ ἐν τρόμῳ πολλῷ (in much fear and trembling) is not to be psychologized, but refers, as in the Old Testament and apocalyptic literature, to an epiphany of judgment. See Bauer on the word τρόμος and Wilckens, op. cit., 47 and n. 3 with references.

30 The textual difficulty is not easily resolved. Wilckens, op. cit., 50 n. 1, reviews the options and provides references. In support of the genuineness of λόγοις are the formulations in 1:17 and 2:1 (against J. Weiss, Der erste Korintherbrief [Göttingen: Vandenhoeck & Ruprecht, 1910], ad loc.). In any case it is language characterized by sophia which Paul rejects here as elsewhere.

and ἀπόδειξις (demonstration), but between demonstration and demonstration, word and word.[31] On the basis of 1:24 (θεοῦ σοφίαν, divine wisdom) and 1:30 (ὅς ἐγενήθη σοφία ἡμῖν ἀπὸ θεοῦ, who has become our wisdom from God), it is also a contrast between sophia and sophia. The earlier antithesis, δύναμις/σοφία, is retained in 2:5, however, where Paul comes at last to speak of faith: his proclamation gives presence to the crucified Christ in order that their faith may rest on the power of God rather than on the sophia of men (cf. σοφία λόγου 1:17, 2:1, 2:3).

We have come far enough in the analysis to observe that the questions of factions, sophia, the crucified Christ, election, and faith are bound up with the question of language. Language precisely not in the sense of words but in the sense of event. To return to a point at the beginning of Paul's discussion which I purposely omitted, it is significant that his first appeal to the dissension-ridden Corinthians is that τὸ αὐτὸ λέγητε πάντες (all of you say the same thing, 1:10). What do these words signify? We will be misled if we suppose that Paul is appealing to them to speak identical words, or to keep to a dogmatically correct, even (by tradition) prescribed, measured, or edifying manner of speaking.[32] Nor does Paul mean primarily that they are to set their special slogans aside and emphasize rather what unites them.[33] Weiss draws nearer the theme when he suggests that they ought to meet in a common confession.[34] It is not probable that the phrase was chosen first of all with an eye to 1:12.[35] Some light is thrown on it by observing that the three clauses of 1:10 are arranged (*a*) positive exhortation, (*b*) negative appeal (antithetical parallelism), (*c*) and then the positive again; (*a*) thus corresponds to (*c*), while (*b*) is the negation.[36] To say the same thing, accordingly, means more than agreement in words.[37] It refers rather to a common mind and intention[38] which would make schism impossible. There is a parallel usage in Phil. 2:2 ff. which Paul elaborates at length: ἵνα τὸ αὐτὸ

---

[31] Noted by Wilckens, *op. cit.*, 50 f.

[32] Correctly noted by Weiss, *op. cit.*, 13.

[33] Against Weiss, *ibid.*

[34] *Ibid.*; Hans Lietzmann (*An die Korinther I–II* in *Handbuch zum Neuen Testament* [4th ed.; Tübingen: J. C. B. Mohr (Paul Siebeck), 1949], *ad loc.*) rejects this view and suggests that it probably only means *consentive*.

[35] Against Weiss, *ibid.*

[36] Weiss, *ibid.*

[37] So Bauer, *op. cit.*, on the word λέγω, I. 1. a.

[38] Rather than judgment or opinion: Bauer, *ibid.*, on the word γνώμη.

φρονῆτε, τὴν αὐτὴν ἀγάπην ἔχοντες, σύμφυχοι, τὸ ἕν φρονοῦντες, . . .
τοῦτο φρονεῖτε ἐν ὑμῖν ὃ καὶ ἐν Χριστῷ ᾽Ιησοῦ (by thinking the same
thing, having the same love, being united in spirit, thinking the one,
. . . be disposed in your common life [as it is necessary to be disposed]
also in Christ Jesus), after which follows the celebrated christological
hymn.[39] To think the same thing, to think the one, is to think Jesus
Christ. To say the same thing, consequently, means to bring the crucified Lord to speech, to establish a "world" in which the Crucified
reigns as Lord. A common confession serves the purpose only when
it is language event. And Paul has evidently failed in part to bring
the crucified Lord to speech among the Corinthians—a failure which
he seeks to rectify in the ensuing discussion.

The view that Paul sets a σταυρός christology over against a σοφία
christology in what follows is therefore only superficially correct. It is
more than a dispute over opinions about Jesus Christ. It is a dispute
about faith itself, and Paul's concern is therefore not so much to correct
a faulty christology but to bring the Christ to stand.[40] By bringing the
Crucified anew into language Paul hopes to confront the Corinthians
again with the word of faith, with the word that is power, in which
case the need for controversy will have ceased. It is of course the case
that Paul must traverse the horizons of their existence *critically* if he is
to be successful. For to bring the Christ to stand means to flesh him out
within *their* horizons. And if within their horizons, within the language that is their home. Such an enterprise is risky at best. The risk
may be avoided by clinging to school wisdom, by repeating the time-
smoothed phrases, and thus by rejecting the task itself. For God acts
only where he comes to speech anew.[41]

---

[39] Ernst Käsemann, *op. cit.*, 90 f., holds that what is to be supplied in the relative clause in
2:5 (ὃ καί ἐν Χριστῷ ᾽Ιησοῦ) is something like φρονεῖν δεῖ (it is necessary to think).
Thus: "Be disposed in your common life as it is necessary to be disposed in your existence in Christ" (parallelism between ἐν ὑμῖν ἐν Χριστῷ). This interpretation
supports his contention that Christ is not an ethical model to be imitated, but that it is
his lordship (as set out in the hymn which follows) that determines existence "in
Christ" ("in Christ" is taken as a technical term in Paul). To put it rather differently,
the lordship of Christ founds a "world" under the jurisdiction of the righteousness of
God; existence "in Christ" is existence in this "world." To this "world" also belong
others in the community; one's disposition to them is determined by the disposition one
is granted by virtue of being "in Christ."
[40] This view does not depend merely on the observation that the text, contrary to
Wilckens, is not overtly oriented to christology, but also on the insight that the
proclamation cannot be reduced to an explicit christology. Cf. Ebeling's remarks in
Theologie und Verkündigung, 79 f.
[41] Cf. Käsemann, *op. cit.*, 274.

To return to the text, it may be observed that the underlying theme of language is carried further in 2:6 ff. "But (δέ) we do speak (λαλοῦμεν)⁴² a kind of sophia, but (δέ) a sophia. . . ." The sophia which Paul speaks is the sophia of God (1:24), which is the word of the cross (cf. 1:30). Λαλοῦμεν is renewed in 2:7 and σοφία further qualified. It is this sophia which God reveals to us (ἡμῖν) through the spirit (2:10). The discernment afforded by the spirit of God makes it possible for Paul to speak (λαλοῦμεν 2:13) in λόγοις informed not by human wisdom, but by the spirit. There follows a noteworthy statement which covers the range of speaking the word of the cross (2:13b: interpreting, comparing, combining).

Nor is this line of thought abandoned in 3:1 ff. Paul is unable to speak (λαλῆσαι) to them as πνευματικοῖς (pneumatics), but must speak as to σαρκίνοις [σαρκικοῖς] (worldly men), νηπίοις (babes). Their inability to discern Paul's speech arises from the fact that they are still determined by the world, by human sophia (cf. 2:4), by human standards (3:3), as is demonstrated by the presence of envy and strife among them (3:3). Paul then attempts, in the elementary fashion called for, to explicate the function of the apostles in relation to each other and to the Corinthians (3:5–17). There follows, as was indicated above, a recapitulation in which the themes of sophia (3:18 ff.) and dissension (3:21 f.) are brought together: "let the one who thinks he is wise in this age become foolish in order that he may become wise" is correlated with "let no one make man a basis for pride."

The climax of 3:21–23 notwithstanding, the more significant break comes not between 3:23 and 4:1,⁴³ but between 4:5 and 6. In 4:1 we have a transitional assertion that confirms the unity of the apostles (ἡμᾶς, us) under the hegemony of their Lord and denies by implication their subjection to the judgment of the church. In what follows (4:2–5) it becomes evident that Paul had come under criticism in Corinth in the course of party strife. He consequently renews the theme introduced in 2:14–16 by bringing it into relation to himself;

---

⁴² The choice of λαλοῦμεν in preference to κηρύσσομεν (1:23) or καταγγέλλων is striking, and suggests that Paul may have certain charismatic gifts in mind (cf. the characteristic use of λαλεῖν in I Cor. 12:3, 30; 13:7; 14:2 ff.), the profusion of which in Corinth he has already indicated (1:5 ff.). The language of 2:6 f., 2:12 f., 3:1 especially brings this context to mind. It is possible that Paul elects the catchwords of *Enthusiasmus* because these were the hallmark of Gnostic sophia. In that case even the choice of the verb heightens the irony.

⁴³ Note the οὕτως (so) which indicates that the train of though continues.

4:5 constitutes a kind of eschatological climax,[44] and with 4:6 we are brought to a programmatic statement which reaches back at least as far as 3:5,[45] but which ultimately, in my opinion, applies to the whole discourse. Is it not the case that dissension among the Corinthians is the occasion for the entire essay? Verse 4:6c ("that none of you may be puffed up in patronizing one and flouting the other" [cf. NEB]) returns, therefore, to the appeal in 1:10. By the same token, ταῦτα (4:6a) may be taken to refer to the entire presentation. "These things" are thus the word of the cross, τὰ βάθη τοῦ θεοῦ (the depths of God, 2:10), the πνευματικά (spiritual things), and the like. Taken strictly, the characteristization of 4:6a suits everything up to this point with the exception of 1:26–31 (for which one could just as effectively substitute Phil. 3:4–14) and remarks in 1:10 ff., 3:1 ff., provided one understands "myself and Apollos" as the apostolic ministry and allows Paul occasionally to personalize it.[46]

---

[44] Cf. Paul Schubert, *The Form and Function of the Pauline Thanksgivings*, Beihefte zur ZNW, 20 (1939); Jack T. Sanders, "The Transition from Opening Epistolary Thanksgiving to Body in the Letters of the Pauline Corpus," *JBL* 81 (1962), 348–62.

[45] Weiss, *op. cit.*, is of the opinion that ταῦτα cannot refer to 4:1–5 since the relation of Paul to Apollos is not under consideration there (he takes his clue, as do most commentators, from 4:6c, where the subject is relations among the Corinthians). Only 3:5–9 fits as the antecedent of ταῦτα. But it is psychologically improbable that Paul passed over the sharp change in mood of 3:10–17, over the conclusion in 3:23, the discussion of 4:1–5, and suddenly reverted to 3:5–9. As a result Weiss can only suppose either that there was a temporal break between 4:5 and 6 (Paul remembered only generally what he had said), or that 4:6 ff. once stood in close proximity to 3:5–9. Lietzmann (*op. cit.*) takes ταῦτα to refer to 3:6–4:5 without meeting Weiss' objections. He, as well as Wilckens (*op. cit.*, 10), assumes that the specific antecedent is defined by 4:6c.

[46] Wilckens' polemic (*op. cit.*, 52 n. 1; *Kerygma und Dogma* 3 [1957], 77 ff.) against H. Schlier (*Die Zeit der Kirche. Exegetische Aufsätze und Vorträge* [Freiburg: Herder, 1956], 214 ff.) with respect to the latter's interpretation of the first person plural (e. g., 1:23) as exclusively apostolic is well taken. However, Wilckens might have learned from Bultmann of the fluidity of the first person plural in Paul, vacillating as it does between apostolic and general Christian (*Exegetische Probleme des zweiten Korintherbriefes*, "Symbolae Biblicae Upsalienses" [Uppsala, 1947; reprinted Darmstadt: Wissenschaftliche Buchgesellschaft, 1963], 3 f., 16). What Bultmann observes in II Cor. is equally applicable to I Cor. There is first of all the singular-plural shift: 1:10–16 is dominated by the singular, 4:6, 8–13 plural (apostolic), 4:14–21 singular. The apostolic singular applies by extension to the other apostles as well as to Christians generally, as our analysis of Paul's mode of discourse indicates. There is the same fluidity in the apostolic plural except at those points where Paul is explicitly speaking of Apollos and himself. Yet even here it is for the sake of the Corinthians (4:6), i.e., it refers indirectly to them also. We have to allow for four levels in Paul's use of the first person plural and only ask which one or combination is uppermost in a given text: (1) I, Paul; (2) apostolic over against the church; (3) apostolic-general Christian; (4) apostolic-Christian over against opponents (both internal and external).

Paul is utilizing a mode of discourse here that is also characteristic of II Cor. 1:3 ff., 2:14—7:4, 10:1—13:13—in his recapitulation he is endeavoring, in full view of the congregation, to attend to the word himself, in order to allow it to determine his vocation as apostle, his proclamation (form and content), his stance as a man of faith, and, indirectly, the disposition of those who are "listening in." In our text he includes Apollos so that the two of them may together hear the claim of the word in view of the interapostolic warfare in the church. This methodology is appropriate to Paul for two reasons. First, for Paul, hearing and proclaiming the word are correlates. Paul preaches as he himself is addressed (cf. the interpretation of his convictions in Phil. 3:4 ff.). If he now speaks the word indirectly to the Corinthians by standing along with Apollos within range of the word, it is because he understands the word as event, an event in which he participates and in which he hopes the Corinthians will participate. He thus refers[47] these things to himself and Apollos for the sake of the Corinthians, so that they may learn, via the apostles, how they are to comport themselves with one another. The second reason arises out of the epistolary medium. He is writing to those to whom he has already preached the gospel and who, for one reason or another, have not grasped its dimensions or have missed it altogether. The apostle is therefore in the mode of recapitulation. Language in this mode is characterized by primary reflectivity, i. e., language which reflects upon its own intentionality in view of its auditory range.[48] In such a mode the apostle cannot merely repeat what he has said; he must reflect on what he himself is hearing in relation to a broader spectrum, or listen more sharply for particular notes. His hearing will be sensitized in direct proportion to his ability to enter into the language context to which he wishes to address himself. We should not be surprised, then, to find two aspects to Paul's primary reflectivity: (1) his own attending anew to the word spoken to him and which he wishes to speak; (2) his attempt to enter into the language context of his auditors more fully and/or precisely.

In 4:7 f. Paul turns to direct and ironic speech (as in 1:26-31) in rebuffing the Corinthians for presuming to transcend the limits of their own historic existence. Thus 4:8b serves as the immediate transition

---

[47] μετασχηματίζω: to transform, change εἴς τι into, as something. In rhetoric it means to say something with the aid of a figure of speech. Cf. Bauer, *op. cit.*, under the word. Paul has transposed direct language into indirect for the sake of the Corinthians.
[48] Cf. chap. 9, *supra*.

back to the mode of speech indicated by 4:6. Paul once more refers "these things to himself and Apollos" for their illumination. In this staccato summary (cf. II Cor. 6:4–10), he recalls some of the catch-words of his earlier remarks (especially in 4:10). Paul's intention is to deprive them of their basis for boasting (4:6c–8), which is precisely the basis of apostolic existence (4:9–13)—1:26–31 in different garb!

Paul is their father, for he has begotten them through the gospel (4:14 f.). He therefore urges them to be imitators of him, i.e., to be determined by the Christ in the way in which he is (4:16). To be so determined, however, is conceived not as possession, but as gift (4:7). The word of the cross, as the power of God, is the means by which man is begotten in Christ, and the appropriation of that word is a "hearing." This is so because for Paul preaching is simultaneously a "hearing," and it follows that the Corinthians, too, must receive the word as a "hearing." This "hearing" is the basis of their κλῆσις (call-ing, 1:26), since it is the means by which they are invoked as κλητοί (called, 1:24) and through which they are saved (1:21b). If the redemp-tive power of the word is broadly asserted in 4:15b, it is more precisely aimed into the situation in 4:18 ff. Some[49] are falsely inflated because they think Paul is not coming to Corinth. In 4:19b ff. he contrasts λόγος as mere talk, prattle with λόγος as δύναμις: the language of the pompous egoists is empty, but the kingdom consists not of talk but of power. He will learn what power their language has, when he comes, should they wish. He therefore puts the matter up to them: shall I come with a rod, i.e., with λόγος δυνάμεως (word of power), or in love and a gentle spirit?[50]

III

Wilckens has emphasized that Paul avoids σοφία in the formula-tion of the basic antithesis in 1:18 ff.[51] There can be no doubt that Paul conceives sophia as belonging to God; every human claim to sophia is therefore precluded (1:31; cf. 3:21). Wilckens insists, ac-cordingly, that sophia for Paul has no anthropological correlate (per-haps as a concept parallel to γνῶσις, knowledge), which I take to be correct, provided it means the preclusion of "any wisdom of one's

---

49 We learn for the first time that some and not all of the Corinthians are involved.
50 Cf. II Cor. 13:2 ff.
51 Wilckens, *op. cit.*, 24, 38, 98. One might expect σοφία θεοῦ in the second member of the formulation, but Paul employs δύναμις.

own."[52] If it is taken to mean that sophia has no anthropological reference for Paul, I Cor. 2:6–16 stands in direct contradiction, as does I Cor. 12:8 (ᾧ . . . δίδοται λόγος σοφίας, to one . . . has been given proclamation of wisdom).[53] This is especially evident if πνεῦμα (spirit) in 2:10 ff. is a synonym for σοφία.[54] Yet Wilckens resists the inference that the sophia of God has an anthropological reference because he rightly wants to exclude a Christian counterpart to Gnostic sophia. But does the Pauline antithesis as it is developed in 2:6–16 permit a secret, esoteric sophia in the Gnostic sense? Wilckens apparently thinks so, and what makes Paul's error so horrendous in his judgment is that he confines it to an inner circle, the τέλειοι (the initiated).[55]

Paul speaks sophia ἐν τοῖς τελείοις (among the initiated, 2:6). This note is introduced parenthetically and then explicated in 2:(13)14 ff.[56] Verse 3:1 makes it evident that τέλειος is synonymous with πνευματικός (cf. 2:15, 13 [?]).[57] Wilckens holds, following Reitzenstein, that τέλειος/πνευματικός belong to the technical vocabulary of the Hellenistic mysteries and especially of the Gnostic mysteries,[58] and mean "complete identity with the transcendent God."[59] On the basis of σοφία and τέλειοι in 2:6 and a congeries of related terms in what follows in relation to comparative material, Wilckens concludes: "In fact Paul suddenly speaks here exactly like a Gnostic. Everything that he says here can be understood without exception as Gnostic wisdom teaching in the sense of the Corinthians."[60]

Bultmann, like Wilckens after him, is equally certain, if not more so, of the contrast between 1:18—2:5 and 2:6–16.[61] In 2:6 ff. Paul speaks of a proclamation which is comprehensible as sophia for human understanding, rather than of σταυρός as sophia in the paradoxical sense. This sophia, moreover, is no longer hidden for Christians but remains

---

[52] *Ibid.*, 39; Bultmann, *Glauben und Verstehen* I, 44.

[53] Wilckens (*op. cit.*, 46) notes 12:8, but does not bring it into relation to this point, except to say that charismatic speech was overvalued in Corinth. But cf. *TWNT* VII (1964), 523 n. 394.

[54] Wilckens, *op. cit.*, 81; cf. E. Käsemann, *op. cit.*, 270 f.

[55] Wilckens, *op. cit.*, 87 and *passim*, following Bultmann, *Glauben und Verstehen* I, 42.

[56] Wilckens, *op. cit.*, 60.

[57] *Ibid.*, 53.

[58] *Ibid.*, 53–60. This is the position of Bultmann, *Glauben und Verstehen* I, 42 f.

[59] Wilckens, *op. cit.*, 56.

[60] *Ibid.*, 60.

[61] *Glauben und Verstehen* I, 42 ff.

hidden for others, while elsewhere in Paul the word of the cross has been revealed and preached to all. The text (3:1 ff.) states clearly that Paul has not yet transmitted this special sophia to the Corinthians. And finally, here the "perfect"/"initiated" alone possess the spirit—and they have it as a possession at their disposal—while elsewhere every Christian has the spirit.

With respect to the Corinthian schismatics themselves the picture has discernible contours. That the Corinthians understood sophia as bringing salvation into the present there can be no doubt (cf. 4:8). Inasmuch as they were united with a transhistorical sophia, they understood themselves to be entitled to transhistorical existence and thus privileged to leap over the mundane realities of historical existence. The basis of divisiveness within the congregation lay in their attachment to the mystagogue, whether Paul, Apollos, Cephas, or Christ,[62] who was their leader in perfect gnosis. The various leaders thus acquired a soteriological function.[63] Whatever the content of sophia for the several parties may have been (Paul does not specify interparty differences), they shared a common understanding of sophia: it was mysterious and hidden in that it was otherworldly[64] and accessible only to the "perfect"/"initiated." For the "perfect"/"initiated," nevertheless, sophia was at the disposal of thought and language, i.e., it

---

[62] Köster, op. cit., 591, has pointed out the exegetical difficulties that arise when one assumes the Corinthian parties to be identifying themselves with the exalted Christ as sophia. One must first strike ἐγὼ Χριστοῦ (I am of Christ) out of the list of passwords (1:12). Further, it is difficult to see how Christ can be divided if he is in fact the content of salvation as sophia for one and all. Allegiance to the several baptizers also becomes problematical when one observes that Christ does not enter into this picture, nor does Peter, and Paul takes pains to emphasize that he baptized virtually no one. That leaves only Apollos, who did not appear in Corinth until after the church was established. J. M. Robinson, however, has attempted to meet this objection by arguing that the association of the baptismal idiom with the parties in Corinth indicates a special kind of baptism, i.e., one especially efficacious, which need only have been carried out by those claiming the succession of Paul, Apollos, Cephas. The special efficacy of baptism administered by those in the right succession is reflected in Acts, and the role of the founding fathers as coredemptors is intimated in Col. 1:24 ("The Sacraments in Corinth," *Journal of the Interseminary Movement of the Southwest* [1962], 19–32; "Kerygma and History in the New Testament" [see n. 9 in this chap.], p. 123). And finally, why does Paul expressly subordinate the entire congregation to Christ (3:23), if, in fact, the Corinthians were already claiming identity with Christ? It would appear to be more accurate to understand Christ as one mystagogue among others. To which may be added that in this case, too, it is then possible to understand why Paul takes an extreme line with the Corinthians: they had subordinated both Christ and the apostles to sophia and thus fallen outside the range of the word of the cross altogether.

[63] Cf. Wilckens, op. cit., 59.

[64] It is otherworldly in the sense both that it brings knowledge of the divine realm and that it has its source there as revelation.

was free-floating speculation. Since the "perfect"/"initiated" were mystically united with sophia, they were above the criticism of men and beyond the judgment of God. And finally, sophia for them was not grounded in Jesus, i.e., in the cross. So much can be inferred from Paul's response. And Bultmann and Wilckens allege that Paul, at least in part, falls prey to these views in 2:6–16.

The primary step in assessing this allegation is to re-examine 2:6–16 *in its own context.*

Δέ (but, 2:6) indicates that 2:6 ff. is an explanation or qualification of what has preceded[65]: "Yet we do speak a kind of wisdom. . . ." The qualifications that follow (δέ οὐ . . . οὐδὲ [but not . . . nor] 2:6b, ἀλλά [but] 2:7) set this sophia off from the sophia that formed the basis of the antithesis, i.e., σοφία λόγου, κόσμου, ἀνθρώπων (wisdom of word, world, men). Paul has prepared the way for this contrast by introducing θεοῦ σοφίαν (divine wisdom) as that which is preached already in 1:24—a link which Wilckens does not take sufficiently into account in his explication of 2:16 ff. In 1:24, of course, θεοῦ σοφίαν = Χριστὸν ἐσταυρωμένον (Christ crucified). The correlation of Christ and sophia also appears in 1:30, where it is again given soteriological significance. Wilckens further assumes that the sophia-phrases in 1:21 are to be understood in the same sense as sophia in 1:24, 30: the sophia (of God) is either the "sphere" in which man exists or the means by which he can come to knowledge of God, and both of these are merely different functions of the one sophia of God.[66] Wilckens' interpretation seems doubtful, however, for the reason that, on his view, the sharp contrast between sophia and the foolishness of preaching in 1:21 is emptied of its significance precisely for the Corinthians. Furthermore, if διὰ τῆς σοφίας (through wisdom) of 1:21a refers to the same sophia of God as 1:24, 30,[67] then the opposition between the sophia through which the world did not know God and the redemptive power of the foolishness of preaching (1:21) is reduced to nonsense (the world did not know God through wisdom, so it pleased God to save the world through wisdom), or a meaningless distinction between the act of God in Christ (as God's wisdom) and the foolishness of preaching is being implied.

It is more likely that Paul deliberately avoids the term sophia in the formulation of the basic antithesis (1:18) as Wilckens thinks, but

[65] See *supra,* n. 12.
[66] Wilckens, *op. cit.,* 34.
[67] *Ibid.,* 33, 34.

takes it up in a pejorative sense in 1:19 f. and then moves via the contrasting uses in 1:21a[68] to the positive formulations of 1:24, 30. That the positive correlation of sophia with the Crucified is taken up in 2:6 is given with the trajectory of thought and confirmed by the qualifying δέ (but, 2:6), which sets this sophia off from the sophia of men in 2:5. It is therefore a peculiar kind of wisdom, which the world will view as foolishness (2:14). That it can be labeled wisdom, however, follows from the way in which the Corinthians suppose their wisdom to function, i.e., redemptively (1:30). The point is corroborated by 3:18: "If anyone among you thinks he is wise in this age, let him become a fool in order that he may become wise." Here Paul utilizes wisdom in two different and opposing senses (1:21 also?). The paradox[69] involved is that such wisdom contradicts the opinion of the world, not that the statement contradicts itself. Thus Paul is using their language against them.[70]

It would be all the more surprising that Paul should correlate sophia with Christ, if this were precisely what produced the unorthodox Corinthian christology.[71] It is not satisfactory to answer that for Paul it was the exalted Christ with whom sophia was identified, for in that case the question "Is Christ divided?" loses its meaning. We would expect Paul to argue for the exclusion of all human ties in favor of an exclusive relationship to Christ (3:21 ff.). It is thus possible, and exegetically more illuminating, to understand the correlation of sophia and Christ as specifically Pauline, in opposition to the Corinthian subordination of all the apostles as well as the Christ to sophia.[72]

---

[68] It may be suggested that sophia of God in 1:21a is used in an ironical sense: in God's "wisdom" it was determined that the world would not come to knowledge of God through wisdom (cf. 3:18). The ironical sense prepares the way for the shift to a positive correlation in 1:24. Köster's suggestion (op. cit., 591) that sophia is parallel here to νόμος (law) is to be considered: Through (or on the basis of) the wisdom of God—just that wisdom which the opponents claim for themselves—it was determined that wisdom was not the way to the acknowledgment of God. Yet not to be ruled out is the meaning "counsels of God" for the first occurrence, a meaning suggested by Rom. 11:33 and assumed by both RSV and NEB. In that case, the second occurrence (διὰ τῆς σοφίας) is to be understood in a pejorative sense (cf. K. Barth, Die Kirchliche Dogmatik, II/1, 490 [Wilckens, op. cit., 33 n. 2]).

[69] Wilckens, op. cit., 40.

[70] It is doubtless the case that sophia is a Corinthian catchword since it is not otherwise typical of the Pauline vocabulary (ibid., 68). This is valid irrespective of whether or not σοφία and γνῶσις are synonyms.

[71] Ibid., 20, 25, 68, 98 f. and passim. Cf. n. 66 above.

[72] This is not to say that there was not precedent for the identification. Köster, op. cit., 594, proposes a possible history of religions context for the Corinthian viewpoint.

The sophia which Paul[78] speaks is not the sophia of this age or of the powers of this age (2:6). No (ἀλλά), the sophia we speak is the sophia of God (2:7), for God reveals it to us (2:10a). It is the sophia by which we identify the Lord of Glory as the Crucified (2:8); we have received the sophia (= πνεῦμα) of God in order that we may discern the gifts given us by God (2:12: transition back to direct polemic). We do not speak sophia, therefore, in language informed by human sophia, but in language informed by the spirit (sophia of God). In so doing we are combining or comparing spiritual things with spiritual things, and thus discerning the spirits, i.e., engaging in substantive criticism. For the spirit not only confers wisdom and spiritual gifts, but it stands in critical judgment upon wisdom and spiritual gifts.[74]

The connection between sophia and the Crucified does not emerge in 2:6-16, according to Wilckens, because Paul has taken over a sophia christology from the Corinthians; since Paul has not defined sophia in 2:6-16, Wilckens assumes that he is using it in the Corinthian sense as a christological title of the exalted Lord.[75] The first fallacy in this argument has already emerged: Paul himself introduces sophia as a christological predicate in 1:24, 30 and connects it there with the Crucified. This stands whether or not Paul has taken over a Corinthian catchword. The assumption which emerges from the sequence of thought analysis is therefore logically the same as Wilckens', but its consequence is quite the reverse: sophia in 2:6-16 is used in precisely the same sense as in 1:18 ff., but that now means as qualified by the Crucified. Although the preceding context is quite sufficient to give definition to sophia in 2:6-16, we are not wholly dependent upon it. The passage 2:6-16 also speaks for itself.

First Corinthians 2:6b clearly appears to radicalize the contrast between the sophia of God and the sophia of the world and men by representing the former as hidden from the powers of this age as well as from the world. Yet on the basis of 2:8b Wilckens is forced to reinterpret: 2:6b is introduced not to radicalize the hiddenness of the sophia of God, "but because the hiddenness of the sophia of God and its non-recognition by the powers is precisely what has made possible

---

[73] On the use of the first person plural see *supra*, n. 46. Given the polemical context, it is obvious that Paul does not propose to embrace his opponents in this "we" without qualification.

[74] Käsemann, *op. cit.*, 274.

[75] Wilckens, *op. cit.*, 68.

the redemptive effect of the revelation and the κύριος τῆς δόξης [Lord of Glory] to lead ἡμεῖς [us] back to δόξα [glory]."[76] From this Wilckens draws the conclusion that the wisdom of the powers is brought to naught at the cross, at the place of their supposed victory, because they were deceived (by the fleshly garb of the redeemer).[77]

To the theme of hiddenness I shall return momentarily. Meanwhile it may be suggested, against Wilckens, that it is doubtful that a sophisticated docetism stands at the beginning of the Christian-Gnostic controversy.[78] However that may be, it is clear that the Pauline assumption underlying 2:8b is that the Lord of Glory was crucified. In the only other place, according to Wilckens, where Paul accommodates himself to the Gnostic redeemer myth, Phil. 2:5 ff., he makes it evident by his own addition in 2:8 where the crucial point lies: in the event of the crucifixion.[79] And it is in I Cor. 2:8b that the same connection is posited: Lord of Glory and Crucified. The theory that Paul accommodates himself to an alleged sophia-exaltation christology in 2:6 ff. is shattered, therefore, by the correlation of 2:8b.

If we inquire why the powers crucified this Lord, we are brought to the question of mystery (ἐν μυστηρίῳ) and hiddenness (τὴν ἀποκεκ-ρυμμένην, 2:7). If Wilckens is correct in thinking that mystery here does not denote "plan of salvation," nor finally the contents of salvation laid up in heaven awaiting the final revelation—of which a little something is already revealed before the eschaton—but rather the revelation of the Christ as the content of salvation, must we conclude with him that the Gnostic redeemer myth determines the cast of the passage?[80] Both Bultmann and Wilckens insist that the Gnostic redeemer myth lies behind 2:8.[81] However that may be, a comparative observation does not exhaust the text. The further observation that 2:7a is formulated in typical Gnostic language (note the parallelism between ἐν μυστηρίῳ and ἐν τοῖς τελείοις 2:6a) and 2:7b in typical apocalyptic language is determinative of nothing beyond that fact. The question remains: in what sense does the hiddenness of the

[76] Ibid., 74 f.

[77] Ibid., 75, 97, 121 n. 1.

[78] Köster, op. cit., 593, 595; cf. C. Colpe, "Gnosis I. Religionsgeschichtlich," RGG II, 1652.

[79] Wilckens, op. cit., 98.

[80] Ibid., 70, 73.

[81] Bultmann, Theology of the New Testament I, 175, 293; Wilckens, op. cit., 70 ff.

sophia of God make it inaccessible to the powers (2:6b, 8) and the ψυχικός (unspiritual) man (2:14) alike?

Ἐν μυστηρίῳ in 2:7a in my judgment picks up μυστήριον in 2:1.[82] In 2:1 f. the superlative word and wisdom are set off against knowledge of the Crucified. The mystery is therefore bound to the proclamation of the word of the cross.[83] A distinction cannot be maintained between mystery in its formal and its substantive senses:[84] it is not the mode of Paul's speech which is itself mysterious, but the substance of what he proclaims, i.e., the word of the cross. In that case, the sophia spoken among the "perfect"/"initiated," the sophia spoken in a mystery, and that which was hidden from the powers all refer to the mystery of the cross. The conditional sentence in 2:8b, consequently, is in a sense redundant: if the powers had understood the mystery of the cross, they would not have failed to recognize the Lord of Glory.[85] Just as Paul carries through a consistent understanding of mystery, he also retains the contrast with μωρία (foolishness): The ψυχικός man cannot receive the things of the spirit of God (= the sophia of God, the mystery of the cross) because they are foolishness to him (2:14). And this same antithesis dominates 1:18 ff.

What the powers did not know, i.e., perceive, was the word spoken to them in the cross. The deception perpetrated on them was thus not merely the fleshly garb of the Redeemer, but his open, i.e., historical, appearance in obedience and weakness (cf. Phil. 2:8 in a similar context). To the Gnostic the foolishness and weakness of the Redeemer must be ephemeral; to Paul they are the substance of his redemptive work. Gnostic wisdom delivers man from the world; the sophia that comports with the word of the cross leaves man, as it were, at the mercy of the world. For Gnosticism hiddenness is transhistorical; for the Christian it is nothing if not historical. Since for Paul the Crucified is the focal point of the discussion (also cf. 2:16b), he grounds the sophia of God in that μωρία (foolishness), ἀσθενές (weakness), which belongs to the cross. On this point the text is everywhere clear.

---

[82] Adopting μυστήριον as the reading, with J. Weiss, Lietzmann, Bornkamm, Wilckens (*op. cit.,* 45 n. 1 for references and discussion). Μαρτύριον can be urged on the basis of 1:6, to be sure, but since the relationship between 1:4-9 and 1:10 ff. is remote, I am inclined to give the weight to the relationship between 2:1, 7 and 4:1. The question cannot be resolved on text-critical grounds alone.

[83] Bornkamm, *TWNT* IV (1942), 825.

[84] Bornkamm, *op. cit.,* 856; Wilckens, *op. cit.,* 64 n. 1.

[85] "Crucified" here is equivalent to rejection. Paul is not speculating about an "if" of history, since the crucifixion is not understood by Paul merely as an event of world history but as an act of God.

Now, of course, there is a sense in which the hiddenness of the revelation is constitutive of its redemptive power. It is hidden that Christ may become faith's wisdom from God, that faith may rest not on the wisdom of men but on the power of God, that no one may boast of men but only of God. As is widely recognized, the doctrine of justification by faith, explicitly set out in Romans and Galatians in relation to a Jewish context, is transported into the atmosphere of a Jewish or Gnostic Hellenism in the Corinthian correspondence and interpreted in relation to its way of framing problems, its terminology, and its line of argumentation.[86] Bultmann long since and now Wilckens[87] have both recognized certain affinities between Gnostic and Christian structures of thought. Wilckens' ostensible complaint is that Paul's language in I Cor. 2:6 ff. could have been taken by the Corinthian Gnostics precisely in their own way, but what he fails to recognize is that within those structures of thought Paul is shattering their intention at the crucial points. For example, Paul deforms the catchwords sophia, Lord of Glory, mystery, in the course of his exposition, as has been noted. He attaches sophia precisely to the Crucified, which produces a radical deformation of the term as the Corinthians understood it, in that it no longer intends a transhistorical Sophia or even the exalted Lord of Glory. He identifies the Lord of Glory as the Crucified, which robs the Corinthian soteriology of its unrelieved glory. He adduces the word of the cross as the mystery, which means that mystery no longer signals an esoteric revelation but the open weakness and foolishness of the Crucified. At these points Paul is obliquely deforming Corinthian language in the interest of gaining a hearing of the word of the cross. It follows' that one must inquire closely after the intentionality of the text.[88]

With 2:13 the previous development is consummated: the what and the how of this peculiar sophia have been sketched in antithetical language. Paul now turns to the negative side and, at the same time, prepares the way for his own defense (4:1–5) by developing the critical note introduced in 2:12 f., a note which he sounds openly against the Corinthians in 3:1 ff. The man who has not received the spirit ($\psi\upsilon\chi\iota\varkappa\acute{o}\varsigma$) is the one who is perishing of 1:18, the Jew and Greek of 1:23, the one who vests his destiny in human sophia (cf. the

[86] Käsemann, *op. cit.,* 267; Wilckens, *op. cit.,* 222 and references in n. 1. Cf. my essay, "The Hermeneutical Problem and Historical Criticism," *New Frontiers* II, 164–97.
[87] *Op. cit.,* 217.
[88] Also recognized by Wilckens, *ibid.*

antithesis of 2:4). In language more characteristic of Paul he is σαρκικός, a synonym he applies to the Corinthians in 3:1[89] and which signifies that they are given to the standards of the world, i.e., to human wisdom.[90] Paul softens this designation by adding the term νήπιος (babes, 3:1) and follows it with an appropriate figure of speech. Following Reitzenstein and Bultmann, Wilckens[91] takes τέλειος/πνευματικός as contrasting terms to σαρκικός/ψυχικός rather than to νήπιος, thus understanding the former as technical terms of the mysteries. The contrast with νήπιος is indeed "secondary," as Wilckens insists. Nevertheless, its addition suggests that Paul senses he has drawn the line too sharply: they are indeed σαρκικός insofar as envy and contention, with all that these imply in the Corinthian situation, reign among them.[92] Alongside the radical contrast between those who possess the spirit and those who do not, Paul sets the contrast between mature and immature, and this in the same breath.[93] That their criticism of Paul and his of them lie behind 2:14 ff. is further shown by οὔπω γὰρ ἐδύνασθε. ἀλλ’ οὐδὲ [ἔτι] νῦν δύνασθε (3:2), ἔτι γὰρ σαρκικοί ἐστε (3:3) (You were not up to it. And you are not up to it now, for you are still worldly men), which picks up οὐκ ἠδυνήθην λαλῆσαι ὑμῖν (I was not able to speak to you) of 3:1, and goes back to οὐ δύναται γνῶναι (he is not able to know) of 2:14. The ψυχικός man, then, is he who is able neither to receive nor to know because, lacking spiritual discernment, the things of the spirit are foolishness to him. Into this category at least some (4:18) of the Corinthians fall.

On the other hand, the πνευματικός discerns all things (and what

[89] Wilckens rightly observes (92 n. 1) that σαρκικός is the Pauline synonym for Gnostic ψυχικός.

[90] Defined in 3:3 as κατὰ ἄνθρωπον περιπατεῖν (to behave according to human standards). Cf. Bultmann, *Theology of the New Testament* I, 239 ff. It is important to note that the σαρκικός man is given to boasting as one who puts his confidence in the flesh: *ibid.*, 242 f.

[91] *Op. cit.*, 53 f. n. 3.

[92] P. J. Du Plessis, ΤΕΛΕΙΟΣ: *The Idea of Perfection in the New Testament* Kampen: J. H. Kok N. V., n.d.) is entirely wide of the mark when he wants to distinguish between a Christian–non-Christian dichotomy in 1:18—2:16 and inter-Christian dichotomy in 3:1 ff. He does so, of course, for some of the same reasons that cause Wilckens to want to set 2:6–16 off from the rest of the passage. But, as we have observed, the discussion of sophia in 1:18—2:16 is integral to the problem of factionalism. Verses 3:1 ff. cannot, therefore, be disengaged from what goes before.

[93] That the latter contrast comes in the end to prevail is indicated by the tenor of the discussion in 3:3 ff. (note especially 3:16 f.), 3:21 ff., 4:6, 14 ff. Cf. Lietzmann, *op. cit., ad loc.*

theologian does not pretend to!), but is himself called to account by
no one. This right accrues to the pneumatic by virtue of his receiving
the spirit (2:12) which itself searches all things (2:10b). The explication of 2:15 is to be found in 4:3: it does not matter to Paul in the least
whether he is called to account by them or any other *human* court.
He is, of course, under the judgment of the Lord through the word of
the cross (4:2, 5a; cf. 2:3), as he has indicated by the form he has given
his exposition (4:6; cf. above), but no one has the mind of the Lord,
i.e., God, so as to instruct him in his judgments (2:16a).[94] Only—and
here is Paul's claim—we have the mind of Christ: on this basis he
dares to embark on substantive theological criticism and call the
Corinthian schismatics to book.

Bultmann has rightly observed that the designation of the Corinthians as σαρκικοί in spite of their having been baptized does not involve a contradiction (it is also possible on the basis of Gal. 5:16 f.,
Rom. 8:12 f.).[95] What is contradictory in his view consists in setting
off the pneumatics as a special class which has the spirit at its disposal
(so Wilckens[96]). In view of the fact that τέλειος is a technical term
of the mysteries, the reader is taken by surprise at its appearance in
2:6, the Corinthians more than anybody. For not only is the sophia of
God set in sharp contrast to the sophia of the world, but those who can
hear it are set off from those who cannot.[97] The Corinthians have
drawn a circle from which they now find themselves excluded, because the circle has been redrawn with a new center. The cleavage
between those to whom the word of the cross is foolishness and those
to whom it is the power of God has prevailed since 1:18. If Paul now
introduces a Corinthian catchword to refer to the latter, we cannot
prevent him by referring him to the glossaries in standard Gnostic
handbooks. He must be permitted to establish his own usage.

Τέλειος in 2:6 is synonymous with πνευματικός, as 3:1 shows.[98]
These terms may therefore be considered together. The τέλειοι are
those to whom God has revealed "these things" (2:9-10a): "these

---

[94] Wilckens, *op. cit.*, 95, correctly observes the polemical cast of the rhetorical question, thus necessitating the answer "no one." That Χριστοῦ stands in the next clause
rather than Κυρίου (θεοῦ) comports with the discussion in 1:18—2:5.
[95] *Glauben und Verstehen* I, 43 f. Cf. Gal. 5:2 ff., 3:1 ff., where the criticism is also
radicalized.
[96] *Op. cit.*, 52 ff., 87.
[97] Cf. *ibid.*, 52.
[98] *Ibid.*, 53.

things" refer to the sophia of God, the mystery of the cross (2:6–8).⁹⁹
They are also those who have received the spirit (= sophia) of God
in order to discern the gifts given them by God (2:12): the critical
authority of the "perfect"/"initiated" arises out of the mystery of the
cross and refers to it as norm. And finally, they are those who discern
all things but are themselves examined by no one. Again, no one
could be more surprised than the Corinthians themselves, for Paul is
chastizing them with their own slogan.¹⁰⁰ Taken together with 1:26–
31, 3:16, 4:15, there can be no doubt that "τέλειος for him [Paul] is
the possibility and reality where grace is at work."¹⁰¹ And if for Paul
the τέλειοι, the πνευματικοί, are those who have received the word of the
cross as power, he has reminted the current Gnostic coin of these
terms.

Does not Paul nevertheless make a distinction within the congregation?¹⁰² Indeed he does! The question is what kind of a distinction
and on what basis? There is first of all the possibility that the relation
between those within the congregation having the spirit and those not
is dialectical. This is possible because spirit for Paul is both power and
norm.¹⁰³ There is no contradiction between this view and the assertion
that all Christians receive the spirit at baptism, for, although with the
spirit is created the possibility of faithful existence, this possibility can
only be actualized in concrete deeds. Thus it may be said that Christians both have (insofar as they walk according to the spirit) and do
not have (insofar as they fall short of the norm) the spirit. Paul's
formulation in 3:1 ff. indicates that he has not freed the notion of
sophia from faithful comportment, and thus has not turned it into free-

⁹⁹ Cf. *ibid.*, 75–80, 81.
¹⁰⁰ Weiss, *op. cit.*, 66 f.; Wilckens, *op. cit.*, 94 f.; cf. Wilckens' statement in *TWNT*
VII (1964), 521 n. 387: "a sharper condemnation of the Corinthian position in gnostic
language is not possible."
¹⁰¹ Käsemann, *op. cit.*, 269.
¹⁰² This question troubles Wilckens no end, as his comments (*op. cit.*, 87) indicate.
He cannot surmount Paul's use of a Gnostic term by which he believes Paul's clarity
is comprised: "Have *all* Christians received πνεῦμα (v. 12), or only the pneumatics
among the Christians (v. 10; cf. 14 f.)? Consequently, is the speech concerning the wisdom of God general proclamation (as in 1:24 ff.), or only special charismatic speech?
Are those to whom such wisdom is addressed the world, Jews and heathen, or just a
special circle of charismatics? That no clear answer is to be drawn from the text itself
is what constitutes its peculiar problematic." One can account for this confusion on the
basis of (1) the tyranny of comparative lexicography, and (2) the exclusion of the
larger context.
¹⁰³ Cf. Bultmann, *Theology of the New Testament* I, 336 f., *Glauben und Verstehen*
I, 43 f.

floating speculation.[104] Closely related is the view that distinctions within the congregation are based on degrees of maturity.[105] It has been argued above that this kind of distinction is in fact the one which Paul ends by making in Corinth. But the sharpness of the antithesis in 2:6–16 is to be accounted for in another way. There is, of course, the radical antithesis between those who cling to the ground of faith, the Crucified, and those who substitute human wisdom for faith, i.e., the antithesis of 1:18—2:5. If the Corinthian parties had subordinated both Christ and the apostles to sophia,[106] they would in that case fall into the class of those to whom the word of the cross was foolishness. That many were only superficially converted to the faith (then as now) and that some remained essentially pagan may be taken as certain. The dichotomy between intra-extra- and inter-Christian then loses its validity.[107]

[104] Bultmann, *Theology of the New Testament* I, 327.

[105] *Ibid.*, 160.

[106] Cf. *supra*.

[107] Two further exegetical notes may be appended: (1) Bultmann's point (against Barth) that the text (3:1 ff) says clearly that Paul had not yet preached the sophia of 2:6 ff. to the Corinthians as yet is surely in error. Οὐκ ἠδυνήθην λαλῆσαι ὑμῖν ὡς πνευματικοῖς (I was not able to address you as pneumatics) refers to the auditory perceptiveness of the congregation: he addressed them then (i.e., at the beginning, as with every new audience) and does so now as "fleshly" men, as "babes in Christ," viz., in a way which introduces them to the faith, as though they had not heard of it before. He continues to feed them on the bottle. Bultmann takes this to imply that Paul would, when they matured sufficiently, also speak the higher mysteries to them. But where is there supporting evidence that Paul conceived the word of the cross as anything other than an "open mystery"? And this text cannot be made to stand by itself, as though it had no context. The distinction cannot be referred to the variety of charismata either, for in that case there would be a substantive difference between mysteries spoken in the spirit and the content of prophecy (I Cor. 14:2 ff.). On the contrary, Paul's language in 3:1 ff. is to be understood within the context of the expectations of the Corinthians rather than within his own: it is for this reason that he puts it in *their* language. Paul cannot give them the "mysteries" (which they thought they possessed) because they have been and are "fleshly" (which they thought they weren't) until they become "spiritual" (which they believed themselves to be); when they become "spiritual" they will see that the "mysteries" are nothing other than the word of the cross, which is foolishness, and that the strife and envy among them is the sign of their "fleshliness" (3:3). Paul has simply turned their language, and thus their expectations, inside out in the interest of bringing them face to face with the word of the cross. (2) One further observation may be made with respect to the vacillating first person plural (cf. *supra,* notes 46 and 73): the first person plural in 2:6 ff. is inclusive-exclusive, i.e., hovers between the two. On the one hand, it attempts to pull his readers into his own orbit, to embrace them, as it were, within the fold of the faithful. On the other hand, given the polemical context, it verges on exclusion, particularly as the critical note emerges in 2:12 f. That critical, excluding note erupts in 3:1 f. as the singular.

IV

This examination of the text has endeavored to bring to the surface the path of Paul's thought as it comes to expression in particular and diverse language. At the same time the interpretations of Bultmann and Wilckens have served as the foil of its articulation. The point at which these two cross, especially in the case of Wilckens, is *how* Paul's language is heard. Wilckens is preoccupied with whether a particular word or phrase or sentence is to be referred to Jewish apocalyptic or Gnostic conceptualities, with whether this expression or that sentence calls up this or that context: in this interest he is by no means misdirected. Such careful marshaling of comparative material is a long and necessary step toward the goal. Nevertheless, Wilckens tends to be dominated on the one side by the results of his own comparative investigations, i.e., by how the informed investigator understands the language, and on the other by hearing which takes place in staccato fashion, i.e., which edits. The Corinthians did not hear a phrase or even a sentence in isolation, but were brought under the impact of the whole. Of course, there were doubtless those who fastened on this phrase or that paragraph and thus missed the point. But neither Paul nor the exegete can make himself responsible for selective hearing. What the exegete must take as his responsibility is the intentionality of the language in view of its linguistic horizons.

If one reflects upon the flow of thought, the architecture of the whole section 1:10—4:21, one is struck—so the examination has attempted to show—by the way in which Paul begins with the evident (the strife among them), reflects upon his own proclamation to them, then draws near their language home in particularly biting and stringent criticism. He also knows how to retreat: he does so mildly in 3:1 ff, and almost sentimentally in 4:14 ff. It is not the psychology of this movement that is interesting, but its structure: Paul brings the evident and the language realm of the Corinthians into proximity with the tradition, i.e., proclamation in Paul's own characteristic language. He does so that the Christ may qualify their situation. Now the substance of the argument is that the Corinthians, who stood under the impact of the whole, would not have missed the way in which Paul brings the word of the cross into juxtaposition with their own jargon. It is precisely the proximity of the two in 2:6-16, when taken as a part of the larger movement, that does violence to their language and so shatters the terms that were censoring their hearing.

Preoccupation with how language is heard, however, tends to obscure what language intends. In fact, precisely this preoccupation may give rise to nonunderstanding or misunderstanding. If attention is riveted on what is being said, on the discourse itself, and thus on how it is to be heard, what the discourse is attempting to bring to expression is lost wholly or partially to view. Such misattention is equally fatal to the original auditor and the modern interpreter. What a given text intends is not exhausted or perhaps even grasped in the immediate situation into which it is directed. That does not necessarily qualify its intentionality. The question of intentionality must therefore be raised with respect to what the text fixes attention on, its "object," as that to which it holds fast as a ship sets her prow to the wind. Intention also has a passive side: the subject matter, the "object" of the discourse so to speak, exerts independent power in striving to come to speech; as that which is intended, it sets language on its path. The two go inevitably together: man as the user of language intends what cannot be reduced to the intending act; but what is intended is not constituted apart from the intending act, hence apart from that language in which what is intended comes to expression. It is for this reason that the exegete must take as his proper concern the intentionality of language in view of its linguistic horizons.

When we inquire of Paul what he intends, it becomes evident that he intends Jesus the Crucified as the ground of faith, as 1:18–31 shows. The christological predicates cling to Jesus. The word is referred again and again to the cross. The word which Paul invokes is therefore a word determined by Jesus. As a word determined by Jesus, it cannot be Paul's word. Rather, it must be the word which Jesus gives Paul to speak. By the same token, it cannot be just a word about Jesus, for that would divorce it from its ground and transpose it into the category of sophia. As a result, Paul's intention can be executed only by letting Jesus come to speech, by letting him speak the word which is power. For only as Jesus comes to speech, only as the difference between faith and unbelief becomes acute (1:18, 2:14), is the word a redemptive word at all.

The word which stands on the opposite side of the Pauline antithesis is the word determined by sophia. By implication this word is without power. It is without power, first, because it is cut off from the ground of faith, namely, the crucified Jesus. It is powerless, too, because it has lost its critical function. It is divisive, but not critical. It draws a circle around its own without putting them to the test. It creates in-groups and out-groups, but does not cut across the perversity of man as such. Moreover, it deafens the auditor to the true word (cf. 2:14 f., 3:1 f.). The word of the cross, on the other hand, is indiscriminate in its critical power. It denies to man the right to boast and throws him upon the grace of God. In its weakness, its foolishness, it creates the opening for grace. It is the word of faith because it creates faith. The language of the Corinthians, finally, has been delivered over to the formal test of terminology, concepts, and mythologies. Since it is determined by human wisdom, it becomes the formal basis for parties, which refer themselves not to the ground of faith but to ideological leadership.

How inconsequential the game of language was among the Corinthians is demonstrated by Paul in 2:6–16, where he attempts to play the same game with reverse english. He seeks to shatter the word determined by sophia on the word of the cross. When the latter is given expression in the former, the word of sophia, so to speak, is turned inside out. The irony in his language is patent. Sophia becomes foolishness, the "perfect"/"initiated" are turned into men of the flesh, and those who lay claim to the spirit and the revealed mysteries find themselves in the camp of those without gnosis. In this Paul anticipates his coming with a rod (4:21), i.e., with a word of power.

It remains a possiblity, nevertheless, that Paul failed in his intention. While neither Bultmann nor Wilckens contests the overarching intention of Paul, each alleges that Paul, in 2:6–16, either falls in with the views of his opponents, or leads the Corinthians via his language to think so.

Bultmann's view is that Paul's pride induced him to posit a Christian gnosis on the basis of which he could rival the heathen (and the Corinthian heretics).[108] This is a very real, i.e., human possibility, full of earthiness, and assumes that Paul was not misled by his own cleverness. Paul was by no means above such temptation (cf. II Cor. 11:16 ff.). In response I have attempted to show that Paul's language exerts critical power over the Corinthians in a way which comports with the word of the cross.

Wilckens, on the other hand, refers the problem to a certain terminological precariousness,[109] to a dangerous because manifestly ambiguous unclarity in argumentation.[110] This instability in thought arises out of Paul's intention to engage the basic Gnostic thesis critically, while at

[108] *Glauben und Verstehen* I, 44.
[109] *Op. cit.*, 86 n. 1.
[110] *Ibid.*, 93.

the same time accommodating the pneuma doctrine but without acceding to its consequences.[111] That is to say it is this double purpose, in the same train of thought to take up and to reject, positively to reinterpret and polemically to contest, that produces confusion.[112] Thus put, it would appear that for Wilckens the unclarity and the resulting error reside in Paul's failure to carry through the polemic in Gnostic language and categories. In that case the question is exegetical and turns on a close examination of the text to determine whether such ambiguity does in fact dominate the passage. But consider Wilckens' further remark: Paul wants to distinguish his own preaching from that of the Gnostics in Corinth, but he is evidently not successful in 2:6 ff., "because he is here endeavoring to carry on the discussion in the language and conceptual realm of the Corinthians."[113] Taken strictly, this brings us "to the policy of rejecting not only false implications but also a total theological context and its vocabulary, as was to become standard policy from the Pastorals on."[114] One wonders, then, whether Paul's polemic being lost under an alien line of thought is to be referred to his failure to execute his intention, or whether in fact he could not have executed his intention, given his decision to utilize Gnostic language.[115] The *Sachkritik* which Wilckens proposes may, therefore, be the criticism of one ideology in the name of another.[116] Such an interpretation would make it understandable why Wilckens frames the whole problem as a christological controversy. It illuminates, moreover, a frequent tendency of his to give otherwise admirable comparative judgments a theological value in and of themselves. In any case, Wilckens' explanation of Paul's failure is of a different order from Bultmann's.

The locus of the exegetical dispute in the first instance lies in where one gives weight to the context. It is faulty methodology, as is well known, to interpret a text without reference to its context, a context that expands in ever widening concentric circles. But it is also necessary to grant the text its own integrity, i.e., to allow it to speak for itself over against as well as within its broader frame of reference. Wilckens

111 *Ibid.*, 92; cf. 217.
112 *Ibid.*, 93; cf. 217.
113 *Ibid.*, 98.
114 J. M. Robinson, "Basic Shifts in German Theology," *Interpretation* 16 (1962), 86.
115 Wilckens, *op. cit.*, 88; cf. 60, 87, and *passim*.
116 Cf. the judgment of E. Fuchs, with respect to Wilckens' remarks in *Offenbarung als Geschichte* (Göttingen: Vandenhoeck & Ruprecht, 1961), 63 ff., in *ThLZ* 88 (1963), cols. 259 f.

has cast his net widely in a most commendable fashion. He has also provided a close analysis of the smaller units of the passage itself. It may be asked, however, whether in fact he, as Bultmann before him, has not slighted the middle range of context, i.e., I Cor. 1:10—2:5; 3:1—4:21. This question may be raised in spite of his attention to the inner coherence of the larger section. Going together with this deficiency is his inclination, often unchecked, to allow comparative materials to dominate the detail of the text.

In the second instance—and here the point does not apply to Bultmann—there is the question whether intentionality can inhere in christological ideologies. In the only place where he raises the question explicitly, Wilckens apparently relativizes doctrinal christology.[117] Nevertheless, his whole study attempts to elucidate Paul's conflict with the Corinthians as the conflict between two opposing christologies.[118] It would be disastrous, of course, to depreciate christology out of hand. Yet to direct attention to the theological content of the proclamation without reference to its ground, on the one hand, and the linguistic context in which it is to be heard, on the other, is to turn the word into words, to cut language loose from event. Moreover, it obscures the central issue for Paul: can the Christ come to speech in such a way that he determines the situation, i.e., simultaneously creates faith and unbelief? Without that determination, the proclamation, however orthodox christologically, remains nonkerygmatic.[119] I have attempted to show that Paul's language in I Cor. 1:10—4:21 is not explicit christology, but an attempt to refer the Corinthians to the ground of faith, Jesus, in such a way that their situation is radically qualified. Thus 2:6-16 goes together with the whole in a single movement: it is an effort to bring the Corinthians, via their own language, within hearing range of the eschatological-critical power of the word.

---

[117] *Op. cit.,* 217 ff. Elsewhere he uses intention in the sense of aim or purpose: 52, 98, 216.
[118] Cf., *ibid.,* e.g., 20, 25, 68.
[119] Cf. Ebeling's discussion, *Theologie und Verkündigung,* 76 ff.

INDEX OF REFERENCES

(1) BIBLICAL

INDEX OF NAMES

312

Maybaum, S., 259n
Meland, Bernard E., 107n
Merleau-Ponty, Maurice, xiv, 122, 123, 129, 225, 227–30, 234 f.
Michaelis, W., 184, 185n, 211n
Michalson, Carl, 26n
Michel, O., 257n, 258n, 260n, 266
Miles, T. R., 5
Mitton, C. L., 273 f. n
Montefiore, Hugh, 166n, 167n, 183n, 186n
Moule, C. F. D., 252n, 259n
Mowry, Lucetta, 204, 205n
Müller-Schwefe, Hans-Rudolf, 37 f. n, 41n, 45n
Mullins, Terence Y., 259

Nietzsche, Friedrich, 82, 83
Norden, Eduard, 259n

Ogden, Schubert M., xv, 23n, 36, 73n, 74, 75n, 76, 77, 80, 82, 83, 87–108, 112, 122, 235n, 241n
Ott, Heinrich, 37 f. n, 74, 76, 77, 107, 108–22, 232n

Pannenberg, Wolfhart, 36n

Ramsey, Ian T., 36, 83, 137
Reitzenstein, Richard, 297
Richardson, William J., S.J., 37 f. n, 38n, 39n, 41n, 44n, 51n
Riesenfeld, Harald, 203
Riezler, S., 159n
Rigaux, Béda, 263n
Robinson, James M., xi, 10n, 20n, 21n, 37 f. n, 39n, 41n, 43n, 45n, 47n, 48n, 49n, 53n, 64n, 66n, 109n, 114, 116n, 118, 120n, 121, 129n, 130n, 149 f. n, 151n, 156n, 205n, 241n, 244 f. n, 257, 265n, 269n, 279n, 282n, 290n, 304n
Rosenmeyer, T. G., 159n
Rossetti, Christina, 157

Sanders, Jack T., 257, 263, 264, 265n, 269n, 274n, 286n
Sandmel, Samuel, 277n
Sartre, Jean-Paul, 227 f.
Schermann, Th., 259n
Schlier, H., 286n
Schleiermacher, F. D. E., 10
Schmauch, W., 168n

Schmithals, W., 266n, 272
Schubert, Paul, 256, 260, 263, 264, 286n
Sharpe, Eric J., 216 f. n
Smith, L. P., and Lantero, E. H., 144n, 211n
Snell, Bruno, 159n
Snyder, G. F., 49n
Stein, E., 259n
Stendahl, Krister, 168n, 208n
Strack, H. L., and Billerbeck, P., 212n
Suggs, M. Jack, xv, 265n, 274n

Turner, H. E. W., 166n
Tinsley, E. J., 207 f. n
Tillich, Paul, 140n
Thyen, Hartwig, 256n, 259, 260n
Thevanaz, Pierre, 227n

Van Buren, Paul M., 23n, 74, 76, 77, 78–87, 88, 104, 105, 107, 112, 122, 243
Van Unnik, W. C., 216 f. n, 232n
Vincent, J. J., 145n, 207n
Vögtle, A., 255n
von Eichendorff, Joseph, 119
von Humboldt, Wilhelm, 28
Vycinas, Vincent, 37 f. n

Wackernagel, J., 126
Weidinger, K., 255
Weiss, Johannes, 131, 252, 258, 259, 260, 266n, 272, 274, 282n, 283, 286n, 295n, 299n
Wendland, Paul, 257n, 259n, 263
Westermann, C., 199n
Wheelwright, Philip, 125n, 136n, 138, 141n, 142n
Whitehead, A. N., 106, 235
Wibbing, S., 255
Wilckens, Ulrich, 131, 262n, 264n, 277, 278, 279, 281, 282n, 283n, 284n, 286n, 288, 289, 290n, 291, 292n, 293, 294, 295n, 296, 297, 298, 299n, 301, 303 ff.
Wilder, Amos, xv, 19, 21n, 49n, 124, 127n, 129, 131, 132, 136n, 140n, 145, 146, 153, 155, 156, 203n, 204, 205n, 216 f. n, 230n, 232, 237, 248, 269n
Wilson, R. M., 186n
Windisch, Hans, 255n
Wodehouse, P. G., 156n
Woolf, B. L., 145n, 263n
Wrede, Wilhelm, 22, 33

INDEX OF SUBJECTS

Allegory, 152, 157n, 200, 204, 209n, 214n
christological, 206
Analogy, 80, 104, 136 f., 144, 193
Answer (response), 26, 40, 52, 55, 56, 65, 69, 72, 75, 118, 214
Anthropology, 240, 288 f.
Apocalyptic (–ism), 154, 253, 272 f. n, 280, 294, 301
Art (artist, painting), 3 f., 11, 45, 126, 150, 225, 230, 234

Articulation, 7, 9, 43, 229 ff.
"As," existential-hermeneutical, 231
apophantical, 231
Atheism, see God, death of

Baptism, 277, 290n, 298, 299
Being
call of, 39
and language, 39 f., 41, 42, 44, 47, 51, 52, 54, 55, 60

314

Jesus *(Continued)*
 Jesus-Paul antithesis, 29 ff., 132
 language of, 28, 197, 216, 244 f. n
 memory of, 85
 message of, 31, 61 f., 96, 130, 154
 ministry of, 176, 196n, 197
 relation to, 132
 as text, 57, 60–2
 as word, 68, 197
 word of, 33, 68 ff., 85
John the Baptist, 170

Kerygma, 24, 30–36 *passim*, 60, 61, 72 f.,
 76, 88, 89, 114, 115, 130, 238, 244 f. n
Kingdom (of God), 32, 129, 130, 146, 154,
 155, 194n, 197, 198, 215, 220, 235,
 236, 237

Language (speech)
 alien, 125, 131
 assertive, 26, 34, 36, 37, 51, 75, 105,
 106, 231, 235, 247
 authentic, 40, 44, 54, 56
 biblical, xiii, 6, 11, 22, 47, 50, 53, 59,
 64, 66, 75, 115, 116
 care for, 1, 5, 41, 45
 conventional, 2, 57, 139
 crisis of, 52, 87
 decay of, 43, 55 f.
 deformation of, 7, 141 f., 195, 233, 237,
 238, 247 f., 296
 destiny of, xiv
 discursive, 136, 137–43, 179, 196, 231,
 233, 244 f. n
 doctrine of, 59
 everyday, 229
 failure of, 8 ff., 10, 11, 86, 117
 of faith, 9, 11, 21, 59, 64, 75, 79, 82,
 83, 86, 102, 104
 and faith, 24 f., 26, 63, 68
 foundational, 233, 244, 244 f. n, 246
 fund of, 118 f., 139, 141 f., 233, 237
 future of, xiv
 gain, 50, 55, 57–60
 ghetto, xiv, 122
 gift of, 56
 God-language, 21 f., 49, 67-71, 74 ff., 78–
 84 *passim*, 104, 241
 godless, 70
 history of, 53, 79
 and history, xii ff.
 historical function of, 26
 as house of being, 20, 39 ff.
 I–language, 83
 intentionality of, 142, 276, 287, 301 ff.,
 303 ff.
 "language of," 4
 literal, 86, 194n. *See also* Literal.
 metaphorical, 137, 142 f., 154, 156, 158,
 194n, 195
 mythological, 21 f., 30, 31, 35, 36, 37,
 75, 90, 92, 104, 116, 152 n, 241
 new (birth of), xiv, 9, 28 f., 44, 53, 55,
 56, 59, 65
 non-conceptual, 122
 non-discursive, 132, 143
 non-mythological, 35, 37, 77, 91, 95, 97,
 104

Language *(Continued)*
 non-ontological, 77, 120
 non-religious, 28 f., 93
 non-theistic, 81, 83
 objectifying, 21, 37, 54, 59, 75, 77, 90,
 105 f., 118, 241n
 oral, 248, 249, 264, 265, 268, 269, 272
 passive, 84 ff.
 performative, 26 ff.
 phenomenology of, 224–34, 244 f. n
 poetic, 77, 86, 117n, 119, 120
 power of, xiv, 14, 26, 27, 28 f., 38, 45,
 52, 226, 281, 284, 288, 302 f.
 prattle (idle talk), 8 f., 28, 44, 119, 234,
 288
 primordial, 26, 39, 40, 42–44, 51, 109,
 230, 231, 232, 235
 prose, xv
 and reality, xii ff., 9 f., 86, 104, 117, 140
 rebirth of, 45
 relation to, xiii, 6, 28, 38, 42, 62
 secular, 86, 122
 sedimentation in, 4, 228, 229, 244 f. n
 sophistry of, 281
 steno, 138, 141, 142
 theological, 6, 53, 74, 76 f., 78, 79, 83,
 105, 106, 107, 118, 120
 traditional, 9, 79, 81, 83, 87, 118. *See
 also* Linguistic tradition
 of unfaith, 64
 as *vorhanden*, 42
 written, 248, 264, 267, 268, 269, 272
 as *zuhanden*, 42
Language event, 20, 21–26, 27, 28, 47, 50,
 51, 52, 53, 55, 56, 57, 60, 61, 62, 64,
 66, 67, 68, 69, 71, 78, 107, 119, 128,
 129, 140, 143n, 198, 216, 220, 221,
 237, 283, 284, 287, 305
Lebenswelt, 227, 232, 233
Letter (epistle), 14, 130–32, 224, 233
 benediction *(beracha)*, 256 f., 257, 258,
 263, 270
 body of, 249, 257, 263–70, 269, 270,
 272, 274
 catalogue of virtues and vices in, 255
 chiastic structure, 258, 261 f.
 closing, 252, 257, 258, 264, 270
 conventions, 248, 256, 257, 267 f., 269,
 270
 doxology in, 257, 258, 263, 270
 eschatological climax, 249, 257, 264, 265,
 270, 271, 273, 286
 form of, 131, 224, 237–49, 253, 254,
 263–74, 270
 greetings, 263, 270
 Haustafeln in, 255, 256n
 hymn in, 257
 intentionality of, 237
 kerygmatic formulae in, 257
 language of, 131, 237–49
 paraenesis in, 254–56, 260, 263, 264,
 270 ff.
 prescript, 257
 salutation, 252, 257, 263, 270, 273
 secondary composition, 271 ff.
 structure of, 125, 131, 224, 225, 248
 style of, 254, 255, 272

316